Mary Boleyn

'The Great and Infamous Whore'

Alison Weir

JONATHAN CAPE
LONDON

Published by Jonathan Cape

2 4 6 8 10 9 7 5 3

First published in Great Britain in 2011 by
Jonathan Cape
Random House, 20 Vauxhall Bridge Road,
London SW1V 2SA

www.randomhouse.co.uk

Addresses for companies within The Random House Group Limited can be found at:
www.randomhouse.co.uk/offices.htm

The Random House Group Limited Reg. No. 954009

A CIP catalogue record for this book is available from the British Library

ISBN 9780224089760 (Cased edition)
ISBN 9780224093903 (Trade paperback edition)

The Random House Group Limited supports The Forest Stewardship
Council (FSC®), the leading international forest certification organisation.
Our books carrying the FSC label are printed on FSC® certified paper.
FSC is the only forest certification scheme endorsed by the leading environmental
organisations, including Greenpeace. Our paper procurement policy can be found
at www.randomhouse.co.uk/environment

Typeset by Palimpsest Book Production Limited, Falkirk, Stirlingshire
Printed and bound in Great Britain by
Clays Ltd, St Ives PLC

This book is gratefully dedicated to my editor,
Anthony Whittome, to mark his retirement

Contents

Illustrations

Henry VIII and Anne Boleyn at Hever, engraving by Joseph Nash, 1849. Photo: Mary Evans Picture Library

Henry VIII, artist unknown, *c.* 1520, National Portrait Gallery, London. Photo: Art Media/HIP/TopFoto

Henry VIII by Lucas Horenbout, *c.* 1525/6, Fitzwilliam Museum, Cambridge. Photo: Fitzwilliam Museum, University of Cambridge, UK/The Bridgeman Art Library

Katherine of Aragon with a pet monkey, artist unknown, private collection. Photo: Private Collection/Photo © Philip Mould Ltd, London/The Bridgeman Art Library

Elizabeth Blount, memorial brass, *c.* 1539–40, British Museum, London. © The Trustees of the British Museum

Greenwich Castle, detail from a drawing by Anthony van der Wyngaerde, 1558, Ashmolean Museum, Oxford. Photo: Ashmolean Museum, University of Oxford, UK/The Bridgeman Art Library

Henry Fitzroy, Duke of Richmond and Somerset, miniature by Lucas Horenbout, *c.* 1533–4, The Royal Collection. Photo: The Royal Collection © 2011 Her Majesty Queen Elizabeth II/The Bridgeman Art Library

Letter from Anne Boleyn to her father, written at La Veure, 1514, Corpus Christi College, Cambridge. Reproduced with permission of The Master and Fellows of Corpus Christi College, Cambridge MS 119, p.21

Mary Tudor, Queen of France, sister of Henry VIII, artist unknown, French school, *c.* 1514, Musée des Arts Décoratifs, Paris. Photo: Musée des Arts Décoratifs, Paris, France/Giraudon/The Bridgeman Art Library

Second Section

Tournai tapestry depicting the marriage of Louis XII and Mary Tudor in 1514, *c.*1525, Hever Castle, Kent. Photo: Hever Castle Ltd, Kent, UK/The Bridgeman Art Library

François I, King of France, School of Jean Clouet, Musée Condé, Chantilly. Photo: Musée Condé, Chantilly, France/The Bridgeman Art Library

Claude de France, Queen of France, tomb sculpture by Pierre Bontemps, 1549, Basilica of St Denis, Paris. Photo: Manuel Cohen/Getty Images

Hôtel de Cluny, Paris, print of *c.* 1835. Photo: Mary Evans Picture Library

Charles Brandon and Mary Tudor, wedding portrait by an unknown artist, *c.* 1515, from a private collection. Reproduced with permission

The 'Donjon d'Anne' Boleyn at Briis-sous-Forges. Photo © Véronique Pagnier

William Carey portrait possibly after Hans Holbein, private collection

William Carey, copy of a lost Elizabethan portrait, collection unknown. © reserved. Photograph National Portrait Gallery, London

Greenwich Palace drawing by Anthony van der Wyngaerde, 1558, Ashmolean Museum, Oxford. Photo: Ashmolean Museum, University of Oxford, UK/The Bridgeman Art Library

Nicholas Bourbon, drawing by Hans Holbein, 1535, The Royal Collection. Photo: The Royal Collection © 2011 Her Majesty Queen Elizabeth II/The Bridgeman Art Library

Syon Abbey painting by Jonathan Foyle, 2004. © Jonathan Foyle www.built.org.uk

Sir John Russell, drawing by Hans Holbein, The Royal Collection. Photo: The Royal Collection © 2011 Her Majesty Queen Elizabeth II/The Bridgeman Art Library

Mary Boleyn's signature, The National Archives, Lisle Papers, S.P. 3/6, 23

Anne of Cleves, miniature by Hans Holbein, 1539, Victoria & Albert Museum, London. Photo: V&A Images/Alamy

Probably Katherine Howard, miniature by Hans Holbein, The Royal Collection. Photo: The Royal Collection © 2011 Her Majesty Queen Elizabeth II/The Bridgeman Art Library

Henden Manor, Kent. Photo: Brian Shuel/Collections Picture Library

Rochford Hall, Essex. Photo: Pamaer.org/Getty Images

St. Andrew's Church, Rochford, exterior. Photo: John Whitworth www.essexchurches.info

Henry Carey, Lord Hunsdon, 1591, artist unknown Berkeley Castle, Gloucs. With grateful thanks to the Berkeley Castle Charitable Trust

Elizabeth I by Steven van der Meulen, c.1563. Photo: World History Archive/Alamy

Lord Hunsdon's tomb in Westminster Abbey. Photo: © Dean and Chapter of Westminster

Portrait of a pregnant lady, probably Katherine Carey, Lady Knollys by Steven van Der Meulen, 1562, Paul Mellon Collection, Yale

Center for British Art. Photo: Yale Center for British Art, Paul Mellon Collection, USA/The Bridgeman Art Library
Tomb of Katherine Carey and Sir Francis Knollys in Rotherfield Greys Church, Oxon, Photo: John Ward, Aston Rowant, Oxfordshire

The author and publisher have made every effort to trace and contact the relevant primary copyright holders for each image. The publishers would be pleased to correct any omissions or errors in any future editions.

Preface

I owe a debt of gratitude to several kind people for their assistance with this book. To Nicola Tallis, who is surely destined to be one of our great popular historians of the future, for so generously sending me her research paper and numerous related documents on Mary Boleyn, and for encouraging me to write this book and listening so enthusiastically to my arguments. To Douglas Richardson, for emailing me so much helpful information and for his very judicious observations on the paternity of Mary's Carey children. To Anthony Hoskins, for so kindly sending me copies of his article 'Mary Boleyn's Carey Children' and his unpublished responses to Lady Antonia Fraser's views on that article, with other related essays, letters and press cuttings. Anthony, we may not agree on all points, but it was so generous of you personally to share all this, and your conclusions, with me. To Carole Richmond, who – just as I was finishing revising the text – very kindly drew my attention to, and sent me, Elizabeth Griffiths' ground-breaking article on the Boleyns at Blickling, which has proved invaluable. To Josephine Wilkinson, author of *Mary Boleyn*, for assistance with sources and permission to publish her theory on the 'sister' who was present when Anne Boleyn miscarried in 1536.

I should like to thank my historian friends, Tracy Borman, Sarah Gristwood, Siobhan Clarke and Susan Ronald, for all the lively discussions about this book, and their professional support while I was writing it.

My agent, Julian Alexander – is it really twenty-three years we've been working together? – has been, as ever, enthusiastic and dynamic in his advocacy of my work, and always a friendly and encouraging voice at the other end of a phone. In a year in which we have set up my own historical tours company, at Julian's suggestion, he has worked indefatigably to get us off the ground whilst supporting me in my writing career. That's some feat!

I wish also to thank my professional colleagues, Siobhan Clarke and John Marston, for shouldering many of the administrative burdens of Alison Weir Tours Ltd, so that I could get on with finishing this book. And to my lovely husband, Rankin, the mainstay of my life, thank you for shouldering nearly everything else, and for the occasional glass of wine placed on my desk when the stress gets too much!

I wish to express my deepest gratitude to my dear mother, Doreen Cullen, for all her selfless support of my work over the years, and for her unending enthusiasm, praise and encouragement.

I am singularly blessed in having three outstanding editors. A huge thank-you goes to my commissioning editor, Will Sulkin, and to my editorial director, Anthony Whittome, without whose brilliant creative support and boundless interest and enthusiasm this work would not be in print. I want to thank you also, Tony, for all the excellent work you have done on my books over the past twelve years, and for being such a wonderful friend. I feel very privileged to be one of the authors you have chosen to work with following your much-lamented retirement. I have learned so much from you, and it is thanks to you that I am much more knowledgeable about writing and publishing books than I was twelve years ago.

I wish also to acknowledge all the support and advice given to me by my American editor, Susanna Porter, and her lovely team, who welcomed me so warmly to New York last summer. I'd like to make special mention of my publicists too: Lisa Barnes at Ballantine, Clara Womersley at Jonathan Cape and Ruta Liormonas at Doubleday, and to thank them for all their hard and highly professional work on my behalf, and for making publicity such fun.

Finally, I should like to acknowledge all the efforts put in on my behalf by the unsung heroes of the publishing team at Jonathan Cape and Random House, notably Neil Bradford, Sophie Hartley and Kay Peddle.

I thank you all, from the bottom of my heart.

Alison Weir
Carshalton, Surrey
January 2011

Introduction

Mary Boleyn has gone down in history as a 'great and infamous whore'. She was the mistress of two kings, François I of France and Henry VIII of England, and sister to Anne Boleyn, Henry VIII's second wife. She may secretly have borne Henry a child. It was because of his adultery with Mary that his marriage to Anne was declared invalid. It is not hard to see how this tangled web of covert relationships has given rise to rumours and myths that have been embroidered over the centuries, and particularly in recent years, so that the truth about Mary has become obscured. In all my years of writing women's histories, I have never tackled a subject who has been so romanticised, mythologised and misrepresented.

It may seem strange, in the pages that follow, to see popular history books, some of them decades out of date, compared with serious academic studies, and yet the former are important because it is through them that the mythology of Mary Boleyn has been largely created, nurtured and reaffirmed; and it is helpful to see where and how misconceptions originated.

Everyone knows Henry VIII as the king who married six times. His matrimonial adventures have been a source of enduring fascination for centuries, and the interest shows no sign of abating. On the contrary, in the wake of Philippa Gregory's *The Other Boleyn Girl* (2001), the two film versions of it, and the successful (but alarmingly inaccurate) TV drama series *The Tudors*, it has become elevated to a virtual obsession, as one can see reflected only too clearly in numerous websites and blogs on the internet, where historical personages like Anne Boleyn now have what are virtually fan clubs. We have also witnessed in the public's eye a disconcerting blurring of the demarcation line between fact and historical fiction.

Comparatively little is known or understood about Henry VIII's extramarital adventures. Most recent popular history books have thrown little new light on that subject, or have merely confused it further, and thanks to them, and to the widespread appeal of *The Other Boleyn Girl*, many people have the wrong idea about the woman whom that novel has made the most famous of Henry's mistresses, Mary Boleyn. Was she really such a 'great and infamous whore' with a notorious reputation? Is it true that the King was the father of her children? I am often asked these and numerous questions about Mary, and am constantly being made aware, not only of various misconceptions that are accepted as facts by a majority, but also of the views of many others who *are* well informed on the subject and are wondering why Mary Boleyn is so misrepresented. It is for these reasons – and because I have done a lot of unpublished research on her over four decades – that I have written a biography of Mary.

Mary Boleyn represents only one short episode in Henry VIII's chequered love life; all we can say with certainty is that she was his mistress for a short period while he was married to his first wife, Katherine of Aragon. Mary's true historical significance – and importance – lies in the implications of her royal affair for her more celebrated sister, Anne Boleyn.

My interest in Mary, and my research, goes back to the 1960s, when she was regarded as little more than a footnote to history – in which obscurity she remained until the publication of Philippa Gregory's novel. Since then, I have written about Mary briefly in three books: *The Six Wives of Henry VIII, Henry VIII: King and Court* and *The Lady in the Tower: The Fall of Anne Boleyn*, while my unpublished research comes from my extensive original version of *The Six Wives of Henry VIII*, written in 1974. A serious historical treatment of Mary Boleyn is long overdue. There has been just one admirable, but sadly brief, study by Josephine Wilkinson; I understand that Dr Wilkinson was constrained by a disadvantageous word limit when she had so much more to say, and she has most generously agreed that I can claim that this is the first full biography of Mary.

Recently, in *The Tudors*, Henry VIII has been portrayed as a great lover and sensualist. Many people are asking if this is true! Although the evidence is fragmentary, there are many tantalising references in contemporary sources that can help to provide an answer to the paramount question: what was Henry VIII like as a lover? Was he the virile Adonis portrayed in *The Tudors*? Was he, in fact, a bit of a prude in bed? The answers to these questions necessarily have a bearing on Henry's relations with Mary Boleyn, and they form a part of this book.

Having had some experience in constructing women's histories from fragmentary source material – in, for example, *Eleanor of Aquitaine*; *Isabella, Queen of England, She-Wolf of France*; and *Katherine Swynford* – and having collated information on Mary Boleyn and Henry VIII's extramarital career for earlier books and projects, I had a good basis for crafting what has turned out to be an unexpectedly fascinating – and astonishing – story from the surviving evidence relating to Mary Boleyn's life. In her case, the sources are richer than for those medieval ladies, for she lived in an age of flowering literacy and diplomacy, and we have far more insights into her existence through letters, diplomatic dispatches and archival records than is the case with any medieval woman.

As is my usual practice, I consulted all the primary sources first when preparing this book, researching into the expanding and ever-changing narrative, which is, I have found (thanks to Sarah Gristwood), the most effective way to write historical biography. Only then did I look at the secondary and present-day sources, leaving Josephine Wilkinson's biography of Mary Boleyn until last, as I wanted to research my subject thoroughly beforehand and did not wish to be seen to be drawing upon her work. In this process, I found that some modern historians had reached the same conclusions as I had already, and in such cases that is signified by 'cf.' (compare) in the references section. I have also made it clear where I have benefited from their insights and research.

There is no escaping the fact that an air of mystery pervades every aspect of Mary Boleyn's life.[1] There is so much we don't know about her, and only so much we can infer from the scant sources that have survived. She is in the shadow of her famous sister in more than one way. Furthermore, much that is inaccurate has been written about her. Many of the misconceptions come from novels like *The Other Boleyn Girl* and others of its kind, namely *The Last Boleyn* by Karen Harper (2006) and *Court Cadenza* by Aileen Quigley (1974) (republished as *The Tudor Sisters* by Aileen Armitage) – because people often make the mistake of thinking that what an author of fiction writes must be history – and accurate history.

Yet even historians have often been guilty of making sweeping, unsupported assumptions about Mary Boleyn. This became staggeringly clear when, having researched the original sources, I turned to the secondary ones, which are – with only a few honourable exceptions – littered with inaccuracies. For example, many modern works state categorically that one or both of Mary's children was or were the King's, even though this has never been proven. Time and again, mere assumptions are presented as hard facts – I have lost count of the number of times I have noted a source not being cited – and dubious evidence is accepted indiscriminately, as will repeatedly be highlighted in the pages that follow. Some writers merely recirculate and perpetuate old myths, and even sound and respected, reliable and conscientious historians can be guilty of repeating the same misinformation about Mary Boleyn. I have to confess that I too, in earlier books, have sometimes accepted without question what others have written about her.

It is thanks to such accounts that misconceptions about Henry VIII's private life remain widespread. In fact, it is the persistence of the mythology surrounding Mary Boleyn that has been the most disconcerting aspect of my research. For much of what we might read about Mary, even in history books, should be treated with caution, based as it is on false assumptions. And yet, as will appear in the pages that follow, it is sometimes the case that even the most fanciful and unreliable historians can provide us with compellingly credible – and useful – insights into Mary's character and conduct.

One could go on; the fact is that – as we will see – much of what has been written about Mary Boleyn in history books belongs more properly to historical novels. For this reason, this book is not only a biography but also a historiography of Mary Boleyn.

What follows is a tale that has never fully been told, a rigorous assessment of what we know – and don't know – about Mary Boleyn, which hopefully will enrich our understanding of this much-misrepresented lady and her relations with Henry VIII.

A NOTE ON MONETARY VALUES

All monetary sums quoted in the text are in sixteenth-century values. The approximate modern equivalent (at the time of writing) is given in brackets. For converting old money to new, I have used the National Archives' Currency Converter (www.nationalarchives.gov.uk).

1

'The Eldest Daughter'

Blickling Hall, one of England's greatest Jacobean showpiece mansions, lies not two miles north-west of Aylsham in Norfolk. It is a beautiful place, surrounded by woods, farms, sweeping parkland and gardens – gardens that were old in the fifteenth century, and which once surrounded the fifteenth-century moated manor house of the Boleyn family, the predecessor of the present building. That house is long gone, but it was in its day the cradle of a remarkable dynasty; and here, in those ancient gardens, and within the mellow, red-brick gabled house, in the dawning years of the sixteenth century, the three children who were its brightest scions once played in the spacious and halcyon summers of their early childhood, long before they made their dramatic début on the stage of history: Anne Boleyn, who would one day become Queen of England; her brother George Boleyn, who would also court fame and glory, but who would ultimately share his sister's tragic and brutal fate; and their sister Mary Boleyn, who would become the mistress of kings, and gain a notoriety that is almost certainly undeserved.

Blickling was where the Boleyn siblings' lives probably began, the protective setting for their infant years, nestling in the broad, rolling landscape of Norfolk, circled by a wilderness of woodland sprinkled with myriad flowers such as bluebells, meadowsweet, loosestrife and marsh orchids, and swept by the eastern winds. Norfolk was the land that shaped them, that remote corner of England that had grown prosperous through the wool-cloth trade, its chief city, Norwich – which lay just a few miles to the south – being second in size only to London in the Boleyns' time. Norfolk also boasted more churches

than any other English shire, miles of beautiful coastline and a countryside and waterways teeming with a wealth of wildlife. Here, at
Blickling, nine miles from the sea, the Boleyn children took their
first steps, learned early on that they had been born into an important and rising family, and began their first lessons.

Anne and George Boleyn were to take centre-stage roles in the
play of England's history. By comparison, Mary was left in the wings,
with fame and fortune always eluding her. Instead, she is remembered as an infamous whore. And yet, of those three Boleyn siblings,
she was ultimately the luckiest, and, unlike her sister, the most happy.

This is Mary's story.

Mary Boleyn has aptly been described as 'a young lady of both
breeding and lineage'.[1] She was born of a prosperous landed Norfolk
family of the knightly class. The Boleyns, whom Anne Boleyn claimed
were originally of French extraction, were settled at Salle, near
Aylsham, before 1283, when the register of Walsingham Abbey records
a John Boleyne living there,[2] but the family can be traced in Norfolk
back to the reign of Henry II (1154–89).[3] The earliest Boleyn inscription in Salle church is to John's great-great-grandson, Thomas Boleyn,
who died in 1411; he was the son of another John Boleyn and related
to Ralph Boleyn, who was living in 1402. Several other early members
of the family, including Mary's great-great-grandparents, Geoffrey
and Alice Boleyn, were buried in Salle church, which is like a small
cathedral, rising tall and stately in its perpendicular splendour in the
flat Norfolk landscape. The prosperous village it once served, which
thrived upon the profitable wool trade with the Low Countries, has
mostly disappeared.

The surname Boleyn was spelt in several ways, there being no
uniformity in spelling in former times, when it was given as Boleyn,
Boleyne, Bolleyne, Bollegne, Boleigne, Bolen, Bullen, Boulen, Boullant
or Boullan, the French form. The bulls' heads on the family coat of
arms are a pun on the name. In adult life, Anne Boleyn used the
modern form adopted in this text. Unfortunately, we don't know
how Mary Boleyn spelt her surname, as only two letters of hers
survive, both signed with her married name.

The Boleyn family had once been tenant farmers, but the source
of their wealth and standing was trade. Thomas's grandson, Sir Geoffrey
Boleyn, made his fortune in the City of London as a member and
then Master of the Worshipful Company of Mercers (1454); he was

Sheriff of London from 1446–7; M.P. for London in 1449; and an alderman of the City of London from 1452 (an office he held for eleven years). In 1457, he was elected Lord Mayor.[4] By then, he had made his fortune; his wealth had enabled him to marry into the nobility, his wife being Anne, daughter and co-heiress of Thomas, Lord Hoo and Hastings, and she brought him great estates. Stow records that Sir Geoffrey 'gave liberally to the prisons, hospitals and lazar houses, besides a thousand pounds to poor householders in London, and two hundred pounds to [those] in Norfolk'. He was knighted by Henry VI before 1461.

In 1452 (or 1450), Geoffrey had purchased the manor of Blickling in Norfolk from his friend and patron, Sir John Fastolf.[5] The manor had once been the property of the eleventh-century Saxon king, Harold Godwineson,[6] and the original manor house on the site had been built in the 1390s by Sir Nicholas Dagworth, but it was evidently outdated or in poor repair, because – as has recently been discovered – it was rebuilt as Blickling Hall, 'a fair house' of red brick, by Geoffrey Boleyn.[7] Geoffrey also built the chapel of St Thomas in Blickling church, and adorned it with beautiful stained glass incorporating the heraldic arms of himself and his wife, which still survives today; in his will, he asked to be buried there if he departed this life at Blickling. In the event, he died in London.

Ten years later, in 1462, Geoffrey bought the manors of Hever Cobham and Hever Brokays in Kent from William Fiennes, Lord Saye and Sele,[8] as well as thirteenth-century Hever Castle from Sir Thomas Cobham. Sir Geoffrey now moved in the same social circles as the prosperous Paston family (Norfolk neighbours who knew the Boleyns well, and whose surviving letters tell us so much about fifteenth-century life), the Norfolk gentry and even the exalted Howards, who were descended from King Edward I, and at the head of whose house was John Howard, first Duke of Norfolk; the friendship between the Boleyns and the Howards, which would later be cemented by marriage, dated from at least 1469.[9]

When he died in 1463,[10] Geoffrey was buried in the church of St Lawrence Jewry by the Guildhall in London. His heir, Thomas Boleyn of Salle, was buried there beside him in 1471,[11] when the family wealth and estates passed to Geoffrey's second son, William Boleyn, Mary's grandfather, who had been born around 1451; he was 'aged 36 or more' in the Inquisition Post Mortem on his cousin, Thomas Hoo, taken in October 1487.[12]

The Boleyns had arrived; they were what would soon become known as new men, those who had risen to prominence through wealth, wedlock and ability. William Boleyn, who – like his father – had supported the House of York during the Wars of the Roses, was dubbed a Knight of the Bath at Richard III's coronation in July 1483, became a Justice of the Peace, and made an even more impressive marriage than his father, to Margaret Butler, who had been born sometime prior to 1465,[13] the younger daughter and co-heiress of Thomas Butler, 7th Earl of Ormond.[14]

The Butlers were an ancient Anglo-Norman family, whose surname derived from the office of butler (an official who was responsible for the provisioning of wine), which their ancestor, Theobald Walter, had borne in the household of the future King John in 1185. They too were descended from Edward I, and had been earls of Ormond since 1329.[15] Thomas Butler was one of the wealthiest peers; he had inherited a fortune of £40,000 (£20 million), and was lord of no fewer than seventy-two manors in England. He sat in Parliament as the premier baron and served as English ambassador to the courts of France and Burgundy. His wife was Anne, daughter and heiress of a rich knight, Sir Richard Hankeford.[16]

Before he had come into his inheritance in 1477, Butler had been chronically short of money, and Sir William Boleyn and his mother had continually come to the rescue;[17] Butler repaid his debts with the hand of his daughter, and a dowry that would handsomely enrich the Boleyn family.

Lady Margaret Butler bore Sir William Boleyn eleven children, of whom there were four surviving sons: Thomas, James, William and Edward. Thomas was the eldest,[18] born in 1477,[19] when his mother was probably quite young, although perhaps not as young as twelve, as her mother's Inquisition Post Mortem suggests. After Richard III, the last Plantagenet monarch, was killed at the Battle of Bosworth in 1485, the Boleyns prudently switched their allegiance to the new Tudor dynasty; in 1490, Sir William was appointed Sheriff of Kent, by which time he was probably dividing his time between Blickling and Hever. King Henry VII, the first Tudor sovereign, demonstrated his trust in him by making him responsible for keeping the peace in his locale, delivering prisoners to the assizes, and placing and guarding the beacons that would herald the approach of the King's enemies; he gave William a commission of array against an invasion by the French, and appointed him Sheriff of Norfolk in 1501. The next year, William was made the third of only four Barons of the Exchequer, who sat as judges in the Court of the Exchequer.²⁰

In 1497, Sir William Boleyn and his son Thomas, now twenty, fought for Henry VII against the rebels of Cornwall, who had risen in protest against excessive taxation. Again and again the Boleyn family would demonstrate its solid loyalty to the Crown, and in so doing would win the notice and favour of the Tudor kings, Henry VII and Henry VIII, who valued 'new men' who had risen to prominence through trade and the acquisition of wealth, as opposed to the older nobility, whose power, hitherto boosted by private armies, they strove to keep in check.

The detail in Thomas Boleyn's tomb brass suggests that some attempt was made to reflect his true appearance. It is the image of a dignified man with the long face, high cheekbones and pointed chin that were inherited by his daughter Anne and his grandson, Lord Hunsdon. He has strong features, wavy hair cut straight at chin level, and the hint of a close-cropped beard. His coat of arms, sporting three bulls' heads, while being a play on his name, also symbolised his valour, bravery and generosity. In the case of the latter, it was little more than flattery.

Thomas was a gifted linguist, more fluent in French than any other courtier, and proficient at Latin;²¹ he was also an expert jouster, and these were talents that would make him admired and useful at court. The celebrated Humanist scholar Desiderius Erasmus thought him 'outstandingly learned', and was to dedicate two books to him, one of which was a commentary on the Psalms, in which Thomas Boleyn had shown an interest.²²

Thomas was to prove a highly able and hard-working statesman and diplomat, and Henry VIII himself would say that there was no skilled negotiator to equal him.²³ He was adept at dealing with his royal master, whose liking for him seems never to have died. Yet although normally affable, even congenial, Thomas Boleyn could also be chillingly dispassionate, brusque and even insolent, as he showed when on a crucial diplomatic mission to the Holy Roman Emperor in 1530; and when, during an embassy in Rome, the Pope — as was customary — offered his toe to be kissed, and Boleyn's spaniel bit it, Boleyn refused to kiss it because his dog had defiled it, and so compromised his good relations with the Vatican.

Although he was hard-working and diligent, Thomas Boleyn's besetting vices — by all accounts — were selfishness and avarice; 'he could not risk the temptation of money'.²⁴ It was to be said of him that 'he would sooner act from interest than from any other motive',²⁵ and never was that more apparent than when he showed himself willing to participate in the destruction of two of his children in order to protect himself and salvage his own position and career.

Following in the tradition of his father and grandfather, Thomas Boleyn made a great marriage, to Lady Elizabeth Howard, the eldest daughter of Thomas Howard, Earl of Surrey. Surrey was the son of John Howard, Duke of Norfolk, who had been killed at the Battle of Bosworth fighting on the wrong side for Richard III. Henry VII had declared the title forfeit and cast the heir into prison, but Thomas Howard gradually recovered royal favour and prospered, with the earldom of Surrey being returned to him just four years later, in 1489, and the dukedom of Norfolk in 1514. Had the Howard fortunes not suffered such a reverse, Master Thomas Boleyn might not have gained such a prize as a Howard bride, even though he was the heir to an impressive landed inheritance and the families were on good terms. Elizabeth was a brilliant match for him, and marriage to her made this ambitious esquire brother-in-law to the sister of the Queen of England, for Elizabeth's brother, another Thomas Howard (who succeeded his father as the third Duke of Norfolk in 1524), had, in 1495, married Edward IV's daughter, Anne Plantagenet; Anne's sister Elizabeth was Henry VII's queen and the mother of the future Henry VIII.

   The young Elizabeth Howard was very pretty – in his verses dedicated 'To My Lady Elizabeth Howard', the court poet John Skelton compared her to the mythical Trojan beauty Cressida, whose looks far outshone those of the radiant Polyxena, youngest daughter of Priam, King of Troy, and sister of Troilus, whom Cressida was to betray:

> To be your remembrancer, Madam, I am bound:
> Like unto Irene maidenly of porte [bearing],
> Of virtue and cunning the well and perfect ground,
> Whom Dame Nature, as well I may report,
> Hath freshly enbeautied with many a goodly sort
> Of womanly features: whose flourishing tender age
> Is lusty to look on, pleasant, demure and sage.

Goodly Cressida, fairer than Polyxena,
For to envy Pandarus' appetite:
Troilus, I vow, if that he had you seen,
In you he would have set his whole delight:
Of all your beauty I suffice not to write,
But, as I said, your flourishing tender age
Is lusty to look on, pleasant, demure and sage.

In comparing Elizabeth with the artist Irene, the gifted daughter and pupil of the Greek painter Cratinus (to whom Boccaccio refers in his book *Famous Women*), Skelton is perhaps implying that she had some artistic talent herself.

In the poem in which these verses appear, 'The Garland of the Laurel' (1523), Skelton describes a visit he made to Sheriff Hutton Castle as the guest of Elizabeth's father, Thomas Howard, Earl of Surrey. In the course of it, the Countess, Elizabeth Tylney, was so impressed with Skelton's poetry that, at her behest, her daughters, Lady Elizabeth and Lady Muriel, with some other ladies – Lady Anne Dacre of the South, Mistress Margery Wentworth (who would marry Sir John Seymour and become the mother of Henry VIII's third wife, Jane Seymour) and Margaret Brewes, the wife of Sir Philip Tylney (Surrey's auditor and steward of Framlingham Castle) – made for him a laureate's garland of silk, gold and pearls in honour of his talent. No one could then have dreamed that two of these young ladies would give birth to future queens of England.

'The Garland of the Laurel' is in part an allegorical poem, but its references to the noble ladies at Sheriff Hutton, Skelton's 'court of fame', are authentic. In 1523, when the final version was written, Elizabeth Howard (whose parents had wed in 1472 and who must have been at least twelve by *c*.1498) would have been aged between thirty-seven and fifty-one, far too old in those days to be lauded a beauty. Internal evidence in the poem suggests that it had been originally composed around 1495.[26] It has credibly been suggested that the poem commemorates a pageant that was staged at Sheriff Hutton around May that year, in which Skelton's 'goodly garland' was presented to him. His verses give an illuminating glimpse into the kind of life that Elizabeth Howard led as a young girl growing up in an aristocratic and cultivated household.

In 1523, when Skelton published his poem, it was probably much in its original form, with a few later additions. But by then, his compliment to Elizabeth Howard may have acquired a sting to its tail, as we will see in the next chapter.

Thomas Boleyn's union with Elizabeth Howard may have been socially prestigious, but it was certainly not lucrative. Given that her father had had to buy back his lands from the King, Elizabeth's dowry cannot have been great, and she proved a fruitful wife, which stretched Thomas Boleyn's resources to the limit. In July 1536, in a letter to Henry VIII's Principal Secretary, Thomas Cromwell, he recalled: 'When I married I had only £50 [nearly £25,000] a year to live on for me and my wife, as long as my father lived, and yet she brought me every year a child.'[27] By this reckoning, Elizabeth was producing children annually at least up to 1505. This early struggle to make ends meet may have been responsible for Thomas Boleyn's notorious avarice in later years.

Only four of the children survived infancy: 'Thomas Bullayne', whose grave in Penshurst Church, Kent, is marked by a cross and the date 1520, Mary, Anne and George. Of the rest, we know only the name of one son, Henry, whose resting place is marked by a small brass adjacent to his father's tomb in Hever church; he probably died young. There may well have been others whose names have not come down to us. This constant childbearing renders dubious claims that Elizabeth Howard was a lady-in-waiting to Queen Elizabeth of York, who died in 1503,[28] unless of course she had held that post prior to her marriage, but there is no evidence for this.

Scholars have long disputed which of the surviving daughters was the oldest, some insisting that it was probably Anne,[29] but there survives good evidence that it was Mary.[30] Mary's grandson, George Carey, 2nd Baron Hunsdon,[31] in a letter to Thomas Cecil, Lord Burghley, dated 6 October 1597, was to argue that he ought to be granted the earldom of Ormond in right of his grandmother, stating that 'my grandmother was the eldest daughter and sole heir' of Thomas Boleyn, Earl of Wiltshire and Ormond – and he was in a position to know the truth. He also asserted that Mary 'sued her livery [pressed her claim], as by the record of the same doth and may appear', although that record does not survive. Had she been successful, she and her husband, William Stafford, would have become Earl and Countess of Ormond, but that was never likely, because the earldom had been granted to Piers Butler in February 1538, more than year before Wiltshire's death, and the Butlers still held the title.

But George Carey had been reared in the hope that it would be restored. 'My late lord father,' he wrote (referring to Henry Carey, 1st Lord Hunsdon, Mary's son), 'as resolved by the opinion of heralds and lawyers, ever assured me that a right and title was to descend on me to the earldom of Ormond, which, if he had lived to this Parliament, he meant to have challenged . . . In that Sir Thomas Boleyn was created Viscount Rochford and Earl of Ormond to him and his heirs general [i.e. both male and female], Earl of Wiltshire to him and his heirs male[32] by whose death without issue male the earldom of Wiltshire was extinguished, but the earldom of Ormond, he surviving his other children before that time attainted, he in right left to his eldest daughter Mary, who had issue Henry, and Henry myself.'

George Carey was working on the assumption that, as the heir of Mary, the elder sister, he had a better right to the earldom than Elizabeth I herself, whom he admitted to be co-heir to it in right of her mother, 'Anne, the *youngest* daughter of Sir Thomas Boleyn, Earl of Ormond'. But, he concluded, 'admit now an equality of descent, then is it to be considered whether my Grandmother, being the eldest daughter, ought not to have the whole dignity?'[33]

With Queen Elizabeth's rights to her executed mother's confiscated property having been restored to her by Parliament early in her reign, George Carey, the most loyal of subjects, would hardly have considered claiming a peerage that, by his reckoning, would have been the Queen's by right, had she been the elder daughter. In the event, though, Carey never presented his petition to Elizabeth. Probably he was advised not to pursue the matter, for since the restitution of Elizabeth's rights, Mary Boleyn could now be regarded only as a co-heir to the earldom, not the sole heir;[34] legally, at this date, it did not matter which sister was the elder, since the Butlers had held the earldom since 1538.

Other evidence that Mary was the elder daughter is to be found in a marginal note made by William Camden in the manuscript of his *Annales rerum Anglicarum et Hibernicarum regnante Elizabetha*, published in 1615; here, he states that Anne was begotten by Thomas Boleyn 'among other children'. Had she been the eldest daughter, Camden would surely have described her thus. In 1585, for what his evidence is worth, Nicholas Sander, one of the chief Catholic historians of the Reformation – of whom we will hear more later – called Mary the elder of the Boleyn sisters.

Other later sources have confused the issue. In 1619, Ralph Brooke, York Herald, in his *A Catalogue and Succession of the Kings, Princes, Dukes, Marquesses, Earls and Viscounts of this Realm of England*, wrote that 'Anne . . . was second daughter of Sir Thomas Boleyn', yet contradicted himself by referring elsewhere to 'Anne the eldest, Mary the second daughter'.

Confusion seems to have reigned in one branch of the Carey family. Mary's great-granddaughter, George Carey's daughter Elizabeth, married Thomas, the heir of the Berkeleys, a noble Gloucestershire family, in February 1596. In a manuscript in the Berkeley collection written in 1584, twelve years before Elizabeth Carey's marriage, Mary is called 'the second daughter and coheir of Thomas Boleyn'. This could well be an error, but on the tombstone of Elizabeth Carey, Lady Berkeley, who died in 1635, Mary is again referred to as the second daughter, as she is also described in a manuscript, Lives of the Berkeleys, compiled over four decades and completed in 1618 by John Smyth of Nibley, steward to the family from 1596 to 1640. If Smyth repeated the earlier error in the records, from 1584, it was never corrected, although the occasion may not have arisen. There remains the matter of the epitaph; it may be that, after Lady Berkeley's death, her family merely found this information in their papers, or obtained it from the possibly misinformed Smyth, who was still alive.

It would have been odd if Elizabeth Carey, who was Queen Elizabeth's goddaughter, was under the impression that her great-grandmother was the younger of the Boleyn sisters, when her father, George Carey, had taken such pains to demonstrate that she was the elder. Yet there is no hard evidence that Elizabeth Carey herself did believe that Mary was the younger; or it is just possible that, if she had been told by her father that he had been advised not to pursue his claim, she decided to distance herself from it by pretending that her great-grandmother had indeed been the younger daughter. In either case, it is far likelier that George Carey, Mary Boleyn's grandson, knew the truth of the matter.[35]

As late as 1631, John Weever, in his *Ancient Funeral Monuments*, called Anne Boleyn the eldest daughter, but without revealing his source. Weever was not born until 1576, and his work has been shown to be inaccurate, and plagiarised, in parts, and therefore his evidence, according to Professor Ives, is 'totally implausible' when compared to the claim and arguments of George Carey.

In Harleian MS. 1233, fol. 81, there is a pedigree of the Boleyn family that was probably drawn up in the reign of Charles I: this too describes Mary as 'second dau.'. The College of Arms holds another pedigree, formally attested in 1679 to be 'proved out of certain Registers and Memorials remaining in ye College of Arms', which gives Anne as the 'eldest daur.' and Mary as 'daur. and heir'. Yet Mary's seniority is supported by the wording of the Letters Patent of 1532 creating Anne Boleyn, 'one of the daughters' of Sir Thomas, Lady Marquess of Pembroke.[36] Had Anne been the elder, she would surely have been described as such. Mary was also the first sister to be found a husband, another indication of her seniority,[37] for it was customary in England for landed families to marry off their daughters in order of seniority. Retha Warnicke, relying on Weever, believes that Mary was the younger sister and that the Boleyns flouted this convention because Anne was still in France and they were hoping that she would make a grand match there; but this theory flies in the face of the other compelling evidence to support Mary being the elder of the two, on a balance of probabilities.[38]

It is worth saying that this debate over seniority has raged for well over a century, and is never likely to be resolved to the satisfaction of all historians.

Further controversy surrounds the dates of birth of the Boleyn siblings. The actual date of the marriage of Thomas Boleyn and Elizabeth Howard is not recorded; the dates most often given or suggested are 1498 or 1500.[39] We know, from the evidence of Skelton's poem, that Elizabeth was still unwed in May 1495, but all we can surmise is that she married Thomas sometime between then and 1498, the latest possible date estimated on the evidence for the probable births of their children, as laid out below.

There survives, however, what seems to be the jointure settled on Elizabeth Howard, dating from shortly before 29 November 1501 and granting her manors for the term of her life,[40] which must have been made after her marriage, because at this period, 'the marriage contract created the jointure, which did not exist without it'.[41] Marriage contracts would commonly state that a dowry was being paid 'in consideration' of the bridegroom's family's promise to settle a jointure on the bride,[42] a jointure being the legal provision made for a wife in the event of her husband's death.

It was not until the reign of Henry VIII that jointures had to be made before marriage. Prior to that, they were often settled within a year of marriage, but there was in fact no time limit,[43] and sometimes the bridegroom failed to establish any jointure at all, so this cannot be seen as conclusive evidence for the date of the wedding, although it supports the other evidence that the marriage had taken place in recent years, with 1498 being the date most frequently suggested.[44]

In order to estimate Mary Boleyn's possible birth date, we must look at the evidence for her sister Anne's, which is much more plentiful. According to the marginal note made by William Camden in 1615, Anne was born in 1507, the date also given by Henry Clifford in his memoir of Jane Dormer, Duchess of Feria, printed in 1643, long after it was written; according to the latter, Anne was 'not twenty-nine years of age' at the time of her execution in 1536. That would place her date of birth either in 1507, after 19 May, or in 1508. Jane Dormer, who assisted in the preparation of Clifford's work, had been born two years after Anne's death, and later became one of the maids of honour and close confidantes of Henry VIII's daughter, Queen Mary I. She could have obtained her information from people at court (including Mary herself) who had known Anne – but if she did, it was almost certainly incorrect, for there is good evidence that Anne was not born in 1507.

William Roper, Sir Thomas More's son-in-law, whose biography of More was finished around 1556, went so far as to claim that Anne was born as late as 1512, but that date does not fit with the other evidence and is obviously far too late, because we have records of her at the court of Margaret, Archduchess of Austria, the following year.

Writing more than seventy years later, John Weever, who must have seen a translation of Camden's work, claimed that Henry VIII and Anne Boleyn fell in love when he was thirty-eight and she twenty-two, again placing her birth in 1507.[45] But by June 1529, when Henry was thirty-eight, he had been pushing for an annulment of his marriage for two years, and had been pursuing Anne for at least fifteen months before that; furthermore, Weever states elsewhere that Anne was twenty-two when she returned to England from France early in 1522 and entered the service of Katherine of

Aragon, yet there is no evidence to suggest that Henry VIII fell in love with her at this early date, when he was only thirty-one. It would therefore be unwise to rely on Weever, whose dates are hopelessly confused, yet have been cited to bolster theories that Anne was born in 1507 or 1499.[46]

The identification, in 1876, of the skeleton of a woman aged twenty-five to thirty as Anne Boleyn, during excavations in the royal chapel of St Peter ad Vincula in the Tower of London, was based on her having been born in 1507; other remains, of a woman aged thirty to forty, may well have been Anne's, but were reburied without further examination as those of her sister-in-law, Jane Parker, Lady Rochford.[47] Thus archaeological evidence is of little use in confirming Anne's likely age.

A century ago, James Gairdner accepted Camden's date of 1507, and some modern writers still do.[48] Warnicke has argued that Weever's information was accurate, and that the age gap of sixteen years would have been worthy of comment in Tudor times; but, as any study of aristocratic pedigrees will show,[49] many women did go on bearing children into their forties, and there was often great disparity in age between couples in an era in which marriages were arranged for profit or advantage, so Henry's sixteen years' seniority would not have been seen as exceptional.

Furthermore, if Anne was born in 1507, she would have been only six years old when she was sent abroad to the court of Margaret of Austria in 1513, and seven when she transferred to the court of France the following year. What settles the matter is a well-authenticated letter written by Anne to her father in 1513–14,[50] which is clearly written in the well-formed hand of an educated teenager, not a child of seven.[51]

On the evidence of this letter, Hugh Paget effectively demonstrated in 1981 that Anne was probably born around 1501, a credible date put forward as long ago as 1842 by Agnes Strickland. It is supported by Lord Herbert of Cherbury, Henry VIII's seventeenth-century biographer, who had access to sources lost to us, and states that Anne was twenty when she left the French court early in 1522. William Rastell, the mid-sixteenth-century biographer of Sir Thomas More, and the admittedly unreliable Gregorio Leti, whose life of Elizabeth I was suppressed by the Catholic Church, both suggest that Anne was born around 1499–1500. Any date between 1499 and 1502 would therefore seem to be a reliable estimate, with 1501 being the likeliest date. Certainly that would make sense of the Imperial ambassador describing Anne as 'that thin old woman' in 1536,[52] for in an age in which female life expectancy was around thirty years, women were considered to be middle-aged by their mid-thirties.

It may be that Camden, or someone before him, misread the date 1501 for 1507 – an error easily made – and that other early writers repeated the error.[53]

Mary was older than Anne, so she must have been born in 1500–01 at the very latest, probably earlier, although there may well have been no more than a year between them.[54] Mary's year of birth is usually given as 1498[55] or 1499.[56] On the assumption that, in common with so many little girls in those days, she was named for the Virgin Mary, it has been claimed that her actual birth date was around 25 March,[57] that being the Feast of the Annunciation, popularly known as Lady Day. It has also been suggested[58] that Mary was named after the Princess Mary Tudor, daughter of Henry VII, who was born in March 1496, and whom Mary was later briefly to serve. If so, that might place Mary Boleyn's date of birth (and her parents' marriage) a year or two earlier.[59]

It has been further asserted that Mary's sister Anne was named for St Anne and born around that saint's day, 26 July.[60] She might also have been named after her great-aunt, Anne Butler, the wife of Sir James St Leger,[61] yet Anne was a popular name in the Boleyn family; two, possibly three, daughters of Sir William Boleyn had been named after his aristocratic mother, Anne Hoo, which suggests there was a tradition that the name of the heiress who had been one of the chief sources of Boleyn wealth and status should be kept in the family. However, it is also credible that Anne was named after her aunt-by-marriage, the Princess Anne of York, who had been married to Elizabeth Howard's brother, Thomas, Earl of Surrey, in February 1495.

Given that Anne was probably born around 1501, Mary, who was older, cannot have been born as late as 1503–4, as has been suggested,[62] nor can she have been only about twelve years old in 1520.[63] Furthermore, it has been rightly said that 'the circumstances of Mary's life fit much better' if she had been born in 1500 or earlier, rather than some years later.[64]

We do not know the dates of birth of the other children who died young, and who may have come between Mary and Anne, but

Thomas, named after his father and perhaps his grandfather, the Earl of Surrey, was almost certainly the eldest son, and Henry, perhaps named for King Henry VII, may well have been the second. George Boleyn was probably the youngest of the three surviving siblings: he was described by George Cavendish, Cardinal Wolsey's Gentleman Usher, as being under twenty-seven when he was preferred to the Privy Council in 1529,[65] so he must have been born in 1502 at the earliest, or 1503. This dating is corroborated by a degree by Jean du Bellay, the French ambassador, who expressed the opinion that George was too young to be sent to France as England's ambassador in 1529.[66]

Thomas Boleyn's heir and namesake lived until 1520, and it is probably fair to say that George's other older brother, Henry Boleyn, was still alive when he was born in 1502–3; had he not been, this third son might also have been named after the King. Instead, it seems likely that he was called after England's patron saint, St George, as the name does not appear elsewhere in the Boleyn family tree, and that he was born around that saint's day, 23 April.[67]

These estimated dates of birth suggest that Mary, Thomas and Henry were the three oldest children, born before 1501 (but not necessarily in that order), and Anne and George the two youngest. There were probably others, given that their mother had a child 'every year', so this sequence cannot be conclusive. What it, and the other evidence, does suggest is that Thomas Boleyn and Elizabeth Howard married some years earlier than 1500, and that Mary Boleyn was born between 1496 and 1501.

The surviving Boleyn children were probably born at Blickling Hall in Norfolk. Prior to his death in 1505, their grandfather, Sir William Boleyn, resided mainly at Hever – he is referred to in old records as 'Sir William Boleyn of Hever Castle'[68] – and Thomas and his family appear to have lived in the manor house at Blickling. Anne Boleyn's chaplain, Matthew Parker, who was born in Norfolk, was to refer to himself as her 'countryman', and Sir Henry Spelman, a Norfolk antiquarian writing in the reign of Anne's daughter, Elizabeth I, wrote: 'To Blickling was decreed the honour of Anne Boleyn's birth.' Given that Anne and Mary were almost certainly born before late 1505/early 1506, when their father left Blickling for Hever, Mary is likely to have been born at Blickling too; it is also possible, although less credible, that she came into this world in the old manor house at Mulbarton, near Norwich, another Boleyn property in Norfolk, which was part of the Hoo inheritance, and would be sold by Thomas Boleyn in 1535. The Boleyns, like the Pastons and the Heydons, owned a house in Norwich itself, by the River Wensum in King Street, the site of which is next to the fifteenth-century house now known as Dragon Hall;[69] this could also have been Mary's birth-place; and of course, she could have been born at Hever Castle, although this is less likely, unless she arrived when her parents were visiting.

The Blickling Hall of the Boleyns no longer exists. The absence of a licence to crenellate, and Leland's description – as Griffiths points out, he used the word 'fair' to describe decorated houses – suggest that it had no defensive features and was probably a manor house like the one of moulded brick and tile that survives at East Barsham, Norfolk, which was built around 1520. Possibly Sir William Boleyn or his son, Thomas, carried out improvements at Blickling. Their house was surrounded by yew hedges that still survive today, and was acquired in a decaying state from their kinsman, Sir Edward Clere, by the Hobart family in 1616. By 1619 it had been largely demolished to make way for the present Jacobean house. Parts of Sir Geoffrey Boleyn's house – the western service range and sections of the north wing, including the parlour, withdrawing chamber and one end of the long gallery – were incorporated into the new one and survived until 1767. These parts, including a gabled building with Tudor windows in the north wing, can be seen in eighteenth-century prints by Edmund Prideaux. The old moat is now a flower garden.

By November 1501, possibly through the influence of his Howard in-laws, Thomas Boleyn had begun to make his mark at court. That month, he was present at the wedding of Henry VII's heir, Arthur Tudor, Prince of Wales, to a pretty, golden-haired Spanish princess, Katherine of Aragon, which was celebrated in great splendour in London's St Paul's Cathedral.[70] In August 1503, after Arthur had tragically died at just fifteen, and his younger brother Henry, now twelve years old, had been made Prince of Wales in his stead and betrothed to the widowed Katherine, Thomas Boleyn was among the escort appointed to conduct the King's daughter Margaret to Scotland to marry King James IV.[71] In 1507, Thomas held the post of 'yeoman of the Crown' at the port of (King's) Lynn in Norfolk.[72]

Sir William Boleyn died on 10 October 1505, and was buried in

Norwich Cathedral, in a plain tomb bearing the Boleyn arms, which had been built as a family mausoleum by his mother in 1463, after lightning struck the spire and a great fire had damaged the presbytery.[73] His sister Anne is buried nearby, her tomb being marked by a brass.

Thomas Boleyn's financial problems were solved by his father's death, for he inherited the family wealth and lands, including the manors of Blickling, Calthorpe and Wickmere, which had been purchased by Sir Geoffrey Boleyn, and were all located north of Aylsham in Norfolk. Not far off were Heydon and Baconsthorpe, where there were Boleyn family connections, and nearby lived other relatives, the Calthorpes, the Sheltons and the Cleres. Blickling, the family seat, was by far the most important Boleyn property in the area. To the south lay Norwich, and the nearby manor of 'Micklebarton' (listed in Domesday Book as 'Molkebertuna') or Mulbarton, which was also part of Thomas Boleyn's inheritance; here he may well have stayed on occasions in the original moated manor house on the site of the Elizabethan Old Hall.

Thomas Boleyn also came into possession of other manors in Norfolk: Filby on the Norfolk Broads, bought by his father in 1501; Stiffkey, on the marshes between Wells and Blakeney; Hoe, or Hoo, just north of East Dereham, as distinct from the manor of Hoo in Bedfordshire, which he also inherited; and West Lexham, near Castle Acre; there was also Cockernhoe in Hertfordshire (now part of the urban sprawl of Luton), an estate of the manor of (Great) Offley, three miles to the north, which Thomas sold in 1518, both also from the Hoo inheritance; Seal (near Sevenoaks), purchased by Sir Geoffrey in 1463, and Hever Castle, both in Kent.[74] The Boleyns probably never resided in most of the manors Thomas inherited, but would have lived off the profits instead.

This was the close-knit social milieu in which Mary and her siblings spent their early years, the kind of society described so vividly in the letters of the Paston family. But for all their long tenure there, the Boleyns have left few traces in Norfolk, apart from a few graves.

Thomas Boleyn received royal licence to take possession of his estates in February 1506.[75] Under the terms of his father's will, he was to pay his widowed mother, Lady Margaret, 200 marks (nearly £2,000) yearly for her maintenance. By February 1506, he had left Blickling,[76] which he seems to have been happy to abandon (and for which he paid 3s.6d. (£85) every thirty weeks for castle guard to the Bishop of Norwich),[77] and moved with his family, taking his mother with them, to Hever, which was more convenient for London and the court; in 1538, he would tell Thomas Cromwell that he had lived 'these thirty-three years' in Kent.[78]

Mary Boleyn was between five and ten years old when she came to live in the thirteenth-century castle at Hever, where she would spend the remainder of her formative years. Set amid parkland and forest in the beautiful, undulating Kentish countryside, three miles south-east of Edenbridge, it was – and still is – an idyllic place. Originally a fortified farmhouse and keep built around 1270 by the Norman de Hever family, it was not crenellated until 1384, when it was owned by Sir John de Cobham. The oldest surviving parts are the thirteenth-century three-storey gatehouse, outer defensive wall and moat, and the fourteenth-century battlements.

In 1462–3, Mary's great-grandfather, Sir Geoffrey Boleyn, had begun converting the castle into a moated manor house; his works were carried on by his son, Sir William Boleyn, and some can still be seen today: the ceiling in the room now called 'King Henry VIII's Bedchamber' dates from 1462, while the main entrance from this period still survives opposite the one created by Geoffrey's grandson, Sir Thomas Boleyn, who began making further improvements as soon as he acquired the castle. Around 1506, he installed mullioned windows, added the present entrance hall, the staircase gallery above it, and a ninety-eight-foot long gallery above the great hall (which had hitherto had exposed rafters). This is one of the earliest examples of a long gallery in England.

But the Hever that Mary grew up in was not the Hever we know today, for the decaying castle – which had reverted to use as a farmhouse – was extensively altered and refurnished in the early twentieth century by the American business magnate, William Waldorf Astor, who substantially remodelled the interior and replaced the courtyard façades. A drawing executed by Joseph Nash between 1838 and 1849 shows the courtyard as it was before a disastrous earlier restoration in 1898, when its old mullioned windows were removed and a timber-framed cladding was attached to the walls. In Tudor times, there was a brick bridge across the moat.

The present dining hall was then the great hall (not panelled until 1906); a nineteenth-century narrative painting, *The Yule Log*, by Robert Alexander Hillingford (on display at Hever), shows the Boleyns' great hall with its screens passage still intact, as it was before the restorations.

In Mary's day, the present library was probably a steward's office, the morning room was probably the private parlour, and the Edwardian great or 'inner' hall was the kitchen, which had a large fireplace and a well sunk in the floor. The long gallery was not panelled until Elizabethan times; another of Nash's drawings shows it much as it was in the late sixteenth century. There was stained glass in the Tudor castle, but the only piece that survives is now in the elaborately reconstructed minstrels' gallery above the dining hall. The Tudor stables with their oak balcony and a large ancient barn were demolished in 1898; the balcony and the roof tiles were later incorporated into William Waldorf Astor's Tudor Village. The gardens were extensively remodelled, and the lake dug, in the early 1900s, so they could not, as has been imaginatively claimed, have 'provided a romantic setting for visits paid by the King to Anne Boleyn'.[79]

By 1509, Thomas Boleyn had begun his long career at court when he was appointed 'Esquire of the Body' to Henry VII, a post that brought him into daily contact with the King. The four Esquires of the Body enjoyed great influence, and were usually able and cultivated knights who took turns to wait on the King day and night in his bedchamber, helped him dress, attended to his daily needs, and informed the Lord Chamberlain 'if anything lack for his person or pleasaunce. Their business is in many secrets.'[80] This was naturally a position of great honour and trust, and its occupants were often able to enjoy manifold benefits from being in such close proximity to the monarch. This gave them a distinct advantage over other courtiers, and opportunities to sue for favours for themselves – and for others at a price – and express persuasive opinions. Thus early on did Mary's father become influential at court.

Elizabeth Howard, who was rarely at court, would from now on have been the guiding figure in her childen's daily lives, and a far less distant one than Thomas Boleyn, who was often to be away from home, either at court or on the King's business, and who, in the manner of Tudor fathers, would have had much influence over, yet little hands-on involvement with, the rearing of his children. Thomas was in his element at court, where there was every chance that he could fulfil his ambitions. He can have had little idea of where those ambitions would take him and his family.

2

'The Best of Husbands'

In April 1509, Henry VII died, and his son, the tall and handsome young Henry VIII, ascended the throne to an outburst of popular acclaim. On 11 May, Thomas Boleyn performed his last duty for the old King, serving as Esquire of the Body at his funeral in Westminster Abbey.[1] He was dubbed a Knight of the Bath at the new King's coronation on 23 June – for which occasion his wife, who was in attendance on the Queen, had a new gown[2] – and soon afterwards was appointed a Knight of the Body to Henry VIII,[3] a position that required him to serve as bodyguard to the King, sleeping on a pallet outside Henry's door, in turn with other Knights of the Body. In July 1509, Boleyn was appointed Keeper of the Exchange at Calais – then an English possession – and of the Foreign Exchange in England,[4] and so progressed on what was to be a successful and even glittering career at court.

In addition to the estates he had inherited, Thomas Boleyn had now acquired another important property. In a pardon roll of the first year of Henry VIII's reign, he is referred to as 'Thomas Boleyn of Blickling, Norfolk, Hever, Kent, New Inn without Temple Bar, and Hoo, Bedfordshire'.[5] The Inns of Chancery had originally been founded to train Chancery clerks, this being the preliminary step towards becoming a barrister. New Inn, at Aldwych in the liberty of Westminster, had been founded from Our Lady Inn in 1485 as a hostel, and it had more recently been purchased by Sir Thomas.[6] Stow later called it 'an inn of Chancery clerks' housed in 'a common hostelry [at the] sign of Our Lady'.[7]

With a new and dynamic young King on the throne, it was an

exciting time to be at court. 'If you could see how all the world here is rejoicing in the possession of so great a prince, how his life is all their desire, you could not contain your tears for joy,' wrote the cultivated humanist William Blount, Lord Mountjoy in a private letter; 'the heavens laugh, the earth exults, all things are full of milk and honey, of nectar! Avarice is expelled the country, liberality scatters wealth with a bountiful hand. Our King does not desire gold or gems but virtue, glory, immortality!'

The poet laureate John Skelton was also full of praise for Henry VIII's virtues and good looks:

Adonis of fresh colour,
Of youth, the goodly flower,
Our Prince of high honour,
Our paves,[8] our succour,
Our King, our Emperor,
Our Priamus of Troy,
Our wealth, our worldly joy!

Upon us he doth reign,
That maketh our hearts glad,
As King most sovereign
That ever England had.
Demure, sober and sad,
And Mars's lusty knight,
God save him in his right!

On 11 June 1509, Henry VIII, tall, slim, broad-shouldered, athletic, fair-skinned and red-haired, had at last married his brother's widow, Katherine of Aragon, who, at twenty-three, was more than five years his senior. The marriage was at first happy. 'My wife and I be in as good and perfect love as any two creatures can be', the genial Henry told his father-in-law, while Katherine declared that she loved her new husband 'so much more than myself'.[9] Together they presided over a court that epitomised Renaissance magnificence, celebrated the cult of chivalry and served as an academy of the arts, literature, learning and sciences. It was also a centre of sporting excellence, and the social hub of the realm, attracting visitors from far and wide.

There can be no doubt that Henry loved Katherine of Aragon. Early on, he spoke openly of the 'joy and felicity' he had found with

her, and how he 'desired her above all women', and he was to re-
iterate such sentiments over the years. Whether he was actually *in
love* with her is another matter entirely, although he probably thought
he was at the time of their marriage, not being experienced in affairs
of the heart, for he had led an over-sheltered existence under strict
supervision at his father's court. His sentiments towards her appear
to have been rooted in chivalrous impulses, political expediency and
the desire to reverse Henry VII's unpopular policies.

But there was far more to a royal marriage than love. A queen's
first duty was to ensure the succession, and Katherine happily fulfilled
this by becoming pregnant immediately. Once she was beyond his
reach sexually, for intercourse during pregnancy was frowned upon
and considered risky, Henry began looking elsewhere for gratifica-
tion, establishing a pattern of behaviour that would recur during his
married life.

But five of the six children born in the next eight years to the
royal couple – three of them sons – died young or were born dead,
and as the years passed and Katherine suffered one disastrous pregnancy after another, and consequently lost her looks and her figure,
the age gap between the King and Queen became more glaringly
apparent. Katherine increasingly sought refuge in excessive piety, even
taking to wearing a hair shirt beneath her royal robes, and began
retiring early from the court entertainments beloved of her sociable
and pleasure-seeking husband. Unbearable disappointment led to the
gulf between them widening, and Henry, predictably, turned more
and more to other women.

In order to understand the context of Henry VIII's affair with Mary
Boleyn, it is helpful to trace his extramarital affairs during the years
before it began. What we know about these and later affairs gives
us clues as to how Henry conducted his liaisons with his mistresses,
and to the likely duration and nature of the affair with Mary Boleyn,
and we need such clues, because discretion was Henry's watchword
in his illicit dealings with women. He prided himself on being a
virtuous prince and a man of conscience, and when it came to sex,
he was overly discreet, and possibly even prudish. Contemporary
references to his extramarital affairs are therefore sparse, which
prompted J.D. Mackie to assert in 1952 that 'the story of [Henry's]
promiscuous amours is a myth'.

Mackie's statement itself propagated a myth: for a long time afterwards, historians would assert that the King's extramarital adventures were few. Yet it is clear that Henry did take a number of mistresses, as well as indulging in fleeting sexual encounters; indeed, the evidence suggests that, in private, he was as promiscuous as most Renaissance rulers – it may be that secrecy gave an added thrill to the forbidden. The problem with the evidence for these affairs is that, because Henry was so discreet, it is fragmentary; yet there is enough of it to show that Mackie was wrong.

Lord Herbert wrote that 'one of the liberties which our King took at his spare time was to love. For, as all recommendable parts occurred in his person, and they again were exalted in his high dignity and valour, so it must seem little strange if, amid the many fair ladies which lived in his court, he both gave and received temptation.'

Unlike his contemporary, King François I of France, Henry did not, in these early years, allow any of his mistresses to wield influence that might threaten the position of the Queen; in England, the role of royal *maîtresse-en-titre* did not exist (it did not exist in France either until 1518), and the women who became involved in affairs with the King could expect very little reward for their favours and the potential loss of their honour. Like his Plantagenet forebears, Henry expected them to remain in the background and provide him with unencumbered sexual pleasure, and perhaps entertaining company, when he felt the need.

It has been claimed that many of the ladies with whom Henry had affairs 'never washed, had wooden teeth, bad breath and body odour'.[10] Had that been the case – and there is no evidence for it – it is unlikely that he would have fancied them, for by the standards of his day, the King was one of the most fastidious of men, and would surely have expected the women with whom he became intimate to maintain certain standards of personal hygiene.[11]

Henry's infidelity was not limited to the periods when his wives were pregnant, although he almost invariably strayed at those times. 'The King is a youngling, who thinks of nothing but hunting and girls, and wastes his father's patrimony,' one ambassador recorded early in the reign.[12] Even when Henry was middle-aged, his physician, Dr John Chambers, would describe him as being 'overly fond of women' and 'given to lustful dreams'.[13] The Duke of Norfolk, who knew Henry well (two of his nieces married the King), observed that he was 'continually inclined to amours'.[14] The Emperor Charles

V told his ambassador that it was well known that the King was of 'an amorous complexion',[15] and in 1537, it was said of Henry that all it took to please him was 'an apple and a fair wench to dally withal'.[16] Even the King's admiring apologist, William Thomas, wrote in 1546 that 'he was a very fleshly man' who 'fell into all riot and overmuch love of women'. Another sixteenth-century commentator wrote: 'King Henry gave his mind to three notorious vices: lechery, covetousness and adultery, but the latter two issued and sprang out of the former.'[17] In the reign of Elizabeth I, Sir Robert Naunton famously wrote that Henry VIII never spared a man in his anger, nor a woman in his lust. This evidence seriously undermines fashionable modern notions that the King suffered from erectile dysfunction. Clearly, being 'free from every vice', as a Venetian envoy described Henry in 1515,[18] did not preclude committing adultery.

Katherine's first child, a daughter, was born dead on 31 January 1510, but she conceived again soon afterwards, and by May, she was reported to be 'very large'.[19] Around that time, two sisters of Edward Stafford, Duke of Buckingham, the King's cousin, were living at court. One was Elizabeth, the wife (since 1505) of Robert Ratcliffe, Lord FitzWalter, and a great favourite of the Queen; the other was Anne, who had married George, Lord Hastings in 1507; she was 'much liked by the King, who went after her'. Henry's close friend, Sir William Compton, is known to have lived for some time in an adulterous relationship with Lady Hastings, for whom he later founded a chantry chapel at his country seat, Compton Wynyates,[20] but although some believed that 'the love intrigues were not of the King but of his favourite, Compton', in the opinion of the Spanish ambassador, Luis Caroz,[21] 'the more credible version' was that it was Henry VIII who was discreetly pursuing Lady Hastings at this time, while Compton was providing cover for his master's amorous exploits by pretending to court her himself.

Thanks to Compton, Henry was able to keep the affair secret, until Lady FitzWalter became suspicious of the attention that Compton was paying to her sister. Wishing to spare her family any scandal, she summoned her brother the Duke and Lord Hastings, Anne's husband, and confided her concerns to them. Buckingham went at once to Anne's lodging at court, and when he found Compton there, he used 'many hard words' and 'severely reproached' him. Compton sped off to the King and told him what had happened, upon which Henry, in a rage, summoned Buckingham and so vented his wrath on him that Buckingham stormed out of the court. Meanwhile, confronted by her irate husband, Anne had confessed all, and had been carried off by him to a nunnery sixty miles away, out of Henry's reach.

Furious at being deprived of the lady, Henry sought to apportion blame, having guessed that Lady FitzWalter had been the cause of his misfortune. He summarily banished her and her husband from court, but it appears that before she left, she had her revenge by revealing to the Queen what had been going on. This was the first Katherine had heard of her husband's infidelity, and she bitterly upbraided him, provoking a heated, and very public, row, as Henry, in turn, reproached her for daring to criticise him. Both ended up 'very vexed' with each other.[22]

Henry clearly felt ill done by. By Renaissance standards, he was fairly virtuous, in an age in which it was common for kings and nobles to take mistresses. They married for policy, profit or dynastic reasons, did their duty by their wives, and took their pleasure elsewhere. In this case, he had taken care to be discreet, and been at pains not to humiliate Katherine publicly. It was a wife's duty to maintain a dignified silence if she discovered that her husband was playing away from the marriage bed. The onus was on her to adapt to circumstances.

But Katherine had no intention of being silent, and continued to berate Henry for his betrayal. She also vented her anger on Compton. The Spanish ambassador feared she might compromise her considerable influence with the King through her unreasonable behaviour. In the end, she had to concede defeat. She had learned a humiliating lesson, and never again would she take Henry to task for being unfaithful – at least not in public.

In 1884, Anne Boleyn's biographer, Paul Friedmann, stated that Elizabeth Howard, Lady Boleyn, had been appointed one of the new Queen's ladies, and several modern writers describe her as a lady-in-waiting to Katherine,[23] but all of them have confused her with her sister-in-law, Anne Tempest, the wife of Sir Edward Boleyn.[24] Surprisingly, given Thomas Boleyn's standing with the King, there are no references to his wife being in the Queen's household, aside from joining Katherine's train for the Field of Cloth of Gold in 1520, as one of the many noble ladies attending her. Obviously, therefore, Elizabeth Howard cannot have used her influence with the Queen to further her husband's career, as has been claimed.[25]

It has also been suggested that her willingness to sleep with the King accounted for her husband's rapid rise to favour.[26] Indeed, there have been persistent claims, from her own lifetime to the present day, that she was Henry's mistress. This has been given as the reason why the wife of such an up-and-coming, and later prominent, courtier as Sir Thomas Boleyn was not assigned a post as a lady-in-waiting to the Queen.[27]

There is, as we shall see, some evidence that Elizabeth Howard did have a poor reputation. After the coronation, she is not recorded at court for eleven years, and it may be that she was constrained by her husband, or chose herself, to remain at Hever, presiding over her family and household, supervising the running of the estate and the home and tenant farms – and possibly keeping out of mischief. Maybe she did not desire a place at court, except when she was obliged to go there for the most important celebrations, or in middle age as chaperone to her daughter Anne Boleyn during the King's courtship; otherwise there is barely a mention of her in contemporary sources.

From the 1530s, there were rumours – almost certainly apocryphal – that Lady Boleyn had been Henry VIII's mistress at one time. Friar William Peto, an Observant Friar of Greenwich who had publicly denounced Henry VIII's determination to wed Anne Boleyn in a sermon preached before the King on Easter Day 1532, warned Henry afterwards that it was being said that he had meddled with both Anne's sister and her mother.[28] According to Henry's cousin, Reginald Pole, another who opposed the marriage,[29] Peto had confided to the Papist Sir George Throckmorton, a member of Parliament, that Henry had had affairs with both Mary Boleyn and her mother.

In a letter sent to Henry VIII in October 1537, Throckmorton recalled a conversation he had had in 1533 with Sir Thomas Dingley (who was to be beheaded for treason in 1539). Throckmorton, who did not yet know that the King had secretly married Anne Boleyn, had told Dingley how he had been sent for by Henry after speaking out against the Act in Restraint of Appeals (passed in April 1533) that heralded the break with Rome, 'and that he saw his Grace's conscience was troubled about having married his brother's wife. And I said to him [Dingley] that I told your Grace I feared if ye did marry Queen Anne your conscience would be more troubled at length, for it is thought ye have meddled both with the mother and the sister. And your Grace said "Never with the mother." And my Lord Privy Seal [Cromwell] standing by said "Nor never with the sister either, and therefore put that out of your mind."' This was in substance all that was said. Throckmorton made it clear that he 'intended no harm to the King, but only out of vainglory to show he was one that durst speak for the common wealth; otherwise he refuses the King's pardon and will abide the most shameful death'.[30]

Thomas Cromwell, then well established as the King's chief minister, would have known that there were good reasons for keeping his master's affair with Mary Boleyn a secret. If Mary had not been Henry's mistress, then Henry himself would surely have denied it, as he had denied having relations with her mother. And that he did deny the latter there is no doubt. As Nicholas Sander's editor points out, if this conversation had never taken place, 'it is not credible that [Throckmorton] could have dared so to write to the King, nor is it credible that he invented the story'.

Also in 1533, Elizabeth Amadas, the wife of a royal goldsmith, who had herself once been pursued by Henry VIII, publicly asserted 'that the King had kept both the mother and the daughter', referring to Elizabeth Howard and either to Mary or Anne Boleyn, who was widely reputed in the years before her marriage to Henry in 1533 to have been his mistress. Mrs Amadas also claimed that 'my lord of Wiltshire [Thomas Boleyn] was bawd both to his wife and his two daughters'.[31] However, since she made various other wild and fanciful assertions about Anne Boleyn, of whom she bitterly disapproved, it would be unwise to give too much credence to any of them.

The rumours nevertheless persisted, and spread farther afield. In March 1533, it was recorded that Thomas Jackson, a chantry priest in Chepax, Yorkshire, had claimed that Henry VIII's marriage to Anne Boleyn was adulterous and that the King had 'kept the mother and afterwards the daughter, and now he hath married her whom he kept afore, and her mother also'.[32] The fact that such gossip was in circulation as far away as Yorkshire shows how widespread were the salacious tales about the Boleyn ladies. Yet it appears that Fr Jackson, and possibly Mrs Adamas, were unaware of Mary Boleyn's relations with the King; they would surely have made capital out of them if they had been.

In 1535, John Hale, Vicar of Isleworth – no friend to the Boleyns or Henry VIII, as will be seen – repeated, amongst other calumnies, that 'the King's Grace had meddled with the Queen's [Anne Boleyn's] mother'.[33] Hale, a supporter of Katherine of Aragon, was on a mission to impugn the legality of the Boleyn marriage, but if Henry had had any sexual connection with Lady Boleyn, he would surely have declared it when applying to the Pope in 1528 for a dispensation to marry the sister of a woman (Mary Boleyn) who had been his mistress; congress with the mother would also have made such a marriage incestuous, and rendered it null and void.

Nevertheless, the assertion that Elizabeth Howard and Henry VIII had been lovers was repeated later on by three hostile Catholic writers: Nicholas Harpsfield, William Rastell, who was Sir Thomas More's nephew – More was executed in 1535 for refusing to swear the oath acknowledging the validity of the King's marriage to Anne Boleyn – and an exiled Catholic priest, Nicholas Sander, whose treatise damning Henry and Anne was published in Rome in 1585. All three writers were staunch Catholics who viewed Anne Boleyn as a Jezebel and a heretic and blamed her for the English Reformation; none was the remotest bit likely to give her a good press.

William Camden was incorrect when he fulminated that Sander was 'the first man that broached [a] damnable lie about the birth of Queen Elizabeth's mother'.[34] In fact, it originated with either Nicholas Harpsfield, whose *Treatise on the Pretended Divorce between King Henry VIII and Katherine of Aragon* was published in the reign of Katherine's daughter, Mary I, or William Rastell (*c*.1508–65), who was a contemporary of Mary Boleyn and died a recusant exile at Louvain in Elizabeth I's reign. Harpsfield, an archdeacon of Canterbury, wrote that he 'had credibly heard reported that the King knew the mother of Anne Boleyn' – in the Biblical sense, of course.

Rastell, a printer and a judge, was the editor of Sir Thomas More's works, which he published in 1557. He wrote a life of More, but it was probably never published, and certainly does not survive today. Yet Lord Herbert, whose biography of Henry VIII was published in 1649, certainly saw it, for he refers to it and states that Rastell asserted therein that Anne Boleyn was the fruit of an illicit liaison between her mother and Henry VIII, and had been conceived while Sir Thomas Boleyn was away on an embassy to France.[35]

Nicholas Sander, who lived at Louvain from 1565 and was a zealous priest and missionary whose powerful works have largely informed Roman Catholic thinking on the English Reformation, but who has been castigated at best as credulous, and at worst as a seditious liar and slanderer, by English historians down the centuries, probably also saw Rastell's lost life of More, as well as perhaps Harpsfield's *Pretended Divorce*, for he too went so far as to assert that 'Anne Boleyn was the daughter of Sir Thomas Boleyn's wife; I say his wife, because she could not have been the daughter of Sir Thomas, for she was born during his absence of two years in France on the King's affairs.' According to this version, when Boleyn returned home, he demanded to know who had sired the child, but Henry VIII ordered him to stop persecuting his wife, who admitted to him that 'it was the King who had tempted her to sin, and that the child, Anne, was the daughter of no other than Henry'. The clear implication was that Anne incestuously married her own father.

The 'impudent lie'[36] about Anne Boleyn's paternity was repeated in 1587 by Adam Blackwood, a lawyer defending the good name of Mary, Queen of Scots, whom Elizabeth I had just had executed; he wrote as if the story were well known, and indeed the contemporary gossip referred to above would tend to corroborate that. Of course, Blackwood had an axe to grind against Elizabeth, and the calumny of her being the child of incest would have served him well.

The fact that no fewer than ten people alleged in the sixteenth century that Elizabeth Howard was Henry VIII's mistress would, by most of the rules of historical research, suggest that there was some truth in it, but the King himself denied it, when he did not deny that he had had an affair with Elizabeth's daughter Mary, and this at a time when either relationship would equally have prejudiced his marriage to Anne Boleyn. Moreover, all the sources are hostile, and the story told by Rastell and Sander can easily be proved a nonsense. Sir Thomas Boleyn was not sent as ambassador to France until 1519, and Henry was probably less than ten years old when Anne was conceived.

But the allegations may have been believable because of Elizabeth Howard's dubious reputation. When the poet Skelton – possibly with the benefit of hindsight – compared her to the beautiful Cressida, he may have been hinting at something far less attractive than her looks. For 'False Cressida' appears in medieval literature as the woman who pledged undying love to her Troilus, but, after being captured by the Greeks, had an affair with Diomedes. By the fourteenth century, when Chaucer wrote his version of the legend, her name – as he acknowledges in his text – had become synonymous with female inconstancy. So when hearing any woman compared with Cressida, people would, in the Tudor period, have instantly grasped the *double entendre*. Maybe Skelton *was* merely praising Elizabeth's beauty, but if so, he had chosen a strange and compromising comparison, when there were plenty of others to be drawn.

Skelton was famous for his satirical attacks on the court, and he used allegories such as this fearlessly to criticise the great and the good, even incurring the wrath of the powerful Cardinal Wolsey. If, by 1523, when she was approaching middle age, Elizabeth Howard had gained some ill fame for straying from the connubial couch, then, with her husband riding high at court, she might well have fallen foul of Skelton's scathing wit.

There are other references in the poem that may be barbed allusions to Elizabeth's conduct. Skelton tells her he is bound to be her 'remembrancer', a remembrancer being a person (or official) who caused someone to remember something, or collected debts, or brought them a warning. He describes her as not only virtuous but cunning, which by then had acquired the meaning of artful or skilfully deceitful. The word 'lusty' was associated with desire, having by the sixteenth century lost its earlier, more innocent meaning of 'joyful' or 'merry'. Pandarus, who is mentioned in these verses, acted as go-between for Troilus and Cressida, and after Boccaccio and Chaucer wrote their versions of the story in the fourteenth century, his name gave rise to the word 'pander', which, by the 1520s, meant one who facilitated illicit sex, or supplied another with the means of gratifying lust. Skelton here refers to Pandarus' appetite, which appears to reflect that meaning. The last three lines seem to be ironic and heavy with innuendo:

> Of all your beauty I suffice not to write,
> But, as I said, your flourishing tender age
> Is lusty to look on, pleasant, demure and sage.

Taken together, all these references suggest that Skelton may have reworked his verses in 1523 to reflect what he now knew about the once-fair Lady Elizabeth Howard.[37]

What we can infer about the Boleyns' marriage from the sources does not suggest conjugal happiness. Sir Thomas stayed mostly at court or abroad, Elizabeth lived mainly in the country, visiting the court only rarely, when form demanded it. That was not especially unusual in an age of arranged marriages. But Skelton's comparison with Cressida, Elizabeth's absence from the Queen's household, and the fact that all her offspring became notorious in one way or another for sexual immorality might suggest that she herself had set them a poor example by her loose morals and by betraying her marriage vows.

If so, it is unlikely to have been with Henry VIII. Even when Henry was of an age to have sexual relations, he was supervised so strictly by the King his father that he was not permitted to leave the palace unless it was by a private door into the park, and then only in the company of specially appointed persons. His apartments could only be reached through those of Henry VII, and he spent most of his time in the tiltyard or in a bedchamber that led off his father's, and appeared 'so subjected that he does not speak a word except in response to what the King asks him'.[38] No one dared approach him or speak with him, and nothing escaped his ever-vigilant father's attention. It is likely therefore that he was still a virgin when he came to the throne. Speculation that his first affair had been with Elizabeth Denton, his mother's lady-in-waiting,[39] is unconvincing, and the extraordinary theory that the pious Margaret Beaufort, Henry's grandmother, selected her for his first sexual experience[40] even less so; in fact, the evidence we have suggests that Mistress Denton was rewarded by the new King not for sexual favours, but for faithful service to his family.

Despite Henry's denial and the other strong evidence against his having had an affair with Elizabeth Howard, a number of more recent writers still assert that she had 'briefly graced the royal bed'[41] and that Henry enjoyed 'the sophisticated embraces' of 'Lady Howard (sic.)'.[42] There have been imaginative claims that the affair took place in 1508, when Henry was seventeen;[43] that Elizabeth was 'not averse from instructing her young master in the arts of love';[44] that Thomas Boleyn's advancement in the King's service 'was probably due to a liaison between his wife and Henry';[45] that Elizabeth was 'flattered by the young Prince's attentions' and began preening herself at court;[46] and that Mary Boleyn 'gaily followed her mother into the King's bed'.[47] There is no evidence for any of this.

How did that calumny, that Elizabeth Howard was Henry's mistress, come to be spread in the first place? Possibly there were rumours in the early 1520s that the King was having an affair with one of the Boleyn ladies, and the gossips conjectured that it was Elizabeth Howard, given her reputation. It has been convincingly suggested that some people at court confused Elizabeth Boleyn with Elizabeth Blount – the name Boleyn was variously spelt, and one form of it, 'Boullant', could easily have been mistaken for Blount;[48] given how discreetly Henry VIII conducted his *amours*, this is entirely believable.

There is sounder evidence for Henry having a brief liaison with a French lady during his triumphal sojourn at Tournai in September and October 1513, in the wake of taking the besieged town. There, he entertained Margaret of Austria, Regent of the Netherlands, before visiting her court at Lille, where he is recorded as spending 'almost the whole night dancing with the damsels'.[49] The evidence for this affair is in the form of a letter dated 17 August 1514. Translated from the original French, it speaks of a bird (probably a singing bird) and some (probably medicinal) roots 'of great value, belonging to this country' that the writer has sent the King, then continues:

> When Madame [Margaret of Austria] went to the Emperor her father and you at Lille, you named me your page, and you called me by no other name, and you told me many beautiful things . . . about marriage and other things; and when we parted at Tournai, you told me, when I married, to let you know, and it should be worth to me ten thousand crowns, or rather angels. As it has now pleased my father to have me married, I send [the] bearer, an old servant of my grandfather, to remind you.
>   In your house at Marnay by Besançon, 17 August.
>   The most of your very humble servants, G. La Baume.[50]

According to the seventeenth-century French genealogist Père Anselme, the initial G could have been an E; and the writer could therefore be identified as Étiennette, daughter of Marc de la Baume, Seigneur of Châteauvillain and Count of Montreval; she married, on 18 October 1514, as his third wife, Ferdinand de Neufchâtel, Seigneur de Marnay and Montaigu (1452–1522).[51] Her bridegroom was then sixty-two, and she bore no child during the seven years of their marriage.[52] She died in 1521.[53]

Her letter gives us tantalising insights as to how Henry VIII may have conducted his love-play: the reference to Étiennette pretending to be his page and his calling her by that name reveals him as a young man who conducted his amours with humour and who enjoyed sexual role-playing and, naturally, taking the dominant part. Is there a hint of blackmail here? Did Henry pay up? We have no record of him doing so, but that is not to say that he never did. Nor is there any record of a house owned by him in Marnay. Probably it was just the one in which he had stayed during his visit.

While this letter may be evidence of a sexual affair, it is not conclusive. It could as well point to the King enjoying banter with a young woman whom he much admired. She was of a noble family, and doubtless waiting for her father to find her a husband. Henry told her beautiful things about marriage, which might be thought unusual if he was committing adultery – or did he show her how beautiful the delights of the marriage bed could be? He promised her a dowry. Was that a chivalrous gesture, or was it a reward for sexual favours? Yet she was apparently still living in his house at Marnay a year later, which suggests that he had paid for it and installed her there. On balance, the evidence points to her having been his mistress, and to Henry having done – or promised to do – the 'honourable' thing by her.

Katherine of Aragon was visibly pregnant for the fourth time when, in June 1514, good relations between England and Spain collapsed. Convinced that he had been insulted and betrayed by Katherine's father, Ferdinand V of Aragon, the King 'spat out his complaints against her', and her influence accordingly diminished. That autumn, there was even talk, in Rome and in England, of a divorce. At that time, Katherine's confessor referred to Henry having 'badly used' the Queen.[54]

He might, just possibly, have been referring to the King's latest affair. In October 1514, one of Henry's closest friends and courtiers, not to mention physical double, Charles Brandon, Duke of Suffolk, wrote to the King from France, asking him to remind 'Mistress Blount and Mistress Carew that next time, I write unto them letters or send them [love?] tokens'.[55] From this we may gather that the King, like Suffolk, was on terms of familiarity with both these young women, and probably enjoying flirtations – and perhaps more – with them. Mistress Blount and Mistress Carew may well have shared their favours; the hostile Nicholas Sander, writing in 1585, frequently repeated unsubstantiated calumnies about Henry VIII, but his assertion that the King was often 'living in sin, sometimes with two, sometimes with three of the Queen's maids of honour' may not be far off the mark. Henry gave Elizabeth Bryan, the wife of the rising courtier Nicholas Carew, 'many beautiful diamonds and pearls and innumerable jewels',[56] which strongly suggests that at one time she was more to him than just a mere acquaintance; and certainly, at some stage, he enjoyed a sexual relationship with Elizabeth Blount, for she later bore him a son whom he acknowledged. Significantly, Queen Katherine was well advanced in her fourth pregnancy in October 1514, and Henry had every excuse for straying from the marital bed once more.

Elizabeth, or Bessie Blount, as she was familiarly called, was then sixteen at the most, probably younger; her exact date of birth is unknown, but her father was only thirty-six in 1519,[57] and as boys were then not considered to be capable of cohabiting with their wives before the age of fourteen, she cannot have been born much before 1498. She was one of the eleven children of Sir John Blount of Kinlet Hall, Shropshire, by Katherine Peshall of Knightley, Staffordshire, who had been a lady-in-waiting to Katherine of Aragon at Ludlow for a short spell in 1502, when Katherine had been married to Arthur, Prince of Wales. Lady Blount's father had fought for Henry VII in 1485 at the Battle of Bosworth, which had established the Tudor dynasty on the throne.

Effigies of the five sons and six daughters of Sir John Blount survive on either side of his tomb in the church of St John the Baptist at Kinlet. Elizabeth had probably been born in the nearby manor house of the Blounts, which was demolished in the eighteenth century (the site now being occupied by Moffat House School). Sir John, who died in 1531, was a kinsman of the Queen's chamberlain, William Blount, Lord Mountjoy, the noted humanist scholar. Probably it was Mountjoy who, in 1512,[58] had secured for Elizabeth a post as maid of honour to the Queen.

On the evidence above, it may well have been in 1514 that Henry VIII took Elizabeth as his mistress. According to the chronicler Edward Hall, 'the King, in his fresh youth, was in the chains of love with a fair damsel called Elizabeth Blount, which in singing, dancing and in all goodly pastimes, she exceeded all other, by which she won the King's heart'. Henry, being a gifted composer, musician and dancer, much admired these accomplishments in women. Lord Herbert of Cherbury, writing in the seventeenth century, and in a good position to know, since he was a neighbour of the Blounts of Kinlet,[59] stated that 'Mistress Elizabeth Blount was thought, for her rare ornaments of nature, and education, to be the beauty and mistress-piece of her time'. William Camden, writing in the early seventeenth century, records how the Blounts were 'very famous' for their 'golden locks', so the chances are that Elizabeth was blonde. Jones states that she wrote music, but does not cite her source.

Elizabeth showed Henry 'so much favour' that they became lovers in the fullest sense.[60] But again, the King was discreet – so much so that very little is known about this affair; in 1519, when Elizabeth was still very much on the scene, the humanist Erasmus would even refer to the King as 'the best of husbands' who set his subjects a shining example of 'chaste and concordant wedlock'.

His future pursuit of Anne Boleyn aside, Henry's affair with Elizabeth Blount was the best documented of his affairs – which is not saying much – and the way it was conducted may well throw some light on his later, poorly documented liaison with Mary Boleyn; therefore it is useful to look at the surviving evidence for that affair.

At Christmas 1514, Elizabeth featured prominently at a pageant performed at Greenwich, in which she, Elizabeth Carew, Margaret, Lady Guildford, and Lady Fellinger, wife to the Spanish ambassador, all dressed as ladies of Savoy in blue velvet gowns, gold caps and masks, and were rescued from danger by four gallant 'Portuguese' knights, played by King Henry, the Duke of Suffolk, Nicholas Carew and the Spanish ambassador. Queen Katherine was so enamoured of the 'strange apparel' worn by the performers that, before they unmasked themselves, she invited them to dance for her in private in her bedchamber. Here, Henry partnered Elizabeth Blount, and there was much laughter afterwards when the masks were removed and the identities of the dancers revealed. The Queen thanked the King for such 'goodly pastime' and kissed him.[61]

The fact that Henry partnered Elizabeth Blount on these occasions suggests that they were already lovers. It has been stated that their affair began in 1518,[62] but this fails to take account of this earlier evidence. It may be significant that, on Twelfth Night 1515, only a few weeks before the Queen gave birth to another son who died young, Elizabeth was not present when the same dancers performed in Dutch costume, her place having been taken by another lady of the court, Jane Popincourt.[63] Possibly the Queen had grown suspicious; or Henry had feared to upset her in her condition, or that the affair might be exposed. Instead, Elizabeth appeared in a

'disguising' featuring Sir Thomas Boleyn and his son, from which
the King was notably absent.[64]

Elizabeth Blount appears to have been the King's mistress for at least
four years. For most of this time, there is no mention of her in
contemporary sources. Given the length of the affair, there must have
been more to it than just sexual dalliance; maybe the pair were in
love, which is possible, although it may be overstating things to claim
that Elizabeth 'meant everything' to Henry.[65]

    On 3 October 1518, on the evening after an important treaty with
France was signed in St Paul's Cathedral, Cardinal Wolsey feasted the
French ambassadors and the court at York Place (later Whitehall
Palace), his London residence, in honour of the betrothal of the little
Princess Mary to the Dauphin of France.[66] Afterwards, the King and
his sister Mary, Duchess of Suffolk, led out a troupe of twenty-four
masked dancers, of whom one was Elizabeth Blount.[67] This was the
last occasion on which Henry VIII and Elizabeth were recorded as
appearing together in public; by this time, as Lord Herbert quaintly
put it, 'entire affection [had] passed between them, so that at last she
bore him a son', conceived during the Queen's last pregnancy.

    A convincing theory has been put forward that Henry and Elizabeth
had been using some form of contraception;[68] after all, their affair
had apparently been going on for four years before she conceived.
It has also been suggested that Elizabeth deliberately got pregnant,[69]
presumably in order to profit in some way from her royal lover,
although, given how Henry had maintained the utmost discretion
throughout, she would have been foolish indeed to court such a
scandal. Henry, it is argued, may have felt betrayed by his mistress
purposefully conceiving a child, and this may have sounded the death
knell to the affair.[70] It seems far more likely that the pregnancy was
an accident.

    Elizabeth had to leave court, of course, and Henry sent her to a
house called Jericho, which he had leased from St Lawrence's Priory
at Blackmore in Essex, near Chipping Ongar. It was not given to
Elizabeth, as has been asserted,[71] but made available to her at this
time. It may be that the Augustinian canons at the priory gave her
some support, and in this we might perceive the managing hand of
Cardinal Wolsey.[72]

    Jericho might have been monastic property, but it was a house
that later came to gain a poor reputation. It was surrounded by a

moat and screened by tall brick walls that afforded a high degree of privacy. The moat was fed by the River Can, which was known to the local people as 'the River Jordan'; this was how the place had acquired its name.

Here, at Jericho, the King kept a private suite of rooms, and when he visited, he probably took with him only a few attendants – his 'riding household'. Here, as at his other residences, 'the King's Highness have his privy chamber and inward lodgings reserved secret, at the pleasure of his Grace, without repair of any great multitude'.[73] According to Philip Morant, an eighteenth-century Essex historian, 'this place [was] reported to have been one of King Henry the Eighth's houses of pleasure, and disguised by the name of Jericho, so that, when this lascivious prince had a mind to be lost in the embraces of his courtesans, the cant word among the courtiers was that he was gone to Jericho'. This account may have been somewhat embellished, but certainly no one would have been encouraged to approach the King during his stay, and the pages and grooms of his privy chamber would have been routinely warned 'not to hearken or enquire where the King is or goeth, be it early or late, without grudging, mumbling or talking of the King's pastime or his late or early going to bed'.[74]

It is not inconceivable that Jericho was used by Henry as a trysting place where he could make love to Elizabeth Blount in privacy, and perhaps other women also – possibly even Mary Boleyn herself when her time came. If so, such covert pleasures would have come to an end in 1525, when the priory was dissolved by Wolsey and Jericho was sold.[75]

Elizabeth Blount certainly resided for a time at Jericho, for around June 1519 – and possibly on the 18th, if her child was ennobled on his sixth birthday in 1525[76] – she gave birth there to a son, 'a goodly man child of beauty like to the father and mother'.[77] The infant was given his father's Christian name and the old Norman-French surname of Fitzroy, which meant 'son of the King'.[78]

The tragedy was that this son was born out of wedlock. By then, Queen Katherine's catastrophic obstetric career had ended in failure. Of her six pregnancies, only one daughter, the Princess Mary, born in 1516, had survived. For a king who needed a son to succeed him, this was a dynastic disaster, for there was a widespread conviction that women were not meant to wield sovereign power; that it was against all laws both natural and divine. The birth of a living son to his mistress was a triumphant vindication for Henry. It proved that he could father boys, and that the fault did not lie with him.

It probably signalled the end of his affair with Elizabeth Blount. In accordance with the convention that it was unsafe and ungodly to have sex during pregnancy, he had probably stopped sleeping with her months before, and there is no evidence that they resumed having relations after the birth. Almost as soon as she had recovered from her confinement, Henry enlisted the aid of Cardinal Wolsey in arranging an honourable marriage for her with one of the Cardinal's wards, Gilbert Tailboys. This must have taken place in the latter half of 1519, no later, as the eldest daughter born to the couple, also Elizabeth, was stated to be twenty-two years old in the Inquisition Post Mortem on her brother, Robert, Lord Tailboys, in June 1542.[79] Thus she had been born in 1520. The date of the marriage is not recorded, and Elizabeth is not referred to as Tailboys' wife until 1522.[80]

Gilbert Tailboys was the son of George Tailboys, Lord Kyme, 'an lunatic' whose person and lands had been entrusted to the protective custody of Cardinal Wolsey in 1517, and whose estates were held in trust by the Crown.[81] Lands in Lincolnshire and Somerset were released to Gilbert on his marriage, and Parliament, thanks to Wolsey's influence, assigned Elizabeth Blount a handsome dowry. Wolsey was savagely criticised for his part in this, and accused of encouraging 'the young gentlewomen of the realm to become concubines by the well marrying of Bessie Blount, whom we would yet by sleight have married much better than she is, and for that purpose changed her name'.[82]

'The mother of the King's son' continued to benefit from the King's bounty after her marriage. On 18 June 1522, she and her husband were granted the royal manor of Rokeby in Warwickshire,[83] and in 1524, an Act of Parliament was passed giving her a life interest in many of her father-in-law's estates. In 1534, she was receiving a yearly grant of three tuns of Gascon wine from the port of Boston.[84] Thereafter, Elizabeth received the occasional New Year's present from the King.[85] It is, of course, possible that some of these grants were gifted in acknowledgement of further intimate services rendered by Elizabeth to the King, or as rewards for Tailboys being an accommodating husband – yet it is much more likely that the affair had ended in 1519, and certainly by 1522, because the evidence would suggest that Henry began pursuing Mary Boleyn that year. George, Elizabeth's third child by her husband, was sixteen in March 1539,[86] so he must have been born in 1523 at the latest, which means that her second child, Robert, had arrived in 1521/2. It is hardly likely that her affair with the King had continued through this period of successive pregnancies.

There is no evidence that Elizabeth's father ever benefited materially from his daughter's liaison with the King and its natural consequences. Her husband was not knighted until 1524 and thereafter held the office of Sheriff of Lincoln for two years.[87] He is also recorded as 'belonging to the King's Chamber',[88] so he enjoyed some influence at court, possibly on his own merits. In 1525, Tailboys was appointed Keeper of Tattershall Castle,[89] and he and Elizabeth took up residence in Lincolnshire, where they lived in a house built on to the fourteenth-century castle at South Kyme, his family home; the house was demolished in 1725, and all that remains today is the castle tower. Tailboys represented Lincoln as Knight of the Shire in the Parliament that met in November 1529, and it was in this Parliament that he was created Baron Tailboys,[90] possibly in consequence of his wife's position as mother of the King's bastard son.[91] Tailboys and Elizabeth produced several children, of whom three survived into adulthood, before his death on 15 April 1530. He was buried in the twelfth-century church of the Augustinian priory of St Mary and All Saints at South Kyme, and when it was largely rebuilt in 1805 (only a Norman doorway remains), his leaden coffin was discovered, along with those of three of his children by Elizabeth Blount.[92]

In 1532, still resident at Kyme, Elizabeth turned down a proposal of marriage from Lord Leonard Grey[93] in favour of marrying a royal ward, Edward Fiennes de Clinton, 9th Baron Clinton, who was fourteen years her junior, and would be created Earl of Lincoln in 1572 by Queen Elizabeth I. They had married before February 1534,[94] and Elizabeth bore Clinton four daughters. She was still living on 6 February 1539, but had died by 15 June 1541. She was buried with her first husband at Kyme, and monumental inscriptions to them both were put up in the church.[95]

Henry Fitzroy was Henry VIII's only acknowledged bastard son – 'my worldly jewel', as he called the boy. Lord Herbert makes it clear that Fitzroy was 'much avowed [acknowledged]' by Henry in the years prior to the child's ennoblement at the age of six. Cardinal Wolsey was the infant's godfather at his baptism, and afterwards the

King entrusted Wolsey with overall responsibility for young Fitzroy's care, although it would seem that the child remained with his mother during his early years. Henry provided him with the best education, and, according to William Franklyn, Archdeacon of Durham, the boy grew into 'a child of excellent wisdom and towardness; and, for his good and quick capacity, retentive memory, virtuous inclination to all honour, humanity and goodness, I think hard it would be to find any creature living twice his age, able or worthy to be compared with him'.[96]

Herbert described Henry Fitzroy as 'proving so equally like both his parents, that he became the best emblem of their mutual affection'. From the first, bastard though the boy was, Henry VIII would groom him for kingship.

3

'Into the Realm of France'

Sir Thomas Boleyn was one of the gallant knights who took part in the great tournament held in February 1511 at Westminster to honour the birth of Henry VIII's first son, Henry, Prince of Wales, who had been born on New Year's Day. But, to the great grief of his parents, the infant Prince died only a week later, and Sir Thomas soon found himself one of the bearers at the funeral in Westminster Abbey.[1] That is prime evidence that he was already prominent at court and close to Henry VIII. At a tournament on 23 May 1510 at Greenwich Palace, he had jousted against the King himself.[2] By 1511, Sir Thomas was well established as one of Henry VIII's favourite courtiers, and more lucrative offices were coming his way. He was appointed keeper of the royal park of Bestwood, Nottinghamshire, that year, and Sheriff of Kent for twelve months, then made joint Constable of Norwich Castle on 15 February 1512. He was again Sheriff of Kent from 1517 to 1518.[3]

Boleyn, being a great linguist, an invaluable asset in the world of Tudor diplomacy, was sent in May 1512, with Sir Richard Wingfield – who lived at Stone in Kent, not far from Hever – and John Young, on an embassy to the Holy Roman Emperor, Maximilian I, in Flanders. On 5 April 1513, Boleyn and Sir Edward Poynings concluded a treaty with Pope Julius II and Maximilian's daughter, Margaret of Austria, Regent of the Netherlands, at Malines near Brussels, when they joined forces with Henry VIII as the 'Holy League' to make war against the French. Sir Thomas returned to England in June 1513.[4] Later that summer, when Henry VIII invaded France, Boleyn led a company of a hundred men[5] and took part in the siege of Thérouanne and the Battle of the Spurs, both English victories.

At the turn of the sixteenth century, Andreas Franciscus, a continental visitor to England, observed that Englishmen, 'contrary to nature', showed no love to their children, lavishing all their love on their wives. Thomas Boleyn seems to have lavished little love on either, but he was a cultivated man and he plainly cared about education, seeing it as the pathway to success. He was at the forefront of innovation in having at least one of his daughters tutored to a high standard. That was Anne, whom Lord Herbert states was so 'singular' in 'towardness' that her parents 'took all possible care for her good education'. Because Anne later became Queen of England, we know quite a lot about her intellectual abilities and interests, and can infer from those something of her education, but of her sister Mary's we know next to nothing, save that she was literate, read books and could write a competent letter. No one mentioned *her* singular towardness, and Ives' reference to her 'evident inferior potential' may be apposite. Nevertheless, Sir Thomas Boleyn afforded both his daughters a training that would befit them for court life and good marriages.[6]

There is a consensus of opinion among historians that Mary 'was apparently less of an intellectual than the rest of her family'.[7] It has even been claimed that she was 'neglected from infancy by her parents',[8] although there is no evidence for this – indeed, rather the contrary. Just one historian suggests that, 'to judge from her later history, [Mary] may well have been intelligent and opportunistic'.[9] But others disagree, asserting that Anne was 'far more intelligent and far more applied' than Mary, as 'the respective courses of [the sisters'] lives would amply demonstrate'.[10] Anne 'was clearly the brighter, and considered to be the more teachable',[11] while Mary had 'only a trace of Anne's great vitality, with less brains, and much less determination'.[12] She was 'neither accomplished nor witty'.[13] 'Anne appears to have outstripped Mary in her education, and she quickly became the focus of Thomas Boleyn's ambition for his daughters'.[14] Anne, it seems, was his favourite.[15]

All these assertions – going on purely circumstantial contemporary evidence – are probably percipient, yet it is barely conceivable that Mary, being the elder daughter, would not initially have been afforded an education similar to that which her younger sister received.[16] And even if Thomas Boleyn gave up on that at some point, finding that Mary was a pretty girl but not as bright as her sister,[17] her birth and her father's position would have been sufficient to secure her a good marriage.

This was a time when medieval notions of education being a danger to the moral welfare of girls were being overturned. Sir Thomas More's house in London was virtually a female academy: he afforded his clever daughters a fine classical education, no different from that arranged for his son. More's success – showing that women could be both learned and virtuous – undoubtedly influenced Katherine of Aragon in planning the education of her daughter, the Princess Mary, born in 1516; she took the advice of the Spanish educationist Juan Luis Vives, who prescribed a vigorous curriculum. But that was years after Thomas Boleyn had afforded his daughters a rather advanced education for the period, which also placed emphasis on all the accepted branches of virtuous instruction, such as music, singing and dancing,[18] essential accomplishments for girls who were destined to be the ornaments of courts, as clearly their father intended. The composer Richard Davy was chaplain to Thomas Boleyn from 1506 to 1515, when some of his best church music was written, so the sisters had the benefit of growing up in a household in which music was integral and a sophisticated example was set.[19] Mary (like her sister) may have grown up to be an accomplished musician,[20] but this is only an assumption.[21]

The Boleyn daughters were taught to read and to write in a fine Italianate hand, as Anne's letters prove; only two of Mary's letters survive to show that her style was not as elegant as her sister's, or as grammatical – a failing of which she was aware, for she referred to one being 'scribbled with her ill hand',[22] although it does show her to have been articulate.[23] It was not uncommon, however, for educated aristocrats, both men and women, to write and spell badly.[24] Mary does reveal in that same letter that she read 'old books' about kings and queens, presumably for pleasure, so no doubt she read others also.

All the Boleyn children were taught to speak fluent French. That was clearly very important to their father. As we will see, Anne initially struggled with that language, and only years of living abroad at the courts of Brussels and France made her proficient in it. Mary seems to have had a better aptitude for French, which shows she was not a dullard. There is no evidence to support the assertion that 'both daughters occasionally accompanied their father on his missions abroad'.[25] It was he who accompanied them when they went to foreign courts.

Mary and Anne would have received instruction in the traditional aristocratic pursuits of riding, hunting and hawking, at which their father excelled, and instruction in the rituals and beliefs of the pre-Reformation Catholic Church – doctrines that the Boleyn family would one day challenge. Their lives at Hever Castle would have been conventional, ordered by religious and domestic routines, and the unchanging round of the seasons: Lady Day, 25 March, the official beginning of the medieval year; Lent; Easter; May Day, when young girls rose early to bring in the May; Michaelmas, and the start of the farming year; Harvest-tide; Advent; Christmas and the Twelfth Night celebrations, and Candlemas. The cycle was punctuated by numerous holy and saints' days. There would have been a chapel in the medieval castle, where the family chaplain would have celebrated Mass daily.

Hever Castle boasted a great hall, a symbol of the Boleyns' wealth and status, where the family plate would have been displayed on a buffet, and the prevailing fashion dictated sparse furnishings consisting largely of hangings, chests and side tables. But at this period, when personal privacy was beginning to be seen as more desirable than communal living, such halls were going out of fashion, and were used mainly for celebrations and entertaining, while family life was generally conducted, and meals taken, in the privacy of the parlour.

On wet days, instead of walking in the gardens, riding out on horseback, hunting or hawking, the sisters might take their exercise in the long gallery built by their father. Their parents would have slept in the Great Chamber, which also doubled as a reception room in Tudor times, and they themselves would have occupied lesser bedchambers. We have no way of knowing which chambers Mary and Anne occupied at Hever, but they would probably have had a fireplace, small diamond-paned windows and wainscoted or painted walls. Their beds would have been solid wooden structures with a tester or canopy and expensive curtains and hangings of silk or damask. They would have had a chair or stool, a chest for clothes and linen, a cupboard to hold a basin and ewer, cosmetic jars, a mirror of burnished silver and a chamber pot.

The family's steward held sway in the estate office, where tenants came to pay rent or settle disputes, and accounts were kept, with the aid of a chequered counting table or cloth. This room was very much a male preserve, but Lady Boleyn, the mistress of the castle, would also have had her office, and from here she ruled her household, ordering the servants and overseeing the provisioning and feeding of the family and their large staff of servants. Traditionally, even great ladies had their still rooms, where they might distil sweet waters, or produce confits and conserves, or make medicines and poultices, using the herbs that grew in the gardens. In these tasks, Mary and Anne would have assisted their mother, for it was considered essential that girls of good birth were taught the skills that would enable them to run a great household. They would have learned that a lady should keep her servants busy not only by precept, but by example.

Breakfast in those days was served early, at six or seven o'clock, and consisted of meat or pottage (broth), bread and ale. Dinner – the main meal of the day – was usually eaten late in the morning. The Boleyns, with their rich estates, would have eaten well, if not lavishly, and been offered several courses, with many dishes at each; and they might well have followed the fashion to remain at table until two or three in the afternoon. Supper, a lighter repast, was at five or six o'clock. All the food was organic, and much of it would have been fresh and flavoured with herbs and expensive spices. The parlour where the family ate would have been furnished with a long table, a chair for Sir Thomas Boleyn at its head, and stools and benches for his wife, his children and his mother. The walls would have been panelled with wainscot, perhaps with painted friezes or scenes on the plaster above, and hung with tapestries, painted cloths or pictures.

Rooms were heated by open fires or braziers, and lit by beeswax candles, which were often set in beams or wheel-shaped structures and hoisted into place by a pulley. Only the better-off could afford sufficient lighting to allow them to stay up in the evenings, when Mary and Anne and their brothers probably amused themselves by playing cards, dice or games such as chess or tables (backgammon); or they might have passed their leisure time in reading, singing, making music, sewing, embroidering, writing poetry or teasing each other with riddles, which was a popular pastime. Probably they danced too, practising the latest steps against the time they might be summoned to court, which must have been the greatest desire of their childhood.

The clothes the sisters would have worn in their everyday life were modestly cut, of good quality and the same as those worn by their elders. These comprised a washable linen shift, worn next to the skin, a petticoat lined perhaps with fur, and a long, square-necked gown lined with richer fur; this had a train that they were taught to carry looped over one arm. The sleeves of the gown were either long and hanging, or tight with fur-lined cuffs. Unmarried girls customarily wore their hair long and loose, although they may occasionally have worn caps or hoods with long lappets hanging down over their shoulders. Their stockings were of black wool, and their shoes had double soles and broad toes.

As they grew older, the Boleyn sisters would have enjoyed certain freedoms. English women, noted a Dutch observer, Emanuel van Meteren, did not lead cloistered lives. They were well dressed and enjoyed showing off their finery when shopping and going to market. They employed their time walking, riding, playing cards, visiting friends and keeping company, conversing with their 'gossips' and neighbours, and making merry at childbirths, christenings, churchings and funerals. In these pursuits, Mary and Anne would have been chaperoned by their mother or governess, for unmarried girls were kept 'rigorously and strictly' to protect their virtue.

Above all, the Boleyn sisters would have been brought up to render unconditional obedience to their father and, later, to the husbands he would choose for them.[26] They would have learned that women were subordinate creatures, infants in law and subject to the dominion of men.

Anne grew up to be a talented musician, an accomplished singer and dancer, a competent poet, a trendsetter in fashions, a skilled needlewoman and a witty conversationalist. Mary is not recorded as having any of those gifts, although she probably had some ability in music and dancing, which was desirable at court and would, later, have been pleasing to Henry VIII. And when the tutors he had employed had done all they could, Sir Thomas Boleyn unashamedly used his official connections to secure 'the extra advantage of a continental finish for his daughters'.[27] Yet although Mary was the elder, it was the sparkling Anne who was found a position at court first.[28]

It is possible that Anne was chosen to go to the court of the Archduchess Margaret of Austria, Regent of the Netherlands, because she needed to complete her education, when Mary had already done so.[29] But there was far more than education at stake, for the Archduchess's court offered many opportunities and advantages for a young girl of good birth. Anne's acute intellect is more likely to have been the reason why her father decided that she, rather than her elder sister, should benefit from being educated abroad:[30] whilst at Malines, he boasted to Margaret of Austria of the virtues and accomplishments of '*la petite Boulain*' (as he called his younger daughter in one of his letters[31]) and, as a result, the erudite Margaret offered Anne, then about twelve years old, a place in her household as one of her eighteen '*filles d'honneur*'. The name Boleyn appears on the list of her ladies.

Margaret's court was regarded as one of the finest finishing schools in Europe.[32] According to the Emperor Maximilian, it was usual for maids of honour to be aged about thirteen or fourteen;[33] this was because they were expected to be able to attract advantageous marriages at court, advance the interests and ambitions of their family, and perform the decorative and social functions required of them. Competition for places was fierce, and parents and guardians were prepared to lay out substantial financial inducements in order to secure the honour of an appointment for their daughters. Moreover, there were more chances of success if a girl had the kind of attributes that would make her an ornament of the court; she had to know how to dress fashionably, dance, sing, entertain her royal mistress and important visitors with witty and amiable conversation, and understand how to conduct herself when in attendance in public and on state occasions. It was for this that Thomas Boleyn had provided his daughters with a sophisticated education, and clearly he did not baulk at the considerable outlay required to provide them with suitable court attire. It could never be claimed, as Mary Luke does, that he sought places at court for them to rid himself of the expense of their upbringing.

In the nineteenth century, there was 'no doubt it is Mary, and not Anne Boleyn, who was *fille d'honneur* to Margaret of Austria and the subject of that lady's letter to Sir Thomas Boleyn',[34] and several historians since have repeated the error,[35] but the issue is settled by an undated letter, written in French by Anne to her father (and the first of hers to survive), that must belong to this period.

Sir [she wrote],
    I understand by your letter that you desire that I shall be a worthy woman when I come into the court, and you inform me that the Queen will take the trouble to converse with me, which rejoices me much to think of talking with a person so

wise and worthy. This will make me have greater desire to
continue to speak French well, and also spell, especially because
you have enjoined it on me, and with my own hand I inform
you that I will observe it the best I can. Sir, I beg you to excuse
me if my letter is badly written, for I assure you that the orthog-
raphy is from my own understanding alone, while the others
were only written by my hand, and Semmonet tells me the
letter but waits so that I may do it myself.

Written at Veure by Your very humble and very obedient
daughter,

Anna de Boullan.[36]

For a long time, it was thought that this letter was written at Hever
Castle,[37] but in 1981, Hugh Paget retranslated it, and discovered that
it was in fact written from La Veure (or Terveuren), a royal palace
and hunting park near Brussels, which Margaret of Austria favoured
as a summer retreat. We know the letter is authentic because it was
preserved by Thomas or Anne Boleyn, and bequeathed by Anne's
chaplain, Matthew Parker, later Archbishop of Canterbury, to Corpus
Christi College, Cambridge.[38] Thus there can be no doubt that it
was Anne who was sent to the court of the Archduchess.

'Semonnet' was presumably a governess – possibly called Simonette
– who instructed Anne, and perhaps the other *filles d'honneur*, in
French, or 'she' could conceivably have been a male tutor with that
surname; there was a gentleman called Symonnet in the household
of Margaret of Austria's nephew, the future Charles V, in 1510.[39]
Certainly Margaret had assured Anne's father that, by the time he saw
his daughter again, she would be able to converse with him in French.[40]

It is likely that Anne was present at Lille when the Archduchess
entertained Henry VIII there in October 1513, and she may even
have been one of the 'damsels' with whom the twenty-two-year-old
King spent the night dancing.[41] This may have been the first occasion on which she set eyes on Henry of England – unless she had
seen him when her grandfather entertained him at New Hall in 1510.

It was highly unusual for a younger sister to be advanced before an
elder one, and Anne's appointment has been cited as proof that she
'had to have been the elder';[42] yet it was even more unusual for a
younger sister to be married first, and the fact that Mary did marry
before Anne was found a husband tends to demolish that argument.

It has also been asserted that Anne was not married off before Mary because she was expected to make a good marriage in France,[43] but by 1520, she had been there five years and no husband had materialised. Moreover, by the spring of that year, as soon as her sister had been wedded and bedded, her father was negotiating a marriage for her in England – which immeasurably strengthens the case for her being the younger sister.

Even so, it is strange to find Mary, who evidently spoke good French, being passed over as a *fille d'honneur* to Margaret of Austria. The reason was possibly that her father believed that Anne had what it took to succeed at court in greater measure than Mary. Yet Mary was clearly by no means deficient in that respect, for soon Sir Thomas would find her a place at court too. This leads one to wonder if there was some other reason for Anne being chosen first. Maybe Mary was unwell at the time, or her father had other plans for her, perhaps hoping to place her at the English court.

It may be that Mary Boleyn was jealous of her younger sister going before her into the world of courts, and we may imagine that, after Anne had left for the Low Countries in 1513, Mary perhaps felt resentful and not a little lonely. Yet there is no evidence that the sisters were close,[44] or even friendly, so she may have welcomed some respite from being always in the shadow of Anne. Mary has also been seen as 'a highly sexed young woman who had been desperate to escape from the boredom of her home at Hever Castle',[45] and as 'sensual and precociously attractive'[46] and therefore no doubt frustrated – but no one can say any of this for certain. Yet even if Mary was bored at Hever, she would not have to wait long for her own advancement. And if she did not have the same talents, charm and ambition as Anne, she had clearly been afforded an education that would befit her for a career at court, for in a very short time, thanks to her father's influence, she would make her own début there.

While we cannot be sure what Mary looked like, as she grew towards womanhood the charms that were to inspire lust in two kings must have become evident. Modern writers describe her variously as 'dark-haired',[47] 'stately and golden-haired'[48] or 'dimpled and red-cheeked, with lightish-brown hair and grey eyes' and a 'rosy, soft, blue-eyed fairness';[49] but there is nothing to substantiate any of these confusing statements. All we know is that Thomas Boleyn's chaplain, John Barlow, thought that Mary was by far the more beautiful of the

Boleyn sisters. That is in direct contradiction to claims that she was 'physically not very attractive'[50] and 'not a beauty'.[51]

Portraits of Mary's son, Henry Carey, show a man with a long, thin face, a pointed chin, hooked nose and heavy-lidded eyes. He does not favour his father, William Carey, although the resemblance to Elizabeth I and Anne Boleyn is striking. Possibly Mary herself had similar features, which were inherited from the Boleyns. But sadly, there is no authenticated portrait or likeness of her.[52]

In the summer of 1514, Mary Boleyn would no doubt have been delighted to receive a summons to court. The King's sister, the beautiful eighteen-year-old Mary Tudor, was to be married to Louis XII, King of France, and had need of young girls of good birth who could speak French to attend on her.[53] Mary Boleyn had not had the benefit of specialist coaching in French at the court of Brussels, yet she was selected, which argues that she had not had need of it, having inherited her father's aptitude for languages. The Princess specifically asked for Anne Boleyn also, having heard, presumably from Sir Thomas, that she had made excellent progress in French. 'To this request I could not, nor did I know how to refuse,' the proud father wrote to the Archduchess Margaret.[54] There had been much jostling for places in Mary Tudor's train, and the fact that he was successful in obtaining appointments for both his daughters is a measure of Sir Thomas Boleyn's growing influence and standing at the English court.

This royal wedding was being organised at very short notice. Anne's letter to her father had been written in that summer of 1514, when the Archduchess took her household for a summer visit to La Veure.[55] By then, however, diplomatic relations between England and the Empire were deteriorating. Henry VIII had broken the long-standing betrothal of Margaret of Austria's nephew, the Archduke Charles (the future Emperor Charles V), son of the Emperor Maximilian, to Mary Tudor, and had instead made an alliance with France and affianced an unwilling Mary to the ailing Louis XII, Maximilian's rival. Soon, on 14 August, Thomas Boleyn was writing from Greenwich tactfully to ask the Archduchess Margaret if she would permit his daughter to return to him with his emissaries, explaining that the Princess Mary wanted his daughter as one of the attendants she would take with her to France.[56] Thus the queen to whom Anne had referred in her letter from La Veure was Mary Tudor, who now boasted that royal style after having been married by proxy to the King of France.

There has been much confusion as to whether one or both of the Boleyn sisters went to France in 1514. Several writers correctly state that it was Mary who accompanied Mary Tudor there,[57] but the evidence has perplexed many historians. An 'M. Boleyn' is listed among the group of privileged young ladies who were to form part of Mary Tudor's train,[58] and, for more than a century, there was much learned discussion as to whether the 'M' stood for 'Mary', 'Mistress' or 'Mademoiselle'. We know now that it referred to Mary, for in a recently discovered list of Queen Mary's ladies who were paid for their service during the period between October and December 1514,[59] the name 'Marie Boulonne' is to be found. Anne Boleyn's name, however, is missing.

It is clear, though, that both Boleyn girls went to France at some stage, although Anne is also missing from the list of the English attendants who travelled with Mary Tudor from England. Possibly she travelled direct from Brussels.[60] Thomas Boleyn had written from Greenwich to the Archduchess requesting that she be returned to him. That was on 14 August, the day after Mary Tudor had been married by proxy at Greenwich. Mary would not sail to France until 2 October, while her wedding to King Louis would take place on 9 October at Abbeville; thus there would have been enough time for Anne to come home first and then travel to France with her new mistress, but clearly she did not. It may be correct to assume that the Archduchess, angered at the breaking of her nephew's betrothal, made difficulties about Anne leaving, and delayed her departure,[61] for the absence of her name from the list of payments made to Mary's attendants between October and December 1514 indicates that she did not arrive in France until early in 1515.[62] Unfortunately, no records of similar payments survive for the following quarter.[63]

Whether her departure was obstructed or not, it may be that, in order to serve the Queen of France, Anne had to return home to be fitted for a new wardrobe – she was only in her early teens and probably still growing – and that it was this, and perhaps winter weather, that delayed her arrival at the French court.

Among the new Queen's household of nearly one hundred and fifty persons, Mary Boleyn was initially to be one of four 'chamberers', along with 'Mistress Wotton, Alice Denny and Anne Jerningham'.[64] Chamberers served their mistress in the privacy of her chamber, or private suite, performing the menial tasks that were beneath the

dignity of her ladies-in-waiting. All the same, they were personal
servants who enjoyed a degree of intimacy with her.

It was probably in August 1514 that Mary Boleyn arrived at the
court of Henry VIII, which was then in residence at Greenwich
Palace, the beautiful riverside residence where the King had been
born in 1491. The former palace of Placentia had been rebuilt around
1500, and was one of the chief and most magnificent residences of
the Tudor dynasty. Ranged around three vast courtyards, it was of
red brick with great bay windows, surrounded by exquisite gardens
and orchards, and sumptuously decorated and appointed throughout.

In the splendid but daunting environment of the court, Mary was
entrusted at once to the care of Jane, Lady Guildford, the 'Lady of
Honour'[65] or 'Mother of the Maids', who had charge of all the
Princess's maids-of-honour and was appointed to look to their welfare
and good conduct, and to instruct them in etiquette.[66] Lady Guildford,
widow of Sir Richard Guildford, the comptroller of Henry VII's
household, had formerly been the Princess's governess, and a lady-
in-waiting to her mother, Elizabeth of York, and her grandmother,
Margaret Beaufort. She knew how things were done in courts, and
was not only a long-standing confidante and mentor to her young
mistress, but also ruled her maids and chamberers efficiently.

Mary Boleyn would soon meet her fellow attendants. Some she
already knew, including her step-grandmother, Agnes Tilney, Duchess
of Norfolk, and her cousin, Anne Howard, Countess of Oxford. One
of the maids of honour was Jane Popincourt, a Frenchwoman who
is known to have been maid-of-honour to the King's late mother,
Elizabeth of York, in 1498, and to have transferred by 1500 to the
service of his sister, Mary. It was no secret that Jane was the mistress
of a French prince, Louis d'Orléans, Duc de Longueville, who was
at that time a prisoner of the King, having been captured in battle
in 1513. Since then, while waiting to be ransomed, Longueville had
been comfortably lodged in the Tower of London, and was often
invited to court, where he had negotiated the marriage of Mary
Tudor to Louis XII – and successfully pursued Jane Popincourt.
Together with the Princess's former tutor, John Palsgrave, the illicit
lovers were now helping Mary Tudor to perfect her French. Nothing
that is recorded of Jane Popincourt supports the assertion that she
was 'an uncomplicated young woman, more interested in romances,
fashion and shopping',[67] and it has been calculated that she was then
around thirty[68] – middle-aged by Tudor standards.

Louis XII had been sent for approval a list of those who had been selected to attend upon his bride and accompany her to France, but he struck off Jane Popincourt's name after the English ambassador in Paris had warned him that she was leading an 'evil life' as the mistress of the married Longueville, whose duchess would be attending the King's wedding.[69] Mary Tudor was upset at the prospect of being parted from her friend, but Louis was adamant, insisting that his only concern was for the moral welfare of his new Queen. To quieten her protests, he sent her the famous Mirror of Naples, a huge diamond with a pendant pearl, valued at 60,000 crowns (about £5 million). Poor Jane was destined to lose not only her place in the Princess Mary's household, but also her lover, who was returning to France with the bridal train.

Recent writers have speculated[70] – or even stated as a fact[71] – that Jane Popincourt became Henry VIII's mistress for a short time, and it has been suggested that the affair was 'light-hearted' and 'without deep passion on either side';[72] but there is no evidence to support any of this. In May 1516, after the death of King Louis, Jane was allowed to rejoin her lover in France, and on her departure from England, Henry VIII gave her £100 (£48,000).[73] This substantial gift is the sole basis for the theory that he and Jane had amorous relations; but, contrary to what has been imagined, it was far more likely to have been bestowed in recognition of her sixteen years of good service to his mother, his sister and his wife. In 1519, for a comparison, Henry granted an annuity of £100 to Sir John Wiltshire in consideration of his services as Comptroller of Calais.[74] In any case, Jane seems to have cherished feelings for Longueville, for they resumed their affair as soon as they were reunited in France. Moreover, by October 1514, Henry had begun his liaison with Elizabeth Blount.

Nevertheless, Mary Boleyn, an innocent young teenager first arriving at court, had had a chance to observe at first hand how Jane Popincourt's adulterous relationship had brought her only disgrace and unhappiness. It was a lesson from which Mary might have benefited.

Contemporary observers were unanimously agreed that the Princess Mary was very beautiful; one Venetian called her 'a paradise'.[75] She had a sweet nature to match, and was to prove a kindly and generous mistress. There is evidence that she cared for the welfare and interests of her servants all her life, even those who had left her service.

'Mademoiselle Boleyn' was fortunate to have been placed in the service of such a lady.

Mary Boleyn was probably in attendance on Mary Tudor for her proxy wedding to Louis XII on 13 August at Greenwich Palace, and a witness to the lavish ceremony in the great banqueting hall, which had been hung with cloth of gold embroidered with the royal arms of England and France. The Duc de Longueville stood in for his master, and was kept waiting for three hours by the bride, who arrived in a purple and gold chequered gown that matched his own. After vows, rings and kisses had been exchanged, the couple were escorted to a sumptuous chamber where a great bed had been prepared, and lay down together fully dressed, apart from each having one leg bared to the thigh. When their naked legs touched, the marriage was declared to have been consummated.

Thereafter, preparations for the wedding proceeded at a flurry, and Mary Boleyn would no doubt have helped when her mistress was fitted with the thirty new gowns that would make up her trousseau, and watched in awe as the jewels and furnishings bestowed by King Henry on his sister were delivered, admired and packed.

In the last week of September, the bridal train – numbering over a hundred persons, and reportedly the richest cavalcade ever seen – made its cumbersome way to Dover, escorted by the King himself, riding side by side with the Princess, and accompanied by the Queen and the entire court. Everyone, Mary Boleyn included, was wearing their best clothes.[76] On the way, the vast train lodged at Otford, the great palace of the archbishops of Canterbury near Sevenoaks. High winds detained the royal party at Dover Castle until the sea calmed sufficiently for a crossing to be attempted, and then, on 2 October, in the gloom before four o'clock in the morning, Mary's attendants were awakened and summoned to the quayside at Dover, where the royal fleet awaited. There, Henry kissed his sister and commended her 'to God and the fortunes of the sea, and the government of the King your husband'.[77] Then Mary Boleyn's maternal grandfather, Thomas Howard, Duke of Norfolk, escorted the Princess on board, her entourage following. Sir Thomas Boleyn was also of their number. In all, fourteen ships set sail that day for France.

In one of them, probably the vessel that conveyed Mary Tudor and her personal attendants, was Mary Boleyn. They endured a terrible voyage in gales and foul weather:[78] the fleet was scattered, one vessel was lost with hundreds of lives, and it was four days before the

Queen's ship was grounded on a sandbank at Boulogne, with waves still crashing over the decks. In this tumult, a very seasick and bedraggled Mary Tudor was carried to the beach to be greeted by a reception committee of French dignitaries, who were extremely impressed by the size and splendour of her entourage. Mary Boleyn, like her fellow attendants, had to endure a perilous ride ashore by rowing boat in a turbulent sea, and would no doubt have got very wet in the process.[79]

Once all the scattered ships had made land, the Princess and her train spent a short time recuperating in Boulogne, then set off for Étaples and Montreuil, the ladies riding on palfreys with scarlet saddle cloths, with their clothes and personal effects following behind in covered carts. They were fêted on the way with tableaux and pageants, and as they approached Montreuil, they were formally welcomed by the young man who – unless Mary Tudor bore a son – was King Louis' heir: his cousin, the Dauphin François, Count of Angoulême, come with an escort of royal dukes to escort the new Queen to Abbeville, where a 'surprise' meeting with King Louis, the eager bridegroom, was staged. 'What can an old valetudinarian suffering from leprosy want with a handsome girl of eighteen?' asked Peter Martyr, an Italian observer. She would, he predicted, be the death of Louis. But even if the bride-to-be was dismayed at the sight of her future husband's 'decayed complexion', the meeting went well.

Mary Boleyn was a little way behind her mistress when Queen Mary made her state entry into Abbeville, escorted by a magnificent procession of great lords and two thousand knights. Mary was probably one of the gentlewomen who rode on palfreys caparisoned in mulberry velvet fringed with white and pale blue silk, following in order of precedence behind the great ladies in carriages and the senior gentlewomen on palfreys trapped in cloth of gold and purple velvet. Throughout the day, Mary and her fellow attendants were kept busy assisting the Queen with the many changes of clothing that were required for the various ceremonies.

At Abbeville, Mary Tudor and her retinue attended a Mass of thanksgiving at the church of St Vulfran before joining King Louis at a reception, which was followed by a great feast. Then Louis' daughter, poor, lame, squinting Claude, the wife of the Dauphin François, escorted the new Queen and her party to the ancient Hôtel de Gruthuse, where they were accommodated in fine apartments overlooking a pretty garden. In the evening, young Mary Boleyn attended her first court ball, hosted by the Dauphin and Dauphine, where there was 'dancing and music resounding to the skies'.[80]

The next day was 9 October, the feast of St Denis, France's patron saint. Mary, like her mistress and the English lords in her train, was up more than an hour before the dawn broke to prepare for the wedding ceremony. It was a chilly morning, and many donned fur-lined robes of cloth of gold, velvet, damask and silk. After the bridal procession had formed in the Queen's apartments, Mary Boleyn took her place behind Mary Tudor with the twelve other women of the household, each being escorted by a gentleman as they followed their mistress across the gardens to the great hall of the Hôtel de Gruthuse, which was hung with gold. As the Queen entered, the trumpets sounded a fanfare, and then, resplendent in gold brocade and laden with jewels, she was married to the 'antique and feeble' Louis XII by the Cardinal Bishop of Bayeux, who also celebrated the nuptial Mass.[81] Afterwards, Mary Boleyn would have joined the throng of courtiers feasting in the great hall, while the new Queen entertained the royal ladies of France to a private dinner in her own lodgings.

Tradition has it that the wedding ceremony is depicted in a tapestry dating from *c.*1525 or earlier, now at Hever Castle, and that Mary and Anne Boleyn are among the female attendants portrayed, although there is no way of identifying them; the figure of a maid of honour in a red gown was once said to be Anne. But Anne was almost certainly not present at the wedding.

That evening, the King and Queen threw a nuptial ball at the Hôtel de Gruthuse, which heralded three days of feasting and cele-brations. After his wedding night, Louis claimed to have 'performed marvels' and to have 'crossed the river' three times; one observer, the Seigneur de Fleuranges, could well believe it, as 'he was most uncom-fortable'. The Dauphin François, whose long nose had been much put out of joint by this wedding that threatened his succession, had however set someone to spy on the royal couple in their marriage bed, and was mightily relieved to be told that 'it was not possible for the King and Queen to beget children'.[82]

On the morning after the wedding,[83] Mary's grandfather, the Duke of Norfolk, visited the new Queen's English attendants to discuss which of them should stay with her in France. But King Louis, not wishing his wife to be subject to unwanted foreign influence, pre-empted Norfolk's decision, peremptorily dismissing Lady Guildford and most of Mary Tudor's English servants, much to his bride's distress.

In the face of this, he allowed her to keep only her six youngest attendants as maids of honour: among the six was 'Mademoiselle Boleyne'.[84] That must have been Mary, then aged between thirteen and eighteen, as it was she, and not her sister, who received payment for her service during the months of October, November and December 1514. Mary's retention in the Queen's household was, in the well-informed opinion of Charles Brandon, Duke of Suffolk, who arrived on an embassy to France that autumn, thanks to the machinations of her grandfather, the Duke of Norfolk.[85]

Mary Tudor was most put out at the dismissal of most of her English attendants, and dismissive of the abilities of those, including Mary Boleyn, who were left to her, who – as she complained to her brother, Henry VIII – were immature and 'such as never had experience or knowledge how to advertise or give me counsel in any time of need'.[86] That time of need was to come sooner than she could have dreamed, but in the meantime she had to swallow her annoyance and attend to the demands of her husband, who was soon to fall ill with gout.

Mary Boleyn found herself staying on in France with the King's cousin, Lady Elizabeth Grey, sister to Thomas Grey, the Marquess of Dorset; Florence Hastings, the young Dowager Lady Grey de Wilton; Anne, daughter of Sir Edward Jerningham; Lady Mary Fiennes, daughter of Thomas, Lord Dacre of Gilsland; and Lady Jane Bourchier, the daughter of John, Lord Berners. In a short while, probably some-time after Christmas, Anne Boleyn would join them, and – no doubt because of her youth – be allowed to stay. In place of Lady Guildford, an experienced French noblewoman was appointed *Dame d'Honneur*; this was Françoise de Maillé, Madame d'Aumont, who had formerly served the saintly Jeanne de France, Louis' repudiated first wife, and whose husband, Jean d'Aumont, was one of the King's most trusted seigneurs. From now on, Madame d'Aumont was in charge of Mary Boleyn and the other maids of honour.

After a week spent at Abbeville and a short sojourn at Beauvais, Queen Mary was crowned at the great abbey of St Denis, near Paris, on Sunday, 5 November. The next day, she entered Paris in state, to the rapturous acclaim of the citizens. Every vantage point was deco-rated with lilies and roses, in defiance of the season, and all along the processional route there were lavish tableaux and pageants. Young Mary Boleyn would no doubt have marvelled greatly at them, and at the sights of the city of Paris that she would have seen as she passed: the Church of the Holy Innocents, the Châtelet de Paris, the Palais Royal, the soaring cathedral of Notre Dame, the Sainte Chapelle and, finally, the palace of the Conciergerie, to which they were escorted by torchlight in the evening. Here, there was another lavish ball.

The next day, the Queen and her suite moved with the King to the vast Hôtel des Tournelles, which was set in twenty acres and could accommodate six thousand people with ease. Magnificently decorated and embellished, it boasted twenty chapels, twelve galleries and beautiful grounds. To a young girl like Mary Boleyn, such a palace must have been awe-inspiring. Sadly, its splendours have long vanished, and only its subterranean wine cellars survive today.

A week later, Mary was in attendance on the Queen at the great jousts organised by the Dauphin François in honour of Mary Tudor's coronation. In these contests, which took place in the Parc des Tournelles, the handsome Charles Brandon, Duke of Suffolk, excelled himself, while the ailing Louis watched from a couch. Afterwards, there was a lavish state banquet, then all the English lords, including Mary's grandfather of Norfolk, departed for England, and on 27 November the King and Queen moved to the fourteenth-century château of St Germain-en-Laye outside Paris; only the medieval Sainte Chapelle survives from the palace that Mary Boleyn knew, for it was rebuilt in 1539. Here the ailing Louis could rest, while his Queen represented him at receptions and other functions in Paris.

December saw Mary Boleyn and her companions moving with the royal couple back to the Hôtel de Tournelles in Paris for Christmas. Because of the King's poor health, however, the festivities had to be brought to a halt, which meant that Mary Boleyn's taste of the lavish court life in France was to be brief.

That month, the lascivious Dauphin François began to show a blatant interest in Queen Mary, sparking gossip at court and earning him an angry reproof from his domineering and ambitious mother, Louise of Savoy. But King Louis was seemingly unbothered by the dishonourable behaviour of his heir. On 28 December, he wrote to Henry VIII that he was entirely satisfied with his beautiful young bride.

When Mary Boleyn's sister Anne finally arrived at the court of France, it was to find her new mistress already widowed. King Louis, having supposedly worn himself out by the 'marvels' he had performed in the marriage bed, had died in a fit of vomiting in the midst of a violent storm on 1 January 1515. Queen Mary, whose marriage to him had lasted just eighty-two days, is said to have fainted when the news was brought to her, and it may be that Mary Boleyn was among those of her women who ministered to her at this time, and tried to offer some comfort.

But Mary Tudor's ordeal had only just begun. Clad in the traditional nun-like white mourning – the *deuil blanc* – of French royal widows, she was required by tradition to remain in seclusion in gloomy black-draped apartments in the Hôtel de Cluny, a small Gothic-Renaissance palace in the Rue des Mathurins St Jacques on the banks of the Seine; it had once been the town house of the abbots of Cluny, and now houses the famous Musée de Cluny. Queen Mary had to remain there for the prescribed forty days of mourning, closely watched on the orders of Louise of Savoy, the mother of the new King, François I, until it was established that she was not expecting her late husband's child. As she was permitted to be waited on by her English attendants, both the Boleyn sisters were probably with her at this gloomy time, confined to the richly appointed but dark *chambre de la reine blanche*, with the windows shrouded so that no daylight could penetrate, the walls and mourning bed hung with black, and only candles to light them day and night.

Possibly Anne was 'delighted to see Mary again' after a year's separation,[87] yet the few pointers we have to the nature of the relationship between the sisters suggest a certain rivalry, and anyway their reunion was not in the happiest of circumstances, for they had to witness the Dowager Queen becoming distraught – as her increasingly frantic letters prove – not just because of her dismal surroundings, but as a result of King François' unwelcome attentions. He began by calling upon her daily discreetly to ascertain whether or not she was pregnant – for upon this turned his likelihood of keeping the crown – but when she told him the happy news that he was the only possible King of France, he did not cease his visits. He became amorous, and even hinted that he wished to divorce his wife Claude and marry Mary – when in fact he was scheming to make a match for her that was advantageous to himself, before Henry VIII could bestow his sister's hand on some prince who might be hostile to France. Soon, he dismissed Mary's English attendants, who had no doubt witnessed his overtures and might write home of them, and replaced them with the unsympathetic Countess of Nevers and French maids of honour, whom he commanded to withdraw when he was with their mistress. Tales of his courtship – or attempts at seduction – were later wildly exaggerated by the French court historian, Brantôme,[88] but what happened in reality was enough to drive the Dowager Queen to rash action.

Mary had not wanted to marry Louis. Before leaving England, she had made her brother Henry VIII promise that she could choose her second husband, having already, it seems, discovered that she had feelings for Charles Brandon, Duke of Suffolk. When Henry, knowing this, sent Suffolk to comfort the widowed Mary and escort her home, he warned him not to propose marriage, for, unmindful of his earlier promise, he had other plans for his sister.

By the time the English embassy, with Suffolk at its head, arrived in France, Mary Boleyn was back in attendance on the Dowager Queen. Once released from seclusion and able to receive visitors and order her household once more, Mary Tudor had defied King François, dismissed her French ladies and ordered her English ones to rejoin her service.[89] But now she was being cautious: the Boleyn sisters and their fellow attendants were asked to retire while their mistress gave audience to Suffolk alone.[90]

The young Queen was in deep distress. Desperate to escape François' importunings, and the French marriages he suggested she make for his own political – and personal – advantage, she warned Suffolk that, if he did not marry her without delay, she would retire to a convent. When Suffolk pointed out the difficulties, he provoked a torrent of weeping and emotional blackmail that he was too smitten to withstand. In the end, with King François' approval, he 'married her heartily' in secret, with only ten witnesses present.[91] Since Brandon's two diplomatic companions did not attend the secret wedding, it is quite likely that Mary and Anne Boleyn were among the witnesses to the ceremony, which took place sometime in February 1515, in the chapel of the Hôtel de Cluny.

Henry VIII showed himself outraged when informed of his sister's impetuous marriage. Suffolk had not only broken his promise, but had committed a capital crime in marrying a princess of the blood royal without permission. The announcement of the marriage, coming so soon after the late King's death, caused a scandal at the French court, and obliged Henry to agree to a second, public, ceremony. It was only in return for a crippling fine, and protracted and grovelling apologies, that the King finally forgave his sister for her ill-advised marriage to his friend.

One lesson that Mary Boleyn may have learned from this episode was that a woman could get her own way and marry the man she desired if she was sufficiently brave and determined to fight for what she wanted.[92] It was exactly what Mary herself would do one day.

4

'A Very Great Whore'?

Sometime during her six-month sojourn in France, the teenage
Mary Boleyn apparently succumbed to the temptations of the
court – and they were manifold. The sybaritic and notoriously licentious Dauphin, later King François I, who epitomised all the ideals
expected of, and admired in, a Renaissance monarch, and whose
magnificent court, despite being one of the great centres of European
culture and civilisation,[1] was to become a byword for debauchery,
set the tone. He was habitually 'clothed in women', considered
whoring a daily sport on a par with hunting,[2] and boasted of his
special 'petite bande' of courtesans. From 1518 he acknowledged several
maîtresses-en-titre in succession – an arrangement that would no doubt
have horrified Henry VIII and his courtiers – not to mention indulging
in casual affairs with numerous 'sweethearts', in which he drank 'from
many fountains'.[3] A notorious voyeur, he commanded spyholes and
secret doors to be made in his palaces, so that he could watch women
undressing and making love. He himself declared that 'a court without
ladies is like a year without springtime, or a spring without roses'.

François was then twenty-one, an impressive six feet in height,
and broad-shouldered, with an athletic physique and slim legs,
although already he was putting on weight. He was considered handsome, with his dark, saturnine looks and long Valois nose, his cynical
eyes and sensual, mocking lips, and he was undoubtedly attractive to
women. A contemporary described him as 'young, mighty and insa-
tiable, always reading or talking of such enterprises as whet and
inflame himself and his hearers'.[4] Cultivated, intelligent, artistic and
open-handed, yet at the same time wily and extravagant, he was also

spirited, literate and a brilliant, merry and witty conversationalist who had impeccable courtly manners and boundless ambition. To his contemporaries, he exemplified all the kingly virtues.

He had lost his virginity at fifteen, and thereafter was 'all fire and flame for the ladies'.[5] Married that same year, he grew fond of his wife, the patient, plain, plump and crippled Claude, but treated her chiefly as a brood mare. His were rarely affairs of the heart; he loved women in two ways, for sex and for their beauty, of which he was a connoisseur. On the evidence of portraits of his mistresses, he was attracted to plump brunettes, which leaves one to wonder whether Mary Boleyn fitted that description. It is certainly possible, since her sister Anne was a brunette and her son, Henry Carey, had brown hair.

The French court might have been one of the greatest cultural and artistic centres in Christendom, but English observers often professed themselves shocked at the lax morality that prevailed there. Gallantry was the order of the day, with 'rejoicing and entertainment', but promiscuity reigned. 'Rarely did any maid or wife leave that court chaste,' wrote a contemporary.[6] One of François' princely relations commissioned a gold cup engraved inside with an image of a couple having sex, and he would watch with prurient interest as the lady he fancied drained it to reveal the erotic relief, and await her reaction. The King's own almoner, a priest called Buraud, felt obliged to apologise to his mistress for having satisfied her only twelve times in one night, claiming it was the fault of a medicine he was taking.[7]

There is just one piece of evidence to suggest that, for a brief spell, Mary Boleyn became the mistress of King François himself, but it dates from more than twenty years later. On 10 March 1536, Rodolfo Pio, Bishop of Faenza, the Papal Nuncio in Paris, was to write that 'the French King knew her here in France "*per una grandissima ribalda et infame sopre tutte*"' ('for a very great whore, and infamous above all').[8] It is this statement – bolstered by later gossip that actually referred to Anne Boleyn – that has led numerous writers to assume that Mary acquired a notorious reputation at the French court.

For example, it has been asserted that Mary's 'first venture into the wider world and the dazzling experience of the French court went to her head';[9] that she 'was so liberal with her favours that she acquired a very unsavoury reputation',[10] 'on both sides of the Channel, for

sleeping with anyone'.[11] These, and many more claims of a similar
nature, are dubious assumptions – because, according to the historical
evidence, Mary never incurred notoriety or infamy as a royal mistress.

Pio was demonstrably not the most accurate of sources, often
treating gossip as fact; for example, the information he was to relay
about the arrest of Anne Boleyn in 1536 was incorrect; and he was
the originator of the notorious story that Henry VIII lay uncon-
scious for two hours after a fall from a horse that year,[12] a tale that
was uncorroborated by any observer in England, but is still widely
believed today, even by some historians, who have constructed elaborate theories about this concussion being responsible for brain
damage that would explain the King's 'sudden' change of character
and later cruelties.

As the Pope's official representative, Pio was naturally inclined to
vilify the anti-papal Boleyns, especially in 1536, after Henry VIII's
break with Rome and Anne Boleyn's elevation to queenship. Pio's
letter was written only six weeks after Katherine of Aragon's funeral
and Anne Boleyn's final miscarriage (which occurred on the same
day, 29 January), and his comments about Mary were made after he
averred incorrectly that Anne – 'that woman' – had only pretended
to be pregnant and had faked her miscarriage. He did not scruple,
therefore, to make disparaging remarks about Mary, whom he – again
incorrectly – supposed to have been the only lady in attendance on
her sister during her premature confinement, in order to abet Anne
in her deception and preserve secrecy. No other commentator records
Mary's presence on that tragic occasion, and it is doubtful if she was
even in England at the time.

We might wonder if this statement that François I had known
Mary for a great whore is as suspect as others made by Pio, yet the
inaccuracies in his reports lie chiefly in his accounts of events in
England, which were evidently based on garbled hearsay and rumour.
He was actually present at the French court, so had access to more
reliable information, and the ear of the King, so we cannot lightly
dismiss what he wrote. Yet he did not specifically state that François
himself had described Mary as a great and infamous whore – although
many modern writers[13] have assumed that the King actually called
her that – only that he knew her as one.

This ambiguous wording might imply that the King merely had
knowledge of her being free with her favours, yet it seems odd for
Pio to have singled out only François for knowing this, when

certainly – if it were true – other people must have known it too; and if he had intended that meaning, he would surely have written that Mary was known to be a great whore. No, the word 'knew' is almost certainly meant in the Biblical sense here, and it is used to show that François knew Mary as a whore, rather than as a *maîtresse-en-titre*. How Pio discovered this is unclear; it could well have come from King François himself, speaking man to man of the moral shortcomings of the Boleyns; or Pio could have heard it from any number of people at court. The fact that a minor matter for scandal dating from more than two decades before was brought up at all suggests that there was some substance to the allegation. What is surprising is that Pio does not mention Mary's later relations with Henry VIII; clearly he did not know about them, which shows that that liaison was never notorious either. Instead, he derided her for an earlier affair that must have been of much shorter duration, but – far from conferring infamy on Mary – was of such little consequence that no other source mentions it.

It does not seem likely that François I – an experienced libertine and notorious womaniser – would have called Mary 'a very great whore, and infamous above all'. That was certainly saying something, for the French court was reputed to be the most scandalous in Christendom.[14] If Mary's reputation had been that notorious, we would have other reports of it. What could this young girl have done to shock such a seasoned man of the world as the French King? Only weeks before, her mistress, Mary Tudor, had been complaining about her young attendants' lack of experience and knowledge of the world. Had Mary, in such a short time, become practised enough at lechery to merit such a scathing insult? It seems unlikely.

By March 1536, although François had long been a friend to Anne Boleyn and her faction, his good relations with Henry VIII had become frosty, and the latter was leaning towards an alliance with France's enemy, the Emperor Charles V. At the time Pio wrote his report, François would not have been well disposed towards his English rival. Moreover, Anne had miscarried of a son, and her future now seemed uncertain. One might suspect that, in this political climate, François felt at liberty to denigrate the Boleyns, and that he might have grossly exaggerated what he remembered of Mary. Yet the French court historian Brantôme states that 'King François, who was very fond of the ladies (although he was convinced that they are most changeable and fickle), never would have any slandering of

them at his court, but insisted on their being accorded great honour
and respect.' It is unlikely, then, that he would have spoken so
unchivalrously of Mary.

It seems therefore that the zealous Pio, who, as the Pope's
spokesman, hated everything that the Boleyns stood for, was reporting
what he had been told in private by the French King or someone
else in the know, and himself exaggerated it to score a political point;
and that the description of Mary as an infamous whore comes from
Pio, placing his own construction on Mary's conduct, and not from
François I.

This theory effectively demolishes a reader's thoughtful suggestion that François' cruel jibe about Mary was made because she had
actually spurned his advances. That she did so, at least to begin with,
is certainly possible, given that, later on, she seems to have surrendered to Henry VIII against her will. It has also been suggested that
Pio's remark of 1536 was based on what François had learned, during
Henry's visit to Calais in 1532 (when he was accompanied by both
Boleyn sisters), of Mary's affair with the English King[15] – but Pio
did not mention this, as might be expected if that were the case; or
that a jealous François had been angered to hear that Mary had taken
up with his rival, Henry VIII,[16] although this does not take account
of the years that had elapsed between the two liaisons. Had François
been so enamoured of Mary, he could easily have arranged for her
to stay on at the French court after 1515, yet there is no record of
her there, while there is plenty of evidence for his other affairs –
even short-lived ones.

The complete absence of any corroborative contemporary evidence
to support the claim that Mary was the most infamous of whores
fatally undermines Pio's statement – and all the modern myths about
her reputation. There is no other proof whatsoever that Mary Boleyn
'quickly adapted to the immoral atmosphere' of the French court,[17]
or that she soon learned to enjoy 'sexual dalliance',[18] or became very
free with her favours and adventurous in bed. She has been seen as
'an inviting, eager girl, ripe and nubile'[19] whose 'youth, beauty and
inexperience led her into a series of short-lived encounters as she
was passed from the King, who quickly tired of her, to his favourites',[20]
while jumping into bed with François and his cronies 'seemed to
her to be a dazzling career of advancement'.[21] There is no evidence
to support any of this. One writer has even fantasised about Mary
becoming 'an adept at those Paris refinements which, while they

scandalise, are irresistible to the most virtuous of men. Her heart was generous, her body responsive. At Fontainebleau, at Amboise, she had refused no one.'[22] Small matter that Mary is not known to have visited Fontainebleau and never travelled as far south as the Loire Valley.

This same writer accused Mary's parents of abandoning her to 'the vicissitudes of foreign courts' where she could not protect herself from men,[23] when in fact Sir Thomas Boleyn was affording his daughter the best opportunity of advancement and a good marriage in placing her in Mary Tudor's train. It has been said he had cared little that, in sending his daughters to France, he had exposed them to the most licentious court in Europe,[24] but presumably he had trusted to their youth, their training and Queen Mary's protection. As for the unsubstantiated assertion that he was the first to criticise when word of Mary's 'many affairs' got back to England[25] – what 'many affairs', one might ask? The worst that could be said, on the evidence we have, is that Mary had a brief liaison with François I. The rest is pure imagination.

There is a modern perception, though, that her reputation was soon such that she was 'known to be at everyone's disposal. Even at the lascivious French court, there was a code of discretion; Mary had offended it. She was either sent or withdrawn hastily to England.'[26] It has been imagined that, after being quickly discarded by François I, Mary was 'laughed at by courtiers',[27] that this 'warm-hearted and ductile girl made the mistake of scattering her favours too widely and making her affairs too public'[28] and that she would return to England 'with a colourful reputation for wanton behaviour'.[29] Again, all this is supposition.

In fact, Mary's liaisons with François I and later with Henry VIII were conducted so discreetly that not a single comment was made about them at the time. François I, as we have seen, was notorious for his amours. From 1518, his *maîtresses-en-titre* would preside publicly over his court, attracting much comment. In an era in which few courtiers commissioned portraits of themselves – the number painted by Jean Clouet, for example, was modest – several of these mistresses had theirs done to mark their elevation to the royal bed, among them Francoise de Foix, Dame de Châteaubriant; Marie de Langeac, Dame de Lestraunge; Marie de Macy, Dame de Montchenu; Anne d'Heilly, Duchess d'Étampes; and Marie d'Assigny, Dame de Canaples.[30] Had Mary Boleyn been of any significance in the King's life, there would surely have been some evidence of it. But clearly she was not.

Her affair with François was probably so brief and covert that we might not expect to find a record of it; but there is also no contemporary record of her behaving in such a manner as to incur notoriety or gain a reputation for promiscuity – when there certainly would have been if she was conducting herself so immorally as to earn for herself the dubious distinction of being known as the most infamous whore at the licentious French court. It was acceptable for men to indulge themselves in this way; but in a young, unmarried woman of good birth, it would have been worthy of comment. Furthermore, such conduct would have reflected badly on Mary Tudor, who was responsible for the moral welfare of her female attendants – as Louis XII had been well aware when he dismissed Jane Popincourt from her service.

Pio does not reveal when François and Mary had briefly been lovers, but his statement, written in Paris, that the King 'knew her here in France', must surely indicate that it happened when Mary was at the French court in 1514–15,[31] as most writers[32] have concluded. There is no evidence, however, to back up the statement that, because of her promiscuity, Mary was dismissed from Queen Claude's service in 1519.[33]

It has also been suggested that the affair could have flourished during Mary's two later sojourns in France: at the meeting of the English and French courts known as the Field of Cloth of Gold in 1520, or during Henry VIII's visit to Calais in 1532, when she accompanied her sister Anne and met with King François.[34] Yet in 1520, Mary was newly married, in the train of the virtuous Queen Katherine, and accompanied by her parents and her aunt. It would not have been easy, in such circumstances, to have indulged in a secret affair with the King of France, given the extensive interest that attended the Field of Cloth of Gold, that very public event. In 1532, Calais was an English possession and not part of France, so it is hardly likely that Pio was referring to Mary having an affair with François there: Calais was not 'here in France'. Nor is François likely to have uttered his disparaging remarks about Mary's virtue at this meeting,[35] as they were not reported by Pio until three and a half years later, and in very different circumstances.

When, in 1514–15, might this affair with King François have occurred? Circumstantial evidence might suggest that it was towards the end of that period. It has been said that the liaison was going on for a few brief 'months' in 1515,[36] but that is pure guesswork, and had it lasted that long, it might have attracted interest or comment. In 1515, François' favoured mistress was a beautiful Parisian called Jeanne le Coq,. whom he visited by night, accessing her house in Paris through a neighbouring monastery; but that is not to say that he had renounced other women. There had been opportunities for his affair with Mary to flourish in the three months of Mary Tudor's queenship, and he could also have pursued her during his visits to the Hôtel de Cluny, or wherever she was lodging after she had been temporarily dismissed from the Dowager Queen's household. It has been surmised that Queen Mary's example in marrying for love indecently soon after her husband's death 'gave her namesake *carte blanche* to behave in a similar manner'[37] – but the two cases do not bear comparison, and it is unlikely that Mary Boleyn was more than infatuated with her royal pursuer.

More credibly, the affair could have happened after Mary Tudor left the seclusion of her chamber at the Hôtel de Cluny, and returned to Paris, where, on 13 February, she watched from an upstairs window as the new King made his state entry into his capital, and later attended the celebratory banquet. It has even been claimed that the affair took place when Mary Boleyn was supposedly in the service of Queen Claude[38] – which she never was.

Everything points to her affair with François having been 'extremely brief',[39] – a heat-of-the-moment episode or one-night stand, even – and there is no evidence at all that, when François 'soon tired' of Mary, he 'passed her on to his courtiers',[40] nor that this 'shocked' or 'frightened' Anne [Boleyn].[41] And it may be unsafe to assert that it was probably at this point that Anne discovered 'how women really could be exploited and mistreated, that she decided to protect her greatest asset, her purity, at all costs';[42] for Anne herself, as we will presently discover, had been 'corrupted' at the French court.[43]

We might infer from Anne Boleyn's speedy preferment at the French court – it was she who was appointed a maid of honour to Queen Claude, a highly sought-after position – that she was the cleverer and more charming of the Boleyn girls, the one thought most fitted for the high honour of serving first the Archduchess Margaret and then the Queen of France and, later, the French King's sister; and that Mary Boleyn was less accomplished and able, and therefore somewhat in her younger sister's shadow – in the eyes of her family at least. That may be true, and if so, Sir Thomas Boleyn's disappointment in his elder daughter would surely have been compounded by finding out that she had lost her virtue to the King of France and – as if that was not bad enough – had not received in return any tangible benefits such as a financial reward or even an honourable marriage.

It makes sense of the later events and course of Mary's life to assume that her family did find out what had passed between her and François I. It is unlikely that Mary herself told them – what girl of gentle birth would confess to compromising her honour, unless there were to be consequences that had to be dealt with discreetly? We don't, of course, know that there were not, and it would be fruitless to speculate; but for the rest of her life, as will become clear, there is intermittent evidence to suggest that Mary was held in little account or affection by her family; and one gets a sense that she was a continuing disappointment to her 'outstandingly learned' father,[44] and probably to the rest of the family too.

It would make sense that Mary Tudor also knew about her maid-of-honour's fall from grace – and that she found out towards the end of her sojourn in France. Someone in her household – Madame d'Aumont, possibly, whose duty it was to be vigilant in all matters concerning the conduct of her charges – might easily have noticed something amiss, and may even have tackled the girl, forcing a confession. The matter would then have been reported to Queen Mary, who, responsible as she was for the moral welfare of the young ladies in her household, would have been duty bound to write to Sir Thomas Boleyn. Discretion would have been essential, given the recent scandal of Mary Tudor's marriage to the Duke of Suffolk, and we might imagine that that lady was not best pleased to learn that Mary Boleyn had risked linking her to further scandal. This is all informed speculation, of course, but it is credible because it provides an explanation for subsequent events – and for the Boleyn family's antipathy towards Mary.

Her parents' evident disapproval – their dislike, even – may well have dated from this time.[45] Even Anne Boleyn, who conceivably was taken into Mary's confidence, and would have surely known the reason for her sister's disgrace – may have shared their feelings. As far as the family were concerned, there was good reason for their disapproval, and Sir Thomas Boleyn may have felt compelled to act upon it, as will be discussed shortly. He could not allow Mary to remain where she was; her very presence in the Queen Dowager's household was compromising to that lady, and besides, he was probably of the opinion that his daughter needed to be taught a lesson.

What does all this tell us about Mary? The myth of her 'extremely wanton reputation'[46] has predictably coloured historians' assessments of her character.

Some see her as a generous, amiable, easy-going, warm-hearted but not very clever person,[47] or 'an obliging if colourless girl',[48] but that view presupposes that she fell willingly into royal beds. It has even been said that her reputation 'was gone before she reached seventeen',[49] and that her character was therefore 'beyond rescue'. Even so, she was 'a not altogether unamiable personality'.[50] She has been described as 'pretty but insipid',[51] 'eager to please and generous'[52] and 'charming and agreeable'.[53]

One author writes of her 'docility'[54] where another sees her as 'a high-spirited, rather giddy girl who enjoyed all the pleasures of the court on offer'.[55] She has been called 'racy',[56] and it has been suggested that 'the air of innocence her Rubens-like colouring gave her hid a nature passionate, responsive, thoughtless and weak'; she was 'sexually pliant' and almost certainly 'did not possess the stubborn spirit and bad temper of her sister'.[57]

Others have been even more creative in their assessment of Mary Boleyn. It is evident that she became an object of fantasy for male writers of an earlier generation. One imagined her 'discreetly letting it be known that she was always prepared to continue an interesting religious or political discussion in bed'.[58] Another thought she 'was by nature simple'.[59] She was also called 'a light-hearted and easy-spirited girl, the sort of being who is soon in intimacy with men, knows the morose valleys between the heights of their ardour and the heights of their disdain, and is aware that she must inveigle or humour the beasts, or be beaten. She had not much iron in her character. She was one of those ingratiating yet simple women to whom it would never be of great importance to say no, who are pliant and sweet, who cling like ivy and are as easily detached.' She 'yielded to the happy moment'.[60]

That is a view echoed by some modern writers: one describes Mary as 'a woman who lived for the moment and dived head first into love affairs', someone who was kind and loving and 'followed her heart'.[61] The last statement was self-evidently true, given that, years later, Mary was to defy her family, and the King and Queen, to make a second marriage for love. Another author writes of her 'spirited behaviour',[62] and she is also seen as passionate,[63] on the evidence of a letter written in the wake of that misalliance – which was probably true as well.[64]

There is little evidence to show that Mary was 'serenely sure of herself',[65] and none that she saw her 'road to advancement' as being 'through her use of her feminine wiles to manipulate men' or believed that 'her reputation was to be sacrificed to be close to men of the highest influence'.[66] She was not 'remarkably successful' in realising any such ambitions.[67] Even if this were the case – although there is evidence that she was reluctant to become Henry VIII's mistress – Mary seems to have lacked the ability or will to carry through any grand design; she emerged from her affairs with kings barely the richer, and having wielded little or no influence. As for manipulating men, she was clearly no adept – at least in her younger years.

If, as seems likely, François I was Mary's first lover, we can hardly blame her – reluctant or not – for submitting to him, or even for having her head turned. She was young, inexperienced, living at a licentious court in a foreign land, and the daughter of a mother who may have been known for her infidelities. He was the King of France, all-powerful and commanding – how could a young, untried girl deny him? One brief amorous episode in youth does not define a woman's character. In fact, it tells us very little about her.

Anne Boleyn, it has been claimed, 'must have been horrified at Mary throwing herself away so cheaply'[68] – given, of course, that Mary did, for the chances are that she had little say in the matter. But Anne, too, risked becoming the subject of scandal at the French court. In July 1535, King François was to confide to Rodolfo Pio 'how little virtuously she has always lived, and now lives';[69] he may have been referring to Anne's later reputation, but in 1536, Henry VIII himself would reveal to Eustache Chapuys, the Imperial ambassador in England, that it was only after he had begun having sexual relations with Anne that he found out she had been corrupted in France.[70] After her death, when offered a French bride, the King insisted 'he had had too much experience of French bringing up and manners'[71] – a clear reference to Anne Boleyn. Evidently Anne was discreet and clever enough to ensure that barely a soul knew of these early falls from grace.

Contrary to modern popular opinion, Mary Boleyn too seems to have been discreet; aside from taking her cue from her royal lovers in this, she would no doubt have feared for her reputation, and hopefully had some regard to her future and her family's ambitions and sensibilities. Given the absence of any contemporaneous evidence that hints at promiscuity on her part, it is surely time for the traditional view of her as a willing, even adventurous, sexual partner who cared little for the loss of her good name, and was 'a full participant in the sensual pastimes of the French court',[72] to be rebutted.

In 1512, François' mother had written to a correspondent that her son had a disease in his private parts, which had fortunately been cured,[73] almost certainly by the administration of mercury, which was the standard cure for syphilis at that time. Joanna Denny repeats the oft-told tale that François caught it again from a later mistress, *La Belle Ferronière*, but that is a fabrication dating from the seventeenth century, when the story was put about that the lady's cuckolded husband, Le Ferron, deliberately got himself infected with the pox so that his wife would pass it on to the King. In the 1600s, that legend was spun around a famous portrait of a woman by Leonardo da Vinci, now in the Louvre.

Syphilis was first recorded in 1494, when a French army occupied Naples, and it was soon rampant throughout Europe, particularly in the higher ranks of society. The Italians naturally called it 'the French disease' – the French, of course, called it 'the Italian disease'. Most people referred to it as 'the great pox'; the name syphilis was not used until 1530.

According to some lurid accounts, François I died of syphilis in 1547; others, more convincing, state that his last illness was a disease of the urinary ducts. An autopsy showed that he had a stomach abscess, shrunken kidneys, decaying entrails, an abraded throat and one shredded lung.[74] These conditions are not typical of syphilis, even in its later stages; there had been, for example, no mention of the mental disorders associated with the disease,[75] nor do François' later portraits show any collapse of the bridge of his nose, which can be eaten away by it. Thus, after 1512, there is no evidence beyond rumour that François I had syphilis, or that he was 'known to be heavily infected' with it.[76]

It has been suggested that Mary Boleyn could have contracted the 'great pox' from François and later passed it on to Henry VIII.[77]

That is highly unlikely. Syphilis was endemic in Europe in this period, and highly topical, yet it was not until the late nineteenth century that anyone suggested that Henry VIII suffered from it.[78] Only in 1888 did Dr Currie first put forward the theory that the King contracted it as a young man. The Victorians found it easy to believe that, with his notorious marital record, and his infidelities, it must follow that Henry had syphilis. It has been speculated that he could have caught it from one of his mistresses, including Mary Boleyn, whose favours he had shared with François I[79] – even though there is no evidence that the latter had the disease.[80]

The standard sixteenth-century cure for syphilis was mercury, yet there is no mention of that in the complete set of Henry VIII's apothecaries' accounts that survive today. Furthermore, syphilis was as widespread and notorious then as AIDS is today, and the unpleasant side effects of mercury would have been obvious – and well known – to ambassadors and other observers. Yet not one ever hinted that Henry VIII had the pox. Despite all this, Currie's theory is still widely accepted as fact. It is surely time, therefore, to lay that myth to rest also.

Escorted as far at St Denis by François I, the Duke and Duchess of Suffolk departed from Paris on 15 April, bound for Calais, where they waited to receive Henry VIII's permission to return to England. After a smooth crossing in beautiful weather, they and their retinue landed at Dover on 2 May, and were received by a host of nobles and their ladies, sent by the King to greet them. They were then escorted by Cardinal Wolsey to the royal manor of Barking, Essex, where they were formally forgiven by King Henry,[81] who welcomed the couple home, and afforded them a fine public wedding at Greenwich Palace on 13 May 1515.

Confusion reigns as to what happened to the Boleyn sisters at this point and over the next few years. It is often stated that both girls remained at the French court, transferring to the service of Claude, the wife of Louis XII's successor, François I, after Mary Tudor returned to England.[82] Some say that only Mary Boleyn was found a position there,[83] while one writer – misreading the letter sent from La Veure, quoted above – claims that Anne joined her in 1517, and that Mary finally returned home with the English court after the Field of Cloth of Gold in 1520.[84] The claim that Anne went to France with her father in 1519[85] rests on not 'a scrap of evidence',[86] as does the assertion that Sir Thomas Boleyn, 'far from regarding his daughter's fall from grace as some kind of ambitious career move, swiftly recalled' the disgraced Mary to England 'in the wake of Mary Tudor'.[87] And there is no basis to the claim that Anne was only 'a frequent visitor at the French court',[88] or that, around 1519, her father removed her and placed her in Queen Katherine's entourage.[89] Nor is there any evidence to show that Mary Boleyn came back to England with Mary Tudor in 1515, 'and did not return until her father was appointed ambassador to France in February [*sic.*] 1518. She remained for two years and was so liberal with her favours that she acquired a very unsavoury reputation.'[90] We are once more in the realm of myth here.

There is no mention in contemporary sources of Mary remaining at the French court. There is overwhelming evidence that Anne stayed on. As for Mary returning to England with Mary Tudor in April 1515,[91] that is by no means certain.

In the years after Anne Boleyn supplanted Katherine of Aragon in Henry VIII's affections, her former mistress, Mary Tudor, took the Queen's part and showed nothing but enmity towards Anne. It has been suggested that that enmity may have had its roots in France, with Anne making no secret of the fact that she 'blamed Mary Tudor for her sister's wild behaviour and all its consequences';[92] for although Mary Boleyn's behaviour may not have been so wild, still her virtue had been lost. It is said that, if Anne had somehow conveyed her anger to Mary Tudor, that could have accounted for her remaining at the French court, instead of returning home in the French Queen's service. Yet this seems a highly unlikely scenario, unsubstantiated by any source, and there was probably a much more positive and compelling reason for Anne remaining in France.

It was doubtless due to her own abilities and talents – or to Sir Thomas Boleyn's influence – that Anne was offered a place in the household of the virtuous Queen Claude. To be appointed to serve the Queen was a high honour, as competition for places in her household was fierce, and it is unlikely that Anne Boleyn would have secured hers without having displayed the kind of qualities that the young Claude – and, more importantly, her formidable mother-in-law, Louise of Savoy – admired. For Thomas Boleyn, this placement no doubt brought with it the hope that Anne would secure a rich and titled husband in France.

Anne's life in Queen Claude's household was probably quite dull, for it was like living in a nunnery. It was here that she spent her formative years, in company with nearly three hundred other well-born young ladies. She would have been expected to follow the Queen's example and conduct herself modestly and decorously, and her days were governed by an almost conventual routine of prayers and good works. Above all, she was expected to guard her chastity.

Claude's life had been difficult. A cripple, she had been lame from birth, yet she was constantly pregnant during these years. François I was serially unfaithful to her, and she was dominated by her mother-in-law, Louise of Savoy. Because she was ill at ease in the hothouse atmosphere of the court, Claude resided mainly at the beautiful châteaux of Amboise and Blois in the Loire Valley, and on the rare occasions when she was obliged to go to court, she kept a watchful eye on her female attendants, knowing that they were a likely prey for every predatory male there.

Anne's long sojourn at the French court is well documented. In 1536, Lancelot de Carles, who was attached to the French embassy in London during her lifetime, and was clearly not aware that she had previously been in Brussels, wrote that she 'first went out of this country [England] when Mary [Tudor] left it to go and seek the King of France' in 1514; and that when Mary returned to England in 1515, Anne was 'retained by Claude, the new Queen, at whose court she became so graceful that you would never have taken her for an Englishwoman but for a Frenchwoman born'. This is corroborated by the contemporary author of the so-called *Spanish Chronicle*, who wrote: 'This Anne Boleyn was brought up in France at the court of the King.'[93]

In 1583, Charles de Bourgeville, in his *Les Recherches et Antiquités de la Province de Neustrie*, referred to Anne Boleyn being 'brought up in France' after 'she came there when King Louis XII married the sister of the King of England'. William Camden stated that Anne was maid of honour firstly to Queen Claude and later to King François' sister, Marguerite of Valois, Duchess of Alençon. Lord Herbert also wrote that Anne 'lived some time in France, whither, in the train of the Queen of France, she went A.D. 1514 . . . After the death of Louis XII, she did not return with the Dowager, but was received into a place of much honour with the other Queen [Claude], and then with Marguerite, Duchess of Alençon, with whom she remained till some difference grew betwixt our King and François in 1522.'

The French sixteenth-century historian, Jean du Tillet, also recorded that Anne finally went back to England in 1522. Early that year, François I had complained that the popular 'daughter of Mr Boleyn' had been summoned home. This could not have been Mary, as she had been married in England in February 1520.[94]

George Cavendish, Cardinal Wolsey's gentleman usher, obviously got his information rather muddled when he recalled that 'Mistress Anne Boleyn, being very young, was sent into the realm of France, and there made one of the French Queen's women, continuing there until the French Queen died.' He was not referring to Mary Tudor (who died in England in 1533), but to Queen Claude, who passed away in 1524, two years after Anne returned home, but he clearly knew that Anne had been appointed to serve Claude while in France, and he may mistakenly have thought that Claude had died before Anne left the French court in 1522.

The evidence that it was Anne Boleyn, and not Mary Boleyn, who remained at the French court, and spent several years there, is therefore overwhelming. But historians have sought in vain for any record of Mary's presence at the French court between 1515 and 1520. So what became of her?

We hear nothing of Mary in the five years after her possible return to England. One historian states that she remained at the English court,[95] but there is no evidence of her being there. Some historians assert that when she returned to England, she became one of Queen Katherine's ladies-in-waiting,[96] but again there is no evidence that she was ever appointed a maid-of-honour in the Queen's household. Nor is there any contemporary record of a 'darkening cloud of scandal and gossip' accompanying her return,[97] which might have precluded her being chosen to serve the virtuous Katherine of Aragon.

Did Mary Boleyn remain in the service of Mary Tudor? Although the Duke and Duchess of Suffolk found it a struggle to keep up the payments of their fine owed to the King, and to maintain sufficient state to appear at court, Mary Tudor kept a household appropriate to her rank, and we know that she retained at least one of the girls who had attended her in France. This was Anne Jerningham, who (probably in 1515) married Sir Edward Grey. In 1516, Lady Grey carried her mistress's first-born son, Henry Brandon, at his christening, and she was still in Mary Tudor's household in 1517, when Queen Katherine visited her sister-in-law.

Of the other girls who had served Mary Tudor in France, Florence Hastings had been widowed in 1505, and as genealogies often incorrectly show her as dying after 1511, no one has until now identified her as the only possible 'Lady Grey of Wilton'[98] who could have been in Mary Tudor's household, so clearly she lived at least until the spring of 1515, but nothing further is known of her. Like Anne Boleyn, both Lady Elizabeth Grey and Mary Fiennes stayed on at the court of France, where they served Queen Claude after Mary Tudor's departure. Jane Bourchier seems to have married Edmund Knyvett soon after her return to England, as their son John was born in c.1517–18; there is no record of her in Mary Tudor's English household.

Thus we have a record of just one of those six girls being retained by the 'French Queen' (as Mary Tudor was now known in England), and as there is no further mention of Mary Boleyn being in her service, it seems likely that she had been dismissed with the rest[99] when her mistress returned to England – and dismissed, possibly, for her misconduct. Mary Tudor, having only recently, and with great difficulty, extricated herself from the scandal of her ill-advised marriage, would not have wanted a girl of dubious moral probity in her household. Where she herself had erred merely in making a secret marriage, with the blessing of the Church, Mary Boleyn had committed the sin of fornication, which could not be condoned.

It seems that the termination of Mary's service was managed amicably, and perhaps of necessity discreetly, because Mary Tudor remained – at least for a time – friendly towards the Boleyn family, and in 1517, when her daughter Frances was christened at Hatfield, Anne Tempest, the wife of Mary Boleyn's uncle, Sir Edward Boleyn, stood proxy for the Queen as godmother.[100]

So if Mary was not in the service of Queen Claude, Katherine of Aragon or Mary Tudor, where was she in these years? Maybe she returned to Hever Castle to await the marriage that her father would in time arrange for her.

But there is another possibility – a possibility that arises from her having been confused with her sister by two sixteenth-century writers. According to Lord Herbert, William Rastell – Sir Thomas More's editor and biographer, and therefore a hostile source – claimed that when *Anne* Boleyn was fifteen, she was caught in a compromising situation with one of her father's servants and was sent to France in disgrace. Here, she 'behaved herself so licentious that she was vulgarly called the Hackney of England, till, being adopted to that King's [François I's] familiarity, she was termed his mule'. A hackney, in sixteenth-century parlance, was a horse for hire and another name for a prostitute; the French once derisively called Elizabeth I 'the hackney of her own vassals'.[101] A mule, then as now, was an infertile hybrid breed with a reputation for being stubborn; probably Rastell's reference to a mule was meant to imply an incapacity to bear children – he knew of course that Anne Boleyn had produced just one daughter and not the desired son.

Nicholas Sander – no reliable source, and no partisan of the Boleyns – embellished this story in 1585, stating that, after discovering that fifteen-year-old Anne had had affairs with his butler and his chaplain, her father sent her to France, where she was 'placed, at the expense of the King [Henry VIII] under the care of a certain nobleman not far from Brie'. This place name has been variously given by Sander's translators as Brière, Briare or Brie. The only place called Brière lies in the vast lush, marshy area north of the Loire estuary in Brittany, much of which was forest and only navigable by boat. Paul Friedmann thought that Brière should read Briare, a town situated 240 miles south of Paris, but this sounds improbable, while there is a link between the Boleyns and a town called Brie.

Adam Blackwood, writing in 1587, states that the French nobleman with whom Anne supposedly stayed was a friend of her father's. According to Sander, 'soon afterwards, she [Anne] appeared at the French court, where she was called the English mare, because of her shameless behaviour, and then the royal mule, when she became acquainted with the King of France'. It is easy to see where Sander got some of his information.

Clearly both accounts, Rastell's and Sander's, are flawed, since Anne was probably fifteen in 1516, when, according to most reliable sources, she was in the service of Queen Claude. (Even if one accepts her date of birth as 1507, making her fifteen in 1522, the tale does not fit, because that year saw her returning to England from France.) Sander says that Anne was sent to Brie to be placed in the care of that certain nobleman *before* she went to the court of France; there is, indeed, a gap of four months in which her whereabouts cannot be accounted for, but she went to the French court from Brussels, not Hever. After she arrived there, she served in turn Mary Tudor,

Queen Claude and Marguerite of Valois, before returning to England.
Thus we know what she was doing during those seven years.

Furthermore, if Anne Boleyn, who became Queen of England
and notorious in Catholic Europe, had acquired a licentious reputation in France, we would certainly know about that too. That she
did not is made clear by the fact that neither François I nor anyone
else sought to make political capital out of it, when it might have
been to their advantage to do so. If Anne had been so promiscuous,
it would have been mentioned by her enemies in the years when
Henry VIII was trying to divorce Katherine of Aragon in order to
marry her. So Rastell's account, on which Sander drew, appears to
have been an invention aimed at discrediting Anne,[102] with the reference to a mule probably being made with hindsight. It is hardly
possible, after forty years, that there was any gossip about Mary Boleyn
and François I that he could have heard, which he might have mistakenly thought related to Anne. He may well, knowing that Anne had
been at the French court, have concluded, like Brantôme, that no
woman left that court chaste – and embellished this with a few salacious details.

Yet many historians (with your author following suit in previous
books) have associated these calumnies with Mary Boleyn: it is she
who is invariably assumed to have been called the French King's
'hackney' or 'mule', and this has only served to embellish the myth
of her notorious reputation. Clearly there has long been a consensus
that this could not have been Anne, and that these accounts give
credence to Rodolfo Pio's statement about Mary being an infamous
whore.

Both Rastell and Sander were determined to vilify Anne Boleyn
and her family, while Sander was not above reporting rumour as
fact, and may even have been guilty of making things up to bolster
his case; not for nothing has he been called 'Dr Slander'. It was he,
after all, who had asserted that Anne was her mother's daughter by
Henry VIII. For this reason, little credence can be given to his
assertions.

But could it be that Sander was referring to *Mary* Boleyn being
sent by her father to rusticate at Brie, after compromising her reputation at the French court? Several writers have suggested that he
and Rastell confused Anne with her sister Mary,[103] when referring
to Anne being called the French King's hackney or mule,[104] but
although Sander was probably wrong in following Rastell in this

error, what he says about Brie may be based on truth – and may relate to Mary rather than Anne.

Sander has been responsible for spreading some blatant calumnies about Anne Boleyn – although he himself may have believed them. So it is unlikely that Thomas Boleyn had caught Mary in *flagrante delicto* with a member of his household. If he had found her to be that promiscuous at an early age, he would surely never have risked sending her to France in the train of the King's sister.[105]

There is other evidence for this French connection. In his life of the great French jurist Charles du Moulin (or Dumoulin) (1500– 66), Jean Brodeau, whose work was published in 1654, states that *Anne* Boleyn was brought up in Brie-sous-Forges by a relation of du Moulin. He has been identified as Philippe du Moulin (d.1548), Seigneur of Brie and cup-bearer to François I,[106] who had married one Marie de Boulan, who is said to have been distantly related to the Boleyns a long way back.[107] The *Almanac of Seine-et-Oise*, published in 1790, states: 'At Brie-sous-Forges, we see in this place the remains of the old castle where they claim was brought up the famous and unfortunate Anne Boleyn, the second wife of Henry VIII of England and mother of Elizabeth I.'[108]

Brie-sous-Forges, which lies south-east of Paris, is now called Fontenay-les-Briis, and the Tour Anne Boleyn, which dates from around 1200, is now privately owned. There is a well-established local tradition that Anne Boleyn lived here sometime in her youth – towards 1520, according to one account[109] – and there is even a street named after her. It has been suggested that she may have lodged briefly at Brie-sous-Forges on her way home from France,[110] yet local folklore claims that she lived there for some time, and was even brought up there.[111] Such beliefs are not always reliable – there are historic houses in England that claim royal links that can be disproven – but the tradition in Brie goes back to the sixteenth century. Furthermore, it is documented as fact by other early historians: John Bale, in the sixteenth century, Bishop Burnet in the seventeenth, and David Hume in the eighteenth, as well as by several eminent French historians.

Philippe du Moulin is said to have known Sir Thomas Boleyn when the latter was ambassador to France from 1519–20. Nineteenth-century French historians claimed that Sir Thomas placed Anne, who is described as a child, with Philippe du Moulin at Brie because her mother was having an affair with Henry VIII, and that Philippe promised to bring her up as a 'young lady of high quality'. Later, he is said to have presented her at the court of François I.[112]

There are obvious problems with this version, which does not take into account the four years between 1515 and 1519, when Anne was already at the French court in the service of Queen Claude. Nor was she a child in 1518, but a young woman of marriageable age. Again there is a tale of some scandal having been the cause of her being sent to Brie – this time, nothing to do with her having affairs with her father's butler or chaplain, but concerning her mother and the King of England. Yet it has already been established that Elizabeth Howard is unlikely to have had an affair with Henry VIII, so again, we might infer that Brie had no connection with Anne Boleyn, and that it was in fact Mary Boleyn who was sent to live there with a respectable noble family.

This theory makes more sense – far better sense than any involving Anne. Maybe there was a family connection with the du Moulins; certainly there had been a scandal involved – that of Mary's illicit relations with François I. Possibly, at Sir Thomas Boleyn's behest, Mary Tudor was able to arrange for Mary Boleyn to be taken into the household of the French King's cup-bearer. In the protection of a respectable noble family, her reputation could be preserved and she could learn acceptable conduct. There was nothing remarkable in this: it was not unusual for girls of good family to be sent to live in a noble establishment to learn good behaviour and complete their education. It may be that Mary stayed at Brie until a marriage was arranged for her, more than four years later, and that, in the wake of Anne Boleyn becoming Queen of England, people forgot that there had been two Boleyn sisters, and remembered only that one had lived at Brie – and thus the legend grew that it was Anne. We will never know the whole truth of the matter, yet the theory is credible.

Others have reached a similar conclusion, but offer a different version of this story. It is agreed that the loss of Mary's honour in a brief affair with King François might well have 'horrified her family in England',[113] but it has been suggested that Sir Thomas Boleyn, discovering that his daughter had disgraced herself at the French court, and not regarding that in any way as 'an ambitious career move',[114] arranged for her to disappear from society and enter a convent, ostensibly for educational purposes, but effectively to teach her virtuous behaviour. This echoes Sarah Tytler, who, writing in 1896, referred to Anne – at her father's wish – entering a convent school at Brie to complete her education; Tytler too stated that Anne had been confused with her sister Mary, and that it was Mary who entered the convent. Yet there is no other source that mentions a convent.

One reader has suggested that Mary was perhaps sent to Brie because she was pregnant by King François, but there is no evidence for this, and history credits François, that legendary lover, with only one dubious bastard child, Henri de la Rue.

Given the confusing nature of the evidence for Mary's possible sojourn at Brie, it is hardly surprising that Sander and other historians either mistakenly or deliberately confused her with her sister Anne.[115]

Thomas Boleyn's loyal and efficient service, and the recognition he received at home and in foreign courts, continued to bring its rewards for his children. It was at one time claimed that he sent his son George to be 'educated among the Oxonians',[116] but that is unlikely, because between 1500 and 1600, records show that the age of entry to Oxford University was invariably seventeen.[117] What is certain is that a 'Master Boleyn' took part with his father in the revels at court at the Christmas season of 1514–15.[118] It is invariably assumed that this was George, but it was probably his older brother Thomas, and it may well have been Thomas who was sent to Oxford, for he must have been born before 1500, and lived long enough to go to university. Moreover, it is more likely that Sir Thomas Boleyn would have provided his heir with a university education, rather than his younger son. George, who was only about eleven in 1514, became a page to the King soon afterwards,[119] holding the post until 1524, so it is unlikely that he went to university at all, although he did receive an excellent education, excelling at languages like his father.

There is no shred of evidence that Mary was ever close to her brother George,[120] and the sparse sources we have tend to support the view that neither George nor Anne had much time or use for Mary.[121]

On 3 August 1515, an event that was to have long-term consequences for Mary occurred: her grandfather, the Earl of Ormond, died, aged either eighty-five or ninety.[122] 'I understand to my great

heaviness that my Lord my father is departed this world,' Lady
Boleyn wrote to her son, Sir Thomas. Having no male heir, the Earl
had directed in his will, dated 31 July that year, that his extensive
property (which also embraced the Hankeford inheritance that had
come to him on marriage) was to be divided between his two co-
heiresses, Anne, the wife of James St Leger, and Margaret, Lady
Boleyn.[123] Each daughter received thirty-six manors, and among the
property inherited by Margaret Butler was the great lordship of
Rochford in Essex, including Rochford Hall, a fine manor house
that would one day – briefly – be owned by Mary Boleyn. Another
was New Hall in Essex, which Sir Thomas Boleyn sold in 1516/17
to the King, who rebuilt it as the palace of Beaulieu. To his grandson,
Thomas Boleyn, the Earl left a hunting horn of ivory and gold,
which had been in his family for generations; tradition held that
Thomas Becket, the ill-fated Archbishop of Canterbury, had once
drunk from it.

Control of an heiress's inheritance was usually vested in her
husband, who enjoyed all rights to it, but where the heiress was a
widow, control remained in her hands. Since the fourteenth century,
some landowners had tried to limit female inheritance by imposing
an entail, the most popular form of which was the male tail, which
restricted the descent of land to men, but the Butler lands were not
entailed. Nevertheless, the widowed Lady Margaret appears to have
allowed her son to assume control of her inheritance, for on 26
October 1517, he was granted a licence to export wood and other
commodities 'made within the lordship of Rochford' in his ship the
Rosendell.[124] By 1519 – as we know from later records – Margaret
Butler had become insane and incapable of managing her own affairs,
so Thomas Boleyn assumed responsibility for her estates.[125] That
meant that from henceforth he had substantial landed resources at
his disposal.

The earldom of Ormond should have descended to Thomas
Butler's nearest male relative, his cousin Piers Butler, who assumed
the title, but the late Earl's two daughters, with Margaret being backed
vigorously by her son, Thomas Boleyn, all took steps to prevent Piers
from coming into his rightful inheritance. The dispute would drag
on until December 1529, when Thomas Boleyn, as heir general, was
finally granted the earldom of Ormond, along with that of Wiltshire,
by Henry VIII.

★

Wherever Mary was living between 1515 and 1520, she did not see her sister for several years. Anne Boleyn was to remain in France, in the service of Queen Claude, until early 1522, when a war between Henry VIII and François I was looming. But before then, Mary was to be married. Her family had arranged a most advantageous match for her.

5

'William Carey, of the Privy Chamber'

Mary's marriage to William Carey was probably no hasty affair, as has been claimed by several writers, who assert that it came 'out of the blue',[1] and who believe that the haste is the reason why people think it was arranged as cover for Mary's affair with the King.[2] Negotiations for it must have begun before January 1519, when Sir Thomas Boleyn left for France to serve as England's ambassador. The existence of two receipts, dated 1496 and 1498, to the bridegroom's maternal grandparents, Sir Robert Spencer and Eleanor Carey, Countess of Wiltshire, from James Butler, Earl of Ormond, and Thomas Carey (Mary's future father-in-law), for part payment of an annuity payable during Ormond's lifetime,[3] proves that there was a long-established connection between the Carey and Butler families, and suggests that the marriage was mooted by Thomas Boleyn, or would have been pleasing to him.

The King's attendance at the wedding confirms that the marriage was made with his hearty approval, or even at his behest;[4] there are many instances of his ordering or influencing the marriages of his nobles and courtiers, as was his traditional privilege, and he was to involve himself in negotiations for the marriage of Anne Boleyn later that same year. William Carey was his cousin and one of his intimates in the Privy Chamber, so it follows that he would have interested himself in finding Carey a bride. Of course, Mary, like so many well-born girls of the Tudor era, had little or no say in the matter.

It is likely that the Howards had been involved too;[5] they may well have stood proxy for the bride's father in bargaining over the marriage contract and arranging the wedding in his absence. Boleyn may well have hoped to be back in England in time for the ceremony, arranged for February 1520, but was unable to leave France until he had completed his tour of diplomatic duty there and his replacement had arrived; in the event, he returned home early in March.[6] As marriages were not supposed to be celebrated during Lent, when the devout were expected to abstain from sexual intercourse, it was no doubt agreed that the young couple should not be made to defer their marriage in order to await Sir Thomas's coming.[7]

William Carey, the husband chosen for Mary, was one of the privileged staff of the King's Privy Chamber,[8] an Esquire of the Body to the King[9] – an office that Thomas Boleyn had once held – and a man of good family. There is no evidence that he was ever a member of Cardinal Wolsey's household, as has been claimed.[10]

Contrary to popular belief, William Carey did not have 'little to recommend him as a husband'.[11] He was far more than the 'undistinguished courtier' described by David Hume in the eighteenth century, which has been the prevailing view ever since. Yet it cannot truthfully be said that he was 'of no particular account',[12] 'lowly',[13] a 'fairly undistinguished member of the King's household, never of much importance'[14] or 'obscure'.[15] He did not hold an 'insignificant office',[16] but one of the most coveted positions in the royal household, and he has been described by David Starkey[17] as 'a major figure at court'. He was of good birth, a cousin to the King, who 'highly favoured' him,[18] and all the signs were that he had a brilliant career ahead of him.

The young couple were well matched in age and by birth. Their supposedly 'poor' marriage was not 'surprising',[19] nor was it 'far below the [Boleyn] family's expectations', 'a great disappointment' to them[20] or 'scarcely the great match' they had hoped for.[21] There is no basis for the astonishing theory that Mary's disappointing marriage taught Anne Boleyn 'a cautionary lesson that may have helped to teach her a deep fear of sex, which prevented her fulfilling what her manner promised'.[22] Nor was Carey the kind of man on whom Mary, as 'soiled goods',[23] could be palmed off; there is, in fact, no evidence that her 'reputation' had preceded her. On the contrary, doubtless Carey was pleased to be marrying the daughter of a man of importance like Sir Thomas Boleyn. It has been said that he got an acceptable dowry with her,[24] but no details survive.

Even as a younger son, William could be considered 'a prestigious match';[25] he was a fast-rising star, and we may surmise that Thomas Boleyn found it advantageous to have a son-in-law in such an influential position at court[26] – it may have been thanks in part to Carey's influence with the King that Boleyn would obtain high office there within two years – and that, 'politically and socially, Mary's marriage served to bolster her family's ambitions at court'.[27] It also gave the Boleyns an advantage in their rivalry with Wolsey.[28] So it was, in many respects, 'a good marriage'.[29]

There has been speculation that the couple married for love,[30] with Mary indulging in what Agnes Strickland unfairly called her 'incorrigible predilection for making love matches', but we have no evidence for this,[31] as nothing is known about the personal relationship between her and William. There is no basis to the claim that 'Mary added to the unforgivable errors of her ways by marrying presumably for love', nor was this 'a sorry match for a Boleyn', with Mary having 'spoiled her chances of a good one. Significantly, her father did not attend the wedding.'[32] As we have seen, although Sir Thomas was unable to get back to England in time, the marriage clearly took place with his approval. And, in an age in which marrying purely for love was regarded as akin to insanity, the presence of the King at the wedding argues that it was supported by all parties and considered eminently suitable.

There is no evidence to support the oft-repeated assertion that Carey was 'chosen more for his willingness to have his wife continue to grace the royal bed than for any other reason'.[33] All the evidence points to Mary's affair with Henry VIII having begun after their marriage. Given her misconduct of five years past, she may be considered lucky to have preserved her reputation and secured such a husband. Her father was perhaps aware that he had put soiled goods on the marriage market, but William Carey had probably not heard of Mary's brief affair with the King of France – and probably never would, for no doubt care would have been taken to keep it a secret.

Mary's wedding took place on 4 February 1520[34] at court, with Henry VIII himself attending the ceremony in the newly rebuilt chapel royal[35] at Greenwich Palace, on the banks of the River Thames.[36] The King's Book of Payments records: 'For the King's offering upon Saturday, at the marriage of W. Care and Mare Bullayn, six shillings and eightpence' (£130).[37] Contrary to what some writers[38] have assumed, this was not a gift to the newlyweds but an offering at the altar. Antonia Fraser states that Queen Katherine also 'attended the festivities', but there is no record of this in contemporary sources.

Henry's presence at the wedding is unlikely to have been due to an amorous interest in the bride, as has often been mooted, but probably had much to do with Sir Thomas Boleyn being in high favour and William Carey being the King's kinsman. William's maternal grandmother, Eleanor Beaufort (who had once been married to James Butler, 5th Earl of Ormond), was the first cousin of Henry's grandmother, Margaret Beaufort, and through Eleanor,[39] William was descended from King Edward III and related to nearly every aristocratic family in the land. Indeed, he boasted 'a more immediate royal heritage than the Boleyns'.[40]

The second son of Thomas Carey of Chilton Foliat, Wiltshire, by Margaret Spencer, William was then about twenty-four, an upwardly mobile courtier of some standing, all set for a glittering career at court, and a man of good birth.

His family could trace its lineage back to the eleventh century. In Domesday Book, the manor of 'Kari', which they owned, and from which their name[41] was derived, is described as lying in the parish of St Giles in the Heath, near Launceston, Somerset. The Norman castle they later occupied at Castle Cary, Somerset, stood on the hillside above the village horse pond, but survived only into the twelfth century, and nothing of it remains today. A later manor house of the Careys that stood in the village has also long since disappeared.

The first member of the family to make his mark was Sir John Carey, who supported Richard II after his deposition in 1399, and died in exile in Waterford, Ireland. For this, his lands were confiscated by Richard's successor, Henry IV, and it was only after Sir John's son, Sir Robert Carey of Cockington and Clovelly in Devon, had defeated a knight errant of Aragon and won the post of Champion of Arms to Henry V that they were largely restored. Sir Robert and his descendants, including William Carey, were thereafter authorised to bear the arms of the vanquished knight: 'in a field argent a bend sable bearing three roses of the field'.

The family fortunes suffered another reversal when Robert's grandson, Sir William Carey of Cockington, who supported the House of Lancaster in the Wars of the Roses, was executed in 1471 after the Yorkists won the Battle of Tewkesbury. He left an heir,

Robert, by his first wife, Elizabeth Paulet, and a younger son, Thomas, born in 1460,[42] by his second, Alice Fulford.

This Thomas was William Carey's father. He settled at Chilton Foliat, which lies two miles north-west of Hungerford in Wiltshire, and had links with the Careys going back at least as far as 1407, when a Robert Carey was rector.[43] Thomas sat in Parliament as burgess for Wallingford, Berkshire, in 1491–2, and made a good marriage to Margaret, daughter of Sir Robert Spencer by Eleanor Beaufort; by her he had three sons and four daughters. His date of death is variously given in genealogies: some writers say he died in 1500,[44] but documents in the National Archives show that he was pursuing a lawsuit between 1518 and 1529, and died shortly before 21 June 1536, at Tewkesbury.[45]

Thomas's eldest son, born around 1491, was Sir John Carey,[46] later of Thremhall Priory in Essex, which was granted to him in 1538 at the Dissolution of the Monasteries.[47] In 1522, this John was serving as a captain of one of the ships in Henry VIII's navy, but by 1526, probably through the influence of his younger brother, William, he had been appointed a Groom of the Privy Chamber, a lower rank than that of Esquire of the Body. He returned to his naval career, however, and by 1542 had risen to the rank of Vice Admiral. In 1547, he was knighted by Edward VI. He died in 1552 at Hunsdon House in Hertfordshire, and is buried in Hunsdon Church.

William, who married Mary Boleyn, was John's junior by perhaps five years – if we accept the date 1526 on an Elizabethan copy of his portrait, where his age is given as thirty,[48] which places his birth around 1496. The third son, Edward Carey, was perhaps born in 1498, and died in 1560. One daughter, Mary, married Sir John Delaval of Seaton Delaval in Northumberland, a marriage that was possibly arranged through the good offices of her maternal aunt, Katherine Spencer, Countess of Northumberland. Two others, Eleanor and Anne, became nuns at Wilton Abbey. The remaining daughter, Margaret, appears to have remained unwed.

Chilton Foliat, where the Carey siblings apparently grew up, was – and still is – a small, ancient settlement on the River Kennet, straddling the Marlborough Road and surrounded by lush, unspoilt woodland and gentle hills. It is an area of outstanding natural beauty. There are traces of Neolithic and Bronze Age settlements near the parish church. The medieval manor house stood immediately to the west of the twelfth-century church of St Mary, but was demolished in the 1750s. It was in this manor house that William Carey had probably been born. It was surrounded by a large demesne farm and a deer park, in which there was a hunting lodge.

As the younger son of a younger son, William Carey had no landed estate or affinity, and had had to make his own way in the world, so he must have risen to prominence at court on his own merits, as one of the new men so favoured by Henry VIII: men who owed their success to ability rather than rank.

William had begun his career at court by January 1519, probably gaining entry through the patronage of Henry Courtenay, Earl of Devon, the King's cousin. He had probably come to Courtenay's notice through his Carey connections in Devon.[49] In a very short time, he had won the favour of Henry VIII and secured a post in the King's Privy Chamber, as Esquire of the Body to his royal master,[50] the same post that Thomas Boleyn had once held.[51] In fact, Carey had all the qualities and talents that Henry VIII sought and admired in the young men of his court: he could joust, gamble and play tennis with the best of them, and the chances are that he was learned, witty and good company.

On New Year's Day 1519, the King's Book of Payments records that Carey – who must have quickly proved himself reliable – was entrusted with a thousand crowns (£78,000) for 'playing money for the King' and got 4s.2d (£80) for fetching it.[52] The next month, he is twice recorded as playing – and winning – against the Earl of Devon 'at the King's tennis court'.[53] On 18 June, at Windsor, the King granted Carey an annuity of fifty marks (£4,600).[54]

By October of that year, Carey's name appears on a list of thirty-two privileged persons entitled to 'daily liveries in the King's household', which included 'ordinary breakfasts daily to be served within the counting house': the list included the Lord Steward, the King's and Queen's Lord Chamberlains, the Treasurer of the Household, the Comptroller, the Princess Mary, the French Queen (Mary Tudor), Cardinal Wolsey, the Duke of Suffolk, several Knights of the Body, the Master of the Horse, 'Mr Carey' and some 'young minstrels'.[55] No one under the degree of baron could ordinarily 'have any breakfast in the King's house'.[56] The following month we find Carey listed with Nicholas Carew, Henry Norris and Anthony Poyntz as members of the King's household.[57] 'William Carey, of the Privy Chamber' is also mentioned in a document relating to the household of Henry VIII, drawn up between 1519 and 1522, in which he is recorded as one of the Esquires of the Body 'that lieth upon the King's pallet', 'having wages in the counting house and in the Exchequer', and the right to keep four servants and two horses at court.[58]

William is recorded as taking part in the revels at New Year 1520, when – in company with Carew, Norris and Anthony Browne, prominent courtiers with whom he was already closely associated – he was one of twelve gentlemen who took part in a pageant staged at Havering in Essex, wearing coats in the German fashion in green or yellow satin adorned with gold or silver scales. He got to keep his expensive apparel too.[59]

As a member of the Privy Chamber, which was at once the King's private lodging and an exclusive department of state that centred upon the monarch's person, William received £33.6s.8d (£12,650) a year from the King;[60] this figure relates to 1520, and was the same wage as Henry Norris, a great favourite of the King, received. Carey's duties as Esquire of the Body, which were carried out on a shift basis, included waiting on the monarch hand and foot, attending on him in his bedchamber, sleeping near him on a pallet bed at night, guarding his lodgings when he was absent and sharing his leisure time in the day.[61]

Since 1518, the Privy Chamber had become one of the two power centres in the kingdom, the other being the Privy Council;[62] not for nothing would there be clashes with the all-powerful Cardinal Wolsey, who complained that 'certain young men in [the King's] Privy Chamber, not regarding his estate or degree, were so familiar and homely with him, and played such light touches with him, that they forgot themselves'.[63] In 1519, some of the King's gentlemen – among them Sir Francis Bryan and Sir Edward Neville – had disgraced themselves by indulging in loutish behaviour in the streets of Paris and London, which gave the powerful Wolsey the excuse he needed to purge the Privy Chamber of his rivals, which he was to do again in 1526, with the passing of the Eltham Ordinances. Yet William Carey was secure enough in the King's favour to survive both purges and escape banishment from court. His conduct had clearly not given cause for criticism.[64]

Even so, he and his privileged companions were also the targets of some resentful censure by members of the aristocracy. Edward Stafford, Duke of Buckingham, who was of royal blood and suffered execution in 1521 for plotting to seize the throne, was outraged by the fact that 'the King would give his fees, offices and rewards to boys rather than noblemen',[65] while other peers would disparagingly refer to these gentlemen as 'the minions', a term that then meant a favourite or darling. The minions may also have been satirised by the court poet John Skelton in his interlude *Magnificence*.

William Carey was fortunate enough to be one of this select group of young men who enjoyed a privileged degree of daily access to – and intimacy with – the King, and therefore great influence and the ability to exercise lucrative patronage. No man gained admittance to this small and select band of gentlemen and esquires unless Henry liked and favoured him, for these were the men with whom he enjoyed his 'pastime with good company', as he described it in his own song, in which he speaks of hunting, singing, dancing and 'all goodly sports'. Most of this small, favoured band of courtiers had come to prominence through their expertise at jousting,[66] and shared the King's sporting interests.[67]

Such company could enable Henry VIII to digest 'all thoughts and fancies' and indulge in 'mirth and play'.[68] All Privy Chamber staff were expected to be competent at making music, singing, dancing, cards, dice and even acting. Many had similar intellectual tastes as the King, and dazzled him with their wit and repartee. They were enjoined to be 'loving together' and discreet, and warned 'not to tattle about such things as may be done or said when the King goes forth'.[69]

We may infer from Carey's rapid rise to favour that he had all the requisite talents – and, no doubt, vices – and that the King had taken an instant liking to him and detected in him the kind of qualities that would be useful to him.

The minions were violently pro-French 'in eating, drinking and apparel, yea, and in French vices and brags, so that all the estates of England were by them laughed at; the ladies and gentlemen were dispraised, so that nothing by them was praised but if it were after the French turn'.[70] No doubt it would have suited William Carey very well to acquire a wife who had served a queen of France, and whose father had strong diplomatic links with the French court.

As for Mary, she had married a splendid young man at the height of his powers, an intelligent man who was destined for greatness, and – if William's portraits are anything to go by – good-looking too, with brown hair, a short beard, a strong nose, and eyes that markedly resemble those of his cousin, Henry VIII.[71] It was a fine match, and it might have marked the beginning of obscurity and genteel domesticity for Mary – but for the fact that, some time after her marriage, she became Henry VIII's mistress.

Where did the Careys live after their marriage? William Carey is sometimes described in genealogies as being 'of Aldenham', a small village lying near Borehamwood and Radlett, in Hertfordshire, three miles north-east of Watford; and it has been claimed that, after their marriage, William and Mary, when not at court, resided there. But Aldenham was the property of Westminster Abbey from the eleventh century until the Reformation, when it came into the possession of Henry VIII, who granted it to the Stepneth family in 1546; and the house lived in by the Carey family was not built until between 1576 and 1589. Thus it is clear that William Carey was never lord of the manor of Aldenham, nor is there any record of him owning, or residing in, a house in the village, or ever living there.[72] There is in fact no mention of any Carey living there before 1589. The likelihood is that William and Mary resided at court during their marriage.

On the assumption that Mary was less than twelve years old at the time of her wedding, it has been argued that the consummation of her marriage was 'undoubtedly delayed' for some time, which is said to account for the fact that the couple's first child was not born until 1524.[73] Yet this theory does not take account of the evidence that she was François I's mistress around 1514–15, or the likely date of Anne Boleyn's birth and the fact that Mary was the elder sister, which all suggests that she was probably at least twenty at the time of her marriage, and that it was duly consummated.

There is no record of Mary serving permanently in Katherine's household,[74] but, as the wife of a prominent courtier, she was permitted to lodge at court with her husband, and by virtue of being married to a member of the King's Privy Chamber, she might be called upon to serve as an extra lady-in-waiting to the Queen when needed.[75] Being in such a privileged position normally conferred its own status upon a woman, and afforded her – albeit intermittently – an independent income, for the Queen's ladies received annual fees, occasional perquisites and pensions upon retirement; they also enjoyed special access to royal patronage.[76] However, Mary Boleyn does not seem to have been called upon to serve Katherine of Aragon very often, and may have done so only on one occasion.

Nevertheless, as a member of the inner court,[77] she became part of a close-knit, élite circle of people whose lives revolved around

that of the King. Henry VIII used more familiarity with his infe-
riors than most monarchs – foreign ambassadors were amazed when
he leaned out of a window and shared a joke with them; he was
not averse to playing dice with the master of his cellar, and he
was known to put his arm around a man's shoulder to set him at
his ease. Therefore it was inevitable that most of those who lived at
court would soon become acquainted – and even friendly – with
this highly accessible King.

Coming to court meant embracing an itinerant life, moving from
one magnificent palace to another in accordance with the demands
of state, the necessity for cleansing, or the royal pleasure. As an Esquire
of the Body, in almost constant attendance on the King – and later
as a Gentleman of the Privy Chamber – William Carey was entitled
to a lodging at court, although when on duty he would sleep in the
royal apartments.[78] Mary would have shared his lodging, and been
waited on by the four servants that his rank permitted him.[79] There
were whole ranges of courtier lodgings at the royal palaces; Carey
would probably have been assigned a double lodging, consisting of
two rooms, each with a fireplace, and a garderobe; he and Mary
would have been expected to provide their own furnishings and
ensure that the rooms were kept clean. With servants lodging with
them, space was limited, privacy difficult, and conditions cramped.

After February 1522, when William was appointed Keeper of the
King's house of Beaulieu at Boreham, near Chelmsford, Essex, with
the right to lodgings there,[80] he and Mary may well have resided at
Beaulieu when his duties required it – and perhaps when they wanted
briefly to escape the court and enjoy some privacy. Beaulieu was a
house with which Mary was probably familiar, because it had been
in her family until recently. Originally entitled New Hall, it had
been built as a medieval hall house by the abbots of Waltham, prior
to being acquired by Edward IV. Henry VII had granted it to Mary's
great-grandfather, Thomas Butler, Earl of Ormond, who had entertained Henry VIII there in 1510 – when Mary and Anne Boleyn
may have been present – and in 1515, shortly before he died. His
daughter, Margaret, widow of Sir William Boleyn, then inherited it,
and her son, Sir Thomas, as Ormond's executor, sold it to the King
for £1,000 (£379,500) before January 1516.

Between 1516 and 1523, Henry lavished £20,000 (£7.5 million)
in converting New Hall into a vast and sumptuous palace with eight
courtyards, which he renamed Beaulieu. Faced with red brick, it was

entered via a gatehouse embellished with the King's arms, which led
into a main courtyard with a fountain; the palace boasted a great
hall, a tennis court, a chapel with brilliant stained glass, and beautiful gardens. There was even hot and cold running water in the
royal bathroom. By 1519, the renovations had been sufficiently far
advanced for the King and Queen to entertain noble French hostages
there, and by 1522, when William was made Keeper, they were almost
complete. Being entrusted with the keepership of such an important palace was quite a responsibility for William, and testifies to the
King's trust and confidence in him, and to Carey's proven ability.

Beaulieu later came back into the hands of the Boleyns when
Henry VIII, having decided that it was old-fashioned, leased it to
Mary's brother George in 1531. It is now a school, New Hall, and
has been extensively rebuilt; the only remains of the house that
Mary knew are the cellars, and a stained-glass window now in St
Margaret's Church, Westminster. Beaulieu lay about twenty miles
from another Boleyn property, Rochford Hall, which Mary would
one day inherit.

In June 1520, as 'Mistress Carey', Mary was one of twenty-five
gentlewomen among three thousand 'persons attendant on the
Queen'[81] when the English court decamped *en masse* to France for
the famous Field of Cloth of Gold, the lavish summit meeting between
those great rivals Henry VIII and François I, which took place in a
field between Guînes and Ardres in what is now northern France;
Guînes was in English hands, for Calais and the surrounding area –
the Pale – was an English territory, having been taken by Edward
III in 1347, in the early phases of the Hundred Years War. It then
became part of the great Plantagenet empire founded through the
marriage of Henry II and Eleanor of Aquitaine in the twelfth century.
Over the centuries, successive kings of France had gradually clawed
back the lands, and England's defeat in 1453 at the end of the
Hundred Years War brought about the loss of all the rest but Calais,
which itself would be lost to the French in 1557 by Henry VIII's
daughter, Mary I.

Mary would no doubt have been excited to be involved in such
a great and important enterprise, and been thrown into a flurry of
preparations; and she was to go in some style, for each gentlewoman
was permitted to take with her 'a woman, two menservants and three
horses'.[82] Among the knights of Katherine's household were Mary's
kinsmen John Shelton, Robert Clere and Philip Calthorpe, and several

of her Howard relatives, while Jane Parker, her future sister-in-law, was a fellow gentlewoman.

Mary's husband William also had a role to play in the proceedings; both he and Sir Thomas Boleyn, who had helped to organise the event, were attending on the King,[83] William as one of the Esquires for the Body; while her mother, 'the Lady Boleyn', and her aunt, Anne Tempest, 'the Lady Boleyn junior', were with the Queen.[84]

The King and Queen and their vast retinues, all clad in 'noble apparel',[85] sailed from Dover in a great fleet of ships, then made their way in stately procession to Guînes, where Cardinal Wolsey had arranged for a small temporary palace of wood and canvas to be erected. Here, the Queen was lodged with her ladies and gentlewomen in rooms of unsurpassed magnificence, with most of her people being accommodated in silken tents. Katherine's lodgings were of 'unparalleled splendour', hung with cloth of gold; the altar in her chapel 'lacked neither pearls nor stones' and bore 'twelve great images of gold'.[86] The King's apartments were even more sumptuous.

The two kings met on 7 June in the Vale of Ardres. Attended by vast trains of courtiers, they made a magnificent sight, and the very ground had been levelled so that neither should appear greater than the other. Just to be on the safe side, Henry was accompanied by his guard, 'five hundred in number'. Approaching 'in the field', he and François saluted each other whilst still on horseback, then dismounted and embraced 'with courteous words, to the great rejoicing of the beholders'. The field in which they met was ringed with sumptuous tents and pavilions 'imbued and batoned with rich cloths of silk like fine burned gold' and hung with 'marvellous cloths of Arras'. In every chamber were imposing canopies of estate, also of gold, with 'rich embroidery, with chairs covered with like cloth, with pommels of fine gold and great cushions of rich work'.[87]

Gifts were exchanged, a treaty of friendship signed, and the two kings then passed the day in pleasant conversation, banqueting and 'loving devices',[88] while their courts made each other's acquaintance.

Determined to impress the French, their ancient foe, all the lords of England were decked out in cloth of gold or silver, velvets, tinsel (satin threaded with gold or silver) or crimson silk, often heavily embroidered, and, along with all the knights, gentlemen, esquires and officers of the King, had weighed themselves down with chains, baldricks and SS collars, all of gold.[89]

In company with all the other courtiers, Mary and the rest of the ladies would have spent the seventeen days of the Field of Cloth of Gold 'superbly' dressed in their 'richest and costliest habits', for 'the suites of the two queens were gorgeous in the extreme',[90] although there was snide comment that 'the French ones arranged theirs with more taste and elegance, so that their visitors soon began to adopt the mode of that country – by which they lost in modesty what they gained in comeliness'. Mary had spent months at the French court, and possibly years in a noble French household, so she would no doubt have been used to wearing the nimbus-like French hood that – scandalously – showed off the hair, and necklines that were cut wider, and lower, than those in England.

She would also, no doubt, have enjoyed the endless round of extravagant festivities that attended the seventeen days of the summit, which included jousts, sporting events, feasting, banquets, dancing and excessive drinking from fountains running with free wine. On Sundays, she would have attended Katherine to Mass, celebrated by Cardinal Wolsey, and probably witnessed the touching argument between her mistress and Queen Claude as to whom should take precedence in kissing the Bible first – a contest that looked like ending in stalemate until they spontaneously kissed each other instead.

When Queen Katherine, the Dowager French Queen Mary Tudor and Queen Claude met on 11 June to watch a joust, Mary was one of the 'handsome and well arrayed' ladies who were crowded into wagons or riding on palfreys in Katherine's retinue,[91] and who sat or stood behind her on a stage hung with tapestries or painted cloths and furnished with a costly canopy of estate 'all of pearl', which drew much comment. She would have witnessed her valiant husband – who had been provided with a pair of yellow velvet hose[92] – competing in the lists as one of the Earl of Devon's men,[93] jousting in the same contests as the King, winning prizes in the tournaments and earning the acclaim of the two courts. She would have been present to watch him taking part in the revels alongside his colleagues Henry Norris, Nicholas Carew and Francis Bryan,[94] all intimates of the King's inner circle whom Carey would probably by now have accounted his friends.

On the following day, there was another joust, in which the two kings showed off their talents in feats of skill. It is unlikely that Mary was one of the forty ladies who followed Queen Katherine on palfreys as, clad defiantly in the costume of Spain, France's enemy, she rode in procession to the tiltyard; but she was almost certainly in the six wagons that followed. She would no doubt have thrilled to the sight of King Henry displaying his dexterity 'before the ladies': spurring his horse and 'making it bound and curvet as valiantly as any man could do'. Two more days of jousting followed, with Henry and François vying to impress the two courts; the contest, most fortunately, ended in a draw.

The following evening, Mary would have been in attendance on Katherine when – Henry having gone off to be entertained by Queen Claude at the castle of Ardres – she received King François at Guînes, where he was 'right honourably served in all things needful. Then the ladies came and proffered themselves to dance, and so did in the French King's presence, which done, [he] took leave of the Queen and the ladies of the court.'[95] We do not know if Mary Boleyn was one of the dancers, although it is possible. This cannot have been one of the easiest of social occasions, since François thought Katherine 'old and deformed' (as he had called her the year before), while she was soon to refer to him as 'the greatest Turk that ever was'.

So far, all had been sweetness and courtesy, but it could not be expected that the meeting between the two kings would go off without a hitch. Mary must have been watching when, a couple of days later, Henry VIII, a vain man who believed his athletic prowess was second to none, challenged his royal rival to a wrestling match. At first the fight was equal, but soon the courts were holding their collective breath as the King of France seemed to be getting the better of his opponent.

'Have at me again!' cried a provoked Henry, whereupon the younger François threw him ingloriously to the ground. Consternation broke out among the spectators as the English King rose to his feet and made to lunge at his brother monarch. It was only the timely intervention of Queen Katherine and Queen Claude, who pulled their husbands apart, that averted a serious diplomatic incident.

On 19 and 20 June, there were two more tournaments, in which William Carey probably took part, as the two kings were 'holding tourneys with all the partners of their challenge', watched, as on every day, by the three queens, to whom, as they sat on their 'stages', the kings did reverence before the jousts began. On 22 June, Henry and François did 'battle on foot at the barriers'.[96] At all these functions, Queen Katherine 'and all her ladies were superbly dressed'.[97]

During the summit, Mary may well have been united with her

sister Anne,[98] who was probably in the train of either Queen Claude or Marguerite of Valois. It has been suggested that, after five years, 'relations between the two sisters must have been uncomfortable', with Mary, who had been 'recalled from France in disgrace', now in attendance on Queen Katherine while 'simultaneously warming King Henry's bed'; and that King François 'cannot have failed to notice that King Henry was now riding his English mare'.[99] But there is no evidence for any of this.

Even so, there may have been occasions for awkwardness. Did Mary — and her father — fear that William Carey would hear French gossip about her during the courtly social gatherings that marked the summit and would almost certainly have been attended by people who might have remembered her from the days when she had been King François' mistress? Did she worry that the French King would recognise her in the throng and betray by some look or gesture that he knew her intimately? It is fruitless to speculate, since we know very little about the relationship between Mary and William. Given that the marriage was advantageous on both sides, we might expect Carey to have been conventional enough to have wanted an heir that he could be sure was his own; and, being a prominent man at court, he must surely have cared about his wife's reputation. So it is possible that, for Mary, the Field of Cloth of Gold was something of an ordeal.

The costly pageant came to an end on 24 June, the day after Cardinal Wolsey had celebrated a 'high and solemn' Mass in the open air, which was attended by the two courts and followed by a farewell feast and a magnificent fireworks display. Formal farewells were said, with François visiting Katherine at Guînes, and Henry taking his leave of Claude at Ardres, and the meeting broke up, with very little to show for all the ruinous expense.

For despite the lavish display and protestations of friendship and amity on the part of Henry VIII and François I, the summit had achieved virtually nothing. 'These sovereigns are not at peace,' a Venetian envoy had observed. 'They hate each other cordially.' In fact, Henry had already secretly arranged to meet up with François' great enemy, the Emperor Charles V, after the great long courtly charade was over. Only a fortnight after he had led his court back to Calais, where he and the Queen and their suites lodged in the Exchequer Palace, he rode, with Sir Thomas Boleyn among those in attendance,[100] to Gravelines to meet the Emperor and escort him back to Calais, where he and Katherine hosted a great banquet in his honour. William Carey was in attendance, and Mary Boleyn would almost certainly have been present in the Queen's train. Soon afterwards, the court sailed home to England.

Mary was no doubt able to watch her husband take part in jousts that were held to celebrate the marriage of his patron, the Earl of Devon, to Gertrude Blount, the daughter of Lord Mountjoy, which took place on 25 October 1520. The King had given orders for the making of sleeveless knee-length tunics (known as 'bases') and trappings of russet velvet and cloth of silver 'lozenged and cross-lozenged with cloth of gold, every lozenge embroidered with trueloves of cloth of gold, with saddle covers and harness of the same. These were used by the King, Sir William Kingston and Mr William Carey at Greenwich, the 21st, 27th and 28th October.'[101]

Tragedy struck the Boleyns sometime in 1520, when the eldest son and heir, Thomas Boleyn the younger, died. The cause of his death is unknown. This must have been a terrible blow for his family, for the young man had lived well into his twenties and they had surely envisaged a brilliant future for him. Now he was at rest at Penshurst, and his surviving brother, George, was heir in his stead.

Life, as ever, had to go on. That year, Sir Thomas Boleyn was much occupied, not only by the Field of Cloth of Gold, but in finding a husband for his younger daughter, now that the elder was satisfactorily wed. By the spring of 1520, he was negotiating to marry Anne, then still in France, to James Butler, the son of Sir Piers, who was still calling himself Earl of Ormond. Again, this argues that Anne was the younger sister, whose marriage was not broached until her elder sister was settled in wedlock.

According to Cardinal Wolsey, James Butler was 'right active, discreet and wise', and Boleyn, spurred by the prospect of his daughter becoming Countess of Ormond, joined forces with his brother-in-law, Thomas Howard, Earl of Surrey, the King's Lieutenant in Ireland, to lay the proposal before Henry VIII, who thought it an admirable solution to the Ormond dispute, and gave his 'agreeable consent'.[102] Despite this, the marriage negotiations dragged on for over a year, and in November 1521, Wolsey told Henry VIII that he would endeavour himself to bring them to a conclusion 'with all effect'.[103] He was to do quite the opposite, managing to drag out discussions all through the summer and autumn of 1522, after which the marriage

plans were then abandoned because no agreement on the terms of
the contract had been reached – thanks, no doubt, to the obstruc-
tion of the Cardinal, and to Sir Thomas perhaps deciding that he
wanted the earldom of Ormond for himself after all. This left Anne
no nearer to finding a husband than she had ever been.

By then, Mary Boleyn had probably become Henry VIII's mistress.

6

'The Assault on the Castle of Virtue'

Historically, Elizabeth Blount was by far the most prominent of Henry VIII's mistresses, yet her fame has in recent years been eclipsed by the woman who was probably her successor in Henry's bed, Mary Boleyn.

We can discount an unsubstantiated claim, made in 1879, that Elizabeth was replaced in the King's affections by a Mistress Arabella Parker, the wife of a London merchant.[1] Apart from the fact that she is not mentioned in any contemporary source, Arabella (or, more correctly, Arbella) was then a Scots name and virtually unknown in England until it was given, in 1575, to the Lady Arbella Stuart, Henry VIII's great-great-niece. Because she was perceived to be a dynastic threat to Elizabeth I and James I, the name did not gain popularity, and it was not until the late seventeenth century that it started to become fashionable.[2]

Henry VIII's affair with Mary Boleyn was conducted so discreetly that there is no record of the date it started, its duration, or when it ended.[3] Early in the nineteenth century, the Catholic historian John Lingard put forward the claim that Mary had been Henry's mistress, and backed it with striking arguments; but within thirty years it was being asserted that there was no evidence to prove 'aught against the reputation of Mary Boleyn' and that the 'malicious rumours' about her relationship with the King were invented 'to blacken the fame of Henry while he was seeking to divorce Katherine of Aragon, leading the world to believe that he who could be capable of such enormities could entertain no scruples of conscience on the grounds of consanguinity'.[4] Even the magisterial Froude (and after him, in 1952, Sir Arthur MacNalty) vehemently denied that the affair ever took place. Froude – who miscalled Mary's husband 'Henry Carey' and incorrectly claimed that they were married in January 1521 – wrote, 'The story may have been true, and if it was true it was peculiarly disgraceful, but it is not proved . . . The balance of probability is the other way.' He went on to castigate 'respectable historians' for believing it, and concluded that 'it was a legend which grew out of the temper of the time, a mere floating calumny'.

Friedmann, citing much of the evidence that will be set out in this chapter, exploded that myth in 1884, and since then our knowledge of Henry VIII's private life has advanced immeasurably, so there can now be no doubt that he did have an affair with Mary Boleyn. Indeed, the evidence for it is overwhelmingly conclusive.[5]

Nevertheless the first near-contemporary reference to the relationship dates only from 1527, while other primary evidence is sparse. Henry did not 'flaunt' the affair;[6] we only know about it from later sources, primarily a Papal dispensation granted to Henry VIII in 1528, the testimonies of George Throckmorton (1533) and John Hale (1535), several Spanish diplomatic reports of the 1530s, and a treatise written by the King's cousin, Cardinal Reginald Pole, in 1538 – all of which will be discussed in due course. Froude pointed out in 1891 that the affair was not mentioned in the first draft of 'Pole's Book', *Pro ecclesiasticae unitatis defensione* (*A Defence of the Unity of the Church*), which took the form of an open letter to the King, written at Henry VIII's request and sent to England in 1536, which suggests Pole did not know of it at that time. It was only mentioned in the published edition in 1538, which was sent to England the following year with Pope Paul III's Bull of Deposition. This makes sense, as the Pope could have divulged to Pole what he knew to be the truth about Mary, which prompted Pole to castigate Henry VIII for marrying the sister of his mistress.

As has been noted previously, in 1533, George Throckmorton, a Catholic MP who had opposed Henry VIII's Reformation legislation in Parliament, had the impudence to tax the King with having 'meddled' both with Lady Boleyn and her daughter Mary before pursuing Anne, to which Henry replied, tellingly, 'Never with the mother.' It was Thomas Cromwell who added diplomatically, 'Nor never with the sister either, and therefore put that out of your mind.'[7]

By the 1530s, the Spanish ambassador, Eustache Chapuys, was well aware that Henry's relations with Mary created a bar to his marriage to her sister Anne, while in 1535, John Hale, a supporter of Katherine of Aragon, was to report gossip that Mary Boleyn had borne the King a son.[8] By the reign of Anne's daughter, Elizabeth I (1558–1603), the affair had become common knowledge and was mentioned by several writers.

In the early 1520s, Henry VIII was in his glorious prime, but married to an ageing, childless and increasingly pious wife. Henry had enormous respect for Katherine, and may still have loved her, but it is probably fair to say that 'she no longer satisfied the desires of a virile man just entering his thirties'.[9] With his former mistress, Elizabeth Blount, now married and fully occupied with childbearing, the King, it seems, was ripe for an affair.

It has often been suggested that Mary Boleyn was the reason why the King had lost interest in Elizabeth Blount, or that, once Elizabeth had fallen pregnant and was no longer available sexually, Henry had looked elsewhere. One popular theory, first put forward by Lingard (who, like Froude, gives the date of Mary's marriage incorrectly as January 1521), is that Mary became Henry VIII's mistress at that point, before her marriage, and that she was married off to William Carey because he was insignificant – enjoying, according to one fanciful account, only 'a small place at court'[10] – and prepared to be a sensible, pragmatic and complacent husband.[11] The marriage is said to have been hastily arranged by the King for his mistress 'to cloak their affair'.[12] It is also said that that Carey 'knew all about the affair from the beginning, and was as willing as Mary to comply in order to gratify the King';[13] and even that Mary was married off 'as a precaution' against an illicit pregnancy[14] and 'to protect her honour'.[15] It has further been asserted that 'it is almost certain that she was already Henry's mistress by this time'.[16] Is it?

With very little evidence to go on, historians differ considerably in dating the affair, variously placing its commencement within the fifteen years from 1510 to 1525.[17] With such a broad suggested date range, it is small wonder that there has been much confusion as to when Mary's affair with the King flourished. Going on the sparse surviving evidence, it probably began after Mary's marriage.[18] William Carey, as we have seen, was far from insignificant, and the facts would argue against his having been chosen as Mary's bridegroom just because he was willing to be a compliant husband.

The few pointers we have suggest that Mary attracted the King's interest in 1522.[19] The start of their affair has been the subject of much unsubstantiated, and often romantic, speculation: that Henry was attracted to Mary Boleyn because, like Elizabeth Blount, she was an accomplished dancer, eager to join in the pleasures in which the Queen was no longer interested;[20] or that she resembled her mother, and that that was the real source of her attraction for the King.[21] We cannot be certain that, after acknowledging his bastard by the unmarried Elizabeth Blount, Henry decided that affairs with married women were preferable;[22] that hardly rings true in the light of his later pursuit of Anne Boleyn and other unmarried ladies. It has been suggested that, 'turning from his ageing wife, Henry lost his heart to Mary Boleyn'[23] – yet we have no means of knowing if his heart was involved at all, or that he 'adored' Mary,[24] as has been claimed. Others creatively imagine the King being attracted to Mary as 'a wisp of passion, fresh and winning',[25] and suggest that it was in view of her French reputation, her 'hint of French glamour' and her being sexually experienced that she caught Henry's eye.[26] There is no evidence at all that Mary was 'warmly recommended' to Henry VIII by François I.[27]

It has been thought extremely unlikely that Henry would have had anything to do with Mary if he knew she had been the mistress of his French rival, or was in any way promiscuous.[28] We do not know if he was aware of her affair with François, although what we can surmise of his approach to Mary Boleyn suggests that he may have been – possibly having heard gossip, or even being told it by François himself, at the Field of Cloth of Gold, which is not inconceivable, given that Mary was present – and if he did, he perhaps found an added piquancy in appropriating for himself a woman who had graced his rival's bed. Henry was not so nice in such matters as he was in his prudish attitude to marital sex. There has even been speculation that he quizzed Mary as to how he compared with François in bed.[29]

In the overheated imagination of Paul Rival, writing in the 1930s, it was Mary's Boleyn blood that appealed to Henry, who noticed her 'because of her gaiety, because she was in love with love, and because of other, more intangible things that lent an elusive savour to sentiment'. Rival, who believed that Henry had had an affair with Mary's mother, opined that with Mary, 'he recovered his adolescence', discerning that 'a tinge of incest' added its own piquancy. As for

Mary, 'life had made its mark on her: she was youthful, yet at the same time over-mature . . . With the flesh of this gentle creature slept all the alluring sins of France. Henry, in the security of his rustic retreats, in the pauses between the songs of the nightingale, made it his pleasant business to awaken them. On [Mary's] loving bosom, he pillowed his head. In her arms he savoured a very peaceful happiness.' We are entirely in the realms of fantasy here, and there is much more of the same in the ensuing pages of Rival's supposedly factual book.

Henry VIII's relationship with Mary Boleyn probably flourished in the guise and play of courtly love.[30] On 2 March 1522, the King held a tournament in honour of the ambassadors of the Emperor Charles V, who were then visiting England to arrange a marriage between the Emperor and Henry's daughter, the Princess Mary. King Henry himself took part in the jousts, riding a horse trapped in silver caparisons embroidered with a wounded heart and the motto *Elle mon Coeur a navera* ('She has wounded my Heart').[31] Henry was an adept at playing the game of courtly love by the time-honoured rules, which required a suitor to keep the identity of his beloved a secret, so we cannot be certain who it was that had wounded his heart, only that the lady likeliest to have been the object of such overt yet mysterious symbolism was Mary Boleyn. The date fits, as does the circumstantial evidence. It seems that Mary 'had the King of England entirely enthralled'[32] – at least for a time.

Henry's motto proclaimed the unkindness of the lady in rejecting his advances. It also conveyed the message that he was, or fancied himself, in love with her. What is more likely is that it was a ploy to make yet another sexual conquest.

Henry VIII was no doubt used to women succumbing to him. He was the King, and he was young, handsome, athletic and powerful, an irresistible combination. In 1519, a Venetian eyewitness had described him as 'much handsomer than any sovereign in Christendom. Nature could not have done more for him; he is very fair and his whole frame admirably proportioned.'[33] He was, wrote another, 'the handsomest potentate I ever set eyes on: above the usual height, with an extremely fine calf to his leg; his complexion very fair and bright, with auburn hair combed straight and short in the French fashion, and a round face so very beautiful it would become a pretty woman, his throat being rather long and thick. He speaks

French, English and Latin, and a little Italian, plays well on the lute and virginals, sings from a book at sight, draws the bow with greater strength than any man in England, and jousts marvellously. He is in every respect a most accomplished prince.'[34]

Henry, who was aware of his own attributes and very vain, probably expected Mary to submit to him without a qualm, but it seems that she was not easily persuaded. Maybe the fact that she was now a married woman and feared to offend her husband had something to do with it; or she loved William and shrank from betraying him. Possibly she had regretted her brief affair with François I, and did not want to invite notoriety at the English court, having narrowly avoided it at the French one. Perhaps she didn't want Henry in the way he wanted her. Maybe her sister was warning her not to get involved – given Anne's later refusal to become Henry's mistress until marriage was within her sights, this is a real possibility.

It may be significant that the first of a series of royal grants to William Carey was made in February 1522.[35] Of course, this could have been pure coincidence, an award made on William's own merits, which would not have been unexpected, given his past career and his closeness to the King. But it could also have been a discreet incentive to William's wife, with the implicit message that, were she to be kind to her royal suitor, he was prepared to be generous in return. Given that she was a married woman, Henry could hardly have made grants to her directly; but a grant made to her husband would benefit her too, and serve as compensation to the cuckolded William, whether or not he knew of the affair.

Anne Boleyn had just then returned from the French court,[36] her departure having become necessary after war broke out between England and France. Maybe there was 'another happy reunion' between Anne and Mary,[37] but that is pure speculation. By March that year, Anne was officially attached to the royal wardrobe,[38] and 'her father made such means' that she was soon appointed a maid of honour to Katherine of Aragon.[39] Before long, she had made herself noticed: 'there was presented to the eye of the court the rare and admirable beauty of the fresh and young Lady [sic.] Anne Boleyn, to be attending on the Queen'.[40] But it was not this Boleyn sister who captured the King's attention at this time.

Only two days after the tournament, on Shrove Tuesday, 4 March, Mary and Anne were present at a great feast given by Cardinal Wolsey in honour of the King, the Queen and the ambassadors at his London house, York Place. When dinner was over, the hall was cleared and a pageant was performed, entitled – most appositely – 'The Assault on the Castle of Virtue', and costing £20 (£7,500) to mount.[41] A large model of a castle called *Le Château Vert* was wheeled into the hall. Painted green, it had three towers, from which hung banners: one depicted three broken hearts, one a lady's hand holding a man's heart, and the other a lady's hand turning a man's heart – all possibly significant symbols, given the King's 'wounded heart' of two days before. One might even be tempted to speculate that the whole thing had been designed to turn Mary Boleyn's heart.

From this castle sprang eight ladies, including Mary Tudor, 'the French Queen', Gertrude Blount, the young Countess of Devon,[42] 'Mistress Anne Boleyn, Mistress Carey' and 'Mistress Parker', each clad in a gown of white satin embroidered with Milan-point lace and gold thread. On their heads, these ladies wore 'silk cauls of divers colours' costing 2s.8d (£50) each, and Milanese-style bonnets of gold encrusted with jewels. The eight ladies all had 'strange names' embroidered in gold on their headgear and on the twenty-four yellow satin labels that were attached to each gown. Mary Tudor, who knew the Boleyn sisters fairly well, led the dancers as 'Beauty'; Gertrude Blount was 'Honour'; Jane Parker, the daughter of the erudite Henry, Lord Morley – she was to marry George Boleyn within two years – was 'Constancy', Anne Boleyn was 'Perseverance' and Mary Boleyn was 'Kindness'. Those names seem in retrospect to have suited the Boleyn sisters rather well,[43] and perhaps Mary had chosen hers to convey a message to her royal suitor – or it had been chosen for her.

Beneath the castle there appeared eight choristers of the Chapel Royal disguised as 'ladies whose names [Hall gives only seven] were Danger, Disdain, Jealousy, Unkindness, Scorn, *Malebouche* [Sharp Tongue] and Strangeness, dressed like Indian women' in black bonnets. Then eight lords entered, wearing cloth of gold hats and great cloaks made of blue satin. They were named Love, 'Nobleness', Youth, Devotion, Loyalty, Pleasure, Gentleness and Liberty. This group, one member of which was the King himself, was led by a man dressed in crimson satin sewn with burning flames of gold. His name was 'Ardent Desire'. Was this an allusion to Henry's amorous interest in Mary Boleyn? It seems likely, given the conceit that the King had been wearing at the tournament only two days earlier. Henry himself did not play Ardent Desire – that was probably the court musician and deviser of the entertainment, William Cornish – but nonethe-less 'the ladies were so moved by his appearance that they might have given up the castle'. Mary Boleyn may have been more moved than the others, for the whole theme of the pageant seems to have been an allusion to the King's desire for her.

The 'Indian' women cried out that they would hold the fort, but the gallant gentlemen rushed the fortress to an explosion of gunfire, while the ladies defended it by throwing comfits at the besiegers, or sprinkling them with rose water. The men in turn assaulted it with dates, oranges and 'other pleasurable fruits', and thus in the end over-came it and forced the defenders to surrender. Then they took the ladies by the hand, led them down to the floor as prisoners and danced with them. It may have been a heady – or daunting – expe-rience for Mary, dancing in public with the King in front of the Queen and the whole court, with very few people being aware of Henry's interest in her – or perhaps putting two and two together as they watched the couple together, especially 'when they had danced their fill' and 'everyone unmasked themselves'. Afterwards there was 'an extravagant banquet'.

Yet despite the message apparently conveyed by Mary in the guise of 'Kindness', she seems not to have gone to the King's bed will-ingly – contrary to claims that she was 'pliable, eager to please and anxious to enjoy Henry's caresses'[44] or 'enchanted once more by the glamour of royalty'.[45] Maybe she was making the best of an impos-sible situation, fearing the consequences of refusing the King. Or maybe she was forced.

Cardinal Pole, who may have had access to secret documents relating to the affair in the Vatican Library, or enjoyed the confi-dence of the Pope, put it in no uncertain terms to the King, in his treatise of 1538, that he had 'violated' Mary and then kept her for a long time as his concubine.

The word 'violate' derives from the Latin *violo* – to violate – and *violentia* – meaning 'violence, vehemence, force', and also from the Anglo-French and Old French form, *violence*, meaning much the same things. By the late thirteenth century, it meant using physical force to inflict injury or damage. During the fourteenth century, it also came to mean 'breaking', as in breaking the law, or 'offending', as in offending against the law, or 'outraging', 'attacking' or 'assailing'. By the mid-fifteenth century, when used in relation to a woman, it implied rape, ravishment – which could also mean abduction – or

Two of the six versions of the portrait said, probably
erroneously, to be of Mary Boleyn.

338

Is this Mary Boleyn?
(*Above*) Miniature of
an unknown woman,
sometimes called
'Anne Boleyn'.
(*Right*) Miniature of the
same unknown woman.

Mary's father, the ambitious
Thomas Boleyn, later Earl of Wiltshire.
Brass in Hever Church, c.1539.

Mary's maternal grandfather,
Thomas Howard, 2nd Duke of Norfolk.

Blickling Hall, Norfolk, where Mary Boleyn was probably born. In this drawing of the Jacobean
mansion built in 1619, made by Edmund Prideaux in c.1725, the Tudor gable and windows of
the Boleyns' earlier red-brick house can be seen.

Mary's younger sister, the ill-fated Anne Boleyn.

Hever Castle, Kent, where Mary spent many years of her life, during her childhood and widowhood

'The Yule Log' by Robert Alexander Hillingford, shows the great hall at Hever Castle much as Mary knew it.

The courtyard at Hever: a fanciful but architecturally accurate representation. Drawing by Joseph Nash from *The Mansions of England in Olden Time*, 1849.

The long gallery at Hever, which was built by Mary's father, is here shown as the imagined setting for Henry VIII's courtship of Anne Boleyn. Drawing by Joseph Nash from *The Mansions of England in Olden Time*, 1849.

Henry VIII in *c*.1520, two years before his affair with Mary probably began.

Henry VIII in 1525/6, around the time he fe in love with Anne Boleyn.

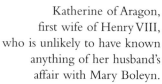

Katherine of Aragon, first wife of Henry VIII, who is unlikely to have known anything of her husband's affair with Mary Boleyn.

Mary's predecessor, Elizabeth Blount, mistress of Henry VIII from around 1514 to 1519. Memorial brass, *c.*1539/40.

Duke Humphrey's Tower, seen on top of the hill behind Greenwich Palace. Henry VIII is said to have had trysts with his mistresses here. Drawing by Anthony van der Wyngaerde, 1558.

Henry Fitzroy, Duke of Richmond and Somerset, natural son of Henry VIII by Elizabeth Blount, the only bastard child acknowledged by the King. Miniature by Lucas Horenbout, *c.*1533/4.

Letter from Anne Boleyn to her father,
written at La Veure, 1514. The handwriting
is that of a teenager at least, which supports a
birth-date of *c*.1501. Mary Boleyn must
therefore have been born before that date.

Mary Tudor, sister of Henry VIII,
in whose train Mary Boleyn went
to France. French School, *c*.1514.

sexual assault. It was only in the late sixteenth century that the word was debased to mean 'improper treatment'. Thus in Mary Boleyn's time, where women were concerned, the word 'violate' still held all its medieval connotations of rape, and it is likely that Reginald Pole was implying that Mary was taken by the King against her will, that she was forced to become his mistress, and that, in so doing, he had taken her from her husband, offended against the laws of the Church and committed an outrage. This, together with Pole's accusation that Henry had thereafter 'kept' her as his concubine, implies that she had very little say in the matter, and undermines the suggestion that Mary became Henry's mistress with the sole intention of obtaining honours and preferments for her family.[46] On the contrary, maybe it was the prospect of possible future rewards that enabled her to make the best of a difficult situation.

An episode recorded in the state papers appears to support the possibility that Henry VIII was capable of taking a woman against her will and overriding any reluctance on her part. In September 1537, five men were interrogated on the orders of Thomas Cromwell, the Lord Privy Seal, after one William Webbe had been accused of treason. Webbe had complained to several people of an incident that had taken place two years before, when he was riding 'a fair gelding with a pretty wench behind him' near Eltham Palace and encountered the King out riding. Henry took such a fancy to the girl that he 'plucked down her muffler and kissed her, and liked her so well that he took her from him, and so lived and kept her still in avoutry [adultery]'. Webbe was furious, and 'cried vengeance on the King' to several of his acquaintances, one of whom reported him for being a traitor.[47] It is possible that his 'wench' was only too pleased to go with the King, but the description of Henry suddenly taking the girl, and Webbe's reaction, suggest that Henry's action was summary, and without thought for the sensibilities of either of them.

Webbe's mistress was obviously from the lower orders of society, and therefore of little consequence, but Mary Boleyn, the daughter of a knight, was no common woman, and her very birth, and the fact that she was the wife of one of his favoured courtiers, should have merited a certain respect. But Henry's behaviour suggests that these things counted for very little, as well as a certain disregard for the conventional sensibilities of ladies, all of which argues that he did know of her affair with François I; so respect clearly had its limits. Those pretty charades – the jousting motto and the

elaborate allegory of the pageant – that almost certainly bear testimony to the King's courtship, may purely have been aids to seduction. And from what Reginald Pole wrote, Henry did not take no
for an answer for very long.

That is not to say that he raped Mary; rather that he manoeu-
vred her into a position wherein she dared not refuse, and thus was
forced to submit to him.

In attempting to chart the course of Henry VIII's affair with Mary
Boleyn, we often stumble upon clues that turn out to be red herrings,
because the facts tend to support more than one interpretation.

We might begin our search for clues by looking at Sir Thomas
Boleyn's career. In Tudor times, it was 'not unusual for the males of
the family to reap the benefits of a daughter's success',[48] and it has
been claimed that 'Henry's lust for Mary' brought 'rich pickings' for
the Boleyns.[49] Many writers[50] have seen these particular awards as
resulting from Sir Thomas's daughter's affair with the King, Henry's
pleasure 'being measured by the pains he took to advance the complacent father'[51] – and a thank-you for Boleyn's compliance, or 'turning
a blind eye'.[52] That is indeed possible, but, again, they could also have
been bestowed on him because he had earned and deserved them,
and because he stood high in favour with Henry VIII and had served
him well.[53] Only one historian has claimed that Mary's connection
with the King 'did not much benefit Sir Thomas'.[54] We cannot say
that for certain.

By the early 1520s, Sir Thomas Boleyn's career was going from
strength to strength, but it could easily be demonstrated that that
was clearly on his own merits, and not necessarily due solely to the
King's interest in both his daughters successively, which came long
after Boleyn had risen to prominence. By 1522, the year in which
Mary probably became Henry's mistress, Boleyn was forty-five, with
a long and distinguished record of service behind him; he had been
a favourite of the King for years, long before Henry's eye alighted
on his daughter. Therefore one could reasonably expect to find Boleyn
receiving a string of honours such as those that were now coming
his way; they were nothing out of the ordinary for a man of his
standing.

In February 1516 – a mark of high honour indeed – Sir Thomas
was one of four persons who bore a canopy over Henry VIII's
daughter and heir, the Princess Mary, at her christening at

Greenwich.[55] When Henry's sister, Margaret, Queen of Scots, visited London in 1517, Boleyn – who had escorted her north to her marriage years before – was appointed her carver,[56] a privilege reserved only for men of rank, the ability to carve being the mark of a nobleman.

In October 1518, Sir Thomas Boleyn was a signatory of the Treaty of Universal Peace between England and France, which provided for the marriage of the Princess Mary to the Dauphin.[57] He was ambassador to France from January 1519, and while there, on 5 June 1519, he acted as proxy sponsor for Henry VIII at the baptism of François I's son, Henri, Duc d'Orléans, carrying out his duties 'with all possible honour', as King François wrote to King Henry a week or so later.[58] Henry VIII was appreciative of Boleyn's good service at the French court, but aware of his limitations, for he was business-like rather than courtly, and pernickety and plodding in his manner. In February 1520, the King replaced him with the more experienced Sir Richard Wingfield, who was better qualified to lay the diplomatic foundations for the proposed summit between the two monarchs that would later become famous as the Field of Cloth of Gold.[59]

In June 1520, Boleyn was present at the Field of Cloth of Gold, which he had helped to arrange. He was now a wealthy man and an active and committed Privy Councillor; that year he was appointed Comptroller of the King's Household,[60] and on 24 April 1522, its Treasurer, a post he held until 1525.[61] On 29 April, he was made Steward of Tonbridge (then called Tunbridge) and Keeper of Penshurst, both near his home in Kent.[62] This was around the time when Mary Boleyn probably became Henry VIII's mistress, so the award of these important appointments may not have been pure coincidence, yet Sir Thomas could equally have been granted such offices as rewards for his long service, and in particular for sitting on the special commission before which the indictment against the Duke of Buckingham had been brought the previous year, an indictment that had led to the Duke's execution for treason and the enrichment of the King through the confiscation of his forfeited lands.[63]

Clearly Boleyn was admired for his diplomatic and linguistic skills: in 1521, Cardinal Wolsey sent him and the Prior of St John's, Clerkenwell, on a 'mission of mediation' to the Emperor Charles V,[64] and Boleyn was present at Windsor in June 1522 at the signing of a new treaty between Henry and Charles. With Dr Richard Sampson, he was joint ambassador to Charles V in Spain from October 1522 to May 1523.[65]

In 1523, 1524 and 1525, Sir Thomas was granted further lucrative stewardships and keeperships in Kent, Essex, Norfolk and Nottinghamshire, and on 23 April 1523, he was made a Knight of the Garter.[66] Given his career, his connections and his closeness to the King, this was not, as has been claimed, 'an unusual honour for a mere knight'.[67] He was also appointed Vice Chamberlain of the Household, then promoted to Chamberlain. In July 1524, the King granted the manor of Grimston in Norfolk to Boleyn's heir, George, who had just married Jane Parker,[68] daughter of the erudite Lord Morley.

It should be remembered that Henry VIII bestowed no comparable honours on Sir John Blount of Kinlet, the father of Elizabeth Blount, the mistress who had borne the King a son, and whose affair with Henry almost certainly lasted longer than Mary Boleyn's. Although Sir John Blount came from a distinguished and renowned knightly family, he has aptly been described as 'unremarkable', and certainly he never enjoyed – and probably never merited – the kind of career and intimacy with the King that was Thomas Boleyn's. After serving in Henry VIII's forces in the French campaign of 1513, he was for a time an Esquire of the Body to the King, but did nothing else of note, apart from serving as Sheriff of Staffordshire in 1526–7, and engaging in a feud with Sir William Compton over property rights;[69] maybe he had long resented Compton's familiarity with his daughter. He was not knighted until 1529.[70] The only grants he received that could be seen as rewards for his daughter's services to his sovereign were those of the keepership of Cleobury Park and the joint stewardship with his father of Bewdley and Cleobury Mortimer; these modest favours were conferred in February 1519,[71] when Elizabeth Blount was pregnant with Henry Fitzroy. This record strongly suggests that Henry VIII was not in the habit of handing out favours simply because a man's daughter had bedded with him, even if she had done him the supreme favour of bearing a son.

Sir Thomas Boleyn was particularly fortunate in that, having broken off an affair with his elder daughter, the King began ardently pursuing the younger. We do not know for certain exactly when Henry VIII first conceived an interest in Anne Boleyn, but it was probably in 1525. Cavendish, who erroneously suggests that the King's eye lighted

upon her in 1523, avers that Boleyn was 'promoted to higher digni-
ties because of the King's love for his daughter'. Yet he was obviously referring to the honours that came Sir Thomas's way after
1525, which were in fact more likely to have been inducements,
because Anne was famously to hold out for marriage, with her family's
staunch support.

It would be unwise therefore to attempt to chart Mary's affair
with the King through instances of royal favour shown to her family.
As has been demonstrated, Sir Thomas Boleyn had already received
many preferments prior to 1522, and the rewards he received thereafter were commensurate with his years of service and his friendship with Henry VIII. However, it is quite conceivable that a father
who, in time, was to show himself willing to be complicit in the
ruin of his children, in order to preserve his own life and position,
should be happy to reap the benefits of a daughter's adultery with
the King. Indeed, Sir Thomas Boleyn would have had good reason
actively to encourage both his daughters in their dealings with Henry
VIII so that he could profit from them and advance himself and his
family's fortunes. Even if he was privately unhappy about Mary
becoming the King's mistress, he may nevertheless have greedily
anticipated the benefits that might well come his way as a result of
it,[72] the gifts of a grateful king. There was every incentive for him
to turn a blind eye to the affair – and perhaps to encourage his son-
in-law, William Carey, to do likewise. As David Starkey points out,
'these transactions might seem to turn Mary into the merest prostitute, with her husband and father as her pimps'.[73]

That is certainly how some of Boleyn's contemporaries saw it. In
1533, Mrs Elizabeth Amadas, whom the King had once tried to
seduce, would claim, amongst many wild assertions, that 'my Lord of
Wiltshire [as Sir Thomas Boleyn later became] was bawd both to his
wife and his two daughters'.[74] We should not place too much reliance
on her words, for she was a hostile and possibly unbalanced witness,
yet her assertion may well reflect contemporary gossip. It has even
been claimed, more recently, that Boleyn 'approved the King's intimacy' with Mary,[75] or that he probably encouraged it.[76] But we
cannot be certain that that was how it was.

Without doubt, Boleyn was an ambitious man. He had wanted
his girls to make good marriages in the Boleyn family tradition;
indeed, he was very well placed to do that. It may seem strange that
he did not make much effort to find rich or titled husbands for

them while they were young, for they had reached marriageable age – which was twelve for girls in those days – long before the King took an interest in them. Prior to 1520, the year Mary was married, and Sir Thomas proposed a marriage between nineteen-year-old Anne and James Butler, there is no hint of any early negotiations or discussion of betrothals, as was customary among the landed classes. As we have seen, Boleyn's own family had a tradition of climbing the social ladder through ever grander marriages, so it seems strange that he did not make more effort to marry his girls off all the sooner, to his advantage. Mary was more than twenty when Sir Thomas found her a husband, and between 1522, when the Butler match fell through,[77] and 1525, when the King probably began pursuing Anne, Boleyn seems to have made no further effort to make a good match for his younger daughter. Is this what one would expect of a man hell-bent on furthering his family's fortunes by any means?

It seems unlikely that Boleyn, that ambitious father, would have approved of Mary sleeping with the notoriously licentious François I, and risking spoiling herself for the aristocratic marriage market in the process. He certainly did not profit from Mary's amorous adventure in France and, as we have seen, he may have taken steps to limit the damage and have her taught better conduct. His explosive reaction in later years to her secret, unsuitable second marriage shows him to have been somewhat contemptuous of her morals and judgement, and angered at the scandal she had brought upon his family, while the vehemence of that reaction – they were probably never reconciled – may have had its roots in these earlier episodes in which she had grievously disappointed him. In each case, there was probably a marked degree of self-interest involved on his part.

Boleyn may have feared further scandal when Mary succumbed to Henry VIII's advances, yet, whatever his private feelings, he was probably content to make the best of things, and, of course, he really had no choice in the matter. Anyway, with Mary being a married woman when the King took her, she was no longer her father's responsibility, but her husband's. Boleyn's grasping soul may have warred with his pride in his family's honour and rising status, but there is no real evidence that he was 'conniving'[78] or actively sought to profit from his daughter's immoral conduct.

It might be argued that Sir Thomas Boleyn did not even know what was going on between his daughter and the King, given the secrecy that surrounded the affair. Yet his subsequent contemptuous and dismissive behaviour towards Mary strongly suggests that he did, and that he did not ultimately approve – not so much on moral grounds, but because this was the second time she had compromised her reputation with a king and come out of it with nothing.

Certainly George Boleyn's rise to prominence owed little to Mary's liaison with the King. He was made Henry's cup-bearer in 1526,[79] at a time when Henry's passion for his sister Anne was increasing; but it was another two years before George was appointed a Gentleman of the Privy Chamber, at a salary of 50 marks (£4,500).[80] Thereafter, like his father, he would accrue various offices and stewardships, as Henry VIII became more and more determined to marry Anne Boleyn. There can be no doubt that the later advancement of the Boleyns had much to do with this, for it was politic to load with honours the family of the future Queen of England, and thus elevate her status. In 1529, following in his father's footsteps, George embarked on a career as a diplomat. By then, he had become enormously influential at court.

As with Thomas Boleyn and his preferments at court, a series of royal grants made to William Carey between 1522 and 1526[81] are often claimed to have been rewards for his complacency in regard to his wife's dalliance with the King.[82] Such generosity on the part of the King was hardly 'casual royal bounty', as it has been described,[83] but, it is said, probably reflected Henry's regard for a man who served him daily.

As we have seen, it may well be significant that these grants began in February 1522,[84] around the time Henry appears to have begun pursuing Mary. The first grant, on 5 February, was of the keepership of the King's house called Beaulieu in Essex, where William was given responsibility for the King's wardrobe, and the right to lodge at Beaulieu whenever the need arose; William was also granted sixty cartloads of firewood annually for Beaulieu, and the right to let the premises to farm and to hire labourers to work in the King's garden and orchard.[85] Clearly the post was no sinecure, but required hands-on involvement. With it came the office of bailiff of the manors of New Hall, Walkeford Hall[86] and Powers (Hall End), Essex.[87]

On 12 May 1522, William Carey and William West, a page of the King's Chamber, were granted the joint wardship of the person and lands of Thomas Sharpe, an 'idiot' of Canterbury, the Crown having a special obligation to care for those who could not care for themselves, notably 'infants, idiots and lunatics'.[88]

In April 1523, 'William Carey of the Privy Chamber' was granted an annuity of fifty marks (£4,500), the grant being signed by Cardinal Wolsey.[89] Later, he would be assigned a much more substantial annuity of £100 (£38,000), and the office of Steward of the Duchy of Lancaster;[90] in this capacity, his role was to preside over local courts and supervise the Duchy's regional officers. On 26 April 1523, William was appointed Receiver and bailiff of the ancient manor of Writtle, Essex, and Keeper of Writtle Park, with certain fees, herbage and pannage,[91] and granted, in tail male, jurisdiction over the large hundred of Kinwardstone that lay mainly in east Wiltshire;[92] this hundred had formerly been held by the executed Duke of Buckingham, and encompassed William's birthplace, Chilton Foliat, suggesting that he had retained links with the area.

Since Saxon times, shires had been divided into administrative divisions called hundreds (so called either because they originally extended over a hundred hides of land – about 12,000 acres – or were intended to support a hundred households), and this one comprised forty-five villages, twelve parishes and the market towns of Hungerford, Marlborough, and Andover in neighbouring Hampshire. Carey's responsibility as lord of Kinwardstone was to act for the monarch in ensuring that justice was administered in the hundred courts that sat at regular intervals, and to maintain the King's peace. In actuality, these duties were carried out by a constable and a reeve, and overseen by the sheriff of the county.

Writtle, also previously owned by Buckingham, and famous as the probable birthplace of Robert the Bruce, King of Scots, boasted only a decaying royal hunting lodge dating from 1211, called King John's Palace after its builder. It is unlikely that William and Mary went there often, if at all.

Carey was also made constable of the royal castle of Pleshey in Essex,[93] where he also had the right to reside with Mary, although he probably rarely did so, as the castle had declined since its medieval heyday and was ruinous by 1557. The post seems therefore to have been something of a sinecure.

On 15 June 1524, William Carey, 'Esquire of the Body', was granted the keepership of 'the manor of Wanstead, Essex, with 2d. [£3] a day out of the issues of the manor'.[94] The royal manor of Wanstead had been purchased by Henry VII in 1499, and Henry VIII, who sometimes stayed there for the good hunting to be had in Epping Forest, placed it in the custody of a succession of keepers, all chosen from among his close associates. Medieval Wanstead Hall, which stood three hundred yards south of St Mary's Church, served as a royal hunting lodge, and Carey, as keeper, had the right to lodgings there, which means that Mary may have stayed at Wanstead from time to time. That month, William and Mary were also granted three former manors of the Duke of Buckingham near Chipping Ongar, Essex.[95]

In August and October 1524 – proof of Henry's opinion of his integrity, and of his increasing importance at court, and that the trust the King reposed in him did not stem from the attractions of Mary Boleyn – William was entrusted with a huge sum totalling £49,000 (£18.5 million), given him by the King 'to be employed upon the wars' with France.[96] In December that year, he was probably the 'Master Karre' who was among the privileged few who were given Gascon wine by the King, while others were required to purchase theirs from the shipment.[97]

On 20 February 1526,[98] some time after the King's affair with Mary had probably ended, William received more substantial grants of estates and manors in Hampshire and Wiltshire: 'To William Carey, Esquire for the Body. Grant of the manors of Parva Brykhill [Great Brickhill], Burton, and Easington, Buckinghamshire, and the borough of Buckingham, part of Buckingham's lands, formerly held by John, Lord Marney, deceased'.[99] With this came a licence to hold fairs and markets, with other liberties, in Great Brickhill and Buckingham.

Plainly William Carey, like his father-in-law, enjoyed Henry's regard for his own sake, being one 'whom the King highly favoured'.[100] However, he was never knighted, and Mary was never 'Lady Carey', as several writers[101] style her.

William's growing closeness to the King, and his importance at court, is underlined by a gift made to him in August 1523, when it was reported that 'the Sieur de Revel has been here, bringing the King twelve Neapolitan chargers, and two for Master Carey, very fine and honourable presents'[102] – and very expensive ones. The fact that Carey was singled out for the gift of such fine horses, horses that had been bred for a king, is evidence that he was well thought of not only in England but also in France, where he had given a good account of himself at the Field of Cloth of Gold.

Just before Christmas 1524, William was one of fourteen lords and gentlemen of the King's household who 'enterprised a challenge of feats of arms', which the King and Queen 'graciously consented' to attend. 'For this enterprise was set up in the tiltyard at Greenwich a castle', and on the appointed day, when Katherine and her ladies had taken their places in the stands, two 'ancient knights' rode up before her, begging her for licence to take part in the contest, despite their age. When she consented, they threw off their robes to reveal the King himself and the Duke of Suffolk. After the jousts, there was supper, a masque and dancing,[103] in which Mary Boleyn may have joined. William's involvement in these jollifications shows that he enjoyed a warm camaraderie with the King, and that he was at the centre of fashionable society at court.

In January 1526, when Cardinal Wolsey drew up the Eltham Ordinances, which were aimed at reducing waste and inefficiency in the royal household, and restricted the number of gentlemen of the Privy Chamber to six, William, who had been promoted to that rank by then, was one of those retained; his older brother John was one of four grooms of the Privy Chamber.[104] The same year, William Carey was appointed Keeper of Greenwich Palace[105] – almost certainly a reward for his own good service – with the right to official lodgings there.

After his promotion, he had been allocated a courtier lodging on the King's side of the court, rather than on an outer courtyard alongside less privileged courtiers; lodgings near the King were the most sought after, and were only allocated to those high in royal favour. It might be argued that such a lodging would be conveniently situated for the King to visit his mistress, but by 1526, Henry's affair with Mary had probably been over for more than a year. Even had this not been the case, and assuming that William Carey was indeed a complacent husband, such an arrangement would surely have given rise to some scandal or comment. In 1536, when the King's Principal Secretary, Thomas Cromwell, vacated his lodging at court for Jane Seymour and her family, so that the King could visit her via a secret passageway, people soon got to hear about it, among them foreign ambassadors.

Years after Mary's affair with the King had ended, Anne Boleyn, ambitious to be Queen, was to consider it well worth courting the influential William's support (see Chapter 9), which suggests that he had earned the favour he enjoyed, and that it owed little to her or her sister.

Possibly the grants made to William Carey were not on the scale of those given to Gilbert Tailboys and Elizabeth Blount,[106] but they were substantial enough, and we must remember that Elizabeth had borne the King a son. William's income was sufficient for him to be assessed for half the amount of tax paid by his wealthy father-in-law, Sir Thomas Boleyn.[107] Yet while it is possible that Henry VIII did grant some gifts to William as incentives to Mary or indirect gifts to her, or even as compensation for his 'indulgent complicity'[108] in his wife's infidelity, it is far more likely that most, if not all, of them were the rewards that an upcoming man in Carey's position might expect to receive.

It is just possible, considering how discreetly the King conducted his extramarital affairs, that William Carey was not even aware of what was going on, despite claims that the arrangement was apparently satisfactory for all involved[109] and that the 'long-suffering' Carey[110] was 'pliant'. The unsupported assertion that he did know, 'and realised that there was nothing to be gained and everything to be lost (including his head) by challenging the King',[111] is a farfetched assumption, as is proved by Thomas Wyatt suffering no ill consequences when, around 1525, he locked with Henry in open rivalry for Anne Boleyn's favours.[112] Yet it is hard to believe that, serving the King as intimately as he did as an Esquire of the Body, one of those who had 'their business in many secrets', Carey did not know what was going on. He may even have been ambitious and cynical enough to hope to profit from his wife's adultery with his sovereign.

All arguments considered, we cannot interpret the grants made to William Carey as hard evidence for the affair between his wife and the King. If they were rewards or inducements, they were 'not such as would raise undue comment'[113] – which they certainly did not. And it seems that, rather than being manipulated by her family, Mary Boleyn was manipulated by the King.

7

'Living in Avoutry'

Mary's experiences as a royal mistress illustrate the moral tone of Renaissance courts and the double standards that prevailed in regard to male and female promiscuity.

The influence of the pre-Reformation Church over moral issues was then considerable.[1] The Church had always taught that marriage was the proper context for sexual relations, and that sexual intercourse was only for the purpose of procreating children. Lust, even within marriage, was seen as evil, and there was an ancient perception, derived from St Jerome, that married couples who had sex purely for enjoyment were no better than adulterers.

Since intercourse was supposed to be purely for procreation, contraception was frowned upon, although rudimentary forms of it were known and practised. Henry VIII's fifth wife, Katherine Howard, for example, admitted that she knew of ways to prevent a pregnancy. Rarely were these methods effective, for many relied purely on superstitions and folk remedies, such as drinking the urine of a sheep or hare before having sex, or taking various herbs, or on *coitus interruptus*. Other methods of preventing pregnancy included inserting pepper or a sponge soaked in vinegar into the vagina, sealing the cervix with beeswax, having anal sex, or doing some 'hard pissing' after intercourse. Condoms as a method of birth control were unknown prior to 1564. Contraception, then as now, was frowned upon by the Church, and because it was often unreliable, if it was used at all, royal love affairs often led to the birth of bastard children. But although the moralists might claim that that 'impoverished the public weal', there was no great stigma attached to illegitimacy and little shame in acknowledging natural children; indeed, royal bastards often enjoyed high status and political importance. It was not until the advent of Puritanism in the late sixteenth century that attitudes to illegitimacy changed and there was greater social disapproval. Even so, as the example of the promiscuous 'merry monarch' Charles II (who reigned from 1660–85 and acknowledged more than a dozen bastard children) shows, kings continued to flaunt their mistresses and advance the living fruits of their affairs.

Morality in the early Tudor period was based mainly on biblical precepts, and the pre-Reformation Church – and often civil law – forbade many sexual practices, including masturbation, prostitution, oral sex, homosexuality and bestiality, and viewed adultery as a grievous sin worthy of stern punishment. Since the fourteenth century, political capital had been made out of the sexual excesses of English kings and public figures, and as recently as 1483, the late Edward IV's mistress, Elizabeth ('Jane') Shore, had been accused by his brother Richard III of sorcery and sentenced to do public penance, dressed as a penitent in only a sheet, and carrying a lighted candle in procession to Paul's Cross in London.

There was a real gulf, however, between the dictates of the Church and what went on in real life, and lay attitudes to sex were often more tolerant, though only to a point. Because the laws of inheritance were generally sacrosanct, especially in the higher ranks of society, a double standard had long been in play, whereby men could sow their wild oats with impunity and get away with it, but women – who were then regarded as more sexually rapacious than men – were expected to remain above reproach. Thus Mary's betrayal of her husband would have been regarded as reprehensible, even with the King.

Fortunately, things had moved on a little since 1483, and the example of Elizabeth Blount showed that, where a gentle- or noble-woman would invariably spoil herself for the marriage market by fornicating with a lesser man, sleeping with the King brought its own advantages, for it could lead to financial rewards and a good marriage. But there was still a moral stigma attached to it, because aristocratic women were key players in the dynastic and landed property market, and were supposed to be above such things.

Yet it was almost acceptable, even expected, for a man of rank to fornicate with women of the lower orders, in order to avoid the kind of trouble that might ensue from liaisons with his own kind;

it was also thought that common women were more satisfactory in bed, and were better formed for experiencing sexual pleasure. In this context, Henry's affair with Mary Boleyn was doubly reprehensible, for she was the daughter and the wife of landed men, and should have been untouchable. But of course, such things did go on in the hothouse environment of a court where men usually outnumbered women by more than ten to one, and where many men – younger sons without real prospects – had little hope of making a good marriage.

Henry VIII prided himself on being a moral man. He would not permit open displays of wanton behaviour at his court, and would command his Knight Harbinger to banish 'lewd women' from its precincts. In 1546, he closed down the brothels in Southwark because of what he termed 'their abominable and detestable sin'. Even so, some considered the ladies of his court to be of easy virtue. In 1536, Eustache Chapuys, the Imperial ambassador, would write cynically to Charles V of Jane Seymour's much-vaunted chastity: 'You may imagine whether, being an Englishwoman, and having been long at court, she would not hold it a sin to be still a maid.'[2] When the King's niece, Lady Margaret Douglas, was found to have been indulging in an illicit affair with Lord Thomas Howard, one observer commented that it would not have been surprising if she had had sex with him, 'seeing the number of domestic examples she has seen and sees daily'.[3]

Mary Boleyn would no doubt have witnessed similar examples of covert dalliance and worse. Yet women who went to court and became royal mistresses were often taking the same kind of advantage of the King's ability to bestow patronage, rewards and favour as the male courtiers who vied for place and precedence by offering good service and congenial companionship.[4]

Certainly there were some who disapproved of ladies who slept with the King. We have seen how people regarded Elizabeth Blount's prestigious marriage as the wages of sin. Nevertheless, there was a general perception that it was normal for kings and nobles to take mistresses. Married off for political or dynastic advantage, there was no guarantee that they would find love with their wives, or satisfaction between the sheets, although of course it was the duty of married couples to love each other, which wasn't quite the same thing. So it was only to be expected that high-born men might look elsewhere for that which they had failed to find in marriage. When

Henry VIII sought out Mary Boleyn, Katherine of Aragon was almost at the end of her childbearing years, had put on weight, and was 'rather ugly', according to one ambassador,[5] and 'old and deformed' in the cruel opinion of François I. Never before had her six years' seniority over Henry been so glaringly apparent. Probably he still loved and respected her, but we can be almost certain that any passion they had shared had long since died; certainly it had never been enough to stop him straying from her bed on earlier occasions.

We know virtually nothing about the manner in which Henry VIII's affair with Mary Boleyn was conducted, or their feelings for each other. Given that, it is probably overstating the case to say that from 1522, Mary 'would continue to be at the centre of Henry's world for the next three years or so'.[6] On the contrary, the King kept the liaison 'very much in the background',[7] and the absence of any references in strictly contemporary sources to Mary Boleyn being the King's mistress is proof that their affair was carried on with the maximum discretion and known only within a small circle that encompassed Mary's own family, the King's closest associates and, no doubt, the all-seeing, all-knowing Cardinal Wolsey.[8]

Contrary to widespread belief, therefore, Henry's adultery clearly did not create 'something of a stir in the court' or lay him 'open to damaging gossip'.[9] Mary did not earn notoriety[10] – at least, not at the time – and there is no evidence that 'in a short time the whole court was aware that [she] had admitted the King to her bed'[11] or that the affair was 'an open secret'.[12] There is no report of any public scandal while the affair was going on; and it is highly unlikely that Mary came to this liaison with a 'reputation for licentiousness' that 'stemmed from her earlier affairs'[13] – because, as we have seen, there is no evidence for any affairs other than a fleeting, unremarked encounter with François I. Later, those in the know about her relations with Henry VIII would have had good reasons for maintaining secrecy. Her poor reputation has been exaggerated, 'thanks to single-source stories'[14] about her conduct at the French court.

In fact, after her appearance in the pageant, Mary faded into anonymity. After 1522 it was *Anne* Boleyn who quickly became one of the bright young stars of the English court, setting trends in fashion, fascinating the gentlemen with her black eyes that 'invited to conversation', and impressing everyone with her graceful accomplishments. But no one thought to praise her sister in a similar way, even though Mary was almost certainly the King's mistress at this time. No chronicler lauded Mary's beauty as Hall had done Elizabeth Blount's, which they might have done had her intimate connection with Henry VIII been known. And Mary seems to have lacked her sister's charm; no one ever claimed that there was anything exotically French about her, and although she must have known a lot about French fashions, she was probably not as stylish as Anne, or as fascinating. In a word, she was eclipsed by her younger sister.

The pageant of 1522 was the last occasion on which Mary Boleyn was recorded at court for many years, so if her affair with the King continued well beyond this date, discretion must have been skilfully maintained. No contemporary source mentions the Queen being aware of it, although it has often been assumed or claimed that she 'and almost everyone else' knew of this 'public' affair.[15] This is just one example of the many unfounded assumptions that have been made about Henry VIII's affair with Mary Boleyn, although in this case we know that the myth originated in the creative imagination of one Victorian writer.

Back in 1858, Francis Lancelott, in his memorials of *The Queens of England and their Times*, had Henry VIII entertaining 'a tender penchant for Mary Boleyn' and being taxed by Katherine of Aragon about it. 'The King denied the charge, but Mary admitted that she had overstepped the bounds of discretion, and, probably by the Queen's advice, was married to William Carey on the thirty-first of January, 1521 [*sic*].' This, of course, was all pure fiction, as indeed are the more modern assertions that the Queen was 'secure in the knowledge that Henry's passion usually grew tepid after the first passionate excitement of the chase and capture', and that she 'waited patiently for his affair with Mary to grow cool and end like the others'.[16] There is no evidence that Katherine was aware that much of Henry's time was spent with Mary, and had more cause to be jealous of her because Mary was 'more acceptable' and better connected than Elizabeth Blount had been;[17] or that the King 'had never attempted to conceal his relations with Mary Boleyn' from his wife, and that Katherine 'more or less philosophically accepted the situation'.[18] There is nothing to say that she 'was forced to look past these indignities without complaint'.[19] Instead, there is compelling evidence that the Queen did not know about the affair.

There is no record of her complaining about it,[20] possibly because Henry 'conceded not one iota of the deference due to her as his consort and wife',[21] and she had learned through bitter experience to keep her mouth shut and endure with dignity his infidelities. But – more significantly – in later years, Katherine did not seek to make political capital out of Henry's connection with Mary Boleyn, when it would have been in her best interests to do so; as Froude put it, Katherine never alluded to Mary 'in the fiercest of her denuncia- tions'; and in all the many letters in which she wrote of the wrongs done to her, there was no word of Mary Boleyn.

This is strange considering that, from 1527, Henry was negot- iating with the Pope for an annulment of his marriage to Katherine so that he could marry Anne Boleyn; he claimed that his marriage to Katherine was incestuous because she had been his brother's wife. Had Katherine known that Mary, Anne's sister, had been Henry's mistress, she could have used that as a powerful argument to demolish his claim that his conscience was troubled by his incestuous marriage, because his marriage to Anne would be equally incestuous, and on the same grounds. She could have exposed his scruples as hypocrit- ical and fatally undermined his case. Yet Katherine did no such thing. It seems incredible that she would not have used such a useful and deadly weapon if it had been readily at her disposal.

All this strongly suggests that Katherine was not aware of any rela- tionship between her husband and Mary, rather than that she had chosen to maintain a dignified silence whenever Henry strayed.[22] Probably their marriage 'was little affected' by this 'transient' affair.[23] It is pure fancy to say that Mary was fearful of the Queen, 'who had always been kind to her', and did not wish to hurt her,[24] for we lack any source that makes us privy to Mary's inner thoughts.

Apart from the pageant of the *Château Vert*, there is no surviving memorial of Henry and Mary being together.

Where then – given that secrecy was the order of the day – did the couple enjoy their trysts? It may not have been too fanciful of Paul Rival to imagine Mary waiting for the King 'in secret cham- bers, in houses concealed in the depths of his parks, far from Katherine and the conjugal bed'.

It is impossible to say whether 'Henry VIII was a regular visitor to Hever Castle at this time', making secret visits in pursuit of 'his romantic involvement' with Mary,[25] for there is no record of him calling upon Mary privately at her family home, where, later on, he probably courted her sister Anne; to be fair, there is no actual record of his courting Anne there either, though the chances are that he did, for there is evidence in his letters of her retreating to Hever at that time. Henry was well placed to visit Hever, for in 1521, after Buckingham's execution, the Duke's property had reverted to the Crown, and one of the houses that Henry had acquired was Penshurst Place, where he had once enjoyed good hunting with Buckingham. Henry had appointed Sir Thomas Boleyn to manage Penshurst, and may have used it as a base for discreet visits to Hever when courting Anne. It has also been stated that, earlier, 'Henry was frequently at Penshurst Place in the company of her sister, dropping in while hunting or to pay a family visit' and that 'much of the affair with Mary Boleyn was conducted at Penshurst'.[26] The King, it is claimed, was often at Penshurst in the 1520s,[27] but no contemporary source supports such assertions, and the evidence we do have strongly suggests that Henry did his courting far closer to home – at court.

Since Mary was married and residing mainly in the court, it is far more probable that she was secretly admitted to the King's lodgings for her trysts with him. It is also possible that he arranged meetings with her at Jericho in Essex, the house where Elizabeth Blount had retired to give birth to Henry Fitzroy.

Henry VIII is said to have installed his mistresses in Duke Humphrey's Tower (later called Greenwich Castle), a moated hunting lodge that had been built in 1433 by Humphrey, Duke of Gloucester, brother of Henry V, on the hill overlooking Greenwich Park, on the site of the present Royal Observatory.[28] It has been seen as significant that, on 12 May 1526, William Carey was appointed keeper of the manor, garden and tower of Pleasaunce at East Greenwich, with his fees being paid out of the issues (royal rents) of Kent[29] – Pleasaunce (or Placentia) being the old name for Greenwich Palace. The tower referred to in the grant could have been the donjon that housed the royal lodgings in the palace ('the manor'), but it is more likely to have been Duke Humphrey's Tower, which was demolished in 1675.

The keepership of the manor and tower of Pleasaunce had been granted in 1517 to Nicholas Carew, whose wife Elizabeth had perhaps enjoyed a brief spell of intimacy with Henry VIII around 1514. There has been unfounded speculation that Duke Humphrey's Tower may have been used later as a rendezvous for Elizabeth Carew's friend Elizabeth Blount and the King,[30] and that it 'must have been Mary Boleyn's lodging during the time she was the King's mistress'.[31] But it is unlikely that Mary Boleyn ever resided there, for her affair with

Henry was almost certainly over by 1525–6, when Henry had the decaying tower 'newly repaired and builded', added a gatehouse, enclosed the whole within a wooden fence, and renamed it 'Mireflore'.[32] It is said that he built a second tower,[33] but it is more likely that he rebuilt the original one, since Anthony van Wyngaerde's drawing of Greenwich Palace, dated 1558, shows only a single square keep on the hill behind, which has recently been confirmed as accurate by archaeological excavations.[34] The tower was only included in this important grant to William Carey because it formed part of the manor of Greenwich, while the assignment of this very important keepership after Henry's affair with Mary had ended is testimony to Carey's growing importance in his own right.

In 1535, the hostile John Hale, Vicar of Isleworth, a staunch supporter of Queen Katherine, who thought the King 'mired in vice', stated that 'Cowsell the porter' had once told him that 'our sovereign lord' kept 'a short of maidens over one of his chambers at Farnham, while he was with the old lord of Winchester'[35] – meaning Farnham Castle in Surrey, the old lord of Winchester being the venerable and devout blind Richard Fox, who had been Bishop of Winchester since 1501 and died in 1528.[36] But there is no other evidence to support Hale's assertion, and it is hardly credible that Henry would have established what was in effect a private royal brothel in the episcopal palace of the bishops of Winchester, or had assignations with Mary Boleyn there.

Mary Boleyn attracted little or no attention at the English court. She was not 'an important person'.[37] As we have seen, while her sister Anne was rapidly gaining a reputation as a setter of trends with her French manners and her innovations in dress, Mary was not deemed worthy of mention. As Friedmann wrote, none of Henry's mistresses (with the notable exception of Anne Boleyn) 'ever held a brilliant position at court'. Mary was not 'in a powerful position',[38] as has been claimed, and it is unlikely that she enjoyed much influence over the King, or that she made many demands on him. She may not have had the ability or ambition to interest herself in affairs of state; certainly she did not exploit her position.[39]

Henry VIII almost certainly did not like or permit his mistresses to interfere in matters of state; on the contrary, he usually kept them very much in the background. His pursuit of Anne Boleyn only became public knowledge after he had decided to marry her. Elizabeth

Blount, the mother of his son, had exercised no political influence that we know of, and her affair with the King lasted at least four years; there are very few references to her in contemporary sources, and even her pregnancy was not commented on. Nor are any lavish gifts to her recorded during the years when she was probably Henry's mistress.

Royal mistresses fell into several categories: some were ambitious, desiring power, wealth and titles. Some did it for love or lust. A few, like Anne Boleyn, were set upon marriage and a crown. Mary was married already, and if she had hoped to profit materially from her affair with the King, she was destined, at the time, to be disappointed. Although it would not be true to say that in the long run she gained nothing for herself or her family, she is not known to have asked for any favours for herself, and – unlike some royal mistreses – she received very little in the way of lucrative gains[40] during her affair with the King, while her husband remained plain Mr Carey.[41] She did not, on the evidence, hold out against Henry's importunings in the hope of some reward for her services;[42] indeed, at the time, she herself received few, if any, benefits,[43] and the affair brought her little profit,[44] unless one counts the grants made to her husband, which could not be said with certainty to be rewards for her compliance. We do not know if she asked the King for favours for her family, and we can only speculate that the Boleyns 'jeered' at her for not having profited from the association,[45] although it is fair to say that Henry was 'never overly extravagant in his extramarital affairs'.[46]

There is nothing to support the imaginative statement that 'triumphant visits' by Mary and her father to Hever Castle made Anne feel like 'the family Cinderella',[47] or the claim that the Boleyns 'looked with complacency if not satisfaction' upon their daughter's liaison with the King.[48] More convincing is the assertion that 'Mary had badly let down [her] father and sullied the family's name. In consequence, she became something of a pariah.'[49] Later evidence would tend to confirm this.

Mary, as the King's mistress, might have seemed to have had everything, yet she enjoyed little in the way of privileges, and no power whatsoever.[50] On only one occasion is she known to have taken advantage of her influence with Henry VIII to exercise patronage,[51] and that was in 1527–8, some years after their affair ended, when she used it to secure the appointment of Thomas Gardiner, one of the King's chaplains, as Prior of Tynemouth, Northumberland. A hostiller's book from Durham Cathedral shows that, in 1527, Peter Lee, the hostiller – an officer who looked after the conventual guest house – was proposed as Prior of Tynemouth; if he ever went there, he was soon replaced by Thomas Gardiner, who was in post by 1528 and held the office until 1536.[52] Gardiner was so grateful to 'Lady [sic.] Mary Carey' for her efforts on his behalf that he granted her an annuity of a hundred marks (£10,700) out of the priory's revenues.[53] Whether Mary received her annuity regularly, or at all, is a matter for speculation, as she was in such 'extreme necessity' after being widowed in 1528 that the King had to order her father to take her under his roof. Possibly she did not begin receiving payments until 1529, in arrears.

The ability to exercise this kind of patronage might suggest that, for a brief period at least, Mary meant more to the King than one of his 'petty dalliances',[54] although even when their affair was going on, she was hardly enjoying royal favour to the full.[55] Given that Henry was hotly pursuing Anne Boleyn when he granted Mary this favour, his bounty may have been spurred by his desire to impress his beloved rather than out of any abiding regard for his former mistress.

Mary has been described as 'a light-hearted lover'[56] who basked in the warmth of the King's amorous attentions and 'scintillated in the gorgeous apparel and jewels that were a sign of his affection';[57] 'a willing, uncomplaining plaything who submitted to a one-sided bargain in which she gave Henry everything he wanted and got nothing in return'.[58] But there is no contemporary source to give credence to such fantasies, no record of gifts of clothing and jewellery.

Mary's function as a kept concubine was, it seems, purely to meet Henry's sexual needs when required, and probably to provide him with pleasant company in private. Theirs may well have been 'an authentic and passionate relationship',[59] but if Henry did have emotional – as opposed to physical – feelings for Mary, they cannot have been enduring, and it would be fair to surmise that he never had for her the all-consuming longing he later felt for her sister Anne.[60] Mary's only recorded comment on Henry, made in 1534, was that he 'ever was wont to take pity',[61] which surely refers to his generous provision to her and her children over the years, and his intervention with her father on her behalf; and it was no doubt a timely compliment paid at a time when she was desperate to regain his favour.

It has been asserted that Mary had flung herself into the affair 'with a passion',[62] and that her later behaviour shows that she had been in love with the King;[63] but it is hard to see how those conclusions were reached, especially since she had probably not gone willingly to Henry's bed, and we have no evidence as to her feelings for him thereafter. The claim that her affair with Henry 'improved a mediocre marriage'[64] is unproven.

There is a theory that William Carey refrained from claiming his marital rights while his wife was the King's mistress,[65] but while this is possible, there is no good evidence to substantiate it. It has been said that Henry expected his sexual partners to be chaste,[66] but that applied more to his wives; the sparse information we have suggests that he was happy to share the favours of Elizabeth Carew and Elizabeth Blount with men such as William Compton.

The four-year gap between Mary's marriage and the birth of her first child, and the three-year gap between her second child's birth and her widowhood have been seen as significant. It has been suggested that Carey delayed the consummation of the union because Mary was twelve at the most when she married,[67] but, as we have seen, she was almost certainly around twenty years old. One opinion is that she was only fertile during her affair with the King, and that her fertility 'resumed' when she married for the second time in 1534.[68] Another view is that she only conceived when she began cohabiting with her husband after her royal affair had ended,[69] and that this suggests that Henry was no longer as potent or fertile as he had been during the earlier years of his marriage to Katherine. But as we do not know for certain when Mary's affair with Henry began or ended, both theories are unsupportable.

Given that Henry probably did not begin pursuing Mary until 1522, we could hardly expect to find William Carey refraining from intercourse with his wife in the first two years of their marriage. During Mary's second marriage, she is known to have borne only one child in nine years. This suggests that, like her mother and sister, she suffered miscarriages or gave birth to unrecorded children who were stillborn or died young – or that, if she was as fertile as her two offspring, who had twenty-eight children between them, she resorted to some form of contraception,[70] possibly deliberately avoiding getting pregnant by her royal lover. As a respectable married woman, she may have feared the consequences of 'presenting her husband with a bastard, even if it was the King's'.[71] The fact that Mary bore Henry VIII 'no acknowledged child' may indicate that she was a good deal more cautious than her undeserved reputation would indicate.[72]

Certainly Henry was still sleeping with the Queen, hoping to conceive an heir, during his affair with Mary. He continued to have sexual relations with Katherine until 1524,[73] and even after 1525, by which year she was 'past the ways of women', he still shared her bed on occasions.

All of this begs the question: what was Henry VIII like as a lover? From youth, he evidently had always seen himself as a knight errant, the embodiment of Arthurian chivalry, and it appears that – to a point – he conducted his relationships with the opposite sex according to the time-honoured rules of courtly love, by which the man was a humble suitor for the favours of his mistress, who was usually above him in station, often married, and supposedly unattainable. The word 'mistress', in this context, did not necessarily imply a woman who lived or bedded with a man outside wedlock, but the female equivalent of 'master'.

When he was not divorcing or beheading his queens, Henry generally treated them with respect and courtesy, unless – like Anne Boleyn – they called him to account for his infidelity and other failings, in which case they got short shrift. After complaining about him being unfaithful to her, Anne was brutally told to 'shut her eyes and endure as more worthy persons have done', and that he could lower her as speedily as he had raised her.[74] But Henry's views on marriage, and on sex within marriage, were more profound than those angry words would suggest. 'Who does not tremble when he considers how to deal with his wife?' he asked, in his treatise *A Defence of the Seven Sacraments against Martin Luther*, written in 1521, just before he became interested in Mary Boleyn. 'For not only is he bound to love her, but so to live with her that he may return her to God pure and without stain, when God who gave shall demand His own again.'

The King was probably 'not a man of adventure in regard to women'.[75] Proceedings in the royal marital bed are likely to have been conducted with a certain reverence and restraint, and it was perhaps for this very reason that Henry took mistresses, so that he could indulge his baser lusts. Yet the fact that Anne Boleyn was able to hold him at arm's length for at least six years proves that – faced

with an unequivocal 'no' from a woman he believed to be virtuous
– Henry was too much of a knight and a gentleman to resort to
rape. This restraint, however, did not extend to all women, particularly those of the lower orders, as the episode of William Webbe's
'fair wench' may demonstrate; and it apparently had not been exercised for very long when the King was pursuing Mary Boleyn.

Henry's unusual discretion about his amorous affairs might suggest
that he was an inhibited man. There is evidence that he was even
prudish and embarrassed by references to sex.[76] He was shocked
when he found out, after marrying Anne Boleyn, that she had been
'corrupted in France',[77] although it is not clear exactly what he
meant by that. He was never coarse in speech – he was recorded to
have blushed when, in 1538, a French ambassador suggested he might
like to try out several potential brides before choosing one.[78] Once,
when visiting 'a fair lady' at Duke Humphrey's Tower, in true courtly
fashion, he challenged a courtier, Sir Andrew Flammock, to complete
a verse in praise of her beauty, and began it:

> Within this tower.
> There lieth a flower
> That hath my heart . . .

Whereupon Flammock added:

> Within this hour
> She pissed full sour
> And let a fart.

Henry was deeply offended, and waved the man out of his sight,
growling, 'Begone, varlet!'[79] It has been claimed that the lady in question must have been Mary Boleyn,[80] but – as we have seen – her
affair with the King had probably ended before the rebuilding of
Duke Humphrey's Tower, and Sir Andrew Flammock did not come
to prominence until much later in Henry's reign,[81] so the story
cannot belong to the early 1520s. In 1542, the diplomat Sir William
Paget felt bound to apologise to the King for repeating François I's
'unseemly' reference to 'a strumpet of the bordello'.[82]

Yet Henry's seventeen surviving letters to Anne Boleyn prove that
he had it in him to be a passionate and importunate lover. He could
not make sufficient demonstrations of his infatuation with his fifth

wife, Katherine Howard, and openly caressed her 'more than he did the others'.[83] According to the disapproving Reginald Pole, the King was 'soon tired [or 'sated'] of those who had served him as his mistress',[84] but that could not be said of Elizabeth Blount; possibly she, like Anne Boleyn after her, was sparing with her favours. The fact that Elizabeth retained Henry's interest for four years or more suggests that theirs was not just a physical affair. Maybe Henry was truly in love with her, and this was the first grand passion of his life. Its longevity is probably witness to Henry's heart being engaged as well as his loins.

As for Mary Boleyn, it has been observed that, while it is often assumed that she was 'colourless and insipid, the docile willing dupe of those who took advantage of her', she may in fact consciously – and calculatingly – have opted for a more obscure role than her sister did, 'out of a wise instinct not to tempt fate too far'.[85] It would be her saving grace in the long run.

Yet that begs another question: how far did Mary have control over her life? If she had had little choice in succumbing to two kings, would she really have chosen not to take advantage of the situation, given whose daughter she was? Or did she just not have what it took to exploit her position to her own advantage? Given the fact that the King expected her to remain invisible and without influence, she may have had little choice in the matter. Indeed, she may have welcomed the anonymity. Being a married woman, and the wife and daughter of prominent men, she seems to have felt it was best to hide her shame behind a veil of discretion and wait until such time as her royal lover had tired of her. As time would tell, that proved to be by far the wisest choice.

8

'Hiding Royal Blood'

During her marriage to William Carey, Mary Boleyn bore two children. The elder was Katherine, born probably in March or April 1524[1] and almost certainly named for the Queen.[2] It has been claimed that this was in gratitude for Katherine's 'politeness and forbearing',[3] although it is by no means likely that Katherine knew that there was anything to be forbearing about.

The younger child was Henry Carey, born on 4 March 1525.[4] Even allowing for the dating of the Tudor year from Lady Day, 25 March, the inscription on his tomb in Westminster Abbey states that he was in his seventy-second year when he died on 23 July 1596; that would place his date of birth in March 1525, which is corroborated by the inscription on his portrait at Berkeley Castle (the seat of his descendants), painted in 1591, which records his age as sixty-six. His father's Inquisition Post Mortem, taken in 1528, states that on 22 June that year, his heir, Henry Carey, was aged two years, fifteen weeks and five days,[5] but the ages of heirs given in Inquisitions Post Mortem are not always accurate, and it is much more likely that he was *three* years, fifteen weeks and five days, since the epitaph commissioned by his family and the portrait commissioned by himself are far more likely to bear the correct date, which is 1525.[6] Young Henry was almost certainly named in honour of the King, as were so many boys at that time. It is possible that Henry VIII and Katherine of Aragon were the respective godparents of the Carey siblings, but there is no record of this.

On the assumption that the affair between the King and Mary Boleyn was flourishing through the early 1520s, it is often suggested or claimed that one or both of Mary's children was fathered by the King.[7] One writer has even gone so far as to assert that news that she was to have a child 'caused a smile',[8] while another believes 'there is no smoke without fire in these matters'.[9]

In popular culture, there is little doubt that Mary's affair with Henry VIII bore fruit. In the 1969 film, *Anne of the Thousand Days*, Valerie Gearon played a bitter Mary Boleyn who is great with the King's child and banished to her bedchamber at Hever Castle when he visits. In both filmed versions of *The Other Boleyn Girl*, Mary is shown as bearing the King a son. Film is such a powerful medium that many now believe that Henry Carey was Henry VIII's child.

But the relationship produced no acknowledged offspring,[10] and there is no reliable contemporary assertion that either of Mary's two children was the King's issue.[11] The evidence for Henry's paternity of the Carey siblings is mostly circumstantial and inferential – 'positive proof is lacking'[12] – and there are good historical reasons why some of it should be rejected. Contrary to what has been claimed, close analysis of the circumstantial evidence does not make 'a powerful case' for *both* the Carey children's royal paternity,[13] and there is no contemporary source that suggests that either the King or his successors at any time acknowledged those children as his issue. Mary 'was not known to have borne him any child',[14] while, with one dubious exception, 'no claim was ever made that any of [her children] were sired by the King'.[15] Furthermore, as will be seen, there is clear evidence that Henry Carey was the lawful issue of William Carey.[16]

It is simply not true that there were 'serious doubts' about the paternity of Mary's son, that 'rumour was busy' at the time of his birth, or that 'many' people maintained that Henry VIII was his father.[17] There is no reference to rumours of the King's paternity circulating in 1525, at the time of Henry Carey's birth,[18] and in fact the first and only reference to a rumour dates from ten years later. In November 1531, a Venetian diplomat, Lodovico Falier, after describing the Princess Mary to his masters, reported: 'The King has also a natural son, born to him of the widow of one of his peers; a youth of great promise, so much does he resemble his father.'[19] It has been suggested that this might refer to Henry Carey,[20] since Mary was a widow in 1531, but so also was Elizabeth Blount, whose husband, unlike William Carey, had been a peer of the realm; thus Falier must have been referring to Henry Fitzroy.

In fact, there is only one dubious contemporary source for Henry Carey being the King's son.[21] On 20 April 1535, John Hale, Vicar of Isleworth, confessed before the Council that bills laid against him by four gentlemen were true, and admitted, 'I have maliciously slandered the King and the Queen's Grace and their Council, for which I ask forgiveness of God, King Henry VIII and Queen Anne, and shall continue sorrowful during my life.' He excused his rash words by saying he had suffered 'a fervent ague [and] several falls from my horse, from one of which was troubled my wits, as also by age and lack of memory'. Then he tried to shift the blame to one of his accusers, 'Mr Skidmore', alleging that he had conversed with him 'concerning the King's marriage and other behaviours of his bodily lust', and claiming that 'Skidmore' had pointed out to him 'young Master Carey, saying he was our sovereign lord the King's son by our sovereign lady the Queen's sister, whom the Queen's Grace might not suffer to be in the court'.[22] Hale was at least correct on the latter count, for it was probably common knowledge by then that Anne Boleyn would not 'suffer' her sister Mary to come to court after they fell out for good in 1534.[23]

This same John Hale was a member of a group of dissidents who had been fed salacious calumnies about the Boleyn family by Richard Reynolds, a monk of Syon Abbey who had denied the King's new title of Supreme Head of the Church of England,[24] granted him by Parliament in the wake of the breach with Rome. 'Mr Skidmore' was in fact Thomas Scudamore, a priest at nearby Syon Abbey,[25] a religious house that had once been highly favoured by Katherine of Aragon, who had visited frequently to make her devotions;[26] it is therefore unsurprising that malicious gossip about Anne Boleyn's family was rife there, and the community would have known that, in asserting that Henry Carey was the King's son, they were impugning the legitimacy of Anne's marriage.

Hale himself was violently opposed to that marriage, and had accused the King of indulging in 'foul pleasures' and being 'mired in vice', fulminating that Henry's life was 'more stinking than a sow', and lambasting him for 'wallowing and defiling himself in any filthy place. For how great soever he is, he is fully given to his foul pleasure of the flesh and other voluptuousness.' Hale also asserted that Henry had violated most of the women of his court, and married Anne Boleyn 'out of sheer fornication, to the highest shame and undoing of himself and all his realm'. It was he who had claimed that Henry kept his own brothel of maidens at Farnham Castle 'when he was with the old Lord of Winchester' – which, as we have seen, was highly unlikely – and that 'the King's Grace had meddled with the Queen's mother'.[27]

It was because Hale refused to take the oath acknowledging the royal supremacy, and the invalidity of the King's union with Katherine of Aragon, that he was hanged and disembowelled at Tyburn in May 1535. He was not executed for claiming that Henry Carey was the King's son, as has been implied.[28] Nor can that one statement show 'at the very least . . . that contemporary opinion in 1535 believed that the affair had been ongoing just nine years earlier in 1526'.[29] One man's seditious opinion was not necessarily the view of others, and Hale's tirade can be dismissed as that of a hostile and unreliable witness.

It has been noted that Henry VIII was so discreet in his extra-marital affairs that we know very little about them. Had he been indulging in wholesale fornication with every woman at court, as Hale appears to imply, there would undoubtedly be plenty of surviving testimony to it. But despite present-day claims that Henry Carey was 'widely rumoured' or 'commonly supposed' to have been the King's son,[30] there is no evidence beyond Hale's highly suspect testimony that there were *any* rumours circulating about Henry Carey's paternity – and even if there had been, 'court gossip is not always a reliable source of information'.[31]

Infinitely less compelling as evidence of Henry's paternity is the grant of the borough of Buckingham 'in tail male' to William Carey on 20 February 1526,[32] nearly a year after Henry Carey was born; 'tail male' was the most popular form of entail, limiting the grant to the recipient and the male heirs of his body, who, crucially, must have been lawfully begotten.[33] Fee tails were created in order to ensure that lands and grants made by the Crown remained in the family of the beneficiary; 'the male entail kept land in the hands of men as long as it was biologically possible'.[34] Had Henry Carey been the King's son, no fee tail would, or could, have been created.

When one compares the pattern of grants made to William Carey with the birth dates of the Carey siblings, there are no grants that coincide with Henry Carey's birth and could consequently be seen as possible evidence of the King's paternity. Most arguments in favour of the latter rest on Carey having been born in 1526, not 1525,[35] and thus the grant of 1526 cannot be connected with his birth.

Moreover, in 1538, Henry VIII stated to the Emperor Charles V that Henry Fitzroy – who had died of a pulmonary infection two years earlier – was 'our only bastard son'.[36] In the case of Katherine Carey, however, a grant was made only two or three months after her birth,[37] which may be significant, and has credibly been seen as a reward to Carey 'for his compliant role as nominal father to the King's bastards'.[38]

It has been said that 'the most compelling argument' against Mary's children having been sired by Henry VIII is 'the apparent low fertility of the King'.[39] Henry's fertility has been the subject of much popular and learned debate in recent years, with his genetic make-up, health or possible impotence being held responsible for the deaths of many of his children in the womb or in infancy – and it is time to set the record straight.

Henry Tudor was one of eight children. Only four lived beyond infancy: Arthur, Margaret, Henry and Mary. The others were Elizabeth (died aged three), Edmund, Duke of Somerset (died aged fifteen months), Edward and Katherine, who both died soon after birth. This was not unusual in an age of high infant mortality.

By Katherine of Aragon, Henry had six children: three sons who died soon after birth, Mary, who lived to maturity, a daughter who was born dead, and one who died soon after birth. Katherine of Aragon came from a family of ten: five of her siblings had died at birth or been stillborn. Thus there was a history of proportionate infant mortality on both sides, which may or may not be significant. Furthermore, Giles Tremlett has recently put forward a convincing theory that Katherine suffered from anorexia, which would have had a bearing on her fertility.

Henry's second wife, Anne Boleyn, became pregnant four times. Her first child was a daughter, Elizabeth I. Her second died at or near full term, and was almost certainly a son. Her third and fourth pregnancies ended in miscarriages, the latter of a son. This suggests to me that Anne may have been rhesus negative.[40] Anne herself was born of parents who had had a child 'every year', yet only four lived to adulthood. Again, there is a history on both sides of infant mortality.

Henry had a son by Jane Seymour, who might have presented him with more children had she not died in childbed,[41] for she came from a family of ten, which may have been one reason why he decided to marry her. This successful mating might suggest that Henry's first two wives had been genetically 'at fault' for the premature loss of their children. The King also had one acknowledged bastard son by Elizabeth Blount, and evidence that will be presented later in this chapter strongly suggests that he also had two bastard daughters, both of whom married and bore children. By the time Henry married his three last wives, he was prematurely ageing, ailing and grossly obese; a report by the French ambassador, Charles de Marillac, that his fifth Queen, Katherine Howard, was *enceinte* was probably unfounded, as we hear no more of it. There is an ongoing debate about the King's possible impotence in his later years.[42] Even if he did suffer from it then, it can have had little bearing on his relations with Mary Boleyn, since the earliest possible 'evidence' dates from the 1530s.

Thus it could not be said with any certainty that Henry – a man who fathered fourteen children, seven of them sons – suffered from 'low fertility', allegedly caused by performance anxiety related to the need to sire an heir.[43]

There was no stigma attached to royal bastards – even those born in adultery – in those days, and owning them would not normally have had 'manifold catastrophic effects'.[44] Kings and princes unashamedly acknowledged their illegitimate issue in this period, and there were good pragmatic reasons for that. Natural sons could help to enforce the sovereign's authority and assist him in government, as young Fitzroy did when he was appointed to preside over the Council of the North, in an area that Henry VIII would visit only once in his reign; later, Fitzroy would use his influence on his father's behalf in the remote Welsh Marches, a region in which the King never set foot. Edward IV's natural son, Arthur Plantagenet, Viscount Lisle, was Henry VIII's deputy in Calais. Royal bastards could also be useful in making advantageous marriage alliances to gain land, loyalty and financial gain; Richard III, for example, married off his natural daughter Katherine Plantagenet to secure the allegiance of the powerful Herbert family. A king's sons could serve as commanders in war, or in the diplomatic field, or as channels of patronage at court. For Henry VIII, the father of just one surviving legitimate daughter so far, a bastard son was also living proof of his virility and his ability to sire boys. As Henry was not blessed with numerous surviving legitimate issue, it might seem reasonable to suppose that 'he needed all the children he could lay claim to'.[45] But that is rather a sweeping assumption.

Henry had not delayed acknowledging Henry Fitzroy; it is clear that, right from the time of Fitzroy's birth, people knew that the boy was the King's son – it is just not true that there is no record of his existence before his ennoblement in 1525, or that Henry kept it a secret;[46] indeed, the very name bestowed on the boy – Fitzroy: son of the King – proclaimed his royal paternity, and from birth, he was called 'Lord Henry Fitzroy'. His godfather, Wolsey, gave the young child New Year gifts,[47] and five months before the boy's ennoblement in June 1525, a Venetian envoy reported that the King 'loves him like his own soul',[48] which suggests that the child was very much in evidence.

Yet there were reasons why Henry would not openly have acknowledged any bastard child that Mary Boleyn bore him. Unlike Elizabeth Blount, she was a married woman, and owning up to a bastard born in adultery, and the betrayal of one of the gentlemen who were closest to him at court, would have provoked scandal and undermined the King's image of himself as a virtuous prince with a conscience. And Henry had no need to acknowledge any child by Mary, for there was a presumption in law that any issue born to a married woman was the child of her husband.

It has been argued that, although Henry did not acknowledge the Carey siblings (on the assumption that they were his), 'they remained close to the throne, for they shared the same father as Mary and Elizabeth Tudor'.[49] Yet even if they had been Henry's children, they could never have been close to the throne in the sense of having a claim to it, for royal bastards could not succeed. Unlike nowadays, there was a rigid distinction in Tudor times between legitimate and illegitimate children. Bastards, simply, had no rights of inheritance, and it would have taken an Act of Parliament to settle the succession on a royal bastard, which would have meant acknowledging him or her to begin with, and persuading the landed establishment – and the commons of the realm – that the normal laws of inheritance should be overlooked. This was what Henry VIII was planning to do for Henry Fitzroy, in the event of Queen Katherine failing to bear a son, but it is debatable whether his subjects would have accepted a bastard for their king.

Had Henry claimed Mary's children as his own after 1527, he would have jeopardised his plans to marry her sister, Anne Boleyn, since his sexual relationship with Mary placed him within the forbidden degrees of affinity to Anne, and rendered any union between them as incestuous as the King now believed his marriage to Queen

Katherine, his brother's widow, to have been.[50] Living proof of the King's affair with Anne Boleyn's sister would not only have raised the embarrassing issue of incest, but would also have been evidence of a canonical impediment to any union with Anne and compromised the nullity suit he was pursuing in Rome, which turned upon the fact that Katherine had been his brother's wife and was therefore forbidden to him. The existence of a bastard born to him by her sister would have undermined his moral arguments, as well as his scruples of conscience. As time went by, and he married Anne in defiance of the Pope, he would have wanted to suppress any evidence that might impugn the legitimacy of that marriage. From 1534, after he was proclaimed Supreme Head of the Church of England, he could not have risked any slur on his moral probity.[51]

Thus Henry had every reason to maintain discretion – and probably neither he, nor Mary Boleyn and her family, would have wanted publicly to embarrass her husband William Carey and inflict on him the shame of being publicly branded a cuckold.

That there was a need to maintain discretion is likely. Although, given the almost conclusive evidence, we can be fairly certain that Henry Carey was not the King's child, and that the grants made to William Carey a year after his son's birth were not of any significance in this respect, those made in June 1524 – notably the three manors lately held by Buckingham – and later were perhaps – although this is not proven – discreet provision for Katherine Carey, who was probably the King's daughter.

Some historians[52] believe that Mary never conceived a child by Henry VIII, but there are good grounds for arguing that Katherine Carey was fathered by the King.

The recent discovery of a Latin dictionary in which Katherine's husband, Sir Francis Knollys, listed the births of their children, in order, has assisted the debate about Katherine's birth date and paternity, although it provides no real proof of the latter. This dictionary, which had originally been produced in 1551 in Venice, and was probably acquired by Sir Francis during his exile in the 1550s, is now in a private collection, and its existence only recently came to light.[53] The handwriting has been verified in comparison with a letter written by Knollys in 1575, now in the British Library. The dictionary provides first-hand evidence that Katherine's youngest son, Dudley, was born in May 1562, which tends to corroborate the

traditional identification of a portrait of a pregnant Elizabethan lady
as Katherine Carey.

This portrait, by Steven van der Meulan (d.1563), is dated 1562;
it is now in the Mellon Collection at the Yale Centre for British
Art in New Haven, Connecticut, U.S.A., and has been traditionally
identified 'probably' as Katherine Carey, whose last child, as we have
just seen, was born in May 1562.[54] Some perceive 'a plausible resemblance' between the sitter and the effigy of Katherine at Rotherfield
Greys, Oxfordshire,[55] which may not be apparent to everyone, but
what is striking is that both sitter and effigy are wearing what appear
to be identical pendants, fashioned from pearls and diamonds in a
circular setting around a central stone.[56] This is fairly convincing
evidence that they both depict the same person, and that the sitter
in the portrait is indeed Katherine Carey, although the evidence in
the diary does not conclusively 'prove for the first time that the
details on Katherine's portrait are correct'.[57] Nevertheless, the provenance of the picture tends to support that identification, as it was
in the possession of Katherine's descendants until 1974, when it
was sold, along with other Knollys family portraits, at Sotheby's.[58]
This is bolstered by the existence of a portrait of Katherine's brother,
Henry Carey, Lord Hunsdon, also attributed to Steven van der
Meulan,[59] which has been dated to 1561/3, the same period. Van der
Meulan painted Elizabeth I and luminaries of her court, so it is credible that both her Carey cousins commissioned him to execute their
portraits.

The portrait of the expectant lady bears what is almost certainly
a contemporary inscription – *Aetatis suae 38 Ao Dom 1562* – which
shows that the sitter was in her thirty-eighth year when it was painted.
If this is a heavily pregnant Katherine and her child was born on 9
May 1562, the picture must have been painted in the weeks before
she gave birth, probably in March or April, and she would therefore
have reached the age of thirty-eight between spring 1562 and spring
1563; thus she must have been born between spring 1524 and
spring 1525, and conceived between summer 1523 and summer 1524.
Given that her brother was born in March 1525, she was probably
born in March or April 1524. It is possible that Mary Boleyn's affair
with the King was still going on in the summer of 1523;[60] possible
too that Henry VIII was indeed Katherine's father, and that Mary's
pregnancy put an end to the affair, as seems to have been the case
with Elizabeth Blount. The taboo against sex during pregnancy would

have created a natural distancing between the couple; furthermore, Henry may have wanted to disassociate himself from a gravid Mary so that no one would question the child's legitimacy.

Possibly Mary became pregnant by William Carey, and that put an end to her relationship with Henry; or she conceived 'as soon as she left Henry for her husband',[61] for it is also possible that the affair had ended in 1523, before Mary became pregnant with Katherine. The information in Sir Francis's dictionary is not, therefore, 'evidence that his wife, the Lady Katherine, was Henry VIII's daughter', nor does the discovery of the dictionary put it 'beyond reasonable doubt that Mary's daughter, at least, was a royal bastard';[62] such evidence as the dictionary provides is purely circumstantial. It does not confirm 'that Katherine was born in the years when Mary was the King's mistress'[63] because we do not know exactly when Mary *was* the King's mistress, or if their affair was still going on in 1523. Nor does it follow that, even if Katherine was Henry's child, 'there is but one conclusion: both of Mary's children were Henry's bastards'.[64]

If the King was Katherine's father, Mary would have had every reason to keep that as secret as she had her royal liaison. Naming the child after the Queen could have been a ploy to deflect any covert speculation or gossip, or to forestall Katherine's suspicions, and anyway there was that presumption under English law that her children were the lawful issue of William Carey. Henry VIII could not have taken advantage of that in the case of Henry Fitzroy, whose mother had not been married when she bore him; he had had to acknowledge the boy, and seems to have been proud to do so, if only to prove to the world that he could father sons. Yet if Mary Boleyn had borne him a child, whatever rumour whispered, it could easily have been passed off as her husband's, and the King would have been absolved of all responsibility for it – and Mary protected from the stigma of bearing a bastard. Henry would have had good reason to be relieved that his paternity of Katherine did not have to be acknowledged; he could preserve his carefully cultivated image of a virtuous king, and he was not obliged to own another bastard 'whose existence only emphasised his lack of legitimate heirs'.[65] And Katherine was, after all, a mere girl, and therefore unimportant.

It would have taken an Act of Parliament to nullify the legal presumption of paternity,[66] and there was no reason why Henry VIII would have wanted to pursue this course, or court scandal by doing so.

What is persuasive about the portrait called 'Katherine Carey' is that the sitter bears a striking facial resemblance to both Henry VIII and Elizabeth I. This is subjective evidence, of course, but there is a strong similarity in the setting of the eyes; the Tudors had distinctive heavy lower lids, and this, and the familial winged eyebrows, can be seen in portraits of Henry VII, Henry VIII, Arthur Tudor and Henry Fitzroy, and came from the Plantagenets, as portraits of Henry VIII's grandfather, Edward IV, show. Katherine Carey has these same features. She also has a prominent chin and rounded jowls, like those that are apparent in portraits of Henry VIII and his mother, Elizabeth of York. She has red hair, as did nearly all the Tudors, whereas William Carey's was brown; the colour of Mary Boleyn's hair is not known, nor is it known if red hair featured in the Boleyn and Carey families. Katherine's nose is not hooked like Henry's, and her mouth is wider, but those characteristics could have come from her mother's side, while her resemblance to Elizabeth can be explained by the fact that their mothers were sisters.

This is not, of course, conclusive evidence, for it could be entirely coincidental that Katherine resembled the King in some facial respects; they were already related by blood, and portraits of William Carey show that he too had distinctive lower lids and winged brows, heavy jowls and a wide mouth like Katherine's. Yet her overall resemblance to Henry VIII, especially around the eyes, is stronger, and impacts immediately on the viewer.

Apart from this portrait, there is no other known likeness of Katherine to aid the debate.[67] There is no resemblance to Henry VIII in portraits of Henry Carey, despite assertions to the contrary;[68] and we can ignore unfounded claims that 'contemporary rumour said Master Carey looked very much like the King',[69] for he had the dark hair and the long, thin face of the Boleyns.

Even more compelling evidence that Katherine Carey was the King's child was to emerge after William Carey's death, long after Mary Boleyn had ceased to be Henry's mistress, in the form of an annuity granted to her, as will be seen.

Recently, Sally Varlow uncovered further evidence suggesting that Katherine's royal paternity was no secret to some at the Elizabethan court. In 1582, Sir Philip Sidney was amorously pursuing Katherine's granddaughter, Penelope Devereux, Lady Rich, and it has long been established that he addressed Penelope as Stella in 'Astrophil and Stella', his famous cycle of poems and songs about lovers. Varlow cites one possibly significant reference, in which Sidney calls Stella 'rich in the riches of a royal heart'.[70] But there are other, perhaps more blatant, hints: he gives her the royal title of 'her Grace' in two places, and, in a verse that refers to strange tales 'broidered with bulls' – a clear reference to the Boleyn arms – speaks of 'hiding royal blood full oft in rural vein'. He calls her 'Princess of Beauty', or 'a princess high, whose throne is in the mind', refers to Stella being 'so right a princess', or 'a queen', and says how her 'humbleness grows one with Majesty', which are possibly other allusions to her royal blood. In fact, the royal theme, and the language of majesty, recurs throughout the cycle. We might infer from this that Sidney knew that Tudor blood ran in Penelope's veins, and although his poem is not *prima facie* proof of that, given that poetic language is subject to various interpretations, taken with the other evidence it acquires a certain significance.

If Katherine were the King's child, again, discretion was deliberately maintained, even after the deaths of Anne Boleyn, Mary Boleyn and Henry VIII, with only a very few people being in on the secret. By then, Mary Boleyn's name had acquired a certain notoriety, and Katherine, as she grew older, probably had no wish to blacken it further or dishonour the memory of both her parents; in this, she may have showed respect for her mother's wishes.

Contrary to what has been portrayed in films, there is no evidence whatsoever that Mary, pregnant with the King's child, ever 'took to her chamber' for six weeks, as was the custom prior to a royal birth. This tradition had been laid down in the previous reign by Henry VIII's grandmother, the Lady Margaret Beaufort, for the births of legitimate royal children. Great ceremony surrounded a queen taking to her chamber, with all her male officers being replaced by female ones; this was virtually a state occasion, and one of the King's mistresses usurping that queenly role would have provoked outraged comment. Nor would it have been in keeping with Henry VIII's policy of complete discretion in regard to his extramarital affairs.

The rest is speculation. We cannot ever know for certain the truth of the matter, only that there is a strong possibility that Katherine was the King's child.

There have been claims that Henry VIII fathered other bastard children, although only one is based on compelling evidence.[71] It has often been said that Henry would have had good reason to acknowledge any natural child born to him, and this has been used as an argument against claims that Mary Boleyn's children were his. But it seems that Henry had another bastard whom he did not acknowledge, which strengthens the theory that Katherine Carey was his daughter.

In all but that one case, the evidence for Henry's paternity is slender indeed. In 1592, Sir John Perrot (1528–92), when on trial for high treason, 'boasted that he was King Henry's son'.[72] The husband of his granddaughter Penelope Perrot, Sir Robert Naunton (1563–1635), in his *Fragmenta Regalia*, published posthumously in 1653, also claimed that Perrot was Henry VIII's son. 'Compare his picture, his qualities, gesture and voice, with that of the King's, which memory retains yet amongst us,' Naunton wrote. 'They will plead strongly that he was a surreptitious child of the blood royal.' The portrait of Sir John Perrot in Haverfordwest Town Museum, Pembrokeshire, certainly does bear a resemblance to Henry VIII.

However, it seems more likely that Sir John was the son of Thomas Perrot, who died in 1531, and whose Inquisition Post Mortem[73] shows that his son and heir, John, had been born on 7 November 1529. Yet an inquisition made on 14 April 1549, terminating John's minority, states that he had reached the age of twenty-one in November 1549, in which month he had been knighted. This is likely to be the more reliable source – Inquisitions Post Mortem were not always accurate – so we may safely assume that Sir John Perrot had been born in November 1528.[74]

It is unlikely that Henry VIII would have fathered a bastard in February 1528, when he was headily in love with Anne Boleyn and desperate to marry her, and doing his very best to prove to the Pope and the world at large that he was a moral man and that his scruples of conscience over his marriage were genuine ones. At such a crucial juncture, he would hardly have risked compromising a happy outcome to his 'Great Matter', or his relationship with his 'entirely beloved' Anne (as he called her in a letter sent in June 1528), by taking a mistress. That year, the Pope's legate, having observed Henry and Anne together, reported to his master: 'He sees nothing, he thinks of nothing, but Anne. He cannot do without her for an hour.' Is a man in such thraldom likely to take a mistress? It has been suggested that he did, that he continued 'to enjoy other brief, light-hearted affairs', and that the births of the children that perhaps resulted were probably 'accidents'.[75] But a closer look at the facts would suggest otherwise.

Thomas Perrot's wardship had been purchased by Maurice, Lord Berkeley, in 1523. Berkeley had also bought the wardship of his niece, Mary, the daughter of his brother, James Berkeley of Thornbury, Gloucestershire. Mary had been born around 1510, and Berkeley married her to Thomas Perrot, probably after the latter attained his majority and was knighted in 1526. As Berkeley's wards, they had lived at Berkeley Castle, but after their marriage, they resided at Haroldstone St Issells in Pembrokeshire, the home of Perrot's fore-bears. Mary bore a son, John, and two daughters who married Welsh gentlemen. After Thomas Perrot died in 1531, she married twice more, dying after 1586.

All this places Mary Berkeley very firmly in the West Country and Wales in the period when she is supposed to have slept with Henry VIII, but the only visit Henry ever paid to the western parts (he never went further than Gloucestershire) was in 1535, by which time John Perrot was seven years old. Nor is there any record of Mary ever coming to court. Some modern writers[76] state that she was a lady-in-waiting to Katherine of Aragon, but I can find no contemporary evidence for this. In fact, there is no evidence at all, beyond his own boast – made perhaps in the hope of saving his life – to show that Sir John Perrot was Henry VIII's natural son.

Perrot was 'a tempestuous and choleric character of Shakespearean proportions',[77] a larger-than-life man in every sense who enjoyed a varied and (for a long time) successful career. He served three Tudor monarchs: Edward VI – in whose reign he first came to court under the patronage of William, Lord Paulet – Mary I and Elizabeth I. Edward knighted him, and Elizabeth appointed him one of the bearers of her canopy of estate at her coronation. In the years to come, she would reward him handsomely for his royal and military service. In 1570, he was appointed the First Lord President of Munster and in 1584, Lord Deputy of Ireland. Perrot was now riding high, but he was a forceful and plain-spoken man, and his reckless conduct, blunt manner and candid remarks proved his downfall. Often at loggerheads with the Queen, he angrily criticised her in public for not following a consistent policy in Ireland and for failing to give him adequate support in his difficult role. After four years, he was recalled and preferred to Elizabeth's Privy Council.

In 1592, thanks to the machinations of the former Lord Chancellor, Sir Christopher Hatton, whose daughter he had seduced, Sir John was tried for entering into a treasonable correspondence with Philip

II of Spain, England's enemy, and for making disparaging remarks about Queen Elizabeth, whom he had memorably called a 'base bastard piss-kitchen'.[78] There is a story that, when he was found guilty, he cried, 'God's death! Will the Queen suffer her brother to be offered up a sacrifice to the envy of his frisking adversaries?'

Sentence was deferred. Had Perrot, already ailing, not died in custody in September 1592, Elizabeth might well have pardoned him; instead, she restored his estates to his son. Maybe there was some question in her mind about his paternity, but she too may not have been aware of the circumstances of his birth. Or perhaps she remembered his long and loyal service.

The notorious spy, mercenary, rebel, pirate and recusant adventurer, Sir Thomas Stucley (or Stukeley) (1525?–78) – whose chequered life would require another book to recount – was rumoured, towards the end of his life, to be Henry VIII's son. James FitzGerald, an Irish exile who met him in Rome in 1577–8, wrote that some said he was 'an illegitimate son of Henry VIII', although others described him as the son of an English knight or the offspring of Irish parents.[79] Not knowing FitzGerald's sources, we cannot place too much credence upon what he said. Again, the weight of evidence suggests that Thomas was fathered by the man whose surname he bore, Sir Hugh Stucley, a Devon knight whose wife, Jane Pollard, presented him with five sons. We have seen that Henry VIII never set foot in Devon, and only once travelled as far as the West Country, in 1535.

The theory that Stucley was Henry's son appears to rest on that one report of his rumoured parentage, the fact that he was treated pretty leniently by the Tudor monarchs when he got into trouble – which could be explained in several ways, although Jones states that he, like Perrot, 'got away with almost anything' – and a remark that Stucley made to Elizabeth I when he was presented to her in the early 1560s. He told her he would prefer to be sovereign of a mole-hill than the subject of the greatest king in Christendom, and that he had a presentiment he would be a prince before he died. She is said to have replied, 'I hope I shall hear from you when you are installed in your principality.' Stucley retorted that she surely would.

'In what language?' she asked, referring to his foreign exploits.

'In the style of princes, to our dearest sister,' was the cheeky reply.[80]

Stucley's allusion to the correct form used in letters between princes has been misinterpreted.[81] When he referred to Elizabeth as his 'sister', he was using the word in this context, as one monarch would to another, and probably mischievously to boot.

Despite his skill and daring in battle, Stucley was killed fighting in Morocco in 1578, when a cannon ball took off both his legs. Queen Elizabeth's chief minister, William Cecil, Lord Burghley, later called him 'a defamed person almost through all Christendom', and wrote that 'whole volumes' could be written 'to paint out the life of a man in the highest degree of vainglory, prodigality, falsehood and vile and filthy conversation of life, and altogether without faith, conscience or religion'.[82] He would hardly have spoken thus of a man he knew to be the Queen's half-brother. It is hard to take seriously claims that Stucley, a constant thorn in the side of the Tudors, was Henry VIII's son.

According to a tradition maintained by his descendants,[83] the poet and playwright Richard Edwards (or Edwardes) is supposed to have been Henry VIII's son by Agnes Blewitt, born in the early 1520s, possibly around 1523–5.[84] Agnes is said to have been permitted to display the Tudor rose on her coat of arms. She was the wife of William Thomas Edwards of North Petherton, Somerset, and she herself hailed from Holcombe Regis, Devon. It is claimed that she was at court before she became pregnant – which seems unlikely – and that Henry VIII provided a stipend for Richard's upbringing, gave Agnes land in Scotland (even more unlikely, as he did not own any in that kingdom), where the boy was brought up, and paid for him to be educated at Oxford University, where he studied law. Edwards did not practise as a lawyer, but entered the Church of England, and later wrote plays such as *Palamon and Arcite*, which were performed before Elizabeth I. He died in 1566.

Agnes is said to have stayed with Henry VIII at the royal hunting lodge at Huntworth in Somerset. Her son was born at North Petherton. The family's claim that Edwards was the King's son rests solely on the fact that he received a university education that his family could never have afforded,[85] but that could be explained in any number of ways.

The first problem with this tale is that, as has been noted, Henry VIII only ever visited the West Country in 1535; and the second problem is that there is no contemporary evidence whatsoever on which to base Henry's paternity.

★

Henry VIII is convincingly credited with the paternity of just one of these alleged bastards, Etheldreda (or Audrey, or Esther) Malte, although he did not acknowledge her as his daughter. She is said to have been born in the late 1520s – again, at the time when Henry was deeply involved with Anne Boleyn, so the date is suspect – and to have been the fruit of a liaison between the King and a royal laundress called Joan Dingley (or Dyngley).[86] We know, from the experience of William Webbe, that Henry was not above seducing women of the lower orders.[87]

There has been a credible suggestion that the little girl was named Etheldreda because she was born on the feast of the Saxon royal saint of that name, 23 June.[88]

Henry is said to have persuaded John Malte, his tailor from at least 1527 to 1545,[89] to raise Etheldreda as his own bastard daughter, and paid him well to do it. Joan Dingley had probably married a Mr Dobson by then. Etheldreda took the surname Malte. In his will, drawn up on 10 September 1546, John Malte left a sum of money to 'Audrey Malte, my bastard daughter, begotten on the body of Joan Dingley, now wife of one Dobson'.[90]

In 1545, Etheldreda was betrothed to Richard Southwell, but the contract was formally broken. In autumn 1546, she married the cultivated poet John Harington, who held office as treasurer of the King's camps and buildings at Stepney, enjoyed Henry's 'good countenance', and later served the Lady Elizabeth (the future Elizabeth I), when she was residing at Hatfield Palace. Even though 'the goodlie Esther'[91] was probably the King's daughter, her mother was of lowly estate, so Henry had done rather well by her in finding her such a husband.

In 1656, Jonathan Lesley, Deputy Clerk, wrote to a descendant of Harington describing how 'the great King Henry the VIIIth matched his darling daughter to John Harington, and though a bastard, dowered her with the rich lands of Bath Priory'; he added that his information had come from Sir Andrew Markham, a collateral descendant of Harington's second wife.[92] The King did indeed make Etheldreda a large grant, as her dowry, of monastic lands forfeited by the dissolved nunnery of Shaftesbury, namely Kelston, Batheaston and St Katharine's in Somerset, and the capital messuage of (St) Catherine's Court. This was a generous gesture indeed when aspiring courtiers and nobles were competing to purchase the estates of dissolved monasteries. The grant, dated 23 September 1546, was made to 'John Malte, tailor, and

Etheldreda Malte, alias Dingley, bastard daughter of the said John by Joan Dingley alias Dobson'.[93]

Is it likely that such a lavish grant would have been made to the bastard daughter of a humble tailor and laundress? It is this that has been seen as *prima facie* – and credible – evidence for Henry's paternity. Moreover, in May 1541, the humble John Malte had received two manors and the revenues of two estates in Berkshire,[94] which he left to Etheldreda.[95] This was probably the King making provision for his daughter.

After their marriage, Etheldreda and her husband settled at Kelston, near Bath, on Etheldreda's estate. In 1554, in the reign of Mary I, they were both in attendance on the Lady Elizabeth when she was a prisoner in the Tower. 'My wife is her servant, and does but rejoice in this our misery, when we look with whom we are held in bondage,' Harington wrote to Stephen Gardiner, Bishop of Winchester, the Lord Chancellor. 'Our gracious King Henry did ever advance our family's good estate, wherefore our service is in remembrance of such good kindness.' Harington went on to describe how Elizabeth 'does honour us in tender sort, and scorns not to shed her tears with ours'.[96] Given the magnitude of Henry VIII's bounty to Etheldreda, and her closeness to Elizabeth (to which this letter is testimony), it is highly likely that she was the King's child.

Etheldreda was still alive in October 1555,[97] but had died before 1559,[98] as her husband remarried probably that year, his second wife being Isabella Markham, a maid of honour to the future Queen Elizabeth; he had been in love with Isabella for some time, probably since 1549, and wrote poems for her.[99] Their eldest son, another John, to whom Elizabeth stood godmother, was christened in August 1560, and became famed as the inventor of the water closet. As Etheldreda left no male issue – she appears to have had a daughter, Hester (or Esther), who lived until 1568[100] at least – Harington inherited all the lands King Henry had granted her, and thus made his fortune.[101] He died in 1582. A portrait of Etheldreda in an embroidered gown is said to have been sold at auction at Sotheby's in 1942 to an anonymous bidder, but its whereabouts is now unknown.

Since Etheldreda was almost certainly Henry VIII's daughter, why did he not acknowledge her? It must have been because her mother was of lowly birth, which would have precluded Etheldreda making a grander marriage; it was one thing to acknowledge the bastard son

he had had with the gently born Elizabeth Blount, but quite another
to proclaim his paternity of the humble Joan Dingley's child.

Establishing that Etheldreda was in all probability Henry's daughter,
even though he did not acknowledge her, bolsters the case for his
having had a bastard daughter whom he also did not acknowledge
by Mary Boleyn. It is therefore not possible to take a broad view
that Henry VIII would have acknowledged all his bastards as he had
Henry Fitzroy, and that his doing so is the only proof of their paternity. Clearly, acknowledgement depended on political considerations,
the sex of the child, the status of its mother and the circumstances
of its birth.

On 18 June 1525, at Bridewell Palace in London, Sir Thomas Boleyn
was advanced to the peerage as Viscount Rochford.[102] This was the
latest in a string of honours bestowed on Mary's father. It has often
been assumed that this ennoblement, like some earlier honours
bestowed on him, was a reward to a complacent father for services
rendered to the King by Mary;[103] but in fact that title devolved on
him through his mother, one of the two co-heirs of the Irish barony
of Ormond.[104] Mary Boleyn had not been recorded at court during
the three years prior to her father's ennoblement, and it was probably in 1525 that the King first became enamoured of her sister
Anne. There is no evidence that the affair was sufficiently serious in
June of that year to account for Boleyn's ennoblement.

On the same day that Boleyn was raised to the peerage, the King
made Henry Fitzroy a Knight of the Garter, which was the most
prestigious honour he could have conferred on his son. He also
created him Duke of Richmond and Somerset. These were two royal
titles: the earldom of Richmond had been held by Henry VII before
he ascended the throne, while the dukedom of Somerset had been
bestowed on Edmund, a short-lived brother of Henry VIII, and before
that had long been associated with the King's Beaufort ancestors.
Although only six years old, Fitzroy was now appointed Lord High
Admiral of England, Wales, Ireland, Normandy, Gascony and Aquitaine
(even though the last three duchies had long been lost to the English
Crown), Lord Lieutenant of Ireland and Warden of the Cinque Ports,
King's Lieutenant north of the Trent, Warden General of the Marches
of Scotland, Chamberlain of Chester and North Wales, Receiver of
Middleham and Sheriff Hutton in Yorkshire and Constable of Dover
Castle. He was also given a magnificent household of his own at

Durham House in London, with 245 liveried attendants, as would have befitted a legitimate prince. 'Great feasts and disguisings' marked the elevation of Fitzroy, Boleyn and others.[105]

The Church, and society at large, expected a man to provide for his bastards, and help them to make their way in the world. Defaulting on this was generally regarded as a moral failure.[106] Henry VIII had more than fulfilled his responsibility in this regard, for never before had an English royal bastard been showered with such honours, and no natural son of a monarch had been given a title since the twelfth century. But the King had had to face the fact that his wife was 'past the ways of women' and would never have another child, and his elevation of Fitzroy suggests that already he was contemplating pushing through an Act of Parliament that would make the boy his lawful heir. There was also talk that Henry meant to make him King of Ireland. From now on, Fitzroy would be 'well brought-up like a prince's child' and 'furnished to keep the state of a great prince'; there was talk of bolstering his status by marrying him to a foreign princess, and at one stage, Henry would even toy with the idea of marrying him to his half-sister, Mary. Ambassadors were instructed to refer to his son as 'one who is near of his blood and of excellent qualities, and yet may easily by the King's means be exalted to higher things'.

The fact that Henry VIII was prepared to do so much for his acknowledged natural son makes it even less likely that Henry Carey was his bastard issue, for the isolated instances of favour shown to Carey are in glaring contrast to the extravagant bounty that was heaped upon Henry Fitzroy.[107] Nor could it credibly be claimed that the King had scruples about upsetting Queen Katherine, for when Katherine had protested at the elevation of Fitzroy, Henry promptly dismissed three of her ladies for inciting her to do so, whereupon she was 'obliged to submit and have patience'.[108]

9

'The Sister of Your Former Concubine'

Although it is often claimed that Mary Boleyn's affair with Henry VIII was of great significance and duration, it does not appear to have lasted very long. Reginald Pole, in 1538, wrote that Henry had 'soon tired' of her, although in the next few lines he rather contradicts that and says the King kept her 'for a long time' as his concubine. Maybe it was a long time compared to his other affairs. Mary is not recorded at court after 1522, which suggests that her liaison with the King was brief. But how brief is a matter for conjecture – the term itself is relative, as is 'a long time'. An affair lasting one or two years could equally well be described as brief as lasting a long time. Did this one last weeks, months or even years? We do not know, although it has been claimed that it was a long-term relationship that endured for four or five years,[1] and that – unusually in the history of Henry VIII's extramarital affairs – it went on longer than any of the others,[2] although that may not have been the case, as Elizabeth Blount was probably his mistress for four or five years. Another claim is that 'the affair with Mary was over well before [her son Henry] was conceived', i.e. before summer 1524,[3] but there is nothing to support that assertion beyond speculation.

It has been pointed out by many writers that in September 1523, Henry VIII had in his navy a hundred-ton ship called the *Mary Boleyn*, and some claim that this had been named in honour of Mary, who was supposedly still his mistress at that time,[4] even going as far as to say that Mary was the King's acknowledged mistress by 1523,[5] although there is no record of him ever acknowledging her. Yet in December 1526, Henry's 'expenses of war' included payment 'to my Lord of Rochford for a ship called the *Anne Boleyn*'.[6] This strongly suggests that both vessels had in fact been owned – and named – by Thomas Boleyn, and that Henry bought both ships from him.[7] The fact that the *Mary Boleyn* was not called the *Mary Carey* implies that she had been built before 1520. In any case, it is highly improbable that Henry VIII, who was so covert in conducting his extramarital affairs, would have blazoned his mistress's identity to the world on the prow of a ship; that would have been against all the accepted rules of courtly love.

Most historians believe that his affair with Mary had ended by 1524–6.[8] It has been suggested that the grant of the keepership of Greenwich Palace to William Carey in May 1526 'must signal the end of the King's affair with Mary',[9] but, as has been demonstrated, it probably had nothing to do with her.

The truth is, we do not know when – or why – it ended; but certainly it was over by February 1526, when the King gave a very public signal that he had a new love. If one accepts that Katherine Carey was Henry's child, and Henry Carey was not – as the evidence strongly suggests – then the chances are that relations between Henry VIII and Mary Boleyn had ceased by 1524.[10]

Possibly Henry simply tired of Mary. Pole implies that she was not successful at holding his interest, and it has more recently been suggested that she 'did not have that sharp, incisive mind that enabled her sister Anne to hold on to her conquest' in the years to come,[11] and that she had probably 'begun to bore' the King.[12] The most convincing theory is that Henry lost interest[13] – or was scared off – when Mary became pregnant – probably by him – in 1523,[14] since, earlier on, he seems to have broken off with Elizabeth Blount when she was having his child, pregnancy having had 'the effect of dampening his lust'[15] – which it surely would have done if Mary had been expecting her husband's baby. It may be that Mary did not want the King near her during her first pregnancy,[16] sex being regarded as potentially harmful to the unborn child, and that Henry sought satisfaction in other arms.

It is unlikely that Mary – or Elizabeth Blount before her – got pregnant deliberately, after practising contraception with her royal lover for years, and that Henry felt betrayed, as has been suggested;[17] what would Mary have achieved by doing that? Not a good marriage, like Elizabeth Blount, for she was already wed, but scandal and notoriety – exactly what the King, in maintaining strict secrecy, and Mary, by her absolute discretion, had tried to avoid.

There is also nothing to support the assertions that, when the affair ended, Mary 'wasn't too upset about it',[18] or that she 'settled back into court life quite contentedly as Carey's wife'.[19] There is no evidence that she was 'pensioned off' by the King[20] or 'paid off'[21] when he tired of her. The later grants to Carey have been seen as 'a gesture of thanks' to a mistress who had not been 'exactly seduced and abandoned'.[22] Nor is it true that, after Mary had been 'cast off', her husband 'was obliged by the King to send her away from court',[23] or that she voluntarily left.[24] In all probability, Mary did not leave the court when the affair ended, but remained there, living with her husband as before. Nor did she 'fade into obscurity',[25] for she had never been flaunted publicly as the King's mistress.

It is often assumed that Mary was replaced in the King's affections by her sister Anne,[26] who was to be the great love of his life, and whom he began courting probably in 1525[27] – and certainly by February 1526.[28] Again, we cannot say for certain that Anne supplanted her sister, or that Mary was jealous when she witnessed 'the man she loved' falling for her sister,[29] for, as has been argued, her affair with the King was probably over by the end of 1524, many months before Henry set his sights on Anne.

The Gentleman Usher George Cavendish, who wrote a biography of his master, Cardinal Wolsey, clearly got his dates wrong in claiming that Anne returned to England after Queen Claude's death in 1524, and that the King then set his sights on her, and ordered Wolsey to put an end to her dalliance with Lord Henry Percy, heir to the 5th Earl of Northumberland (and a first cousin of William Carey), because he wanted her for himself. Anne had come home in 1522, and the courtship with Percy probably developed in 1523, for he had been employed in the north as Warden of the East and Middle Marches from late 1522 to early 1523.[30] His kinship with William Carey, Anne's brother-in-law, would have been a good pretext for contriving an introduction to Anne.[31]

The affair between Anne and Percy cannot have lasted long, for Wolsey must have intervened in the late summer of 1523. The young couple had indeed wished to marry, but Percy was already promised to Lady Mary Talbot;[32] his father was sent for, to talk some sense into the boy, and the formal betrothal to Lady Mary had been arranged by September 1523.[33] Anne, burning with resentment against Wolsey, was sent home in disgrace to Hever.[34] There is no evidence that Henry VIII showed any interest in her for some time after that, so it is more likely that he – or Wolsey – had objected to her making marriage plans with Percy, on the grounds that the daughter of the Earl of Shrewsbury was a much better match for Northumberland's heir than Anne Boleyn, the daughter of a mere knight.

It is possible that, between ending his affair with Mary Boleyn and falling for her sister Anne, Henry pursued Elizabeth Amadas, the wife of the goldsmith Robert Amadas, who was made Master of the Jewel House in 1524; and that it was only after Henry VIII had tired of chasing Elizabeth Amadas, or been spurned, that he embarked upon his pursuit of Anne Boleyn.

Robert Amadas was the most successful goldsmith working at the Tudor court, and indeed, the richest in England. By 1521, he was supplying commissions to the King, Cardinal Wolsey and many lords and courtiers. Elizabeth Amadas was of Welsh descent, the daughter of a courtier, Hugh Bryce, whose father had also been a royal gold-smith. Her date of birth is not known, but she was still unmarried and not yet of age in 1498. Her daughter, of the same name, was born in 1508, and married Richard Scrope of Castle Combe in 1529, so if Elizabeth Amadas had married at twelve, the youngest age at which the Church permitted a wife to cohabit with her husband, and bore her daughter a year later, she would have been in her mid-twenties in the early 1520s, and – more realistically – may have been about the same age as the King.

A volatile woman, given to tantrums and strange visions, she was not prepared to maintain the kind of discretion required by Henry, and later had no compunction in revealing that 'the King had often sent her offerings and gifts, and that Mr Dauncy had come as bawd between the King and her to have had her to Mr Compton's house in Thames Street'.[35] She did not say whether she had actually gone there, and, as a supporter of Queen Katherine, it is unlikely that she would have wanted to, or that she in fact did. In the absence of any other evidence for her having an affair with the King, we should assume the latter.

'Mr Dauncy' was probably Sir John Dauncey, a Knight of the Body and Privy Councillor to Henry VIII, whose son William married Sir Thomas More's daughter Elizabeth in 1525. Sir William Compton, it will be remembered, had abetted Henry in his intrigues with the Stafford sisters in 1510 and seems to have shared his amorous interest in Elizabeth Carew and Elizabeth Blount in 1514; he may well have acted as 'bawd' between these ladies and the King. Given this, Mrs Amadas's account of Henry's pursuit of her does ring true. Since Compton died in 1528 (Dauncey died many years later), the affair (if affair it was) with Mrs Amadas must have been played out well before that year, because the King almost certainly began courting Anne Boleyn in 1525, and thereafter had eyes for no one but her; and, of course, this episode with Mrs Amadas may even have belonged to the earliest years of his reign.

It was in July 1533 that Elizabeth Amadas, calling herself 'a witch and prophetess', publicly predicted, along with many other wild prophesies, that 'my Lady Anne [Boleyn, then Queen of England] should be burned, for she is a harlot'. Mrs Amadas had even drawn up a painted roll of her predictions, and asserted that they had been known to her for twenty years. Naturally, her 'ungracious rehearsals' incurred the wrath of the authorities, but she remained unbowed. Under interrogation, she asserted that because the King – the cursed 'Mouldwarp' (an ancient name for a mole, one who works in darkness) – 'has forsaken his wife, he suffers her husband to do the same'. She insisted that she was 'a good wife', in common with Queen Katherine and Elizabeth Stafford, Duchess of Norfolk, for her spouse had forsaken her like theirs; and, to underline the King's perfidious nature, she revealed that she had once been the object of his amorous interest.

Robert Amadas might have abandoned his wife, but immediately after she was arrested, he was sued by the King – on the 'information of certain words spoken by Mistress Amadas' – for a huge sum of money in respect of some plate that was conveniently found to have been missing from the Jewel House; it may have been the price of his wife's freedom.[36]

Mary Boleyn almost certainly 'went quietly',[37] but even if she was not supplanted in the King's affections by Elizabeth Amadas, by 1526 there can be no doubt that Henry had eyes only for her sister.

In February 1526, on Shrove Tuesday, Henry VIII appeared in the tiltyard at Greenwich in a magnificent jousting outfit of cloth of gold and silver embroidered in gold with the words *Declare je nos* – 'Declare I dare not' – which was surmounted by a man's heart engulfed in flames.[38] There can be little doubt that the object of his new passion was Anne Boleyn. In one of Henry's love letters to Anne, probably written in 1527 (or possibly even earlier),[39] he wrote of having been 'struck by the dart of love' for more than a year. In the spring of 1526, having in mind the kind of courtly symbolism that he had displayed four years earlier when probably pursuing Mary Boleyn, he ordered from his goldsmith four gold brooches: one represented Venus and Cupid, the second a lady holding a heart in her hand, the third a gentleman lying in a lady's lap, and the fourth a lady holding a crown.[40]

It would be foolish to conjecture that Henry had already envisaged making Anne his second queen, but a crown could also symbolise aloofness or virginity, which would both have been more apposite, for – unlike her sister – the bolder Anne seems from the first firmly to have proclaimed her virtue and to have kept her royal suitor at arm's length. No doubt Henry initially expected the younger sister to fill the same role as the elder had done,[41] but Anne had learned a salutary lesson from the experiences of Mary Boleyn and Elizabeth Blount – Mary was a 'living example of Henry's fickle nature'[42] and had gained little personal advantage or material benefits from taking the King as a lover,[43] at least while their affair was going on. Although there is no evidence to support the claim that Anne had 'witnessed her own sister in tears, the scapegoat of Henry's black mood or whim',[44] Mary's failure to hold the King's interest and affections was a salutary warning to her younger – and sharper – sister, and evidence of 'the pitfalls of court life'[45] – and clearly Anne did not intend to risk becoming another discarded royal mistress.

That was the way her contemporaries saw it. In 1538, the King's cousin, Cardinal Reginald Pole, from the safe haven of Italy, where he had chosen exile in January 1532, unwilling to become embroiled in Henry VIII's 'Great Matter', published his treatise, *Pro ecclesiasticae unitatis defensione* (*A Defence of the Unity of the Church*), addressed to the King (and based on an earlier letter to Henry), stating in no uncertain terms Pole's views on his sovereign's marriage to Anne Boleyn:

At your age in life, and with all your experience of the world, you were enslaved by your passion for a girl. But she would not give you your will unless you rejected your wife, whose place she longed to take. The modest woman would not be your mistress; no, but she would be your wife. She had learned, I think, if from nothing else, at least from the example of her

sister, how soon you got tired of your mistresses; and she resolved
to surpass her sister in retaining you as her lover.

Now what sort of person is it whom you have put in place
of your divorced wife? Is she not the sister of her whom first
you violated and for a long time after kept as your concubine?
She certainly is. How is it then, that you now tell us of the
horror you have of illicit marriage? Are you ignorant of the
law which certainly no less prohibits marriage with a sister of
one with whom you have become one flesh, than one with
whom your brother was one flesh? If one kind of marriage is
detestable, so is the other. Were you ignorant of the law? Nay,
you knew it better than others. How did I prove it? Because,
at the very time that you were rejecting your brother's widow,
you were doing your very utmost to get leave from the Pope
to marry the sister of your former concubine.

No one had ever dared to address Henry VIII in such accusatory
terms. Pole's treatise infuriated the King, and was to have fatal repercussions for his family, but that aside, we might wonder how he had
come to know about Henry's affair with Mary Boleyn. He was
abroad in Italy from February 1521 to 1527, so was not in England
when it was flourishing. Of course, he could have found out about
it at the English court, where he was active from 1527 until he went
into voluntary exile in 1532; but his letter suggests that he got his
information later at the Papal Curia, where he had seen, or been
shown, a dispensation issued in 1528 (see below), at the King's request,
permitting him to marry within the forbidden degrees of affinity.
Without it, Mary Boleyn having been his mistress, Henry's proposed
marriage to her sister would have been incestuous.

With Anne in attendance on the Queen, the King would have seen
her often about the court, while his friendship with her father and
her brother-in-law, William Carey, and his dalliance with her sister,
had already brought the Boleyns firmly into the royal circle, so Henry
probably already knew Anne socially. Thus far can it be said that she
'owed much of her swift rise to favour at court to her sister'.[46]
Her banishment to Hever appears not to have lasted too long; if
Mary was still the King's mistress at that time – around 1523–5 –
she may even have interceded on Anne's behalf with Henry and
asked him to let her sister return to court; and it was probably after

Anne re-entered the Queen's service that Henry's courtship began. The psychologist J. C Flügel has suggested that, in pursuing the sister of his former mistress, the King was unconsciously impelled by his 'craving for sexual rivals, for incest, and for chastity in his wives, thereby making his marriage couch a nightmare of recriminations, fears and frustrations'.[47] That is pure speculation; a more credible theory is that Henry saw much of Mary in Anne – 'it is even possible that at first he saw little else,'[48] especially if the Mary he had known had been lost to him through pregnancy and motherhood.

We can only conjecture as to how this impacted on the relationship between the sisters. In a letter written by Mary in 1534 (see Chapter 11), there is more than a suggestion that there was some rivalry between them. Maybe what had passed between the King and her sister, the bastard child that may have resulted from their affair, and the affinity created by their relationship, made it difficult for Anne to consider taking Henry as a lover – unless, of course, she welcomed the opportunity to compete with her sister and, 'if possible, to surpass her'.[49]

Of course, Mary might not have been abandoned by Henry: the decision to part may have been mutual, or even hers. At the other extreme, Anne may have stolen her sister's lover, and that certainly would not have made for good relations between them, and might have left Mary seething with jealousy.

It is unlikely that Anne Boleyn feared being 'tarred with the brush of her sister's reputation',[50] because, as has been established, there is no evidence that, as a result of her affair with the King, Mary had 'entirely lost her reputation'[51] – how could she have done that, with discretion having been so rigorously maintained?

It may well be that Mary's passive acceptance of the situation angered the Boleyns, for it would have flown in the face of years of the social and political advancement that was their creed. Ambitious as they were, they would have found it hard to understand. We might conjecture that, after the affair had ended, Mary's father and brother felt only scorn and contempt for her[52] – and Anne may have too. Anne was not one to arouse her family's disapprobation for not making the most of Henry VIII's interest, and they would have no cause to complain of the way she handled it to her – and their – advantage. It has been suggested that, when the King lost interest in Mary, her father, 'in his selfish greed', may 'have sought to maintain his power by the means of the charms' of his younger daughter, Anne.[53] Again, there is no evidence, but, given how suggestible Henry was, the theory might just be credible.

According to Sander, when Mary saw that Anne was 'preferred to her, and that she herself was slighted not only by the King but by her sister', she went to the Queen 'and bade her be of good cheer; for though the King, she said, was in love with her sister, he could never marry her, for the relations of the King with the family [Sander is here alluding to both Mary and her mother having been Henry's mistresses] were of such a nature as to make a marriage impossible by the laws of the Church'.

'The King himself,' Mary is supposed to have said, 'will not deny it, and I will assert it publicly while I live; now, as he may not marry my sister, so neither will he put your Majesty away.' Katherine is said by Sander to have thanked her 'and replied that all she had to say and do would be said and done under the direction of her lawyers'.

As has been explained already, the fact that Katherine did not use the canonical impediment created by Henry's affair with Mary Boleyn, either in an attempt to block his marriage to Anne, or to discredit his doubts of conscience in regard to their own marriage, is strong evidence that she knew nothing about his relations with Mary Boleyn. So it is almost certain that this conversation with Mary never took place, and that Sander made it up or repeated gossip that was informed by the benefit of hindsight. Moreover, the chronology is all wrong. Sander has Mary reacting to Henry abandoning her for her sister, but even if their liaison ended as late as February 1526, Henry did not pursue an annulment until the spring of 1527, and then in only the greatest secrecy.[54]

Maybe Mary did feel slighted by both Anne and Henry, but if so, she probably had the good sense to hide it well, for it seems that the King continued to hold her in some affection, especially since she was probably the mother of his child;[55] the grant of the office of Prior of Tynemouth in 1527–8 to Thomas Gardiner, at her behest, and Henry's care for her in her coming time of penury, suggests that, some years after their affair had ended, some warmth remained.

Henry might have finished with Mary Boleyn, but he could not have known that their affair was to have complicated repercussions, and that he was to have bitter cause, in the short term, to regret it – and, in the longer term, to be thankful that it had happened.

★

Sometime after 1522, William Carey had been promoted from Esquire of the Body to the important and prestigious post of Gentleman of the Privy Chamber.[56] This was a significant promotion, a further indication of the high regard in which Carey was held by Henry VIII. As has been noted, in January 1526, under Cardinal Wolsey's reforms of the royal household enshrined in the Eltham Ordinances, which were approved that month by the King, William Carey features high on the list of members of the King's household; despite the Cardinal's purges, he was one of six Gentlemen of the Privy Chamber allowed to remain in post, alongside Sir William Taylor, Sir Thomas Cheyney, Sir Anthony Browne, Sir John Russell and Sir Henry Norris.[57] The fact that Carey was retained in this office after his wife's liaison with the King had ended and Henry began courting Anne Boleyn is proof that his rise at court was due chiefly to his own merits.

The post of Gentleman of the Privy Chamber had been established in 1518. The King's Gentlemen were with him twenty-four hours a day, whether 'waking, sleeping, eating, drinking, working [or] relaxing'; they were mostly 'expert and superbly qualified manipulators',[58] and among the most influential people at court – which was why Wolsey feared their influence.

On 12 May 1526, William Carey received the last of the grants made to him by the King; an unforeseen tragedy would preclude him from receiving any more, although it is more than likely that they – and a knighthood at the very least – would have come his way. He was appointed 'Keeper of the manor, garden, tower &c. of Pleasance, East Greenwich, and of East Greenwich Park';[59] this effectively made him responsible for Greenwich Palace – Henry VIII's birthplace and one of his most important and favoured residences – and its environs, with the right to lodgings there whenever he needed them.

On that same date, Carey was assigned the keepership of 'the manor and park of Ditton, Bucks., and all foreign woods belonging to the same, with 3d [£4] a day'.[60] Ditton Park was another royal property, often used as a nursery palace for the Princess Mary; later, in 1533, it would be given to Anne Boleyn as part of her jointure as Queen. Some authors have seen these two last grants as tokens of gratitude on the part of the King to a man who had so patiently been cuckolded,[61] but they assume that Mary's affair with Henry had only just ended, when the likelihood is that it had finished more than two years earlier. It is possible, even likely, that the grants were discreet provision for the upbringing of the King's bastard daughter, made to ensure that she would be brought up in sufficiently royal surroundings.

By 1527, William Carey was a man of moderate substance, with a landed estate worth £333.6s.8d (£107,500), as assessed that year for a subsidy.[62] Yet he was not rich in terms of income. Even with board and lodging provided, it was expensive to keep up appearances at court, with the cost of decking oneself out in appropriate dress being very high. Sumptuary laws restricting the wearing of fine materials and jewellery to the upper ranks of society were strict, but a gentleman like William, attending on the King in his privy chamber, would be permitted – indeed expected – to be well turned out, in silk shirts, gold and silver ornaments, furs and good-quality fabrics, and of course, he would need armour for jousting. A man's worth was judged on outward display, and no doubt there was competition when it came to raiment and the furnishing of courtier lodgings. And a courtier's wife, like Mary, would have had to be provided with attire that reflected her own status and her husband's rank.

In the spring of 1527, as Keeper of Greenwich Palace, Carey was involved in mounting a lavish reception there for the French ambassadors who had come to negotiate a 'Treaty of Eternal Peace' between England and France, which would be sealed by the marriage of the Princess Mary to Henri, Duc d'Orléans, the second son of François I. The German artist Hans Holbein, recently arrived in England, executed his first royal commission for this occasion, designing at Greenwich two triumphal arches and painting a ceiling showing the earth environed by the seas, and a vast picture depicting – somewhat tactlessly – Henry VIII gaining victory over the French. He also executed portraits of all the prominent courtiers who were responsible for organising the ceremonies and celebrations to mark the event, and he probably painted William Carey too.[63]

As Carey's wife, Mary Boleyn was no doubt present at the tournaments, recitals, masques, dances and plays that were put on at Greenwich and Hampton Court to entertain the ambassadors. And no doubt she, like everyone else, was shocked when the celebrations were abruptly curtailed when news arrived that the city of Rome had been brutally sacked by mercenaries in the pay of the Emperor Charles V, and that the Pope himself was now the Emperor's prisoner.

★

It was during the festivities at Greenwich that one of the French ambassadors ventured to question the legitimacy of the Princess Mary – or so Henry VIII later claimed. The ambassador did not give offence, but merely voiced a concern with which the King had become increasingly preoccupied.

For some years now – long before his eye had lighted upon Anne Boleyn, and perhaps even Mary Boleyn, for he insisted he had first raised the matter with his confessor in 1522 – Henry had been fretting about the validity of his marriage. Katherine was his brother Arthur's widow, and although she had sworn that Arthur had left her a virgin, the Book of Leviticus prohibited a man from marrying his brother's wife; those who did, it warned, would be childless. With only one daughter surviving from Katherine's six pregnancies, Henry considered himself as good as childless – and professed himself in dread lest he had offended God by this marriage.

By 1527, with Katherine no longer fertile, he was genuinely desperate for a son to succeed him, and passionately in love with Anne Boleyn. He was also conscious of the unpalatable fact that Anne was forbidden to him, just as he believed Katherine to be, for, thanks to his affair with Mary Boleyn, he had placed himself in the same degree of first collateral affinity to Anne as existed – so he was protesting – between himself and Katherine, and created 'an adamantine Levitical barrier'.[64] More so, in fact, because Katherine's first marriage had not been consummated, whereas Henry had had sexual relations with Mary, and therefore any marriage between him and her sister would have been incestuous without doubt.[65] The impediment in Leviticus was categorical: 'Thou shalt not take the sister of thy wife as a concubine, nor uncover her turpitude whilst thy wife still liveth.' It did not actually matter that Mary had never been Henry's wife; what counted was the 'unlawful intercourse' that had taken place between them. It was that which had created the affinity. This was Mary Boleyn's greatest historical significance.

But Henry was determined to marry Anne, and in 1527, he commenced proceedings to have his union with Katherine annulled, and thus embarked on his celebrated – some would say infamous – 'Great Matter', which would end in the Reformation and the severance of the English Church from that of Rome. Those events are beyond the scope of this book, but as they form the backdrop to Mary's story, they will be referred to where appropriate.

With Pope Clement VII still a captive of the Emperor, Katherine's nephew, there was little chance of a 'divorce' being granted, but the King was nevertheless optimistic. One thing was troubling him, though. In September 1527, he had sent his secretary, Dr William Knight, on a secret mission to Rome to discuss his 'Great Matter' with Pope Clement VII. After Knight had left, the King, clearly worried about the canonical difficulty in marrying Anne, evidently realised that he should have been more specific about his relations with Mary Boleyn, so in late October or early November, he drafted a bull of dispensation himself, its object being to remove the impediment of 'affinity arising from illicit intercourse in whatever degree, even the first' in respect of any marriage the King might make in the event of his union with Katherine being annulled. Neither Mary Boleyn nor Anne was named. The reason for his discretion, and for the need for secrecy to be maintained, was that the last thing Henry wanted was the Pope or anyone else pointing the finger and saying that his scruples over his marriage 'had little to do with God and more to do with Anne Boleyn'.[66] It was essential, now more than ever, that his affair with Mary Boleyn did not become common knowledge.

The granting of this bull would allow the King to marry Anne, as soon as he was free, despite the affinity that his adultery with her sister had brought into being.[67] Henry sent this document after his secretary, with instructions to maintain all secrecy concerning it, and his covering letter is testimony to how secret his affair with Mary had been kept:

> I do now send you a copy of another [bull] which no man doth know but they which I am sure will never disclose it to no man living . . . Desiring you heartily to use all ways to you possible to get access to the Pope's person and then solicit this bull with all diligence; and in doing so, I shall reckon it the highest service you ever did me . . . This bull is not desired except I be legitimately absolved from the marriage with Katherine.

In December, Cardinal Wolsey – who was clearly privy to his master's concern – wrote to Sir Gregory Casale, Henry VIII's envoy at the Papal court in Rome:

> Though the King does not fear the consequences which might arise, yet, remembering by the example of past times what false

claims have been put forward, to avoid all colour or pretext of the same, he requests this of the Pope as indispensable.

But the Pope was of course a prisoner of the Emperor, Katherine's nephew, whose mercenary troops had sacked Rome the previous May. In December, Charles ordered Clement not to annul his aunt's marriage, effectively tying the Pontiff's hands. But dispensations such as Henry had requested were commonly granted,[68] and Clement had no wish to alienate the King of England, who had always shown himself to be a good, devout and loyal son of the Church. That month, he escaped to Orvieto, where he set up his court, and when Dr Knight arrived and was received in audience, Clement – as a sop to the English – sanctioned the bull authorising Henry VIII to wed within the prohibited degrees, should the occasion arise, provided his first marriage was proved unlawful.

On 1 January 1528, the dispensation was issued, specifically allowing Henry, whenever he was free to marry again, to take to wife any woman, 'in any degree [of affinity], even the first, *ex illicito coito* [arising from illicit intercourse]'.[69] Effectively, Clement, who – for fear of Charles V – could not bring himself to annul Henry's marriage to his sister-in-law, was actually giving him permission to marry not only the sister of his former mistress, but even his mother or his daughter. In 1533, Dr Pedro Ortiz, a Spanish doctor of theology who was sent to Rome by the Emperor to defend Queen Katherine's interests, was in no doubt as to why the bull had been granted, and reported: 'It is certain that some time ago, [Henry VIII] sent to ask his Holiness for a dispensation to marry [Anne Boleyn], notwithstanding the affinity between them on account of his having committed adultery with her sister.'[70]

Given that, for the present, there was no realistic prospect of the Pope annulling Henry's marriage to Katherine, the bull was utterly worthless.[71]

On 3 March 1528, there is a mention of William Carey in a letter sent from Windsor Castle by Thomas Heneage, one of his fellow gentlemen in the Privy Chamber, to Cardinal Wolsey: 'Mr Carey and Mr [Anthony] Browne are absent, and there is none here but [Henry] Norris and myself to attend the King in his bedchamber, and keep his pallet. Every afternoon, when the weather is fair, the King rides out hawking, or walks in the park, not returning till late in the

evening. Today, as the King was going to dinner, Mistress Anne spoke
to me, saying she was afraid you had forgotten her, as you had sent
her no token. I was requested by my Lady her mother to give her
a morsel of tunny [tuna].'This is one of the few references to Elizabeth
Howard, Lady Boleyn being at court. She was there at this time as
a chaperone for Anne.

Anne Boleyn was always actively to promote her family connections, and clearly she felt the need to court the support of her
brother-in-law, the influential William Carey. It has been said that,
although Carey was married to her sister and thereby aligned with
the Boleyn faction, he also owed a debt of gratitude and allegiance
to his powerful patron, Henry Courtenay, who was supporting
Katherine of Aragon, which would have placed Carey, and Mary too,
in an invidious position involving a conflict of loyalties;[72] but in fact
Courtenay openly (if not inwardly) supported the King until the
late 1530s, and even his wife, Gertrude Blount, a friend of Queen
Katherine, was not to engage in subversive activities until after Anne
Boleyn became Queen in 1533. Thus, in the spring of 1528, when
Anne was afforded an ideal opportunity of securing Carey's allegiance, she seized it, not in order to wean him from his affinity with
the Courtenays, but purely because he was an influential courtier
who was useful to the Boleyns.

On 24 April, Wolsey had learned that Dame Cecily Willoughby,
Abbess of Wilton, had died.[73] St Edith's nunnery at Wilton was an
ancient and rich foundation, as well as being fashionable and aristocratic,[74] and its Abbess enjoyed great prestige and standing. Most
of the convent favoured the election of the Prioress, Dame Isabel
Jordan, an 'ancient, wise and very discreet' woman,[75] to the vacant
abbatial chair, but two of William Carey's sisters, Anne and Eleanor,
were nuns at Wilton, and their brother, John Carey, was keen to see
Eleanor promoted to be head of the house; it was not Mary Boleyn[76]
who nominated her, as has been claimed. One of Wolsey's corre-
spondents had warned him that 'there will be great labour made for
Dame Eleanor Carey, sister of Mr Carey of the court'.[77]

It may have been at the behest of John Carey – or of Mary
Boleyn,[78] for it seems that she was actively pressing her sister in this
matter[79] – that Anne immediately recommended to the King that
he put pressure to bear on the convent to have Dame Eleanor elected
Abbess, and Wolsey promised the Careys that he would push for her
election as Prioress, in the event of her not being elected Abbess;

the letter clearly states 'Prioress' rather than 'Abbess', prioress being the subordinate office. [80] For the present, however, Dame Eleanor would have to be patient, as a prescribed interval had to be observed between the death of the Abbess and the election of her successor.

Late May 1528 saw the worst ever outbreak of the 'sweating sickness', an epidemic peculiar to Tudor times, which had first appeared in 1485, the year in which the Battle of Bosworth had been fought and the Tudor dynasty established. Some had seen it as the judgement of God on the victor, the usurping Henry VII. It had reappeared in 1508 and 1517, and its return in 1528, at a time when Henry VIII was pursuing his collusive suit, was seen as ominously significant. Abroad, the disease was called 'the English sweat' because it was more prevalent in England.

The sweating sickness was deadly, and no respecter of persons; it could kill with terrifying speed. 'One has a little pain in the head and heart. Suddenly, a sweat breaks out, and a physician is useless, for whether you wrap yourself up much or little, in four hours – sometimes within two or three – you are despatched without languishing.'[81] Victims might suffer violent sweats, virulent fever, shivering fits, tachycardia, pain in the back, stomach and limbs, vertigo, rashes, headaches and nervous prostration, and many succumbed on the first day. A man could be 'merry at dinner and dead at supper'.[82] There was no cure, and only those who survived the first twenty-four hours could hope to live. Needless to say, the disease brought panic in its wake: one rumour might cause 'a thousand cases of sweat',[83] and some people 'suffered more from fear than others did from the sweat itself'.[84]

Today, it is impossible to be certain what the 'sweating sickness' actually was, as no cases were reported after the last outbreak in 1551. Some have speculated that it was a miliary fever such as malaria, or a particularly virulent form of 'prickly heat', or even what later came to be known as 'trench fever',[85] while another suggests it was a strain of influenza or typhus, or 'a viral infection transmitted by rats'.[86] Given that bacteria can mutate, it may even have been a simple infection that, with time, ceased to be fatal.

The King had a horror of illness: he was 'the most timid person in such matters you could meet with',[87] and the very words 'sweating sickness' were 'so terrible to His Highness' ears that he dare in no wise approach unto the place where it is noised to have been'.[88] No one who had come into contact with an infected person was permitted to approach the court.

Henry was therefore aghast to learn of this latest outbreak. In great fear, he dismissed most of his courtiers and servants and left Greenwich Palace for Waltham Abbey in Essex, taking Queen Katherine and Anne Boleyn with him. In London, the epidemic raged, with forty thousand cases reported. Nor was Waltham safe. George Boleyn (who was to recover) sickened there of the sweat, and on or shortly before 16 June, learning that one of Anne's maids had also succumbed to the disease, Henry uprooted himself 'in great haste' and rode off to Hunsdon House, twelve miles away, having sent Anne home to her father at Hever, because she was 'suspected of having been infected'.[89]

At Hunsdon, Henry remained isolated in a tower with his physicians. 'The King shuts himself up quite alone,'[90] no doubt fretting about his beloved. Each day, his household became further diminished, as more and more of his attendants were sent away, and wherever he went, he had his lodgings 'purged daily with fires and other preservatives'.[91]

Wolsey, seeing the epidemic as the manifestation of God's wrath, begged his master to abandon all thoughts of divorce, but 'the King used terrible words, saying he would have given a thousand Wolseys for one Anne Boleyn. "No other than God shall take her from me!"' he shouted.[92] But God, it seemed, was not on Henry Tudor's side, for by 22 June, the King had been given the dread news that Anne and her father had fallen victim to the sweating sickness and taken to their beds at Hever. Immediately, Henry sent his own physician, Dr William Butts, to attend her.

This was a difficult time for Mary Boleyn too, for that same day, William Carey also contracted the dread disease. It is clear, from an exchange of letters between Cardinal Wolsey and Thomas Heneage, that Carey had not accompanied Henry to Hunsdon; the King was now retaining very few attendants, their number having diminished daily as he moved from house to house to escape the contagion.[93] William had probably been one of the courtiers dismissed at Greenwich, as Henry VIII (in a letter written to Anne Boleyn after the court left Waltham Abbey) does not include him in the list of those of their acquaintance who had sickened there. It has been claimed that he was taken ill while playing truant from court to go hunting,[94] but there is no contemporary evidence to support this, or the assertion that Carey was one of those 'left to die in manors Henry successively abandoned in his scramble for safety'.[95]

If William Carey had been left behind at Greenwich – which seems probable, as Thomas Heneage was with him – the likelihood is that Mary was there too. If she, Heneage or anyone else had had the courage to minister to William, they would probably have followed contemporary advice to tuck the fully clothed patient warmly in bed in a room with a roaring fire, so that he could sweat out the illness, which must have been misery on a June day; or to give him beer, treacle, herbs, or exotic potions made from powdered sapphires or gold. Or they might have tried the King's own herbal remedy for the sweat, and the pills of Rhazis (named after an Arab physician) that he had recommended to Cardinal Wolsey.[96] At all costs, the patient was to be kept awake and not allowed to lapse into a coma.

In this case, any curative measures were in vain, for on Monday, 22 June 1528, 'in this great plague, died William Carey Esquire, whom the King highly favoured'.[97] He was thirty-two. The end had come with deadly swiftness: Jean du Bellay, the French ambassador, reporting that 'many of [the King's] people died within three or four hours', names Carey as one of them.[98] Thomas Heneage, who was apparently present at the end, informed Wolsey the next day that the dying Carey had uttered a final wish, humbly beseeching the Cardinal 'to be a good and gracious lord to his sister, a nun in Wilton Abbey, to be Prioress there, according to your Grace's promise'.[99] Evidently William had not expected Eleanor to be successful in her bid to be Abbess, and he may have had good reason for that.

'This night, as the King went to bed, word came of the death of William Carey,' wrote Cardinal Wolsey from Hunsdon to Heneage. Henry must have been deeply saddened by the news, which would surely have filled him with dread, knowing that his beloved Anne was suffering from the same deadly illness. Anne, however, was luckier than her brother-in-law: by the time Dr Butts arrived, she was on the mend, and the following morning the King was given the good news that she and her father were 'past the danger' and making 'a perfect recovery'.[100] Henry wrote to Anne to tell her that John Carey, William's brother, had also fallen ill of the sweat – and recovered.

The epidemic had carried off not only William Carey, but also two more of the King's most favoured gentlemen of the Privy Chamber, Sir William Compton and Sir Edward Poyntz. In each case, a promising career was cut tragically short – and Henry had lost three of his friends.

William Carey's last resting place is not recorded. Probably his body was hurriedly consigned to a grave pit with others who had succumbed to the sweating sickness. Given the danger and fear of contagion, it is unlikely that his remains were accorded a more fitting burial with his ancestors in Wiltshire.

Mary may not have mourned her husband deeply. Their arranged marriage was probably not a love match to begin with, and there is no evidence that it ever became one. Nevertheless, had William Carey lived, and continued in the King's favour, he could, on past form, have risen very high indeed, and might – once Anne Boleyn became Queen in 1533 – have won greater rewards[101] and possibly even been elevated to the peerage. Then Mary's life would have been very different. Instead of incurring further opprobrium and fading into obscurity, she might well have ended her days as one of the great ladies of the land.

Instead, she had been left poor and in debt by the death of her husband, who died intestate; and she had two young children to support.

10

'In Bondage'

The lands granted to William Carey by the King were inherited by his lawful, acknowledged heir, three-year-old Henry Carey.[1] William had not been a man of substance. In March 1527, as we have seen, his lands had been valued for a subsidy at just £333.6s.8d (£107,500).[2] These became the property of his heir. His lucrative offices and keeperships, along with their revenues, immediately reverted to the Crown, and suit was at once made for them after his death.[3] For Mary, there was nothing, and probably nowhere to live, as she had no right to stay in the courtier lodging that had been assigned to her husband. All she had to survive on were the rents from his Essex manor,[4] and the annuity from Tynemouth Priory.

She appealed several times to her father for succour, but Thomas Boleyn remained impervious to her pleas, and would not even receive her. It may well be that, as has been suggested, 'his affection for his children lasted only as long as they were useful to him',[5] for he appears to have proved that, in regard to Mary, on several occasions. Possibly he felt there was no mileage in wasting his wealth on someone who could bring him no advantage, even if she was his daughter; he might too have realised that, as she was poor and probably past thirty – middle-aged by Tudor standards – Mary would now find it hard to secure a worthy husband, and could end up being at his charge for good. Or they may have quarrelled, possibly because he had disapproved of her affair with the King. She had not only compromised her honour a second time, but 'had not collected on her investment'.[6] This theory is even more credible if, outraged at her risking her good name at the French court, Thomas had sent Mary to rusticate at Brie in 1515.

By Tudor standards, Mary had been promiscuous, and it is easy to see why her father, her sister, her family and Henry VIII all saw her as an embarrassment. It has credibly been suggested that her ambitious parents had even 'developed feelings of dislike' for her,[7] and that Sir Thomas's treatment of Mary strengthened Anne's resolve not to give in to the King and so end up like her sister.[8]

It is unfair to state that 'William Carey dead made rather more impact than he had living',[9] yet his death revealed how fully Henry trusted Anne Boleyn's 'judgement and ability to manage things'.[10] Early in July, the King granted her the wardship and marriage of Henry Carey.[11]

Making provision for fatherless heirs to estates was the responsibility of the sovereign. In Tudor times, a grant of wardship gave the guardian custody of the lands of his or her ward during the child's minority, until he reached the age of twenty-one, and the right to use the income from them. In return, the guardian was obliged to maintain the estates of the ward and ensure that he was properly cared for and educated. Putative guardians usually paid a hefty fee for the privilege of acquiring a wardship, which could prove highly lucrative and repay the investment with interest. Wardships were vigorously enforced by the Tudor monarchs, who used them to increase their personal revenue. In 1535, Henry VIII passed the Statute of Uses, which asserted the rights of the Crown over wards, and in 1540, he founded the Court of Wards to regulate the system. In the case of Henry Carey, it is likely that the wardship was a gift from the King for the lady with whom he was by now so besotted that he would have given her anything within his power.

Thraldom aside, Henry was right in thinking that Anne would be far more more able and better placed to do much for her nephew than his impoverished and possibly unambitious mother, whom he clearly judged less competent and in no good position to exercise control of her son's lands and income. This would hardly have taken 'a great weight off Mary's mind',[12] and relieved her of the burden of providing for her son,[13] for it deprived her of the use of his revenues, which had been diverted to her sister, and left Mary in penury and with no legal authority over her child. Above all, it can only have caused bad blood between the sisters, and given Mary further cause for envy or jealousy.

To his credit, the King made Thomas Boleyn face up to his responsibilities as a father. Around 15 June, having evidently discussed the problem of Mary with Anne, he wrote to her: 'As touching your sister's matter, I have caused Walter Walshe to write to my Lord [Rochford] mine mind therein; whereby I trust that Eve shall not have power to deceive Adam; for surely whatsoever is said, it cannot so stand with his honour, but that he must needs take her, his natural daughter, now in her extreme necessity.'[14]

The King's reference to Eve deceiving Adam has been seen as moralising on Henry's part about Mary as 'a sinful Eve',[15] or as evidence that Mary had been unfaithful to her husband. It has been asserted that the words 'whatsoever is said' refer to gossip about Mary's poor reputation, and suggest that questions were being raised 'as to whether she [Eve] would prove to be pregnant', and, if so, whether or not the child was her husband's – or if Mary was pretending to be pregnant in order to obtain help from her father.[16] Whilst these possibilities are all plausible, there is no proof to support them, or that Mary had 'drifted from one unsavoury situation to another at the Tudor court',[17] and a deeper reading of the letter suggests that Henry's words probably do not refer to Mary at all, but imply that some female – possibly Mary's own mother – was influencing her father against her.[18] Clearly Henry did not want 'Eve' – whoever she was – to prejudice Sir Thomas Boleyn against his daughter. If he had been referring to Mary, he would surely have wanted her to keep quiet about anything that might do that, because he wanted Sir Thomas to help her. This was hardly a 'cavalier attitude'[19] towards his former mistress.

Boleyn now had no choice but to take Mary under his roof and maintain her, and it seems that she returned to Hever Castle. But on 10 December 1528, again at Anne's behest, Henry assigned Mary a substantial annuity of £100 that had formerly been paid to her late husband.[20] This was a generous gesture, since £100 in present-day values would be the equivalent of at least £32,000. It gives the lie to those who claim that Mary got nothing out of her affair with the King. For Henry had no need or obligation to assign that allowance to her. Her father had been constrained to be responsible for her, and she was living under his roof, at his charge. Her son's future had been assured by the grant of his wardship to her sister Anne. Why, then, was Henry so generous?

Was it to please his new love, Anne Boleyn? Probably, to a degree. But it is also possible that the King was making provision for Katherine Carey, now that William Carey was no longer around to be a surrogate father to a royal bastard. That would certainly account for Henry's open-handedness, which is comparable to the inexplicably large grant that he made to Etheldreda Malte, who was almost certainly his bastard daughter, some eighteen years later. Bolstered by the other circumstantial evidence, this is one of the most compelling arguments for Henry's paternity of Katherine Carey.

Mary now had a comfortable income – her father, with his ever-expanding family, had once existed on half that amount. There is no record of her leaving the parental roof for a house of her own, though; it seems she stayed at Hever Castle, notwithstanding her father's diffident attitude towards her, and, probably, her mother's. Later, she was to refer to her life at this time as being 'in bondage'. Maybe she stayed for the sake of her daughter, so that she could put money by for her – Katherine would need a dowry one day, and the greater it was, the more chance she would have of making a good match. And Thomas Boleyn was often away at court, leaving behind him a household of women: his burdensome daughter Mary; his possibly estranged wife, who may have resented Mary's presence at Hever; his insane and ageing mother; and his four-year-old fatherless granddaughter. It cannot have been the happiest of households.

No one seems to have made an effort to find Mary a second husband, even though she now had a reasonable fortune and powerful connections.[21] But Thomas Boleyn had shown himself somewhat laggardly in arranging marriages for both his daughters when they were younger, so may not have felt inclined to bestir himself now on the unrewarding Mary's behalf; and it may be that, as the 1530s approached and her affair with the King became the subject of whispered court gossip, prospective suitors were put off. Few landed Tudor gentlemen wanted flighty wives who might compromise their inheritance.

With William Carey dead, Anne Boleyn was ready once more to take up the cudgels on behalf of his sister Eleanor's advancement, using it to score a point over the man she regarded as her secret adversary, Cardinal Wolsey. Wolsey, however, had pre-empted her and sent a commissioner, Dr John Bell, Archdeacon of Gloucester, to Wilton to examine the nuns and arrange matters to his satisfaction;

he supported the view of most of the convent that the Prioress, Dame Isabel Jordan, was the best candidate.

At the abbey, Bell interviewed Eleanor Carey, and (as Henry VIII later informed Anne Boleyn) she 'confessed herself to have had two children by two sundry priests', and that she had recently left her convent for a time to live with a servant of Lord Willoughby de Broke as his mistress.[22] Bell then considered the merits of Eleanor's older sister, Dame Anne Carey, but she too was found to have loose morals. Clearly, both sisters were prime examples of women with no vocation who had been pushed into a convent by their family, possibly because the latter could not afford a dowry for them, or because they wished to dedicate a child to God in return for blessings they believed He had bestowed on them – or even, in this case especially, to hush up scandal.[23] The Carey sisters' conduct is symptomatic of the kind of laxity that would soon be made *prima facie* grounds for the dissolution of the monasteries.

The fact that William Carey, on his deathbed, had asked for Wolsey's help in making Eleanor Prioress, rather than Abbess, suggests he had been aware that she would be lucky to get either. It might be inferred from this that he had known about her promiscuous life; if so, then pushing for her election to high office marks out both him and his brother John as pragmatic men with few ethical scruples. One is tempted to wonder if William had taken a similar view of Mary's adulterous affairs, and if his ambition had overridden any resentment or distaste he may have felt.

When the King found out the truth about Eleanor Carey and her sister, he commanded – in the interests of placating his beloved – that neither they nor Isabel Jordan should be Abbess, on the grounds that all three had at some time been guilty of misconduct; possibly Anne's partisans had either made it up about the Prioress or had raked up some old scandal,[24] but in the light of this revelation, Henry wrote to Anne to explain the situation, saying he would not, 'for all the gold in the world, clog your conscience nor mine to make [Dame Eleanor] ruler of a house which is of such ungodly demeanour; nor, I trust, you would not that, neither for brother nor sister, I should so distain mine honour or conscience'.[25] His reference to 'brother or sister' implies that Mary had put pressure on Anne, on her sister-in-law's behalf, and that George Boleyn too was supporting Eleanor. From this, it might be inferred that the King was irritated by Mary's interference.[26]

And [Henry went on], as touching the Prioress [Isabel Jordan], or Dame Eleanor's eldest sister, though there is not any evident case proved against them, and that the Prioress is so old, that of many years she could not be as she was named; yet, notwithstanding, to do you pleasure, I have done that neither of them shall have it, but some other good and well disposed woman, [and] the house shall be better reformed, and God the much better served.[27]

Anne was most put out, therefore, when, in July 1528, Wolsey forced the election of the Prioress, Dame Isabel Jordan.[28] This earned him, on 14 July, a scorching reproof from the King, who had been well aware of Anne's preference for Eleanor Carey,[29] for it seemed that the Cardinal had gone out of his way to offend her. The next day, Wolsey made a grovelling apology to Henry for his hasty action, and hastened to send Anne 'a kind letter' and a 'rich and goodly present', for which she thanked him profusely in an extravagantly worded response;[30] and thus the matter was diplomatically brought to a satisfactory conclusion – for Wolsey at least. Even the late William Carey could not have complained about the passing over of his naughty sister.

By November, when the furore had died down, Isabel Jordan had been quietly installed as Abbess.[31]

For a time, Mary Boleyn apparently resided at Hever, living on the King's pension, rearing her daughter Katherine and coming to terms with her widowhood. Her son may have been left in her care until it was time for his education to begin; he was, after all, rather young to be parted from his mother.

Very little is recorded of Mary during the six years of her widowhood. She was a silent witness to the meteoric career of her sister Anne and the ascendancy of her family, but either she preferred to remain in the background, or it was deemed fitting by others that she should do so. It has been perspicaciously observed that, 'in the brilliant advancement of her sister, she seems to have been eclipsed and neglected'.[32] She is not mentioned at court for a long time, and it may be that, while Anne remained in her anomalous position – neither mistress nor wife and queen – she was not wanted there, even to attend upon her sister. Secrecy about Mary's affair, and the dispensation covering it, had been successfully maintained for several

years, but somehow or other, as the furore over the divorce esca-
lated, word got around that the King had kept Anne Boleyn's sister
as his mistress. Although their affair would never become an open
scandal, there was talk of it at court, at the very least. The presence
of the former mistress with whom Henry shared a compromising
bond of affinity might have been just too uncomfortable for him,
and the Boleyns, at a time when a favourable decision from the Pope
was eagerly anticipated.

Gossip was already lively in 1529. After the new Imperial ambassador, Eustache Chapuys – a man who was to prove indefatigable
in Queen Katherine's cause – arrived in England that year, it did
not take him long to find out about Henry's relations with Mary
Boleyn. In December, he wrote to the Emperor: 'Had [the King], as
he asserts, only attended to the voice of conscience, there would
have been still greater affinity to contend with in this intended
marriage than in that of the Queen, his wife; a fact of which everyone
here speaks quite openly.'[33]

As he often did, Chapuys was probably exaggerating when he
referred to 'everyone', as many courtiers would surely not have deemed
it politic publicly to cast aspersions on the King's doubts of conscience;
and the gossip could not have been that widespread, since other
sources would have recorded it, and Henry's opponents – not to
mention the Queen – would have made more political capital out
of it. As it was, only two people are known to have spoken of Mary
Boleyn: George Throckmorton and John Hale. As we have seen, in
1533, Elizabeth Amadas, whose husband was goldsmith to the King,
and the priest at Chepax, Yorkshire, were not aware of Henry VIII's
affair with Mary Boleyn. Yet even with all this discretion being maintained, the revelation that Henry stood in the same degree of affinity
to Anne as he did to Katherine must, in certain privileged circles,
have undermined his credibility, integrity and sincerity. Nor can the
inevitable besmirching of Mary Boleyn's public reputation have done
anything for that of her sister, which had already, in the eyes of many,
been severely compromised.

In January 1530, when Charles V received Chapuys' report, he
summoned Dr Richard Sampson (later Bishop of Chichester), the
English ambassador at his court, and declared that Henry VIII's scruples of conscience did not appear to be justified, especially 'if it were
true, as his Majesty had heard (although he himself would not posi-
tively affirm it), that the King had kept company with the sister of

her whom he now wanted to marry'. Sampson, who enjoyed Anne
Boleyn's patronage, did not respond to this challenge.[34] The Emperor,
understandably, was not satisfied, but he let the matter rest there,
being preoccupied with other, more pressing business and about to
leave for Bologna for his long-delayed crowning by the Pope.[35] It is
one of the great enigmas of the divorce that Charles V never made
an issue of the King's affair with Mary Boleyn; yet the reason may
lie in Charles's doubts as to whether there had actually been one.

On 8 December 1529, Thomas Boleyn was created Earl of Wiltshire
and Earl of Ormond,[36] and Mary became entitled to style herself
Lady (or Dame) Mary Rochford, after his subsidiary title,[37] which
would soon pass to his son, George, who had been knighted in 1529
and was created Viscount Rochford before July 1530. All the Boleyn
siblings now used the badge of a black lion rampant, as previous
heirs to the earldom of Ormond had done.[38] From henceforth,
Thomas Boleyn, Earl of Wiltshire, would be one of the chief peers
of the realm, and would continue to serve the King energetically at
home and abroad, and to advance the fortunes of his daughter Anne
and himself.

In November 1530, Henry VIII gave Anne Boleyn £20 (£6,500)
to redeem a jewel from Mary;[39] either it was one he had given her
during the course of their affair, or – more likely – she had won it
from him by gambling.[40]

The following summer, Henry VIII sent Katherine of Aragon away
from court; he would never see her again, nor would she be permitted
contact with her daughter, the Princess Mary. That Christmas, people
remarked on the absence of mirth from the festivities at Greenwich,
without the banished Queen and her ladies being present; even Anne
Boleyn was absent, but on New Year's Day 1532, she returned to
court and was 'lodged where the Queen used to be, and is accompanied by almost as many ladies as if she were Queen'.[41] For his
New Year's gift, Henry gave her a room splendidly hung with cloth
of gold and silver and heavy embroidered satin. All the Boleyns
presented Henry with gifts, and in return for her present of 'a shirt
with a black collar', which she may have stitched herself, 'Lady Mary
Rochford' received from Henry a piece of gilt plate, either a cup,
salt cellar, bottle or goblet.[42] Being the recipient of such a gift on
this occasion strongly suggests that Mary was back at court, probably as one of Anne's vast train of ladies, and other evidence shows

that she was periodically in attendance on her sister from this time – if she had not been before.

The name 'Mary Rochford' also appears in the list of recipients for New Year's gifts in 1534; the list for 1533 is missing, but doubtless she featured in that too.[43]

On 7 October 1532, when Henry VIII rode out from Greenwich on the first stage of his journey to Calais to meet once more with François I, taking with him Anne Boleyn and two thousand lords, gentlemen and attendants, Mary went too, as one of the twenty or thirty[44] ladies whom the King had summoned to accompany his 'dearest and most beloved cousin', as he diplomatically referred to Anne.[45] The Boleyn sisters' uncle, Thomas Howard, Duke of Norfolk, was also in the King's entourage.[46]

When Anne had assembled her train of ladies in August, she had written to Mary, bidding her to prepare for the journey, and confiding to her that 'that which I have so long wished for will be accomplished'.[47] She had high hopes of King François using his influence with the Pope on Henry's behalf, and she was also aware that, with the death of William Warham, Archbishop of Canterbury, that month, a major obstacle to Henry's taking matters into his own hands had been fortuitously removed. Even before that, there had been speculation at court that the King himself would declare his marriage to Katherine null and void and marry Anne. But, Chapuys wrote to the Emperor on 9 August, 'even if he could separate from the Queen, he could not have her, for he has had to do with her sister'.[48] Evidently Chapuys did not know about the dispensation issued in 1528, while Charles V seems to have continued to pay little heed to what he probably dismissed as scurrilous gossip.

After spending a night at Stone in Kent, where Bridget, Lady Wingfield, entertained the royal party at her castle, the great cavalcade, more than two thousand strong, rode on to Canterbury, where Mary probably witnessed Elizabeth Barton, the notorious 'Nun of Kent', publicly declaiming her seditious prophecies before the King, who merely ignored her and went on his way to the house of Sir Christopher Hales, where he and Anne, and probably Mary too, lodged overnight.

Before dawn on 11 October, after spending the third night of the journey in Dover Castle, Mary sailed to France on *The Swallow* with her sister and the King; the weather was good. It was a smooth

crossing, and the royal party made land at Calais at ten o'clock in
the morning, to be greeted by a thunderous royal salute.[49] They were
afforded a civic reception by John Bourchier, Lord Berners, the
Governor of Calais, and then conducted in a torchlit procession to
the church of St Nicholas to hear Mass. Mary was accommodated
with Anne's other attendants in the seven fine rooms assigned to her
sister in the Exchequer Palace in Calais.[50] This was a large residence
with a long gallery, a tennis court, and gardens on both the King's
and Queen's sides of the building.[51]

Being in such close daily proximity to Anne and the King, Mary
may well have been aware that Henry and Anne had interconnecting
bedchambers,[52] proof that Anne – who now had marriage within
her sights, with the prospect of the Boleyns' chaplain, the sympathetic reformist Thomas Cranmer, becoming Archbishop of
Canterbury – had at last surrendered to the King. '[He] cannot be
an hour without her,' Chapuys observed,[53] while a Venetian envoy
reported that Henry was now accompanying Anne to Mass *and every-
where* [author's italics], as though she were Queen already.[54]

François I was to bring no train of ladies with him to Calais; his
second Queen, Eleanor of Austria, was the Emperor's sister and
Katherine of Aragon's niece, and under no circumstances would she
have been willing to receive Anne Boleyn. The other French royal
ladies had shown equal disdain, and so Anne and her female attendants perforce had no official place in the proceedings, and had to
be left behind at Calais when Henry sallied forth to Boulogne to
spend four days with his brother monarch. But Anne made the best
of a bad situation, and throughout the ten days of merrymaking that
marked their stay, Mary would have joined the courtiers in hawking,
gambling and feasting on delicacies sent by the French: carp, porpoise,
venison pasties, choice pears and grapes.

On Friday, 25 October, King Henry arrived back at Calais, bringing
King François with him. It seems that Anne and her ladies were not
present at the lavish welcome ceremonies, although they would have
heard the three-thousand-gun salute fired in the French King's honour,
and Anne would have been gratified to receive the costly diamond
he sent her by the Provost of Paris.

François was lodged in the Staple Inn on the main square of
Calais, some way from the Exchequer Palace. Here, on the evening
of 27 October, Mary attended her sister at a lavish supper and banquet
given by Henry in the great hall in honour of the French King. The

hall looked magnificent, hung with gold and silver tissue and gold wreaths glittering with pearls and precious stones, which reflected the light from the twenty silver candelabra, each bearing a hundred wax candles. A dazzling display of gold plate adorned a seven-tier buffet. Henry VIII was dressed to impress too, in purple cloth of gold with a collar of fourteen rubies and two great ropes of pearls, from one of which hung the famous Black Prince's ruby (now set in St Edward's crown, which is used for coronations). The company feasted on 170 dishes, with a lavish variety of meats, game and fish cooked according to English or French recipes.

Afterwards, Mary and five other ladies took part in a masque led by Anne, who made her entrance in an outfit of cloth of gold slashed with crimson satin, puffed with cloth of silver and laced with gold cords. 'My Lady Mary' followed immediately in Anne's wake,[55] having been given precedence over the ladies of higher rank, no doubt to underline the fact that her sister was soon to be the Queen of England. Mary and her fellow performers were dressed alike in gorgeous costumes 'of strange fashion', comprising loose gowns of cloth of gold slashed with crimson tinsel laced in gold, and all wore masks. Among these ladies were Mary's sister-in-law, Jane Parker, Lady Rochford, her cousin, Lady Mary Howard (Norfolk's daughter), her Howard aunts – Dorothy, Countess of Derby, and Elizabeth, Lady FitzWalter – and Honor Grenville, Lady Lisle. These ladies were escorted by four maids of honour wearing crimson satin and black tabards of cypress lawn.

The ladies danced before the two kings, and afterwards, Anne boldly advanced to King François and led him out on to the floor, at which Mary and her companions invited King Henry and the other gentlemen present to join them, the Countess of Derby choosing Henri d'Albret, King of Navarre, François' brother-in-law. We do not know if Mary actually danced with Henry VIII on this occasion, but the King did take great pleasure in removing the ladies' masks afterwards 'so that [their] beauties were showed'. After an hour spent dancing, King François had a long private conversation with Anne.[56]

The next day, the two kings met to attend a chapter meeting of the Order of the Garter and to watch a wrestling match, and on the morning of 29 October, Henry escorted François to the French border, where they said their farewells.

It is possible that, during her sojourn in Calais, Mary met William Stafford, the man who was to become her second husband, who was

then one of two hundred persons in the King's retinue.[57] It is sometimes averred that he was serving as a soldier with the Calais garrison
at this time, but he does not seem to have taken up that post until
after June 1533.[58] Mary was later to reveal that it was Stafford who
pursued her and fell in love with her before she did with him; but
although William was distantly related to the noble family of Stafford,
he was no match for the daughter of an earl and sister of a future
queen. And even if some attraction and kindness – and perhaps a
more intimate connection – did spring up between him and Mary
in Calais, nothing was to come of it for some time.

Violent storms in the Channel forced the English court to stay
on at the Exchequer for a further fortnight,[59] allowing Henry and
Anne time to enjoy what was essentially their honeymoon, and
perhaps affording Mary and her new suitor the opportunity to get
to know each other better. The idyll came to an end at midnight
on 12 November, when the King seized the opportunity afforded
by a favourable wind to sail home to England. The voyage took
twenty-nine hours, and after landing at Dover, Mary rode through
Kent with the royal party at a leisurely pace, lodging at Leeds Castle
and Stone Castle before finally arriving at Eltham Palace on 24
November.[60] Soon afterwards, the King returned to London.

In January 1533, learning that Anne was pregnant, Henry secretly
married her in a turret room in York Place, with her parents, her
brother, Lord Rochford, and 'two favourites'[61] as witnesses; it has
been suggested that Mary was one of them,[62] but if so, she would
surely have been listed with the family members, rather than being
described as a 'favourite'. Certainly contemporary sources do not
convey the impression that she was a favourite with Anne and the
King, and although it might follow that Anne would have her sister
and perhaps her sister-in-law as attendants, there were others to
whom she was closer; the favourites might even have been gentlemen
of the King's Privy Chamber, men such as Sir Henry Norris, Sir
Nicholas Carew or Sir Francis Bryan.

The King, convinced that his marriage to Katherine was invalid,
and aware that his longed-for heir was on its way, had not waited
for the formalities. Even so, it was some weeks before his new
Archbishop of Canterbury, Thomas Cranmer, declared his marriage
to Katherine null and void, and his union with Anne lawful. Anne
first appeared in public as Queen at Easter 1533, much to many

people's shock and consternation, and Henry afforded her a lavish coronation in June.

Prior to that, when Anne was assigned a household of two hundred persons, Mary Boleyn was among her ladies-in-waiting, in company with their sister-in-law, Lady Rochford; Lady Margaret Douglas, the King's niece; Lady Mary Howard, daughter of the Duke of Norfolk and cousin to the Boleyn sisters; Frances de Vere, who was married to another cousin, Norfolk's heir, Henry Howard, Earl of Surrey; Mary Shelton, daughter of Sir John Shelton by Mary Boleyn's aunt, Anne Boleyn; another aunt, Elizabeth Wood, wife of Sir James Boleyn; Anne Savage, Lady Berkeley and Elizabeth Browne, Countess of Worcester,[63] whose testimony would help to bring about Anne Boleyn's downfall three years hence. One of the maids of honour was Jane Seymour, who would one day become Henry VIII's third wife.[64]

The fact that Anne was willing to have her sister wait upon her is perhaps further evidence that Mary's liaison with Henry VIII was more a passing fancy than a grand passion, or an affair of the heart. Anne is hardly likely to have wanted a woman for whom her husband had entertained strong feelings brought into daily proximity to him, sister or no. And Mary is hardly likely to have wanted to be in that position, especially if she had loved Henry, or he had abandoned her.

Aware of the need to give the lie to her poor reputation, Anne demanded that her ladies be above reproach. She gave them each a little book of prayers and psalms to hang at their girdles. She kept them busy sewing garments for the poor for hours on end. They were to attend Mass daily and display 'a virtuous demeanour'.[65] Anne's silk-woman later claimed that she had never seen 'better order amongst the ladies and gentlewomen of the court than in Anne Boleyn's day'.[66] Yet Mary's life was not all dullness, for there was much 'pastime in the Queen's chamber'[67] as well as courtly revelry, dancing and feasting. And, as the Queen's sister, she must have enjoyed a certain status.

Yet it is clear that Mary did not feel appreciated by Anne, or by anyone else for that matter. In contrast to her successful siblings, Mary was the one who had compromised her reputation and done very little since to win respect or admiration. Only a year later, she was to write, 'I saw that all the world did set so little by me.'[68] That implies a lack of self-worth, and we might even go so far as to imagine her not only having to endure the disapproval and disappointment of her family, but also secretly being despised by the courtiers who flocked around the brilliant Anne.

Mary's presence at court may have been disturbing to the King, not because he still cherished feelings for her, but because the implications of their affair continued to haunt him. Now that he had broken with Rome, he was clearly concerned that the legality of his marriage should be beyond question, and in 1533, he had Parliament pass an Act permitting marriage with the sister of a discarded mistress.[69] But the Act did not put a stop to gossip about his affair with Mary, which now seems to have spread beyond the court, for that year saw several people arrested for accusing the King of marrying the sister of his former mistress.[70] The weight this lent to public disapproval of the marriage should not be underestimated.

Mary was one of the 'divers ladies and gentlewomen' who attended Anne at her coronation. The celebrations began on 29 May with a magnificent river pageant. At three o'clock, royally garbed in cloth of gold, the new Queen stepped into the barge she had appropriated from Katherine of Aragon, at Greenwich Palace, and was conveyed along the River Thames to the Tower of London, where – as tradition decreed – she would lodge before her coronation. Mary and the other ladies travelled with her, along with their father and many other noblemen. As Anne alighted at the Tower, to be greeted 'with joyful countenance' by the King, the cannon on Tower Wharf were fired in a 'marvellous' salute.[71]

Two days later, Mary was in Anne's train as she went in procession through the streets of London to Westminster. She was not among the six ladies who rode on horseback immediately behind the new Queen and the chief officers of her household, although her sister-in-law, Lady Rochford, by virtue of her rank, was of their number. Mary, in a rich gown of scarlet velvet – a costly material that, as the daughter of an earl, and a lady of the Queen's privy chamber, she was entitled to wear – was relegated to the third of the chariots that followed, travelling with other ladies of the Queen's household: her aunt, Lady Boleyn;[72] Elizabeth Wentworth, Lady FitzWarin; Mary Zouche; Margery Horsman and Alice St John, Lady Morley.[73]

Along the route, the Queen and her entourage were entertained by lavish pageants, tableaux and music. But Anne was not popular, and although crowds had gathered, they watched in silent disapproval. According to one account, fewer than ten people greeted the Queen with 'God save your Grace!' In fact, when they saw the entwined initial letters of Henry and Anne on the triumphal arches along the route, they jeered, 'Ha! Ha!'[74]

The triumphal progress ended at Westminster Hall. Here, Anne was led to the high dais under the cloth of estate, where 'subtleties with Hippocras and other wines' were served to her, which she sent down to her ladies. When they had drunk their fill, she gave them hearty thanks, and then withdrew with a few of the most privileged – of whom Mary must have been one – to the White Hall, as the great hall at the Palace of Westminster was known.[75]

The next day, 1 June 1533, Anne was crowned in a magnificent ceremony in Westminster Abbey. Dressed in crimson and purple velvet, she was received by the clergy at Westminster Hall and escorted by them to the abbey, followed by several noblewomen on palfreys or in chariots, and then by Mary and the Queen's other ladies, all attired in 'robes and gowns of scarlet'.[76] After the crowning, these ladies accompanied her back to Westminster Hall for the solemn feast that followed.

Despite all that Henry had done in order to marry her, Anne presented him, on 7 September 1533, not with the son he so desperately desired, but with a daughter, named Elizabeth for the King's mother, Elizabeth of York, and probably for Elizabeth Howard also. Her birth must have been a cataclysmic disappointment, but Henry put on a brave face and arranged a splendid christening in the church of the Observant Friars at Greenwich Palace. The Boleyns were there in force, with Wiltshire supporting his granddaughter's long train and his son Rochford helping to carry the canopy of estate above her head. Mary Boleyn was probably one of the 'many ladies and gentle-women' who followed in the procession. It may be significant that she was assigned no important role either at the coronation of her sister or the christening of her niece – which one might reasonably have expected, given her closeness in blood to the Queen. Maybe that was her own wish, given her growing reputation, but her family too, for other reasons, probably did not want to draw public atten-tion to the sister who had been the King's mistress. Perhaps Mary was content to have things that way, for the Boleyns were not popular. 'There is little love for the one who is Queen now, or for any of her race,' observed the French ambassador that November.[77]

It is possible that Katherine Carey, who was nine when the Princess Elizabeth was born, spent the next six years, until she was summoned

to court, in her little cousin's household,[78] which was set up at
Hatfield Palace, Hertfordshire, in December 1533, and thereafter
perambulated between the nursery palaces of the Thames Valley. Being
in this early close proximity may in part account for Elizabeth's great
affection for Katherine in later life.[79] For Mary, this would have
meant separation from her daughter, but for women of the aristocratic class, that was nothing unusual, for girls of good family were
often sent to be reared and educated in great households, and Mary
would have had the consolation of knowing that she was affording
her daughter the very best grounding for the future.

But Elizabeth was not long to enjoy her exalted status as Henry's
legitimate heir. Even before her birth, cracks had appeared in her
parents' marriage. Anne, once won, had clearly been a disappointment. Henry's discovery that she had been 'corrupted' in France[80]
must have disillusioned him early on, while she had clearly found it
difficult to make the transition from a mistress with the upper hand
to the meek and submissive wife he now expected her to be. It took
only months for Henry's long-cherished passion to dissipate, and
during Anne's pregnancy, following true to previous form, he had
taken a mistress, telling her to shut her eyes as more worthy persons
had done, and that he could lower her as much as he had raised
her.[81]

The implications for the Boleyns were chilling.

11

'High Displeasure'

By September 1534, relations between the King and Queen had become even more tense. In the late summer, Anne had lost a baby – probably a son – at full term, another crushing disappointment for Henry VIII, who had strayed again during her second pregnancy, sleeping with 'a beautiful and adroit young lady for whom his love is daily increasing',[1] but whose name is not recorded. Anne's influence was clearly declining, and she must have realised that Henry's great passion for her was dying, so she had many reasons to be humiliated – and furious – when, in September 1534,[2] Mary appeared at court noticeably pregnant. After six years of widowhood, she had done 'the one thing a lady of breeding could not explain'.[3]

Mary could explain, however. She confessed that she had secretly, and of necessity, married – for love – plain Mr William Stafford of Grafton, a younger son of knightly birth with no fortune. Marrying for love – as Mary Tudor had once done, setting Mary Boleyn a dangerous example – was then regarded as the most rash and imprudent conduct[4] – and Anne had good cause to be horrified and furious, for Stafford was certainly no match for the Queen's sister.

Friedmann believed that Mary only pretended to be married to William Stafford to cover the shame of her illicit pregnancy, but there is ample evidence in official documents that the pair were legally wed, and that, besides being in love, and being loved in return, Mary was glad to escape the miserable 'bondage' of her widowhood and her dependence on her avaricious and begrudging father.[5]

William Stafford had been present as one of 'the knights and gentlemen summoned to be servitors' at Anne Boleyn's coronation on 1 June 1533,[6] and it was probably on that occasion – or at the great feast in Westminster Hall that followed – that he encountered Mary Boleyn, possibly not for the first time. As has been mooted, they may have met before, when they were both in Calais in the autumn of 1532, but it is unlikely that they had become acquainted much earlier, even though William was in the King's retinue and had relatives residing in Kent,[7] for Mary hints in a letter written late in 1534 that she had known him only for a 'little time'.[8]

Fit and strong, as became one of his soldierly profession,[9] and apparently a man of loyalty with a volatile temperament, William was probably at least twelve years younger than Mary, yet – as she was to reveal in 1534 – he became smitten and eager to marry her, while she at length responded to his ardour and high regard, which clearly went a long way towards restoring her sense of self-esteem. Theirs was obviously a true love match – it may have been Mary's first experience of being in love[10] – and their feelings for each other were strong enough to override any fears they may have had for the consequences of their secret marriage, and the hardships they might – and would – endure in the face of William's poverty.[11]

William Stafford was a minor courtier, a Gentleman Usher to the King,[12] and the second son of a relatively obscure member of a family that, despite sharing the same surname, was related only through two marriages, made in the thirteenth and fourteenth centuries,[13] to the noble house of Stafford. William's father, Sir Humphrey Stafford of Cottered and Rushden, Hertfordshire, some-time Sheriff of Northamptonshire, was the son of an attainted traitor who had perished at Tyburn in 1486, on the orders of Henry VII, for having supported Richard III, and whose confiscated lands were given to Sir Edward Poynings. Sir Humphrey had then been just eight years old,[14] but he had laboured long and hard to restore his family to royal favour, until finally, in 1515, Henry VIII reversed his father's attainder and restored some of his lands, including the manors of Milton Keynes, Buckinghamshire; Bourton-on-Dunsmore, Warwickshire; and Chebsey in Staffordshire.

Sir Humphrey married well, his first wife being Margaret, the daughter of Sir John Fogge of Ashford, Kent, and London, Treasurer of the Household to King Edward IV (Henry VIII's grandfather), Privy Councillor, Keeper of the Writs, Knight of the Shire for Kent and M.P. for Canterbury. Margaret Fogge's mother was Alice, who was the daughter of William Haute by Joan Wydeville, and therefore first cousin to Elizabeth Wydeville, Edward IV's Queen. William Stafford, born in or before 1512, was thus third cousin to Henry VIII.

Despite this, and the loyalty, pragmatism and talents that would later make him a good husband, courtier and diplomat, William had little to recommend him. He was not even a knight at this time, but a mere freeholder of Cardinal Wolsey's manor of Tickford,[15] now part of Newport Pagnell in Buckinghamshire. His name was doubly tainted by treason, for he was a distant relation of Edward Stafford, Duke of Buckingham, who had gone to the block in 1521 for allegedly conspiring to seize the throne. Since then, Henry VIII had looked with suspicion on the Staffords, for the senior line had Plantagenet blood and were too close for comfort to the throne – and they had been over-supportive of his first wife, Katherine of Aragon.

William's chief disadvantage, though, was that he was a landless nobody, a simple soldier. His older brother, another Sir Humphrey, was Esquire of the Body to the King and heir to the Stafford lands; in 1517, he inherited the manors of Blatherwycke and Dodford, both in Northamptonshire, from his great-uncle, Thomas Stafford.

William is often referred to in genealogies as 'William Stafford of Grafton' or 'William Stafford of Chebsey', but this is not wholly correct. Grafton in Worcestershire, part of the manor of Bromsgrove, had been one of the Stafford properties forfeited to the Crown in 1486; subsequently, it had been granted to Sir Gilbert Talbot, in whose family it remained. Chebsey in Staffordshire was demised by Sir Humphrey Stafford to his younger brother William in a will drawn up in 1545; William inherited the manor three years later, on Humphrey's death, and it was in the possession of his second wife after his own demise.[16] Thus, William never held lands in Grafton, and not in Chebsey during Mary's lifetime.[17]

He had perhaps been born at his father's manor of Cottered, a pleasant village situated on undulating chalk hills near Royston, with a fifteenth-century church boasting an embattled tower and medieval wall paintings. The Lordship, a magnificent moated hall house – probably the former manor house, given its name and prominent position near the church – also dating from the fifteenth century, but much altered since, survives as one of the most ancient buildings in Hertfordshire.[18] It is more likely that William was born here, as his father's other manor, nearby Rushden, was just a tiny settlement.

In November 1527, after the King had been shown evidence that 'more scarcity of corn is pretended to be within this our said realm than, God be thanked, there is in very truth', William, then fifteen or more, was one of several men commissioned to search the barns and stacks in Berkshire, 'putting at the same time into execution the Statute of Winchester against vagabonds and unlawful games'.[19] In April 1529, he and one Richard Andrews bought the lands (which were worth less than £5 (£1,600)) and marriage of a royal ward, William Somer, for 20 marks (£2,100).[20] The following November, Stafford was appointed joint Sheriff of Oxfordshire and Berkshire with John Brome and Henry Bruges, Stafford's name being personally pricked by the King with his pen on the deed of grant.[21] Clearly he had been the royal choice, and must therefore have already impressed his monarch with his good service or personal qualities.

On 2 June 1533, Arthur Plantagenet, Viscount Lisle (an illegitimate son of Edward IV, and thus cousin to Henry VIII), the new Deputy Governor of Calais, took up residence in that town,[22] and it would appear that Stafford transferred to his service as a spearman in the Calais garrison.[23] Possibly, after his visit the previous autumn, he had pursued the idea of a post in Calais, and seized the opportunity when it came, which suggests that, whenever he and Mary had met, whether it was in Calais or at the coronation or earlier, he either had not fallen for her sufficiently to mind the prospect of long partings, or he saw his new posting as a means of raising enough money to marry her.

It seems he proved himself able, reliable and trustworthy, as he was soon being singled out to perform special errands for the Lisles. In December 1533, John Husee, Lisle's man, met with Stafford in Dover, Stafford having evidently been to England to purchase a gorget (a metal fillet worn around the head), ribbons and lawns for Lady Lisle.[24] In a letter to Honor Grenville, Lady Lisle, dated August 1534, one Leonard Smyth wrote: 'Since my coming to London from Hampshire, I hear that Stafford your servant, to whom I gave the letter, was in London long after, so I wish to know whether it has been received.'[25] Evidently Stafford was now travelling to and fro across the English Channel, entrusted with the business of his employers, and it was probably during these visits that his romance with Mary Boleyn flowered. Probably it was at William's behest, on behalf of a friend or acquaintance of his, that Mary wrote to Lord Lisle in February 1534:

> I desire you and my good lady to be good unto Thomas Hunt, a poor man at Calais, for the room [post] of soldier with 6d (£8) a day in the King's retinue, when any such is vacant. From the King's manor of York Place at Westminster, 13 Feb.[26]

Her letter is countersigned by Sir William Kingston, Constable of the Tower and a favoured courtier and Privy Councillor with a military background, who had probably known and approved of Thomas Hunt prior to the latter's going to Calais. Mary's somewhat regal and peremptory tone suggests that, as the Queen's sister, she expected her request to be met.

Yet, despite the position of trust in which 'young Stafford' was clearly held, he had nothing to offer beyond himself, and was no match for the Queen's sister. Even with her increasingly dubious reputation, Mary could have contrived to marry more advantageously, and thereby increased still further the Boleyn affinity and the family's standing; but she had dared to marry merely for love in an age in which society in general considered that to be an offence against 'God, good order and all', and wayward and foolish in the extreme. Furthermore, she had not even had the courtesy to ask her father, her sister or the King for permission to remarry, but had gone ahead regardless of her family's sensibilities and interests and the King's likely displeasure. Nor did it apparently occur to her that the scandal of her marriage would 'darken Anne's reputation'.[27]

Above all, Mary had disregarded her sister's position; Anne, by virtue of her queenship, was now the effective head of the Boleyn family, and in marrying without first obtaining her permission, Mary had failed to recognise this, or the implications of her ill-advised marriage for Anne and for herself, as the Queen's sister.[28] Both the King and Queen had every reason to be angered by this misalliance, but it was Anne who was the more incensed, and also perhaps because Mary not only had hopes of a child when hers had just been cruelly dashed, but also a husband who loved her. The King, by contrast, was 'tired to satiety' with the wife he had ardently pursued for so long, and openly dallying – if Chapuys is to be believed – with his latest mistress.[29] Here was Anne, the darling of her family, applauded by them all for her success in becoming Queen of England, but not at all 'the most happy', as her empty motto claimed; and there was her despised sister, who had done nothing except spoil her reputation and bring derision upon herself, proudly proclaiming her happiness with the lowly man she had married. Small wonder that Anne now refused to see her sister. Mary, somewhat ingenuously, was to write soon afterwards: 'As far as I can perceive, her Grace is highly displeased with us both'.[30]

Wiltshire was just as furious – indeed, the whole Boleyn family, and Mary's uncle, the Duke of Norfolk, were up in arms, doubtless fearful of how Henry would react to this misalliance, which made a landless soldier his brother-in-law. As soon as Wiltshire realised that Mary's child had been conceived out of wedlock and that her marriage had been a necessity – Chapuys confirms that she had been 'found guilty of misconduct'[31] – he immediately cut off the allowance he had reluctantly paid her throughout her widowhood, knowing that there was little risk of his being ordered to reinstate it. Worse still, Anne and her father had no compunction in persuading the King instantly to banish the disgraced couple from court.

Maybe – scandal aside – the sight of her sister, happily married and pregnant, was too much to bear in the wake of Anne's own disappointment and anxiety. Perhaps she was angry that Mary had thrown herself away on this man of low status when she could have made a marriage that was advantageous to the Boleyns.

Probably, although evidence is lacking, Henry was also persuaded to cut off Mary's royal pension, because, in a letter written three months later, she refers to having to beg her bread with her new husband, and twice mentions living 'a poor honest life with him'.[32] Now that she was a married woman, she would be her husband's responsibility, and even if her daughter Katherine was the King's, there was a legal presumption that she was William Carey's, and there was nothing Mary could do about the loss of her annuity, unless she wanted to court scandal and opprobrium.

'The Lady's sister was banished from court three months ago,' Chapuys informed the Emperor on 19 December, 'it being necessary to do so, for besides that she had been found guilty of misconduct, it would not have been becoming to see her at court *enceinte*.'[33]

Mary seems to have been crushed by the reaction to her marriage. Once banished the court with William Stafford, neither certainly would have been welcome at Hever Castle, so they perhaps took refuge with William's father at Cottered – and then waited three

months before Mary attempted to plead her case, by which time her
penury was probably beginning to bite, and she had begun to realise
that the anger and displeasure occasioned by her marriage was no
transitory thing. It was probably for this reason that she judged it
best to make her appeal through the King's principal secretary, Thomas
Cromwell, whom she evidently knew fairly well, frankly revealing
to him how her ill-judged marriage had come about. Her letter is
undated, but seems to have been written in the latter part of 1534,
in which case her marriage had probably taken place in the late
summer, which is apparently corroborated by Leonard Smyth's letter
of August that year, by which time Stafford was back in Calais.[34]
Either Mary and William were married before then, or he returned
to London soon afterwards.

The full text of Mary's letter, the second of only two written by
her to survive, is as follows:

Master Secretary,

   After my poor recommendations, which is smally to be
regarded of me, that am a poor banished creature, this shall be
to desire you to be good to my poor husband and to me. I am
sure that it is not unknown to you the high displeasure that
both he and I have, both of the King's Highness and the Queen's
Grace, by reason of our marriage without their knowledge,
wherein we both do yield ourselves faulty, and acknowledge
that we did not well to be so hasty nor so bold, without their
knowledge. But one thing, good Master Secretary, consider: that
he was young, and love overcame reason; and for my part, I
saw so much honesty in him that I loved him as well as he did
me; and was in bondage, and glad I was to be at liberty.

The grovelling tone is typical of letters of the period sent by those
suing for favours or forgiveness: in each case, petitioners laid on the
flattery with a trowel, or abased themselves. But this is more than a
begging letter. Mary's reference to being 'in bondage' betrays how
unhappy she had been living for so long under the strict control of
a father who evidently had a low opinion of her – and in the shadow
of a sister who also appears to have thought her of little account.
No wonder that, in her early to mid thirties, she had seized what
might be her only opportunity of happiness and freedom, and escape
from a family who, while paying lip service to her position as the

Queen's sister, apparently expected her to remain invisible in case the sight of her gave people cause to question the legality of that sister's marriage.

It is clear from this letter that Mary, at last, was loved for herself, and that William – a considerably younger man – had fallen in love with her before she, in time, came to reciprocate; this boost to her confidence would have been incalculable, and no doubt it gave her the courage, for once in her life, to defy those who had always dictated to her.

Maybe, in the mayhem and excitement of Anne's coronation day, she had grasped the rare chance to enjoy a little dalliance, and gone on grasping it whenever she could escape Wiltshire's vigilance, which would have lent a certain spice to her love affair and invested it with the excitement of forbidden fruit. It would have been easy, in the chaotic world of the court, to indulge in clandestine meetings, or go missing for a short time . . . and it only required two witnesses and a compliant priest to make a secret marriage.

Mary's sense of liberation must have been powerful, and although she freely admitted that she had erred in marrying so impulsively, she was clearly not regretting it. Her letter continued, rather poignantly:

> So that for my part, I saw that all the world did set so little store by me, and he so much, that I thought I could take no better way but to take him and to forsake all other ways, and live a poor, honest life with him. And so I do put no doubt but we should, if we might once be so happy to recover the King's gracious favour and the Queen's. For well I might a had a greater man of birth, and a higher, but I ensure you I could never a had one that should a loved me so well, nor a more honest man. And besides that, he is both come of ancient stock, and again as meet (if it was his Grace's pleasure) to do the King service as any young gentleman in his court.

Mary's statement, that 'all the world did set so little store by me', betrays just how unhappy and unloved she had felt, probably for years. Small wonder that she felt such love for, and pride in, her husband, the man who had rescued her, which comes across so movingly in this passage.

Nevertheless, she knew that, if her plea was to succeed, she must acknowledge herself to be grievously at fault:

> Therefore, good Master Secretary, this shall be my suit to you, that, for the love that well I know you do bear to all my blood, though for my part, I have not deserved it but smally, by reason of my vile conditions, as to put my husband to the King's Grace that he may do his duty as all other gentlemen do.

Here, Mary was asking for Stafford to be restored to his post at court, even though she knew she could merit little consideration as a result of the 'vile conditions' of her disgrace. She continued:

> And, good Master Secretary, sue for us to the King's Highness, and beseech his Highness, which ever was wont to take pity, to have pity on us; and that it would please his Grace, of his goodness, to speak to the Queen's Grace for us; for, so far as I can perceive, her Grace is so highly displeased with us both that, without the King be so good lord to us as to withdraw his rigour and sue for us, we are never likely to recover her Grace's favour, which is too heavy to bear. And seeing there is no remedy, for God's sake, help us, for we have been now a quarter of a year married, I thank God, and too late now to call it again; wherefore it is the more alms to help us. But if I were at my liberty and might choose, I ensure you, Master Secretary, for my little time, I have spied so much honesty to be in him that I had rather beg my bread with him than to be the greatest queen christened. And I believe verily he is in the same case with me; for I believe verily he would not forsake me to be a king.

It is clear from this that Mary believed the King to be more likely to show compassion than Anne, which suggests that her relationship with him had been less complicated than that with her sister. It also suggests that she was sensible of his kindnesses to her, and that there was still some affection between them.

She concluded:

> Therefore, good Master Secretary, seeing we are so well together and does intend to live so honest a life, though it be but poor,

show part of your goodness to us as well as you do to all the world besides; for I promise you, you have the name to help all them that hath need, and amongst all your suitors I dare be bold to say that you have no matter more to be pitied than ours; and therefore, for God's sake, be good to us, for in you is all our trust.

And I beseech you, good Master Secretary, pray my Lord my father and my Lady my mother to be good to us, and to let us have their blessings, and my husband their good will; and I will never desire more of them. Also, I pray you, desire my Lord of Norfolk [her uncle] and my Lord my brother to be good to us. I dare not write to them, they are so cruel against us. But if with any pain I could take my life [that] I might win their good wills, I promise you there is no child living would venture more than I. And so I pray you to report by me, and you shall find my writing true, and in all points which I may please them in I shall be ready to obey them nearest my husband, whom I am bound to; to whom I most heartily beseech you to be good unto, which, for my sake, is a poor, banished man for an honest and goodly cause. And seeing that I have read in old books that some, for as just causes, have by kings and queens been pardoned by the suit of good folk, I trust it shall be our chance, through your good help, to come to the same; as knoweth the [Lord] God, Who send you health and heart's ease.

Scribbled with her ill hand, who is your poor, humble suitor, always to command,

Mary Stafford.

The letter was addressed to 'The right worshipful &c. Master Secretary.'[35]

J.S. Brewer, writing in the Victorian age, and believing that Mary was a woman of loose morals, thought that this was not the letter of 'a woman of strong character or decided principles'.[36] But that is hardly fair, because, in defying her family and making a marriage of which she must have known they would disapprove, and in defending it passionately, Mary was probably calling upon strengths in her character that she may not hitherto have known she had. It could be said that she was now paying the price for showing a reckless disregard for the wider consequences of her actions, yet today we would hardly blame her – as the Victorians might have done – for seizing her chance of happiness and freedom. It has been claimed – somewhat fancifully – that the letter betrays 'liquidity, an April-like glisten and quiver' to Mary's character, and shows her to be 'without calculation',[37] and it has also been convincingly described as the work of 'an articulate and passionate woman'.[38]

Yet some passages in Mary's letter do reveal a glaring lack of tact and insight, and also anger at the way she had been cut off by her family. One can sympathise with her for being unable to hide that, yet she probably did herself no favours by her sometimes defiant, unrepentant tone, and her rather self-centred claim that her plight was more deserving of pity than anyone else's; or by making so many peremptory demands of Cromwell, as if she were still riding high in favour as the Queen's sister. Yet the erratic nature of the letter – the veering from pleading to defiance – strongly suggests that Mary was in turmoil when she wrote it, and not thinking clearly about the consequences. There is a sense of her rushing to commit all her thoughts and emotions to paper, without calculation, and perhaps unaware that she was revealing rather more than she had intended.

What drove her to write the letter was probably the final collapse of her hopes that the story of her impulsive marriage would have a happy ending, with everyone coming to understand how beneficial it really was, and receiving her back into the fold; and, more immediately, her fear of rapidly encroaching poverty – because it is doubtful that she found the loss of Anne's favour 'too heavy to bear' on a personal level. If she was really hoping for a reconciliation with her sister, she was surely going the wrong way about it, deliberately highlighting the fact that, even in disgrace, she now enjoyed a far happier marriage than Anne did. 'For well I might a had a greater man of birth,' she had written, 'but I ensure you I could never a had one that loved me so well. I had rather beg my bread with him than to be the greatest queen christened.'

It is this letter that provides the best clue to the relationship between the sisters. Maybe there had never been much love lost between them, or they clashed often, flaring up in anger or resentment, only to make up just as readily, as sisters do. Maybe Mary had always been unable to restrain herself with Anne, and was given to venting her feelings with biting honesty. Almost certainly, she had been jealous. That jealousy may have had its roots in Anne, the more charming and intelligent of the two, being found a court position before she, the elder sister, did, and shining in that milieu; it would have been fed by Anne snaring the King who had perhaps rejected Mary, and becoming

Queen; it must have festered as a result of Mary being treated as if she were of little account. Now she was making the rather cruel point that she had done better in marrying for love than Anne had done in marrying for ambition. She must have known that that was unlikely to impress her family, or Cromwell, or the King, so she had probably dashed it all down angrily in revenge for Anne's treatment of her. Her words exposed the bitter irony of their respective situations: here was Mary, the King's discarded mistress, who had never sought more for herself, but who had ended up happily married – and Anne, who had held him off for years in order to gain the ultimate prize, but had ended up trapped in unhappy and insecure wedlock.[39]

Anne almost certainly got to see what Mary had written, or Mary had said as much to her face to face,[40] and she was incensed at the obvious jibe, which shattered any possibility of Mary being restored to favour. It seems that she and her new husband were never again received at court, for there is no record of her being there after that time; in April 1535, as we have seen, John Hale mentioned that 'the Queen's Grace might not suffer [her sister] to be in the court',[41] and so it is unlikely that Anne and Mary were ever reconciled.

Mary's letter evidently did her no good with Cromwell either, for he apparently lifted no finger to help her.[42] His reply – if there was one – does not survive, but there was little advantage for him in supporting such an errant couple and risking incurring the royal displeasure.

Anne, however, may secretly in the long run have come to wonder if dismissing her sister was foolish,[43] for it would, in a short time, become clear that many of her supporters were abandoning her and that she needed all the friends she could get, especially in her own privy chamber, although it is unlikely that Mary had the influence to be 'a potentially useful ally', as has been suggested.[44] This may explain why Anne did relent slightly and perhaps gave Mary money and a gold cup;[45] or maybe her conscience was troubled at Mary's plight. But there is nothing to support the claim that she 'provided assistance through Cromwell',[46] and it is unlikely that the sisters ever met again.

Mary may well have been relieved to be gone from the court, with all its 'hypocrisy, backbiting and intrigue',[47] and indeed she would have good cause to be thankful for it within a year or so, for time would prove, dramatically, that she was to end up by far the more fortunate of the two Boleyn sisters.[48]

Mary and William were to pass the rest of their married life in relative obscurity – and, for some years, in 'obscure poverty'.[49] Unless Mary miscarried, a child was born to them in 1535. There has been speculation that this was probably a daughter called Anne, after the Queen, and that the couple also had an unnamed son who had died by 1543.[50] But there is no contemporary evidence for a second child, or for the sex and name of the child Mary may have borne in 1535, the fruit of her scandalous pregnancy. We do not even know if she carried it to term. If it was a boy, he must have predeceased Mary, otherwise the manor of Abinger and other properties and rights, which William Stafford inherited from her at her death, would surely have passed to their son.

By 1535, Mary's elder son, Henry Carey, now ten, had been removed from her care, and – as John Hale's testimony suggests – was living at Syon Abbey, a Bridgettine nunnery at Isleworth in Middlesex, once much favoured by Katherine of Aragon. Founded in 1415 by Henry V, it was one of the wealthiest abbeys in England, and was renowned for its magnificent library of over fourteen hundred books, its spiritual ethos and the quality of its preachers. It would not be suppressed until 1539. Syon Park – as it is now called – has been remodelled several times over the centuries, and all that remains today of the abbey where Henry Carey resided is the quadrangle (the site of the former cloisters), the vaulted undercroft below the great hall, and a brick barn. Contrary to what has been suggested, young Carey was not 'kept out of sight' here and 'given no attention whatsoever'[51] – he was at a great abbey, which enjoyed royal patronage, to be educated, and 'benefited enormously from his position as ward of the Queen'.[52]

For Anne Boleyn took her responsibilities as her nephew's guardian seriously. In 1535, she found him a distinguished tutor, the celebrated French humanist and poet Nicholas Bourbon (1503–50). Before May of that year, Bourbon had been granted asylum in England after falling foul of the French authorities for attacking the worship of saints and for his evangelical reformist beliefs – beliefs that Queen Anne shared. After the French ambassador, Jean de Dinteville, had drawn the King and Queen's attention to his plight, they secured his release from prison and extended to him a warm welcome and their patronage. Bourbon was first lodged in the house of the King's physician, Dr William Butts, a fellow humanist, and later moved in with the King's goldsmith, Cornelius Heyss.

Butts recommended Bourbon to Anne as tutor to her ward Carey, and thus Anne was doing Bourbon a favour when she appointed him to teach her nephew and two other boys: Henry, the heir of Sir Henry Norris, Groom of the Stool and Head of the Privy Chamber; and Thomas, son of Sir Nicholas Hervey, another reformist courtier of the Queen's circle.[53] 'You, O Queen, gave me the boys to educate!' a thankful Bourbon enthused, in the book of verse (dedicated to Henry VIII and François I) he was to publish two years later. 'I try to keep each one faithful to his duty. May Christ grant that I may be equal to the task, shaping vessels worthy of a heavenly house.' Young Carey could not have had a more respected tutor, for Bourbon was the friend of modern thinkers such as Thomas Cromwell, Archbishop Cranmer, Hugh Latimer, Bishop of Worcester, Nicholas Kratzer, the astronomer and mathematician, and the painter Hans Holbein, for whom he sat.[54] In December 1535, Anne Boleyn visited Syon Abbey, possibly to see her ward, and while there harangued the nuns about their popish forms of worship.

It is entirely credible that Bourbon did a good job of imparting his staunch reformist and evangelical principles to Henry Carey, as Anne had surely intended, and indeed, his teachings probably found fertile ground in which to take root. It has been asserted that – 'with the possible exception of Mary', which is hard to believe – the Boleyns were devoted to 'the reformed faith',[55] but athough a study of the books owned by Rochford suggests that he came quite near to becoming a Lutheran, Anne and her father died as orthodox Catholics, so it would be more accurate to say that the Boleyns were zealous for the cause of reform within the Catholic Church.

Given her background as a member of a family notorious in Henry VIII's reign for its aggressive reformist opinions, and rumoured to be 'more Lutheran than Luther himself',[56] Mary probably shared these views and approved of the education afforded her son, especially after her second marriage. For William Stafford later revealed himself to be so staunch a Protestant that he was prepared to choose exile in Geneva during Mary Tudor's reign rather than suffer persecution for his beliefs, and there became a friend of the austere reformer John Calvin. It is entirely plausible that he had embraced the cause of reform, if not the Lutheran faith, before or during his marriage to Mary Boleyn. Indeed, part of her attraction for him may have been the fact that she came from such a famously reformist family. Mary's daughter, Katherine Carey, would marry a man who was 'well affected to the Protestant religion'. It would be surprising therefore if Mary herself did not support the cause of reform, at the very least. Since she died before it became acceptable – and safe – to 'come out' as a Protestant, there is no way of proving this, but in view of her background and her family connections, it is a credible supposition. Like her sister Anne, however, she probably remained, outwardly at least, an orthodox Catholic to the end of her days, dying in the faith of her forefathers.

There is no source that gives credibility to the statement that Mary was reconciled to her father, who allowed her and William Stafford to reside at Rochford Hall,[57] or the assertion that she 'was never fully forgiven, but persuaded her father to let her live with Stafford in one of the Boleyn properties, Rochford Hall in Essex'.[58] Prior to her clandestine marriage, Mary had apparently lived at Hever Castle or at court. Before his death in 1539, Wiltshire was considering cutting Mary off and leaving her share of his property to his niece, the future Elizabeth I, so clearly they remained estranged. It is unlikely, therefore, that he would have permitted her to live at Rochford Hall with the husband of whom he deeply disapproved.

So where did the couple live in the six years between their banishment and Mary coming into her inheritance? The answer is, probably at Calais, for William seems to have been retained by Lord Lisle: in February 1537 we find John Husee writing: 'Coffin would fain have a good hawk; he liked not that [which] Stafford brought him.'[59] And in 1539, William, as one of 'the retinue of that town', was among the welcoming party appointed to receive Henry VIII's fourth wife, Anne of Cleves, on her arrival in Calais.[60] Calais, where Mary had perhaps first become acquainted with William, might have held happy memories for both of them.

Thanks to the establishment of a wool staple and corporation in 1362, Calais was a prosperous town and 'an impregnable fortress'. As a strategic springboard for the debarkation and marshalling of troops, and 'the key and principal entrance' to England,[61] it was of the highest importance to that kingdom, and no expense was spared in maintaining its defences.[62] That was why there was a strong garrison, which comprised 'a force of five hundred of the best soldiers, beside a troop of fifty horsemen'. William Stafford was one of twenty-one mounted spearmen of the garrison; the 'spears' were all men of good family, many of whom progressed upwards through the ranks, as William probably did. The inhabitants of Calais were seen as men of 'unshaken fidelity' and the Governor who guarded it was always 'one of the most trusty barons which the King has'.[63]

The walls of Calais stretched from Beauchamps' bulwark to the castle of Rysebank, with its fort and tower. The chief buildings of the town were the Exchequer Palace, the churches of St Mary and St Nicholas, the splendid Renaissance Hôtel de Ville with its distinctive tower in the marketplace – visible in the distance in the painting of the Field of Cloth of Gold now at Hampton Court (the present Hôtel de Ville is a replica) – and the guildhall of the staple, known as the Staple Inn. Many ships and boats were moored by the Watergate on the quay, where a round tower guarded the entrance to the harbour.[64]

This was the place that Mary probably called home for nearly six years, and where she would have been able to enjoy domesticated obscurity as an 'army wife'. During those years, her brother, Lord Rochford, and her uncle, the Duke of Norfolk, were to visit Calais more than once,[65] but, given their hostility towards Mary, it is doubtful if they made any effort to see her.

A letter sent by Robert Blakeney, the new Prior of Tynemouth, to Cromwell in April 1537, would lend credence to the theory that Mary had moved to Calais. The Prior reminded Cromwell: 'My lady Mary Carey, now Stafford, had an annuity of 100 marks, under convent seal of my house, for no cause except it should be for preferring my predecessor to his room [position]. The said lady can now demand no such annuity, as she can do no great good for me or my house, which is now onerate by first fruits and charges. I once stopped the payment, but could not continue through the command of my Lord Chancellor. These be to desire your Lordship that the said convent seal may be reversed, as this bearer shall declare. For your kindness herein your annuity of 20 nobles shall be made 20 marks.'

Despite this overt bribe, the annuity continued to be paid to Mary, which, along with the Lord Chancellor's earlier intervention, and the fact that the annuity continued to be paid by the Court of Augmentations after the priory was dissolved in January 1539, is further proof that it represented the King's provision for his daughter.[66]

If Mary and William did move to Calais, as seems likely, that would explain the absence of any reference to her in contemporary records at this time. It would explain how the couple managed to subsist during the time of their disgrace. And it would also explain why there is no mention of Mary in the numerous sources documenting the cataclysmic fall of the Boleyns in 1536.

Tapestry depicting the marriage of Louis XII and Mary Tudor in 1514. Mary Boleyn may be among the female attendants. Tournai tapestry, *c*.1525.

Francois I, King of France. It is likely that Mary was his mistress for a brief spell. School of Jean Clouet.

Claude de France, the virtuous Queen of François I. Tomb sculpture by Pierre Bontemps, 1549, Basilica of St Denis, Paris.

The Hôtel de Clu[ny]
Paris, where Mary
and Anne Boleyn
attended upon Ma[ry]
Tudor during the
enforced seclusion
of her widowhood[.]
Print c.1835.

'Cloth of Gold do not despise,
tho' thou art matcht with Cloth of Frieze;
Cloth of Frieze, be not too bold,
tho' thou art matcht with Cloth of Gold.'
Wedding portrait of Mary Tudor and Charles
Brandon, Duke of Suffolk, 1515.

The 'Donjon d'Anne Boleyn' at
Briis-sous-Forges. It is possible that Mary was
sent here after leaving the French court.

William Carey, Mary's first husband,
a man set for a glittering career at court.
Possibly by or after Hans Holbein.

William Carey. Elizabethan copy
of a lost portrait of 1526.

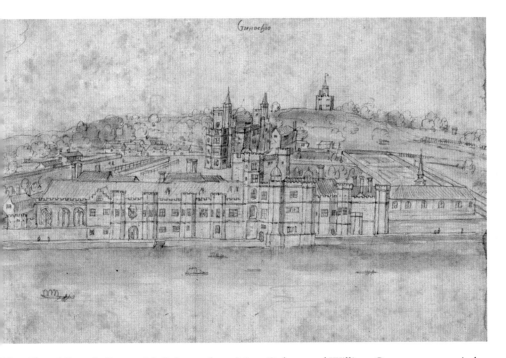

The Chapel Royal, Greenwich Palace, where Mary Boleyn and William Carey were married,
can be seen to the left of the picture, behind the wall, with the great hall behind.
Drawing by Anthony van der Wyngaerde, 1558.

Syon Abbey, as it would have looked around 1535, when Henry Carey was sent there to be taught by Nicholas Bourbon. Painting by Jonathan Foyle, 2004.

Nicholas Bourbon, the reformist tutor of Mary's son, Henry Carey. Drawing by Hans Holbein, 1535.

Sir John Russell, who may have been Henry Carey's guardian for a time. Drawing by Hans Holbein.

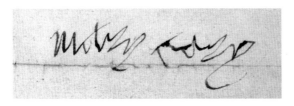

Mary Boleyn's signature, 'Mary Carey', from on a letter dated 13 February 1534.
Only two of Mary's letters survive.

Anne of Cleves, who was welcomed to Calais in 1539 by, among others, William Stafford and probably Mary Boleyn. Miniature by Hans Holbein, 1539.

This portrait may well depict Katherine Howard, against whom William Stafford may have testified. Miniature by Hans Holbein.

Henden Manor, Kent, where Mary perhaps lived for a short time with her second husband, William Stafford.

Rochford Hall, Essex, much altered now, which Mary inherited from her grand-mother, Margaret Butler, and which was in her possession for just four days.

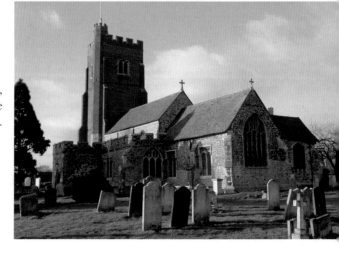

St Andrew's Church, Rochford, where Mary may be buried.

(*Above right*) Mary's son, Henry Carey, Lord Hunsdon. Artist unknown, 1591.

(*Above left*) Elizabeth I, who was close to her Carey cousins. Steven van der Meulan, *c.*1563.

Lord Hunsdon's magnificent tomb in Westminster Abbey.

Portrait of a pregnant lady, probably
Katherine Carey, Lady Knollys.
Steven van der Meulan, 1562.
(*Detail*) This close-up shows a
striking resemblance to Henry VIII.

The empty tomb
of Katherine
Carey and Sir
Francis Knollys
in Rotherfield
Greys Church.

12

'A Poor Honest Life'

On 29 January 1536, Anne Boleyn gave birth to the stillborn male foetus whose survival would have guaranteed her safety. The secrecy surrounding this event spawned widespread rumours. In Paris, Rodolfo Pio, Bishop of Faenza, the Papal Nuncio – as has been demonstrated, a man not notable for the accuracy of his reports – claimed that 'that woman' had never even been pregnant, but had faked a miscarriage, and 'to keep up the deceit, she would allow no one to attend on her but her sister'.[1] This is the only mention of Mary Boleyn being in attendance on Anne after the former's banishment, and no English account mentions her being there. Given the dubious source, Pio's wild assertion that Anne had never been pregnant (when we have a reliable description of the foetus'),[2] and the probability that Mary was then living in Calais, it is, sadly, far more likely that the sisters were never reconciled. Nevertheless, some historians still claim that 'in this sad time, the only comfort came from Anne's sister Mary, who overcame her differences with Anne in order to be with her',[3] with one going so far as to state that Mary 'most certainly was at Anne's side' when she miscarried.[4]

Mary and William would soon have cause to be very grateful for being banished the court, for the fortunes of the Boleyns suffered a fatal crash on 2 May 1536, when Queen Anne was arrested on charges of plotting the death of the King and committing adultery with five men, one of whom was her brother, Rochford, who was arrested that same day. Another was Sir Henry Norris, William Carey's former colleague in the Privy Chamber. Both were imprisoned in the Tower of London with the other accused men. The evidence strongly suggests that they were the victims of a court coup masterminded by the King's principal secretary, Thomas Cromwell, who knew Anne and her faction to be his mortal enemies.[5]

On 15 May, in the great hall of the Tower, Anne and Rochford were arraigned for treason before a committee of their peers that probably included their own father, Wiltshire.[6] Both were condemned to death. The evidence for incest rested chiefly on the testimony of Rochford's wife. We can only conjecture what Mary thought of her father's complicity in the legal process against her brother and sister, and her sister-in-law's part in their fall. Maybe Wiltshire was already the *bête noire* of her life, and even if he was not, she would surely have been chilled to learn that he had it in him to abet the destruction of his own children. It would not be surprising if she never wanted to see him again after this.

Rochford was beheaded, with his sister's other alleged lovers, on 17 May on the public scaffold on Tower Hill, and his body buried beneath the altar pavement of the royal chapel of St Peter ad Vincula within the Tower of London. On his death, all his honours and property were forfeited to the Crown.

Before he sent Anne to the scaffold, the King had their marriage declared invalid, and their daughter Elizabeth legally deemed a bastard. The grounds were kept secret, but Eustache Chapuys, the Imperial ambassador, shrewdly guessed that it had been Henry's sexual relations with Mary Boleyn, which had created a barrier to his union with Anne, and which was without doubt the means by which their marriage was annulled[7] on 17 May, the day Mary's brother Rochford had died on the block. This would also explain the secrecy surrounding the annulment.[8]

According to a new Act of Succession passed in July 1536, the marriage had been void from the first on account of 'certain entirely just, true and unlawful impediments hitherto not publicly known, and since that time [of the marriage] confessed by the Lady Anne before the most reverend father in God, Thomas, Archbishop of Canterbury', and by the King himself, presumably also to Cranmer.[9] These impediments must have been Henry's carnal relations with Mary Boleyn, about which both Henry and Anne certainly had known at the time they were wed.

The Pope had, of course, dispensed with the affinity thus created, so the King and Anne had entered into their union in good faith (in which case their daughter could have been deemed legitimate on its dissolution), but the Dispensations Act passed afterwards, in 1534, provided that existing dispensations issued for causes 'contrary or repugnant to the Holy Scriptures and the laws of God' were invalid.[10] Evidently it had been made clear to Henry VIII that the dispensation of 1528 came under that category, even though Archbishop Cranmer must have found it to be good – and indeed relied on it – when he confirmed the marriage in 1533,[11] and never ventured to question its validity in 1534 – when to do so would, in fact, have been treason. But now, Cranmer found it politic to follow the old canon law in reaching his decision.

Henry may have felt that his affair with Mary Boleyn had provoked divine wrath after all;[12] or, as it has been pithily put, he forgot that an adulterous relationship created kinship 'when it suited him to forget, and remembered it when it suited him to remember'.[13] Soon after the annulment, he restored the old canon law forbidding marriage with the sister of a former mistress.[14] The affair with Mary had therefore served a useful – and entirely unforeseen – purpose.

Two days after her marriage was annulled, Anne was beheaded within the Tower. It is highly unlikely that Mary Boleyn was a witness to her sister's fall, for no source records her presence in the Tower or at the execution. In all her recorded utterances during her imprisonment, Anne never mentioned her sister – but she did not refer to her little daughter either, so we can infer very little from her silence.

In fact, in all the many documents pertaining to the fall of Anne and Rochford, there is no mention of Mary Boleyn, except (briefly) in the context of the annulment. She was almost certainly not at court at the time, but probably at Calais, at a safe distance from the maelstrom that engulfed her siblings. The whole process against them had happened so quickly that she probably received no warning as to what was to happen, and heard news of the unfolding events days after they had taken place. And once she knew of the legal process against Anne and George, she probably realised there was nothing she could have done to help them, and that it was safer to remain in Calais in blessed obscurity. She may have felt that she had no choice but to follow the lead set by her father and her uncle Norfolk, and distance herself from the doomed pair.[15] There is no record of any member of the Boleyn family trying to contact Anne and Rochford while they were in the Tower, or attempting to intercede for them; even had they been inclined to do so, either action could have had unhappy consequences. Yet the loss of her sister and brother

cannot but have affected Mary – and indeed her whole family –
dreadfully.

For more than a century, a tale has circulated that Mary's daughter,
Katherine Carey, was one of the four distressed young ladies who
attended Anne Boleyn in the Tower during the four days after her
condemnation, and accompanied her to the scaffold.[16] The story
appears to derive from Augustus Hare, writing in 1878 of Katherine's
tomb in Westminster Abbey, but he does not cite his source; there
is no contemporary evidence to support the tale, and surely Katherine,
at twelve, would have been considered too young for such a grim
duty. There is no record of her serving Anne Boleyn, and she is not
recorded as a maid of honour until 1540, when she entered the
service of Anne of Cleves, Henry VIII's fourth wife. At the time of
Anne's fall, she may have been in the Princess Elizabeth's household,
and a witness to her little cousin's loss of status, for after being
declared a bastard, the two-year-old was now to be styled the Lady
Elizabeth, and her household was accordingly reduced. It was still
royal, by any standards, and she continued to be served as if she were
still a princess.

  After Anne Boleyn's death, the wardship of Katherine's brother,
Henry Carey, reverted to the Crown, and Henry VIII, as sovereign,
took on responsibility for the boy. When Carey's tutor, Nicholas
Bourbon, returned to France after the execution of his patron, Queen
Anne, the King asked Sir Francis Bryan – who had replaced Sir
Henry Norris as Chief Gentleman of the Privy Chamber – to send
Henry Carey and his fellow royal wards, Henry Norris the younger
and Thomas Hervey, to Woburn Abbey in Bedfordshire. Here, they
lived with the lay community, at the expense of the monks – the
abbey would not be dissolved for another two years – and Bryan
appointed his protégé, James Prestwich, as their schoolmaster. Soon
another boy joined the little school: George Basset, who was 'merry,
and applieth his learning very well'[17] – probably better than Henry
Carey did.

  Master Carey 'was not badly educated: he wrote fluently, in a
simple, expressive style, full of proverbs and homely sayings much to
the point'.[18] But he did not do well in his Latin lessons – it would
later be said of him that 'his Latin and his dissimulation were both
alike equally bad'.[19] And although, in adult life, he owned a copy of
Jean Froissart's *Chronicles*[20] – standard reading for a noble soldier – in

which he entered the dates of birth of his children, it seems he did not shine intellectually: it would be said of him that he 'neither was wise nor seemed wise'[21] and, according to an anonymous Elizabethan poem, 'fool hath he ever been' with 'his wits dull as lead'.[22] It may be that he took after his mother in these respects, although he cannot have been a stupid man, as he managed to retain a succession of important posts for more than thirty years in the reign of Elizabeth, who was never prone to handing out offices and favours to the undeserving, however close they were to her in blood. Thus these slurs may have been purely malicious or provoked by envy.

Henry and his young friends remained at Woburn for two years, but their schooling was dramatically disrupted in 1538, when the abbey was dissolved after the Abbot, Robert Hobbs, had made 'treasonable utterances' that were reported to Thomas Cromwell, and was duly hanged. The tutor Prestwich was now discovered to be a staunch Catholic who 'always stiffly maintained the Bishop of Rome's part', could 'never assent to the new learning',[23] and was indoctrinating his pupils with subversive religious and political beliefs. He was also found to be associating with 'certain persons inhabited near to Woburn and other places thereabouts' who had been under government surveillance.[24] Already, Thomas Hervey had succumbed to Prestwich's teachings, and would remain a life-long Papist.[25]

Maybe Sir Francis Bryan had deliberately intended that the evangelical teachings instilled by Nicholas Bourbon in his pupils should be overlaid by more traditionalist views. John Longland, Bishop of Lincoln, had promised him that God would reward him for 'redressing and punishing such errors as hath been used in this worldly country, of children',[26] but such defiance in the climate of the Reformation bordered on treason. The King must have been horrified when he learned how his wards were being fed such sedition, and Mary and her family would no doubt have felt the same. On 25 May 1538, Bryan dismissed Prestwich from his service, on the pretext that Henry Carey was being transferred to the guardianship of Sir John Russell, who was Comptroller of the Household and soon to be a Privy Councillor. Prestwich fled north, where he was executed for denying the royal Supremacy the following year.[27]

If Henry Carey was taken into the care of Sir John Russell, he could not have had a more eminent guardian and exemplar. Honest, pleasant and adroit, Russell was created a baron in March 1539 and then appointed – as part of Cromwell's administrative reforms – Lord

President of the Council of the West, being thereby invested with responsibility for Devon, Cornwall, Dorset and Somerset; in April 1539, he was made a Knight of the Garter, and in July, High Steward of Cornwall. Although the Council of the West toppled with Cromwell in 1540, Russell remained a great power in the west, and was appointed Lord High Admiral in 1540. He resigned that office in 1542 to follow his military career. During Henry VIII's invasion of France in 1544, he failed to take Montreuil, but was Captain General of the vanguard of the army when the English took Boulogne in 1545. He was a close companion of Henry VIII during the latter's declining years, and was named one of the executors of the King's will, and one of the sixteen councillors appointed to govern England during the minority of Edward VI, who created him Earl of Bedford and gave him Woburn Abbey. Prior to that, his chief seat had been at Chenies, Buckinghamshire, which he had acquired on marriage; when in the west, he resided at Tavistock Abbey in Devon, which had been given to him by the King in 1539. Nothing is left of it today apart from the refectory, two gateways and a porch; the imposing church had entirely disappeared by the eighteenth century. Russell also owned Covent Garden in London, with seven acres in Long Acre.

There is no record of Henry Carey actually being placed with Sir John Russell, and perhaps going to live at Chenies, or in Covent Garden, or even at Tavistock; yet it is credible that he was given into the Comptroller's care, for he was to follow in Russell's footsteps in so many ways, loyally serving a sovereign to whom he was close, and who trusted him; holding responsibility for regional administration; pursuing a distinguished military career; and enjoying a prominent place and high offices at court.

Mary's father, Wiltshire, survived the coup that had destroyed two of his children, at whose deaths, chillingly, he had expressed 'no protest or hint of sorrow'.[28] Understandably reluctant to support his widowed daughter-in-law, Lady Rochford, who had been left destitute when the husband she had betrayed was attainted, he was forced, at the direct solicitation of the King and Cromwell, to make out of his own diminished resources a more ample allowance to her.[29] By 1537, Lady Rochford had returned to court to serve Queen Jane Seymour, who died in October that year after bearing Henry VIII his longed-for son, Prince Edward; Lady Rochford was one of the ladies in

attendance at her funeral in November.[30] She would serve two more
of the King's wives, and in 1539 two Acts of Parliament restored her
jointure and other lands, among which was the manor of Blickling
in Norfolk,[31] where she seems to have resided from this time.

The late 1530s brought more tragedy to Mary. Not two years after
the brutal deaths of her estranged brother and sister, she lost her mother
too – probably without ever having been reconciled to her. Elizabeth
Howard died on 3 April 1538 at the Abbot of Reading's house beside
Baynard's Castle in London; four days later, she was buried with suitable state in the Howard aisle in Lambeth Church.[32] Apparently she
had already been ailing at the time of her children's arrests in 1536,[33]
so the horror of their executions, the pain of their loss and the humil-
iation of the family's disgrace had perhaps broken her.

Not so her husband, Mary's father. The only clue as to his state
of mind in the wake of the savage destruction of two of his children, in which he had been complicit, was his request to the humanist
scholar Erasmus, in the year after their deaths, to write a short
commentary on the 23rd Psalm, to be dedicated to himself. But
Wiltshire was a survivor. Although he was deprived of his office of
Lord Privy Seal after Anne's fall, he retained his place on the King's
Council. Only months after Anne and Rochford died, he was helping
to suppress the rebels who led the northern Pilgrimage of Grace
against the King's religious reforms. In October 1537, he attended
the christening of Prince Edward, the son born to Henry VIII's third
wife, Jane Seymour, who had supplanted his daughter in the King's
affections, and whom Henry had wed only ten days after Anne's
execution.

Wiltshire kept in with Cromwell and other influential people at
court, was prominent at state functions and in the ceremonies of the
Order of the Garter, and, by 1538 was again 'well entertained' at
court, where it was rumoured that he was about to wed the King's
niece, Lady Margaret Douglas.[34] But he did not long outlive his wife,
passing away on 12 March 1539, at Hever Castle, aged sixty-one.[35]
There is little evidence to support Sander's assertion that he 'died of
grief', yet it might be fair to assume that grief had played its part
in hastening his end.

'My good lord and master is dead,' wrote his auditor, Robert
Cranewell, to Cromwell. 'He made the end of a good Christian man.'
The letter was dated 'Hever, 13 March'.[36] Wiltshire was buried in
thirteenth-century Hever Church, where a fine memorial brass

showing him wearing his Garter insignia marks his resting place. The King himself ordered Masses to be said for his soul.[37] If Mary had been in Calais since 1534–5, which is likely, then she would never have seen her parents again, or made her peace with them. It is probably significant that it was only after their deaths that she came back to England, so that she could take possession of her inheritance.

Wiltshire had left no male heir. In February 1538, the disputed earldom of Ormond had been granted to his cousin, Piers Butler. Because Boleyn's heir had died under attainder, the viscountcy of Rochford and the earldom of Wiltshire, which had been granted in tail male, fell into abeyance, the latter being bestowed in 1550 on William Paulet, later Marquess of Winchester. It would not be until 1621 that the viscountcy of Rochford was revived for Mary Boleyn's great-grandson, Henry Carey, 4th Lord Hunsdon.[38]

Wiltshire's two co-heiresses were his daughter, Mary, and his granddaughter, Elizabeth, daughter of Henry VIII by Anne Boleyn. Anne's share of his estates had been confiscated by an Act of Attainder passed in June 1536 after her execution, and her child had been declared illegitimate and unfit to inherit. So when Boleyn's extensive property was divided, half of it, including Hever Castle, Seal and Blickling, reverted to the Crown. It has already been noted that Blickling was transferred by Act of Parliament in 1539 to Lady Rochford.

The Crown did not wait long to seize what was due, but when Cromwell's letter arrived at Hever Castle on 26 March, just two weeks after Wiltshire's death, Boleyn's man in Kent, John Tebold of Seal, had to confess that 'much of the goods in the manor place of Hever had been removed by advice of the Archbishop of Canterbury'.[39] By a royal grant of July 1538, Archbishop Cranmer enjoyed 'the full jurisdiction and authority of the Crown' in many 'churches, vicarages, villages and parishes' in Kent, including Hever;[40] thus he was able to save some of Wiltshire's goods for the elderly Margaret Butler, Lady Boleyn, and her granddaughter Mary, proving himself once again a friend to the Boleyns, whose chaplain he had been. 'Part of the stuff and all the implements yet remain,' Tebold assured Cromwell. He had 'stayed them', on the advice of Sir Thomas Willoughby, 'till the King's further pleasure'. Willoughby himself wrote to Cromwell that very day to say he would 'give Tebold his aid in taking possession of the manor of Hever, and in entertaining the old Lady Boleyn there in best wise to her comfort'.[41]

★

By the end of that year of 1539, Mary and William had come home to England, and he was back at court. In November, 'young Stafford that married the Lady Carey' had been among those appointed to attend upon the Lord Admiral, the Earl of Southampton – the former Sir William FitzWilliam, who had been active in the overthrow of the Boleyns – on 11 December, at St Pierre, a mile south of the Lantern Gate at Calais, for the reception of Henry VIII's fourth bride, Anne of Cleves, upon her arrival in Calais, *en route* to England. Wearing their 'best array', these lords and gentlemen escorted Anne into the town, and as she passed through the Lantern Gate, the cannon along the quayside exploded in a salute. Just inside the gate, Lady Lisle and a host of ladies and gentlewomen sank into deep curtseys as the Princess appeared. Mary Boleyn may well have been one of their number, for she was acquainted with Lady Lisle, who had danced with her in a masque during Henry VIII's visit to Calais in 1532; they must have known each other at court before then, and it follows that they had met in recent years in Calais, William being in the Lisles' service.

After Anne of Cleves had inspected the King's ships in the harbour, she rode through the narrow streets of Calais to the Exchequer Palace, escorted by the Admiral and his chosen gentlemen, with William Stafford among them. And so they brought her to her lodgings, and 'there attended on her daily' until she was ready to sail to Dover. William and Mary would probably have been present at the jousts held on the day after Anne's arrival, and, with bad weather delaying the future Queen's departure, they may also have been present at the banquets and tournaments that were subsequently organised to keep her entertained. It was not until 26 December that a fair wind blew up and the Admiral was finally able to escort the Princess on board the ship that was to take her to England. The crossing was to take seventeen hours.[42]

It seems that Mary and William returned to England with Anne of Cleves. We can only speculate that Lord Lisle must have praised William's good service and given him a very warm recommendation, and that Southampton acted on it; or that William's prominence at the reception of Anne of Cleves implied that his return to royal service had already been approved. It would have been known that he needed to return to England to take charge of his wife's inheritance, and his immediate restoration to the King's good graces, and promotion to a sought-after place at court, might not only have

been well deserved – given the abilities he was to show in royal
service in the years to come – but could also have been a reward
for the care he had taken of Henry's bastard daughter since his
marriage to her mother.

In January 1540, Stafford is recorded as a Gentleman Pensioner
in the King's household. It seems that his appointment had taken
effect almost as soon as he arrived in England. The Gentlemen
Pensioners had been refounded the year before (they had originally
been instituted in 1509), as an élite guard for the King, and it was
their duty to keep watch in the presence chamber. Their members
were the scions of noble houses or from the greatest gentry families, and they were well paid. The equivalent of a household cavalry,
they were fifty in number, and served under the captaincy of the
respected courtier, diplomat and statesman Sir Anthony Browne. They
wore either dark velvet doublets or liveries of red and yellow damask,
with gold medallions on chains of office around their necks, and
were expected to provide their own weapons: a poleaxe, a dagger
and a sword.

There was so much demand for places among the Gentlemen
Pensioners that the King had to create a separate band called the
Gentlemen at Arms, but that did not satisfy the clamour, and by the
end of his reign there were one hundred and fifty Gentlemen
Pensioners. Stafford had been very lucky to secure such a prestigious
post, and to be one of the company of fifty Gentlemen Pensioners
drawn up on Blackheath as the King passed through their ranks to
receive Anne of Cleves on 2 January 1540.[43]

With one half of her father's estate now in the hands of the Crown,
and the rest in the hands of executors, pending its transfer to herself
as his sole surviving heiress, Mary, now probably in her early forties,
may have had concerns as to where she would live on her return
to England. Gentlemen Pensioners were entitled to lodgings at court
only when they were on duty, which was on a rota basis, so it would
not now have been possible for her to live there with her husband.

She may have gone to her grandmother for a short time. Old
Lady Boleyn did not long survive her son, dying sometime between
30 September 1539 and 20 March 1540. An Inquisition Post Mortem
on the Earl of Wiltshire, taken on 30 September 1539, while his
estate was being wound up, reveals that the elderly Lady Boleyn had
been incapable of managing her affairs for the past twenty years,
during which time Wiltshire had assumed control of her estates;

shortly before his death, 'my Lord [of Wiltshire] covenanted that my Lady his mother should have 400 marks [just £130] a year out of them. The deed was made last year and enrolled in Chancery'.[44] This was a mere pittance, given her rich estates, which had enabled her son to live in wealth for years. Thus, if Lady Boleyn was still alive when Mary returned to England, it is therefore unlikely that she was able to offer her granddaughter much support.

We might infer from Sir Thomas Willoughby's undertaking to entertain 'the old Lady Boleyn [at Hever Castle] in best wise to her comfort'[45] that the King had permitted her to live out her days there. Thus Mary may have returned to Hever to succour the old lady until she died – or, if she was already dead, then Mary possibly went to stay temporarily with her father-in-law, Sir Humphrey Stafford, at Cottered. Lady Boleyn's death, at the age of seventy-five, must have come as a merciful release,[46] and meant that Mary could look soon to inherit her grandmother's share of the rich Ormond inheritance, and become a wealthy woman.

In July 1540, Henry would grant the manors of Hever and Seal to his fourth wife, Anne of Cleves, as part of their nullity settlement; Hever Castle would never revert back to the Boleyns, and now passed into peaceful obscurity, in which state it would remain until William Waldorf Astor purchased it in 1903 and set in train its lavish transformation.

In November 1539, when Katherine Carey was fifteen, she had been appointed, against great competition, a maid of honour to Anne of Cleves. Her great-uncle, the Duke of Norfolk, had secured similar positions for two of his other great-nieces, Katherine Howard and Mary Norris, at that time,[47] but he had not visited Calais for some time, and was probably still estranged from Mary Boleyn, so it is unlikely that Katherine's appointment owed anything to his influence.[48] However, if Katherine was the King's daughter, then Henry VIII himself may have ordered her appointment. Unlike her brother, Katherine was not the King's ward, and he was not obliged to make provision for her, although, of course, if she was his child, his interest in her is easily explained; if not, he may have shown her favour for the sake of her brother or her good service to the Lady Elizabeth. But it is perhaps telling that, of all the girls of noble and gentle birth who might have been lucky enough to gain places in the new Queen's household – and the clamour for such places was great –

Katherine, who had little merit as the daughter of Henry's former mistress and niece of his executed wife, was one of the few that were chosen. Soon afterwards, she was to make a good marriage to an up-and-coming courtier. This all points to Henry doing his duty as a father in providing for her.

Katherine came to court ready to serve the new Queen prior to the latter's arrival in January 1540. It turned out that she, the daughter of one of Henry VIII's mistresses, was to serve alongside another, for one of Anne of Cleves' ladies-in-waiting was Elizabeth Blount, now the respectable Lady Clinton.

When, in April 1540, William Stafford, on Mary's behalf, petitioned Thomas Cromwell for 'the profits of the Ormonds' lands in Essex', he was probably shocked to be told, 'That cannot be.' As Wiltshire's auditor, Robert Cranewell, explained to Master Secretary, 'After my Lady's [the Countess of Wiltshire's] decease, my Lord often told me that he had promised the King to make all the Ormond lands sure in fee simple to the Lady Elizabeth for default of issue male of his own body.'[49] Evidently Wiltshire was still sufficiently angry with Mary to consider depriving her of her share of the Ormond inheritance and arranging for it to go to his niece. But an unwritten promise to the King had no force in law, and it seems that Wiltshire had either had second thoughts, or just never got around to formalising his wishes. Even so, it seems that the Crown pressed its claim, presumably in the hope that some documentation of Boleyn's promises actually existed. As a result, Mary and William were obliged to wait three years before they could take 'livery', or possession, of her grandmother's property.[50]

It is often claimed that when her grandmother died, Mary inherited Rochford Hall in Essex and made it her home. Rochford Hall was 'an important building on a grand scale', situated four miles east of Rayleigh and three miles north of Prittlewell (the south end of which became the modern Southend-on-Sea). The Hall had been built in the fifteenth century on the site of an earlier house (of *c.*1216) by Mary Boleyn's forebears, the Butler earls of Ormond, who owned the property until 1515, when it passed to Wiltshire's mother, Lady Margaret Butler.[51] The nearby church of St Andrew, standing only a hundred yards from the house, was probably built by her father, Thomas Butler, 7th Earl of Ormond, whose arms appear on a stone shield above the west door.

Ormond's Rochford Hall was extended and upgraded in Tudor times. In 1923, the Royal Commission on Historical Monuments concluded that the present fabric dates probably from 1540–50. It is unlikely, however, that the rebuilding began under the auspices of Mary Boleyn and William Stafford; it was probably Henry Carey who was responsible for ordering the works, which were carried out according to the very latest architectural fashions and building techniques.[52]

Fragments of carved stonework found in the walls indicate that spoils from dissolved monasteries were used in the rebuilding of the house; these were perhaps acquired by William Stafford, who later, during the iconoclastic holocaust unleashed in the reign of Edward VI, would gain a bad reputation for forcibly carrying off the bells of the churches of Rochford, Ashingdon, South Shoebury, Hawkwell and Foulness for his own benefit; he sold off three of them to raise money to repair sea walls on the nearby coast.[53]

Rochford Hall stood in an eight-acre walled park; the northern boundary wall, with its Tudor diapered bricks, still survives today. Tradition has it that, in 1540, Mary had a circular dovecote with a thatched roof erected in a meadow to the south of the hall – but Mary was not living at the hall in 1540. The dovecote was taken down after being struck by lightning in 1888. In the latter half of the sixteenth century, Rochford Hall was turned into one of the most palatial houses in the country, and thus it remained for a century and more, but in 1760, about half of it was destroyed by a disastrous fire and either pulled down or left in a ruinous condition; in 1893, the place was said to have 'a ghostly air about it, even more so than most decayed mansions'.[54] Further damage was done by German bombers in 1940. Rochford Hall was partially restored in 1987, but nevertheless, substantial parts of the house that Mary and her family knew survive today, although the great hall and chapel have long since disappeared.

Desirable property that it was, Mary could not inherit Rochford Hall until the matter of the Ormond inheritance was resolved, and she and William must have been frustrated at the delay, for gaining possession of her grandmother's lands would have brought them considerable wealth.

However, it was not long before they came into the Boleyn inheritance, the legacy of Mary's father. On 15 April 1540, at Hampton Court, the King granted to 'William Stafford and Mary, his wife, livery [possession] of lands, the said Mary being daughter and heir of Thomas, late Earl of Wiltshire and Ormond, and kinswoman and heir of Margaret Boleyn, widow, deceased, late wife of Sir William Boleyn, deceased'. The lands in question were 'the manors of Southt, alias Southtboram [Southborough, between Tunbridge Wells and Tonbridge] and Henden in Henden Park,[55] and all lands in Hever [excepting the castle] and Brasted,[56] Kent, which belonged to the said Earl'.[57] These lands were worth £488 (£150,000) annually.[58]

The Boleyns had long had a connection with the manor of Brasted (pronounced Braystead). Along with Tonbridge, it had been one of the manors of the Duke of Buckingham that the King retained after the Duke's execution in 1521, appointing the then Sir Thomas Boleyn a life interest in their management.[59] In 1531, the King granted the manor of Tonbridge to Boleyn, now Earl of Wiltshire, and in default to his daughter Anne. A little later, Wiltshire was also given the manor of Brasted. There is no surviving record of this grant, which is known only through a subsequent grant of 1540. On Wiltshire's death in 1539, Brasted and Tonbridge reverted to the Crown along with Hever and other lands, and the following year, Henry VIII bestowed Brasted on Sir Henry Islay. What the Staffords received from the King in April 1540 were certain detached lands in Brasted, Hever, Chiddingstone and Sundridge, as well as the manors of Henden and Southborough in Kent.

Southborough, which had been held by Sir Thomas More before it was granted to Lord Rochford in 1535, was some distance from Hever, but Henden, at Ide Hill, the highest point in Kent, was nearby. Henry VIII had granted it to Sir Thomas Boleyn in 1516. The sixteenth-century timbered manor house, with a moat that may have surrounded an earlier building, still survives, much altered; in Mary's day, it stood in a park of three hundred acres. The Staffords may have resided there for a time, but their tenure would be brief.

On 26 April 1540,[60] Katherine Carey, aged sixteen, was married to Sir Francis Knollys, aged twenty-six, a Gentleman Pensioner of Henry VIII's household and a colleague of William Stafford. No royal grants or gifts marked the marriage, although the King's influence may be perceived in an Act of Parliament that was passed that same year confirming the couple's title to the manor of Rotherfield Greys, near Henley in Oxfordshire, previously held by Knollys's father.[61] It was here, at Greys Court, a fourteenth-century manor house and tower with a Tudor house added on, that Katherine and Francis made their home. In 1542, Francis was elected MP for Horsham. The couple's first child – Mary Boleyn's first grandchild – was born in 1541 and named after the King, as was the popular custom among courtiers.[62]

In July 1540, after Anne of Cleves' marriage had been annulled – Henry VIII, finding her physically repellent, had refused to consummate the union – Katherine Carey transferred to the service of the King's fifth wife, Katherine Howard.[63] Her aunt, Lady Rochford, was also in the new Queen's household as a lady-in-waiting.

William Stafford must also have given satisfaction as a Gentleman Pensioner because in 1541, he was made an Esquire of the Body to Henry VIII. Prior to that, on New Year's Day, at Greenwich Palace, he and five other gentlemen had each presented the King with two bows as New Year's gifts, and been given 10s. (£150) each in return.[64]

In October 1541, in exchange for the manor of Henden, Kent, 'and the park called Henden Park, [with] lands in the parishes of Brasted, Sundridge and Chiddingstone, Kent, and other lands sold by him to the Crown on 5 July', Henry VIII granted William Stafford, 'Esquire of the Body', the manor of Ugthorpe, near Whitby in Yorkshire, and 'divers tenements thereto belonging in Lythe,[65] Yorkshire, parcel of the late priory of Gisborne, Yorks'.[66] After exchanging Henden, Mary and William probably lived at Southborough or at one of their Kentish properties.

Stafford also received in exchange 'the messuage or mansion commonly called the "Unicorn," alias "Unicorn's Horn," in Cheapside in the parish of St Mary le Bow, London, in tenure of John Droke', which was part of 'the possessions of the late priory of Ely; and that part of a tenement usually called the "Unicorne", alias "Goodcheapfield," in West Cheap, in the said parish of St Mary le Bow, in tenure of Leonard Ewe, part of the possessions of the hospital of St Mary without Bishopsgate'.[67] The Unicorn was a substantial building that stood on the corner of Cheapside and Queen Street; in Elizabethan times it became a mercer's shop – 'at the sign of the Unicorn' – and in the eighteenth century it was the workshop of the engraver John Boydell. Goodcheapfield was named after the local family of Goodcheap, one of whom had been Lord Mayor of London. It is unlikely that the Staffords ever lived in these London properties, as they were rented out to Messrs Droke and Ewe, but they would have received substantial rents from them.

Nor is it likely that Mary ever visited Ugthorpe, for William sold it almost immediately to Roland Shakerly, citizen of London.[68] William probably had a general plan to 'trade up' as, hard upon the heels of the grant of exchange, the King granted him permission to alienate the properties he had received.[69] Certainly the couple got rid of other lands, because in October 1542 we find a pardon issued to William Stafford and Mary his wife, and their son-in-law Francis Knollys and Katherine his wife, for the alienation without licence of two messuages (dwelling houses with outbuildings and a courtyard or garden), seven hundred acres of land, fifty acres of meadow, sixty acres of pasture, one hundred acres of furze and heath, common of pasture for a thousand sheep and 59s. 2½d. (£910) rent in Fulbourn. The case was heard before Sir John Baldwin and his colleagues, justices of Common Pleas, at Westminster on 23 October, and the parties were fined.[70] What this document does suggest is that Mary's was a united family and that its members worked together for its common interests.

In 1542, Mary confirmed the transfer of the manor of Filby in Norfolk, which she had inherited from her father, to her uncle, Sir James Boleyn, having probably conveyed it to him in order to raise money; her claim to her grandmother's estate was still in dispute. In April 1541, by Letters Patent of Henry VIII, William Stafford and 'Dame Mary Carey', his wife, had received licence to alienate the manors of Roding, Great Holland, Hawkwell, Foulness Island, Great Wakering, and Rochford, Essex, to William Neville and John Hever, clerk to the Privy Seal; but they were 'to be re-granted to the said William and Mary, and the heirs of the body of the said William', and if he left no issue, they were to go to 'the said Mary and her heirs'. This, however, was not done until May 1543, when Mary finally received formal livery (transfer of possession) of her grandmother's estates.[71]

It is said that Mary made a gift of these Essex manors to her husband between 1539 and 1542, and that they took up residence at Rochford Hall.[72] But, as it turned out, Mary was in possession of that house for only a matter of days.

Queen Katherine Howard went to the block for crimes of adultery in February 1542. It is possible that William Stafford gave evidence against her, and against her former lover, Francis Dereham, whom she had appointed her secretary, for in November 1539, Margaret, Lady Howard, deposed 'to much familiarity between Dereham and the Queen before marriage, and since the marriage has heard one Stafford say, "If I were as Dereham, I would never tell to die for it," and that "there was a thing that stuck upon his stomach"'.[73] That same month, we find this 'Stafford' telling the Privy Council that he had heard 'either of the [Dowager] Duchess of Norfolk or the Lady Howard that she said once in the Queen's chamber to a lady or gentlewoman, "This is he [Dereham] that went into Ireland for the Queen's sake."'[74] In December, Stafford – evidently questioned again – stuck to his story.[75]

Identifying this witness as William Stafford begs all sorts of questions. If it was indeed him, then we might conclude either that he gave this evidence in the hope of currying more favour with the King, or out of gratitude for his recent preferment at court; or, which is more likely, he felt that he had a moral duty to report this information – which chimes with what we know of him in later life. As we have seen, Stafford was more than a reformist – in the not too distant future, he would become the friend of John Calvin, having chosen to go into exile for the sake of his strict Protestant faith. It is entirely credible that he already held such views in 1541, when it was dangerous to profess them publicly, as they were heretical and the penalty was burning at the stake. It is also credible that Stafford collaborated with the reformists at court in bringing down the Catholic Howards.

If that were true, it was not Mary's only family connection with the scandal. In 1541, when evidence of Queen Katherine's infidelity was uncovered, 'that bawd, Lady Rochford'[76] was discovered to have acted as her procuress and go-between. Committed to the Tower and attainted for treason, she 'had shown symptoms of madness till they told her she must die',[77] but seemed lucid enough when she went to the block on 13 May 1542.

On her death, Blickling Hall passed to Mary's uncle, Sir James Boleyn, who had been Anne Boleyn's chancellor.[78] He died in possession of it in 1561, and was buried in the nearby church, after which Blickling came into the possession of his great-nephew, Sir Edward Clere (1536–1606).[79]

These years of tragedy and loss must have blighted Mary's life. In a short space of time she had lost her brother, sister, mother, father, grandmother and sister-in-law. She may well have come to hate Lady Rochford after what she had done to George Boleyn, but the scandal of her crimes, and the horror of her end, must have had some impact, resurrecting painful memories of the fate of Anne and Rochford.

It seems too that, as a consequence of Anne's fall and her own probable years abroad, Mary had little contact with her niece, Elizabeth; we know, however, that in adult life Elizabeth warmly recalled having known William Stafford when she was a child; she would no doubt have seen him about the court when he was in service there, guarding her father. We might pause to wonder if Elizabeth showed life-long favour to her Carey cousins not only for their own sake, but on account of her affection for her aunt, Mary Boleyn. She evidently came to know and love her cousins in youth, so, even though there is no record of Mary visiting the court after Anne Boleyn's death, or of her seeing Elizabeth, it is conceivable that they had some contact, or were in touch with each other through the good offices of Stafford.

Given Elizabeth's enduring affection for her Boleyn relatives, and her evident belief in her mother's innocence,[80] a belief that appears to have been instilled in childhood, probably by members of her household who had known (or been related to) Anne Boleyn, a relationship with Anne's sister, however tenuous, may have brought her comfort. Possibly – although this can only be speculation – Mary Boleyn was one of those who imparted to the future Queen Elizabeth a sympathetic view of her mother's conduct.

Rochford had had no children with his wife, but he may have left a natural son, another George, who was appointed Dean of Lichfield by his cousin or kinswoman, Elizabeth I. This George was a poor scholar, and it seems he received no succour from his aunt Mary, who may not even have known of his existence. The fact that he was called George – a name known to have been borne in the family only by Lord Rochford – and that he chose Henry Carey, Lord Hunsdon, whom he called his 'kinsman' in his will, to be one of his executors, suggests that he was Rochford's bastard.

Mary's husband was to enjoy royal favour for some years to come, but in 1543, he was briefly in disgrace. At a meeting of the Privy Council at St James's Palace on 5 April that year, William Stafford, along with his wife's kinsmen Sir John Clere and Thomas Clere, and a Mr Hussey, was committed to the Fleet prison 'for eating flesh on Good Friday'. On 19 April, the Privy Council ordered that all these prisoners were to 'have the liberty of the garden' at the prison,[81] and on 1 May 1543, dismissed William Stafford, Sir John Clere and Mr Hussey 'from attendance' at council meetings.[82]

It is likely that these misfortunes came at a difficult time, and that Mary was ill when her husband was in prison and dismissed from attendance at court. But he was not out of favour for long, and on 15 May, at long last, a grant was made to 'William Stafford and Mary his wife, kinswoman and heir of Lady Margaret Boleyn, widow, deceased, viz. daughter of Thomas, late Earl of Wiltshire and Ormond, son of the said Margaret, giving them livery [possession] of lands of the said Thomas and Margaret and of those held by Jane, late wife of Sir George Boleyn, Lord Rochford, deceased, by way of jointure'.[83]

It had taken three years to secure livery of Mary's inheritance, and fifteen months to secure livery of Lady Rochford's jointure, which had been seized by the Crown on that lady's attainder – but the grants came too late for Mary. She was either dying, or about to suffer a fatal accident or seizure.

It is often stated – on the premise that she had come into possession of it on her grandmother's death – that she died at Rochford Hall in Essex, a house she would have known from childhood, and where she is said to have made a home with William Stafford. But as Mary owned Rochford Hall for precisely four days, there would surely not have been time for her to take possession, and the most she could probably have managed was a visit of inspection – given that her health permitted; so it is doubtful if she ever lived there. She died on 19 July 1543,[84] leaving her eighteen-year-old son, Henry Carey, to enjoy the Butler inheritance in her stead. It is possible that her death was sudden,[85] but the cause is unknown. We might even speculate that the stresses and tragedies of the past decade had hastened her end.

In her will, Mary left William Stafford the manor of Abinger, Surrey, and messuages called Whithouse and Londons, both formerly held by 'Lady Mary Carewe' in Essex,[86] together with the advowsons – the right to present a nominee to a vacant benefice – of the churches of Paglesham, Foulness, Hawkwell and Leigh.[87]

Mary's last resting place has never been identified. The tale that she was buried somewhere within the grounds of Hever Castle[88] can be instantly dismissed on the grounds that it would have been unheard of then for someone other than a suicide to be interred in unconsecrated ground – and there is no evidence at all that Mary killed herself. It has also been suggested that she was buried in Westminster Abbey, where her children would later be laid to rest[89] – but Mary died long before they found favour with Elizabeth I, and her name does not occur in the detailed records of burials within the abbey. Another claim has been made for St George's Chapel, Windsor, as her last resting place, but again, there are detailed records of interments and she is not among them.

Possibly she was buried in St Andrew's Church at Rochford, which had been built in the late fifteenth or early sixteenth century by her grandfather on the site of an earlier church where, in 1380, the future Henry IV may have married Mary de Bohun, mother of Henry V.[90] The church built by the Earl of Ormond has since been subject to much Victorian restoration, and if Mary was laid to rest there, all trace of any memorial has disappeared. There would be no record of her burial as the parish registers only go back as far as the seventeenth century. However, as we do not know where she was residing at the time of her death, we can only speculate where she was laid to rest.

It would be in keeping that Mary Boleyn was buried quietly and without fanfares, in peaceful obscurity, as she had lived her last years. Probably this was what she had wanted all along. She did not die an infamous woman – no one commented on her end – and even though her affair with Henry VIII had long since become public knowledge at court and beyond, circumspection had nevertheless been maintained. Certainly it has now surely been established beyond doubt that Mary was never the great and infamous whore described by Rodolfo Pio and, perhaps, François I. The sheer lack of evidence is testimony to that. She probably had little choice in becoming the mistress of two kings, and barely anything is known about her supposedly scandalous relations with them – yet, to this day, she enjoys posthumous notoriety as the 'hackney' whom the King of France boasted of riding, and who thereafter happily hopped from bed to bed until she was seduced by the King of England, at whose court she won infamy for a brief, glittering spell. It is time to lay that myth to rest.

Unlike her sister, Mary had not tempted fate too far. There is some irony in this, as Anne had been the one who had flown high and won all the plaudits, while Mary, for much of her life, had done the 'wrong' things, and had probably been a disappointment to her ambitious family, who saw her as a failure. But Mary's letter to Cromwell proves that she had learned what really mattered in life. Where Anne suffered much unhappiness and a cataclysmic fall, Mary – in the end – found love and stability. It has been said, with truth, that 'there was not in her the stuff of tragedy; she passes out of history with a happy ending', married to the man she loved.[91] All things considered, she had managed rather well. And of all the three Boleyn siblings, she alone lived into middle age and died in her bed.

Appendix I

'Of Her Grace's Kin'

When Mary died, all that William Stafford inherited from her was the manor of Abinger in Surrey, which he sold in the early 1550s.[1] In the month of her death, July 1543, at the head of a hundred foot soldiers he himself had furnished, he began four months' military service in France, when Henry VIII took Boulogne,[2] and in 1545, he fought under Edward Seymour, Earl of Hertford, when the English invaded and laid waste southern Scotland. There he distinguished himself by gaining for the King 'two prizes, viz., the *François of Dieppe* and the other Scottish ship', which were 'taken by Mr Stafford'.[3] It was probably for this that he was knighted, on 23 September that year.

Having converted to the Protestant faith – which may have come about as a result of his connection with the reformist Boleyns, if not before – William found favour under his old commanding officer, Edward Seymour, when the latter became Duke of Somerset and Lord Protector during the minority of Henry VIII's heir, Edward VI. Stafford sat in the new King's first parliament in 1547. Edward retained him as a Gentleman Pensioner, and he became the young monarch's standard bearer. He seems not to have suffered as a result of Somerset's fall in 1549; in 1550, after John Dudley, Duke of Northumberland, had seized power, Stafford was granted an annuity of £100 (£20,000) in recognition of his good service to Henry VIII, and entrusted with securely conveying three noble French hostages from Dover to London. He seems to have had no problem in shifting his allegiance, and voluntarily reported to Northumberland the words of a servant who had spoken out in defence of the fallen Somerset.

In 1551, Stafford accompanied Edward, Lord Clinton (Elizabeth

Blount's widower), to Paris to represent Edward VI at the christening of a son of Henri II of France, and when he returned to England, he took part in a great tournament held at court to mark the new year of 1552. But his career foundered after he was involved in a fight with Adrian Poynings, a fellow soldier, in November 1552, which resulted in Stafford being briefly incarcerated – yet again – in the Fleet prison in London. That cost him the Privy Council's respect and confidence.

William apparently mourned Mary for nearly nine years. It was not until 1552 that he remarried, his bride being fifteen-year-old Dorothy Stafford, a distant connection; she was one of the fourteen children of Henry, Baron Stafford, by Ursula Pole. Ursula was the granddaughter of Edward Stafford, Duke of Buckingham, a descendant of King Edward III who had been executed for treason in 1521; her mother had been Margaret Pole, Countess of Salisbury, a niece of Edward IV and Richard III and therefore also of the old Plantagenet royal blood; in 1541, the Countess, at the ripe age of sixty-seven, had been executed by Henry VIII simply because he saw her as a threat to his throne. Her father, George, Duke of Clarence, had been attainted for treason and executed in the Tower of London – probably drowned in a butt of Malmsey wine – in 1478.

Aside from her dangerous pedigree, Dorothy had no dowry to speak of, and we might wonder why William married her. He was now a staunch Protestant, while many members of her family were devout Catholics. Her grandfather, grandmother, great-grandfather and uncle had been executed for treason, and another uncle, Cardinal Reginald Pole, had been an exile in Italy since speaking out against Henry VIII's marriage to Anne Boleyn. We might conclude therefore that this outwardly unsuitable union was yet another love match, as William's marriage to Mary Boleyn had been, and perhaps, again, an impulsive one.

They had little else to offer each other. William had incurred increasing debts, and in 1552, he had exchanged a royal annuity he had been granted for a cash payment of £900 (£180,500) to avoid financial embarrassment.

William and Dorothy had three sons and two daughters: the eldest son, Sir Edward Stafford, served for a time as England's ambassador in Paris, while the eldest daughter, Elizabeth, became Lady of the Bedchamber to Elizabeth I.

When Henry VIII's daughter Mary, a staunch Catholic, succeeded to the throne in 1553 and outlawed the Protestant religion, William Stafford quickly realised that exile was preferable to persecution. In March 1554, he left England and settled in Geneva, Switzerland, with his wife and children, his sister, a cousin, and his servants. Geneva was an obvious choice, because it was where the Lutheran theologian and reformer John Calvin had founded a theocracy, controlling the city through his College of Pastors and Doctors and his Court of Discipline. Calvin's stern brand of religious doctrine and his moral severity must have appealed to Stafford. Calling himself 'Lord Rochford', a title to which he had no right, he became involved in the affairs of Geneva, and was nearly killed in the fighting during the uprising in 1555 that confirmed Calvin's autocracy.

By then, with the fires of Smithfield alight in England, so many English Protestants had sought refuge in the city that an English congregation was set up. Stafford became a member, and his son John was the first infant to be baptised into it, on 4 January 1556, with John Calvin standing as godfather.

William survived Mary Boleyn by thirteen years, dying on 5 May 1556 in Geneva. Ten days later, in ignorance of his death, the Privy Council in England ordered that no payment of money was to be sent abroad to him. Calvin took custody of little John Stafford and forbade the child's mother to leave Geneva with him. Only after she had appealed to her brother-in-law, Sir Robert Stafford, and he had threatened to invoke aid from the French, did Calvin back down. Dorothy took her family to Basel, where she lived until 1559, when Elizabeth I, her distant cousin, now having ascended the throne, she knew it was safe to return to England.

Dorothy may have been the 'Mistress Stafford' who was one of four gentlewomen who had attended Elizabeth during her imprisonment in the Tower in 1554.[4] That would account for the established bond between herself and the new Queen, for Elizabeth herself sent Dorothy assistance to aid her return home in August 1559, and in 1563 made her Mistress of the Robes, always treating her as a friend and kinswoman, the widow of her uncle, William Stafford, whom she remembered having known as a child. She would have met him during her visits to court in the 1540s, when she would also have had opportunities to get to know her Carey cousins – and perhaps her aunt, Mary Boleyn.

Around 1544, Elizabeth was painted in a dynastic family group commissioned by Henry VIII, which now hangs at Hampton Court

Palace. She is wearing a pendant in the form of an 'A' that must have belonged to Anne Boleyn, who favoured pendants displaying her initials: three of them feature in portraits of her. The fact that, by the age of ten or eleven, Elizabeth had formed such a positive view of her mother (whose name was not supposed to be mentioned in her presence) that she was prepared publicly to display her connection with her, in defiance of her father, points to her having been fed sympathetic opinions about Anne. There were Boleyn connections in Elizabeth's household, among them her governess, Katherine Champernowne (later Mrs Astley), who might have voiced these, but it is also possible that Elizabeth had been given information about her mother by Mary Boleyn and her children, or even by William Stafford, who shared Anne Boleyn's passion for reform. That would have been one reason why she showed her Carey cousins such warmth. The fact that there is no record of her ever seeing Mary after 1534 does not mean that they did not meet again.

Dorothy never remarried – which, again, might argue that her marriage to William had been a love match. She would serve the Queen faithfully for four decades and survive her by seventeen months, dying in 1604. The epitaph on her plain tomb in St Margaret's Church, Westminster, records that she served Queen Elizabeth 'forty years lying in her bedchamber, esteemed of her, loved of all, doing good all she could to everybody, never hurt any, a continual remembrancer of the sues of the poor'.

This was the lady whom William Stafford had chosen as his second wife, marrying her against the odds, probably for love, as he had Mary Boleyn. That he mourned Mary for nearly a decade – and then paid her memory the compliment of marrying yet again where his heart dictated – is surely testimony to his genuine feelings for her, and the happiness of their union. It speaks volumes for Stafford's own character that he should win such a prize as Dorothy, and that, in an age that put a high premium on dynastic advantage, he should have twice spurned material gains in order to marry the lady of his choice.

Henry VIII, as Henry Carey's guardian, made suitable provision for his ward; this is not 'inexplicable',[5] as has been asserted, because, as King, he had a duty to act *in loco parentis*, looking to the boy's welfare and his future. As we have seen, he also provided for Katherine Carey, which may be more significant.[6] By 1545, Henry Carey was a member of the King's household,[7] and that same year, Henry VIII found a bride for him: Anne, the sixteen-year-old daughter of Sir Thomas Morgan of Arkstone, Herefordshire, a relatively obscure Welsh gentleman. They were married on 21 May 1545.[8] Not for Carey a grand match with the daughter of a duke, as had been arranged for Henry Fitzroy – which is further proof that Carey was not the King's son. Indeed, this marriage with Anne Morgan seems hardly to have been commensurate with the young man's status as a royal ward with a substantial landed inheritance. Nor did Henry VIII bestow any special gifts or favours on his ward, who grew up supported only by a modest income.[9]

The Careys were a prolific family, and Henry and Anne were to have twelve children – nine sons and three daughters; interestingly, none was given the name Mary, in honour of Henry's mother, which might suggest that he was not overkeen on preserving her memory for posterity. Reared under Anne Boleyn's auspices, and then the King's, he may have been inculcated with the wisdom that Mary was best consigned to anonymity, given the compromising nature of her affair with Henry.

Henry Carey recorded details of his family in a copy of Froissart's *Chronicles*.[10] The Carey offspring were called by contemporaries 'the tribe of Dan',[11] which has been seen as a possible allusion to their being descended from Henry VIII.[12] In the Bible, Dan was the son of Jacob by his wife's handmaid, Bilhah, and possibly a comparison was being drawn with Mary Boleyn, although she had never been a 'handmaid' to Katherine of Aragon. But there is another comparison to be drawn: the tribe of Dan sent more men to war than any other of the tribes of Israel, and did not receive their rightful inheritance, just as Henry Carey and his sons felt that he was never properly rewarded by Elizabeth for his decades of loyal service.[13] This is probably the real basis for the nickname. Certainly it weighs lightly against the other evidence for William Carey's paternity.

Henry Carey and Anne Morgan would be married for over fifty years, and the epitaph that she and their eldest son were to place on Henry's tomb describes him as 'the best of fathers and dearest of husbands' – notwithstanding his infidelities over the years.

In March 1546, Carey came of age, and inherited all the lands given by the King to his father in Buckinghamshire, Essex, Hampshire and Wiltshire, including the borough of Buckingham, as well as those left to him by his mother. Rochford Hall was part of that inheritance.

Late that year, aged only twenty-one, he secured his election as Member of Parliament for Buckingham, a seat he would hold four times. He sat in that Parliament with his stepfather, Sir William Stafford, and his brother-in-law, Sir Francis Knollys. He was the first of eleven Members of Parliament to live at Rochford Hall.[14]

Henry Carey seems not to have had any special attachment to Rochford Hall. He set in train restoration works, then sold the manor and estate around 1552 to Richard, Lord Rich, who was greatly to enlarge the house.[15] By coincidence, Rich's great-grandson was to marry Penelope Devereux, Mary Boleyn's great-granddaughter.

Henry Carey would probably have come to know his cousin, the future Elizabeth I, when he was serving in Henry VIII's household, if he had not been acquainted with her before, when he was the King's ward. An entry in Elizabeth's Hatfield accounts for 1551–2 shows that he was already one of her circle, for it records that she made a gift of money 'at the christening of Mr Carey's child'.[16] That child was probably his daughter Philadelphia, born around 1552, who married Thomas, 10th Baron Scrope; she and her older sister, Katherine, Countess of Nottingham, became Elizabeth's favoured maids-of-honour when she was Queen.[17]

The accession of Elizabeth I on November 1558 dramatically changed the lives of Mary's children. Both were immediately made welcome at court, where they were to enjoy glittering careers. Their cousin Elizabeth held them in great affection, leading some writers to suggest that this may – or must – have been because one or both of them were in fact her siblings;[18] but as her cousins, they were her closest blood relatives aside from her cousinly rivals on her father's side: Mary, Queen of Scots; Margaret Douglas, Countess of Lennox; Lady Katherine Grey and Lady Mary Grey, all of whom were too near in blood to the throne for comfort and could never be trusted. The Carey siblings, apart from being no dynastic threat, were unfailingly loyal, and this in itself would account for Elizabeth's love for them, and for the lavish funerals in Westminster Abbey with which she later provided them.[19]

The acknowledged existence of Carey half-siblings would undoubtedly have been a major embarrassment to Queen Elizabeth, and could have compromised the legitimacy of her title,[20] for she had been declared illegitimate in 1536 on the grounds that her parents' marriage had never been lawful on account of Henry VIII's affair with Mary Boleyn having created a bar to his marriage to her sister Anne, and that ruling had never been reversed. In the eyes of Catholic Europe, the new Queen was a bastard, a heretic and a usurper. Unlike her half-sister, Mary I, Elizabeth, on her ministers' advice, had not, upon her accession, had her parents' marriage declared good and valid. Thus she carried the stain of bastardy with her all her life. It would therefore have been politically – and personally – disadvantageous for Katherine to have been openly acknowledged as Henry VIII's natural child by Mary Boleyn, living proof of the impediment to Elizabeth's mother's marriage. Such a revelation would have drawn unwelcome attention to the Queen's bastard status at a time when her throne was insecure; it would have exposed Henry VIII's hypocrisy in pursuing an annulment of his marriage to Katherine of Aragon, and it could have undermined the foundations of the English Reformation, and the Protestant Anglican settlement of 1559 that built upon it.

It would be wrong, however, to compare the Careys' position to that of Edward Stafford, Duke of Buckingham, who had been executed for treason in 1521 for, amongst other things, 'openly boasting his descent from King Edward III', which, it has been said, was 'not a mistake Mary's children were to repeat'.[21] Buckingham had been of legitimate royal descent, and therefore posed a real dynastic threat to Henry VIII; but no one could ever claim that Katherine and Henry Carey had any kind of claim to the throne or represented a similar threat. Even if the Careys were Henry VIII's children, they could never have challenged Elizabeth's position.

If Henry had been Katherine Carey's father, the one person who would surely have known about it was Elizabeth herself, who grew up to be very close to Katherine, as she did to her other bastard half-sister, Etheldreda, and who would have maintained strict discretion, referring to Katherine simply as her kinswoman. Katherine herself may well have preferred to keep her paternity a secret to avoid further sullying her mother's memory; and it is certain that she would never have done anything that undermined her cousin's throne.

Elizabeth's closeness to the Careys can be explained by their kinship. In a letter written in 1579, she referred to Henry Carey as 'our cousin of Hunsdon';[22] she signed letters to Katherine Carey as 'your loving cousin',[23] and Katherine was called the 'kinswoman and good servant' of the Queen by a correspondent.[24] Mary, Queen of Scots,

in a letter to Elizabeth I,[25] referred to 'one of the Knollyses' – that
is, one of Sir Francis's children by Katherine Carey – as 'your relation'. Had Katherine been Henry VIII's daughter, her children would
have been Queen Mary's own cousins, and therefore her relations
too. Mary freely acknowledged her own bastard half-siblings, and at
least one historian has wondered why she never made political capital
out of the blood relationship between her rival Elizabeth I and her
Carey cousins.[26] But if Katherine Carey had been Elizabeth's half-
sister, the Queen of Scots was probably never aware of it.

In the month of Elizabeth's accession, November 1558, Henry Carey
was knighted. On 13 January 1559, his fortunes changed dramatically when the Queen raised him to the peerage as Baron Hunsdon,
granting him the royal palace of Hunsdon House in Hertfordshire,
where she herself had resided at various times during her childhood,
and lands in Hertfordshire, Kent and Hampshire worth a princely
£4,000[27] (£681,000) a year to 'maintain his rank'.[28] There is no
evidence to support the assertion[29] that Henry Carey had spent his
early years at Hunsdon; it was a royal property, and Elizabeth now
had it in her gift. Henry's uncle, John Carey, a Groom of Henry
VIII's Privy Chamber, had been appointed paymaster and overseer
of the King's works there in 1537–8.[30]

Queen Elizabeth was always to show great affection and trust for
Lord Hunsdon: in 1560, she appointed him Master of the Queen's
Hawks, and in 1561, she made him a Knight of the Garter. The
following year, when Elizabeth was thought to be dying of smallpox,
it was Hunsdon who called in a German physician, and then, when
that physician had given up hope, persuaded him to persevere –
some said at the point of a dagger. From what she believed to be
her deathbed, Elizabeth particularly commended Hunsdon to the
kindness of her Privy Council.[31] He was entrusted with important
diplomatic missions, such as when he was sent to convey the insignia
of the Garter to Charles IX of France in 1564, and for many years,
alongside his more able peers, William Cecil, later Lord Burghley,
Robert Dudley, Earl of Leicester, the Queen's favourite, and, later,
Sir Francis Walsingham, he was at the forefront of state affairs.

Those years saw him well endowed with offices: Privy Councillor
(1577), Captain of the Gentlemen Pensioners, the Queen's personal
bodyguard (1583), Lord Chamberlain (1585), Lord Warden General
of the Northern Marches (1587), Chief Justice in Eyre south of the

River Trent (1589), High Steward of Ipswich and Colchester, Chief Justice of the Queen's Army (1591) and High Steward of Oxford (1592). He was also Lord Lieutenant of Norfolk and Sussex, and a member of that legal elite, the Inner Temple, along with his kinsmen Thomas Howard, 4th Duke of Norfolk, and Charles, Lord Howard of Effingham. However, the Queen never advanced him beyond the rank of a baron, and the two titles he wanted all his life were never to be his: those of Earl of Wiltshire and Ormond, which had been borne by his grandfather, Thomas Boleyn, to whom he always insisted he was rightfully co-heir. But Elizabeth remained deaf to his pleas.

The post of Lord Chamberlain was an important one, for it put Hunsdon at the head of the Queen's household and in command of the conduct of the court.[32] It also ensured that he would have the benefit of 'the continual presence of her Majesty, to take any advantage of time and occasion for having of suits';[33] this meant that he was in an ideal position to exercise the very lucrative privilege of patronage. Yet, despite the honours heaped on him, Hunsdon was never a wealthy man, for he had spent several thousand pounds of his patrimony in Elizabeth's service, much of it for her relief during her imprisonment in the Tower in Queen Mary's reign; he was not greedy, and his income, the fruit of Elizabeth's favour, was never exorbitant;[34] moreover, he had a large family to support. Thus he was perennially short of money.

Hunsdon was 'very choleric but not malicious', a plain main 'of an honest stout heart', whose 'custom in swearing and obscenity in speech made him seem a worse Christian than he was';[35] but the Queen liked that in him, and his bluntness. She took it well when, in 1572, angry at her hesitation over sending the Duke of Norfolk, who had been found guilty of treason, to the scaffold, Hunsdon castigated her: 'It is small policy, not worthy to be termed mercy, to be so careless of weighty matters that touch the quick so near!' She knew him to be 'a fast man to his prince, and firm to his friends and servants, such a one that upon occasion would have fought for his prince and country'.[36] His loyalty to the Queen was unflinchingly staunch.

Elizabeth liked the fact that Hunsdon never involved himself in factional politics. In fact, there were long periods when he rarely visited the court, being often deployed far away on his duties, and when he did go there, he was regarded with fear and suspicion by many courtiers. His innate bluntness and lack of tact – traits he

shared with his grandfather, Thomas Boleyn – did not endear him
to them, and he was never popular. His soldiers, however, idolised
and respected him. 'He loved sword-and-buckler men, and such as
our fathers were wont to call "men of their hands", of which sort
he had many brave gentlemen that followed him; yet [he was] not
taken for a popular or dangerous person.'[37]

A distinguished soldier, a good jouster and a 'valiant man',[38]
Hunsdon was appointed Governor of Berwick in 1568, retaining the
post for twenty years. That year, he was in York as one of the English
commissioners at the trial of Mary, Queen of Scots, and Elizabeth
proposed his eldest son, George Carey, as a putative husband for
Mary, who had fled to England some months earlier and been taken
into custody, as she posed a great danger to Queen Elizabeth's security. This 'remarkable' proposal has been seen as indicating that George
Carey must have had royal blood to be considered a suitable match
for the Queen of Scots,[39] but only four years earlier, Elizabeth had
proposed Sir Robert Dudley, her Master of Horse, as a bridegroom
for Mary, and he was certainly not of royal blood.

As Lieutenant General of the Queen's forces in the north, Hunsdon
was instrumental in suppressing the Northern Rebellion of 1569–70,
one of the most dangerous crises of Elizabeth's reign; in February
1570, although heavily outnumbered, he decisively defeated the rebel
army under Leonard Dacre, and chased the latter over the Scottish
border; as he himself put it, it was 'the proudest charge, upon my
shot, that ever I saw'.[40] When Elizabeth was given the news, she added
a note in her own hand to the official letter of congratulation:

> I doubt much, my Harry, whether that the victory were given
> me, more joyed me, or that you were by God appointed
> the instrument of my glory; and I assure you that, for my
> country's good, the first might suffice; but for my heart's
> contentation, the second pleased me . . .
> Your loving kinswoman, Elizabeth R.[41]

The next year, Hunsdon was made Warden of the East Marches
of the Scottish border, and played a key role in striving to keep
Scotland peaceful during the turbulent period of regencies that
followed the flight of the deposed Mary, Queen of Scots to England.
In time, he became Captain-General of all the English forces
defending the northern border.

Hunsdon was not a faithful husband. He kept at least two successive mistresses, and fathered several bastards. While posted in the
north, he lived with a woman who later married one Hodson; she
bore him a son, Valentine Carey, who was to enjoy a successful career
as a soldier under his father's command before becoming Bishop of
Exeter. There is a suggestion, in an anonymous doggerel of the period,
that Hunsdon underwent mercury (quicksilver) treatment for vene-
real disease:

> Chamberlain, Chamberlain,
> He's of her Grace's kin,
> Fool hath he ever been
> With his Joan Silverpin:
> She makes his cockscomb thin
> And quake in every limb;
> Quicksilver is in his head
> But his wit's dull as lead
> – Lord, for thy pity![42]

When the threat of the Spanish Armada was looming in 1588,
Hunsdon was summoned south to command a force of 36,000 men
at Tilbury Fort, and was expressly enrolled by the Queen on 20 July
as Lieutenant, Principal Captain and Governor of the Army 'for the
defence and security of our own Royal Person';[43] in this capacity,
he was present on the day she went to Tilbury to rally her troops
and deliver her famous, inspired Armada speech. 'He had the charge
of the Queen's person both in the court and in the camp at Tilbury.'[44]
In 1590, Hunsdon was appointed joint Earl Marshal of England with
William Cecil, Lord Burghley, and Admiral Charles, Lord Howard
of Effingham. Two years later, he was one of the commissioners who
tried Sir John Perrot, the reputed 'bastard son' of Henry VIII.

Hunsdon was not always in Elizabeth's good books. When he once
outstayed his leave of absence from court, the Queen became incan-
descent with rage, and exploded to his son: 'God's wounds! We will
set him by the feet and set another in his place if he dallies with us
thus, for we will not be thus dallied with withal!'[45] The storm soon
blew over, though, for Elizabeth could not stay angry with her cousin
for long.

Hunsdon shared with his fellow nobles the contemporary passion
for collecting exotic plants and medicinal herbs.[46] He was a patron

of the painter Nicholas Hilliard, and it was he who commissioned one of that artist's finest miniatures of Elizabeth I, which shows her seated on a chair playing a lute.[47] As Lord Chamberlain, carrying his white staff of office, he is depicted posthumously, walking before the Queen's chariot in a painting of *c.*1601, attributed to Robert Peake, which shows her being carried in procession to Blackfriars; it is now at Sherborne Castle.[48]

As Lord Chamberlain, it was Hunsdon's responsibility to arrange masques, plays and other entertainments for the Queen. He clearly had a great love of the theatre and, following in the steps of Elizabeth's favourite, the Earl of Leicester, and other noblemen, he gave his name and his patronage to a company of players, becoming, in 1594, the first patron of the Lord Chamberlain's Men, among whom were such luminaries as William Shakespeare and the actors Richard Burbage, Thomas Pope and William Kemp. It was, initially, a political appointment, because, in the wake of Shakespeare's controversial *Titus Andronicus*, these actors were regarded by the Privy Council as seditious, and the loyal Hunsdon was seen as the right man to keep them in check – as he did.[49] Shakespeare immortalised him as Philostrate, Master of the Revels to King Theseus, in *A Midsummer Night's Dream*, an uncontentious play written to please his patron. He also celebrated Hunsdon's great victory over the Northern rebels in 1569 in *Henry IV, Part 1*.[50]

Hunsdon's company performed at the Theatre in Shoreditch, the first purpose-built London theatre;[51] under his patronage they produced many of Shakespeare's greatest plays and, in 1599, built the Globe Theatre in Southwark. Sadly, Hunsdon did not live to see this.

As Lord Chamberlain, Hunsdon was also in charge of the Queen's Players, and through them, around 1592, he met Emilia (or Aemilia) Bassano, the gifted daughter of Baptista Bassano, musician to Henry VIII and Elizabeth I. The beautiful Emilia, whom A.L. Rowse once identified as the 'Dark Lady' of Shakespeare's sonnets,[52] became the mistress of Hunsdon in his old age. His junior by forty-four years, she was an accomplished player on the virginals and, in publishing a book of religious verse, *Salve Deus Rex Judaeorum*, she became the first professional female English poet. After Hunsdon's death, she told the astrologer and reputed magician Dr Simon Forman that she had been 'maintained in great pride' by her ageing lover, who 'loved her well' and was generous to her with money and jewels. Hunsdon even got her pregnant, and, to maintain discretion, 'she was for colour married to a minstrel', an Italian called Alfonse Lanier (or Lanyer), with whom she was reputedly unhappy. The boy she bore in 1593 was called Henry Lanier, and his doting father settled on Emilia a life annuity of £40 (£5,000).[53] Henry Lanier would grow up to become a court musician to King Charles I.[54]

Hunsdon had always lived in hope that the Queen would bestow on him the earldoms of Wiltshire and Ormond, which had been borne by his grandfather and earlier forebears. There is a story that, as he lay dying on 23 July 1596 in his lodgings at Somerset House (of which he was Keeper) in London, Elizabeth 'gave him a gracious visit' and caused a patent creating him Earl of Wiltshire, and the robes she had had made for him, to be laid on his deathbed. But Hunsdon 'could dissemble neither well nor sick'.

'Madam,' was his characteristically blunt response, 'seeing you counted me not worthy of this honour while I was living, I count myself unworthy of it now I am dying.'[55] His death – coming within a week of that of his brother-in-law, Sir Francis Knollys – plunged Elizabeth into a melancholy mood.

Lord Hunsdon was buried in a princely tomb in St John the Baptist's Chapel in Westminster Abbey[56] that – according to the inscription thereon – was built by his widow, Anne, and his heir, George Carey.[57] It was not, as some writers claim, paid for by the normally parsimonious Queen,[58] although she did pay out £800 (£80,500) for his obsequies,[59] which demonstrates how deeply she held him in affection. At thirty-six feet in height, his monument was – and remains – the highest in the abbey, and it is certainly one of the grandest. It was constructed of marble and alabaster, painted in black and white and then gilded, with a sarcophagus in an arched recess framed by classical columns, trophies, pedestals, obelisks, and heraldic shields displaying the Boleyn bull and falcon, all crafted in the Italian style by an unknown sculptor. The underside of the arch was panelled with Tudor roses, as in Queen Elizabeth's own tomb, and in the centre are prominently displayed the Carey arms, surmounted a domed and balustraded pavilion supporting a swan.[60] All that was omitted was an effigy. The heading of the inscription reads *Sepulturae Familiae de Hunsdon, Consecratum*, and it has been pointed out that the use of the name Hunsdon rather than Carey is 'striking',[61] although in fact members of the peerage were commonly referred to by their titles. Hunsdon's tomb has been called 'an over-whelming example of Elizabethan monumental art'[62] and 'an unabashed celebration of worldliness',[63] and some have seen it as a monument to an unacknowledged prince. That, of course, is unlikely.

Seven of Lord Hunsdon's children survived him. He was succeeded in his title by his eldest son, George Carey, who died in 1603, the same year as Elizabeth I. The next son, John, then became the 3rd Baron Hunsdon. He died in 1617, when his son Henry took the title. It was for Henry that James I revived the title of Viscount Rochford in 1621. Henry was succeeded in 1666 by his son John, who died without male heirs in 1677, when the titles Baron Hunsdon and Viscount Rochford became extinct.

Legend long had it that Katherine Carey, Countess of Nottingham, Hunsdon's eldest daughter, withheld from Queen Elizabeth the famous 'Essex ring', which the Queen had given to her favourite, Robert Devereux, declaring that if ever he found himself in trouble, he was to send it to her. Accordingly, when Essex was sent to the Tower on a charge of treason in 1600, he is said to have contrived to send the ring to his cousin, Lady Nottingham, with a message begging her to take it to the Queen, but his enemy, Robert Cecil, dissuaded her, with the result that Essex perished on the block. When Lady Nottingham was on her deathbed, in February 1603, she is said to have confessed all to the Queen, who had hitherto been a close friend.

'God may forgive you, but I never can,' Elizabeth is supposed to have replied,[64] angrily taking the dying woman by the shoulders and shaking her in her bed.

A ring that Elizabeth had given Essex did exist, and three centuries after her death it was placed under glass at the side of her tomb; it is now in the Norman Undercroft Museum in Westminster Abbey. The rest of the tale is nothing but a legend, and Elizabeth sincerely mourned Lady Nottingham, whose death in February 1603 is thought to have hastened the Queen's own end.

The Careys played a pivotal role in the events surrounding the finale to the Tudor dynasty and the accession of the Stuarts. Two of Mary Boleyn's grandchildren, Robert Carey, later Earl of Monmouth, and Philadelphia Carey, Lady Scrope, supported the ailing Queen Elizabeth in her last illness. Another legend involving a ring had it that when the Virgin Queen finally died at Richmond Palace in March 1603, Lady Scrope removed her coronation ring from her finger and dropped it from a window of the gatehouse to Robert Carey, who was waiting on his horse below, ready to ride north to Scotland to bring King James VI news – and proof – of his accession.

Of course, the Queen did not die in the gatehouse, as the legend claims, and the ring had been sawn from her finger while she still lived, but Carey certainly bore it to Edinburgh, having – as we may infer from his own account – acquired it by stealth.[65]

According to her memorial plaque in Westminster Abbey, Katherine Carey and Francis Knollys had sixteen children – eight boys and eight girls – of whom at least eleven survived infancy. Only fifteen are shown in effigy as kneeling weepers on their parents' magnificent but empty tomb at Rotherfield Greys, built in memory of Francis and Katherine by their son William in 1605. There are seven sons on one side, seven daughters on the other, and an infant lying beside the effigy of its mother.

The births of the children – who may well have been Henry VIII's grandchildren – were recorded 'in order' by Knollys himself in his Latin dictionary;[66] he listed fourteen children: eight sons and six daughters, and the last to be recorded was Dudley, born in 1562, the only one of the brood who is known to have died young, being 'killed' in the year of his birth. It is almost certain that he is the infant lying with the recumbent figure of Katherine Carey at Rotherfield Greys.[67]

So how can we account for the missing daughter? The Westminster Abbey plaque is likely to be correct, as it was mentioned by William Camden in his memorial of Westminster Abbey in 1600, and had probably been in place long before Knollys's death in 1596.[68] Probably the unnamed daughter died at birth, or was stillborn – reason enough for her father not to list her in his diary. Some modern genealogists claim that there was a daughter called Cecilia who served Elizabeth I, but there is no mention of her in the Knollys family papers. It would appear that she has been confused with her sister Elizabeth, whose portrait bore an incorrect inscription in the seventeenth century.[69]

Unlike her brother, Katherine called one of her daughters (the eldest) Mary, almost certainly in honour of her mother, and another was called Anne, perhaps after her aunt, Anne Boleyn. One son was called William, probably after William Stafford, suggesting that the latter had become a much-loved stepfather.

After Edward VI came to the throne in 1547, Francis Knollys distinguished himself in the war against the Scots, and for this he was knighted by the King's uncle, Lord Protector Somerset. A staunch

Calvinist, Knollys was forced – like his stepfather-in-law, William Stafford, to flee abroad when Queen Mary I began burning Protestants for heresy. Katherine followed him before June 1557; there is a gap of nearly three years between pregnancies, which suggests that they were apart for a considerable time. At least five of their children went with them. When Katherine left England, her 'loving cousin', the future Elizabeth I, wrote a sad letter of farewell, and signed it '*cor rotto*' ('broken heart').[70] This is evidence that the two women had already become close and laid the enduring foundations of future friendship. The shared bond of religion had surely brought them closer in the difficult days of Bloody Mary's reign, and Elizabeth's assurance that she would wait 'with joy' for Katherine's 'short return' betrays her hope that her sister's rule would not last long.

On Elizabeth's accession in 1558, the Knollyses deemed it safe to return home, and Sir Francis was made a Privy Councillor, Vice-Chamberlain of the Queen's household and Governor of Portsmouth. Amidst fierce competition for places at court, Katherine was appointed a Lady of the Privy Chamber, alongside her sister-in-law, Anne Morgan; her nieces, Katherine and Philadelphia Carey, were serving as maids-of-honour. The new Queen had a policy of advancing her Boleyn relatives, but only on their merits; she liked Katherine for herself, and the Carey family were her closest blood relations on her mother's side, towards whom she always behaved with far more familiarity than she used to other members of her court. The Knollys children, like their cousins, the young Careys, were all welcomed at Elizabeth's court, and many of them made good careers or marriages there, some of the daughters waiting upon the Queen. They all basked in her favour, and may have been substitutes for the grandchildren she never had.[71]

Elizabeth 'loved Lady Knollys above all other women in the world'.[72] Katherine had an attractive personality, being graced with 'wit and counsel sound' and 'a mind so clean [and] devoid of guile'.[73] In 1560, Elizabeth granted her, jointly with her son Robert, the manor of Taunton for life. After the death of Elizabeth's beloved former governess, Katherine Astley, in 1565, Katherine Carey became chief Lady of the Bedchamber to the Queen, with whom she was 'in favour, above the common sort', according to Thomas Newton, who published *An Epitaph upon the Worthy and Honourable Lady, the Lady Knowles* in 1569. She was given 'some of the most expensive presents Elizabeth ever gave',[74] and entrusted with the safe-keeping of gifts presented to her mistress.[75] However, Elizabeth's love for

Katherine was marred by selfishness: she wanted her in constant attendance, regardless of the needs of her cousin and her family; and the strain of this, balanced with the demands of a large brood of children, often drove Katherine to 'weep for unkindness'.[76]

To make things worse, during the first decade of her reign, Elizabeth kept Sir Francis Knollys busy with diplomatic missions. In May 1568, when the deposed Mary, Queen of Scots fled to England and was placed under house arrest, he was appointed her custodian. During the year that she was in his charge, he did his best to convert the Catholic Mary to Calvinist doctrines, but was ordered to desist by Elizabeth. Generally, though, he got on well with the latter, despite his poor opinion of her statesmanship, which he wisely took care to conceal.

Knollys had pleaded to be allowed to take his wife with him when he was sent north to take charge of Mary in 1568, but Elizabeth had refused to be parted from her. Late that year, learning that Katherine had fallen ill with a fever, he begged in vain to be recalled. His repeated requests for leave of absence to visit his ailing wife were also ignored, and he was distraught at Elizabeth's 'ungrateful denial of my coming to the court'. In his last letter to Katherine, he wrote of how he desired them both to retire from the Queen's service and live 'a poor country life'[77] – much as his mother-in-law had done with William Stafford.

In his absence, Katherine had to make do with being 'very often visited by the Queen's comfortable presence'.[78] At one stage, she felt a little better and asked Elizabeth if she might travel north to be with her husband, but Elizabeth refused to allow it, arguing that 'the journey might be to her danger or discommodity'. She too was fearful for Katherine's health, and when her cousin suffered a relapse, she had her nursed in a bedchamber near to her own, and sat with her often.[79]

The Queen of Scots was to blame Queen Elizabeth for Katherine's early death at the age of forty-three, claiming that it was the consequence of her husband's enforced absence in the north during the last months of her life.[80] But it was probably years of relentless childbearing that had undermined Katherine's health. She passed away on 15 January 1569 at Hampton Court, greatly mourned by the Queen, while Sir Francis was still absent, guarding Mary, Queen of Scots at Bolton Castle. Afterwards, Elizabeth collapsed in 'passions of grief for the death of her kinswoman and good servant, falling for a while from a prince wanting nothing in this world to private mourning, in which solitary estate, being forgetful of her own health, she took cold, wherewith she was much troubled'.[81] As for the bereaved husband, he was 'distracted with sorrow for his great loss. My case is pitiful,' he wrote.[82]

Elizabeth arranged for Katherine to be buried in April 1569 in St Edmund's Chapel in Westminster Abbey, herself outlaying £640.2s.11d (£111,300) for the funeral – far more than she ever spent on burying other cousins, even those of royal birth.[83] Yet – perhaps for a very good reason – this was almost a royal funeral. The obsequies were arranged under the auspices of the Duke of Norfolk, as Earl Marshal, and the Earl of Leicester, the Lord Treasurer. The funerary furniture was so valuable that it became the subject of a dispute between the Chapter of Westminster Abbey and the College of Arms.[84] A mural tablet of alabaster, adorned with armorial shields – one of the first of its kind in the abbey – marks Katherine's resting place.[85]

Katherine's eldest son, Henry, was held in high esteem by the Queen, who was to write, in 1570, that she had good reason for that, 'in respect of his kindred to us by his late mother'.[86] Katherine's eldest daughter, Laetitia, known as Lettice – 'one of the best-looking ladies of the court' – became Elizabeth's lady-in-waiting and close friend – until her secret marriage to the Queen's favourite, Robert Dudley, Earl of Leicester, was made public in 1578, after which a furious Elizabeth never received her at court again. Lettice's son from her first marriage, Robert Devereux, Earl of Essex, became the favourite of the ageing Queen in her latter years, before he led a rebellion against her government and was executed in 1601.

It is often said that Henry VIII's line died out with Elizabeth. None of his legitimate children left issue, and his acknowledged bastard, Richmond, was childless. But if Katherine Carey was Henry's daughter, as seems likely, then his direct bloodline survives in numerous direct descendants.

Under the Stuarts, the Carey family remained prominent until the senior line died out in 1677. Among the illustrious descendants of Mary Boleyn are numbered Sir Winston Churchill, Lord Nelson, Charles Darwin, Sabine Baring-Gould, William Cowper, Lady Antonia Fraser, J. H. Round, Vita Sackville-West, Thomas West, the Baron de la Warre after whom the US state of Delaware is named, Lady Anne Somerset, Algernon Swinburne, Ralph Vaughan Williams, P.G. Wodehouse, Catherine Middleton, Duchess of Cambridge, Sarah Ferguson, Duchess of York, Camilla Parker Bowles, Duchess of Cornwall, Diana Spencer, Princess of Wales (through the Earls Spencer), the late Queen Elizabeth the Queen Mother, and Queen Elizabeth II.[87]

Appendix II

Portraits of 'Mary Boleyn' and William Carey

A half-length portrait in the inner hall of Hever Castle is said to be 'Mary Boleyn, after Hans Holbein', although in the seventeenth century – when it may have been painted – it was labelled 'Anne Boleyn', and only later changed to 'Mary Boleyn'. There is good cause to question the sitter's identity, as this picture is hung as one of a pair with another of similar size called 'Anne Boleyn', yet the latter is now known not to be Anne, for it is based on a Hans Holbein drawing of a lady who was not identified as Anne Boleyn until 1649, and who bears little resemblance to Anne as she appears in authenticated portraits.

The existence of other, later versions of the portrait said to be of Mary Boleyn suggests that there was an original Tudor portrait from which they all derive. No comparable portrait by Holbein exists, although the costume is contemporaneous with his career as King's painter to Henry VIII. At least five other versions survive: one at Warwick Castle is said to date from the Stuart period or the eighteenth century (with a companion one of 'Anne Boleyn', as at Hever); there are two in the Royal Collection, including a cruder version at Holyrood Palace, Edinburgh; another, in a private collection, is inscribed in a later hand 'Mary Bullen Wife to Wm. Carey Esq'; two others are at Southside House, Wimbledon, and Henden Manor in Kent, a house that was briefly in Mary's possession. Most of the versions are very similar. This proliferation of the same image suggests either that there was some demand for a portrait of this lady, whoever she was, or that

after one portrait was misidentified as Mary Boleyn (almost certainly
at a later date), copies were made in the mistaken belief that the sitter
was Mary.

There are clues in the portrait to the sitter's identity. She has a
round face, prominent nose and chin, large dark eyes and a small
mouth with rosebud lips. Her hair is concealed under her hood and
cannot be seen, but her well-defined eyebrows are light brown. She
wears a black velvet, square-necked gown, bordered in red, with an
ermine trim on the neckline and ermine oversleeves, and a short
gable hood of the type fashionable in the 1530s, with one lappet of
its veil thrown over the top in the favoured 'whelk-shell' fashion.
Around her neck is a double rope of pearls with a lozenge-shaped
pendant surrounded by filigree work and pearls, with a drop pearl,
and on her breast an oval pendant with another drop pearl, surmounted
by a leafy sprig of two small roses or carnations.

On costume alone, this portrait dates from long after the period
– the early 1520s – when Mary Boleyn was Henry VIII's mistress;
in the early 1520s, the ends of the gable hood would have been
longer, and the veil left flowing. Furthermore – and this is crucial
– the sitter wears ermine, a fur reserved exclusively for royalty and
peers of the realm. The wife of a commoner, as Mary's two husbands
were, was specifically prohibited from wearing ermine, even if she
were the Queen's sister. Given the ermine trim on her gown and
the ermine sleeves, it is highly unlikely that this woman is Mary
Boleyn. Moreover, the fact that at least six versions of this portrait
survive, two of them in the Royal Collection, suggests that she was
someone far more important, probably a member of the royal family.
Mary Boleyn, by her own account, was held in little esteem by her
family and the world at large. There would not, in the 1530s, when
she was either languishing in courtly obscurity or banished in disgrace,
have been any demand for a portrait of her.

The jewellery in the portrait is indistinct, so no conclusions can
be drawn from that. The sitter is probably in her teens or twenties.
In the Hever and Warwick versions, her face seems to owe more to
seventeenth- or eighteenth-century portraiture than to that of the
sixteenth. She is far too young to be Katherine of Aragon or Henry
VIII's sister, Mary Tudor, Duchess of Suffolk, who died in 1533, aged
thirty-seven, and too round-faced to be Anne Boleyn; in any case,
she bears little resemblance to portraits of Anne or of Jane Seymour.
The other royal possibilities are Mary Tudor's daughters, Frances and

Eleanor Brandon, and the Lady Margaret Douglas, daughter of the King's elder sister, Margaret Tudor, Queen of Scots, by her second husband, Archibald Douglas, Earl of Angus. Frances Brandon was sixteen when she married Henry Grey, Earl of Dorset, in 1533, Eleanor eighteen when she married Henry Clifford, Earl of Cumberland, in 1537. Margaret Douglas, who spent many years at the English court and was a friend of the Princess Mary, was twenty-one in 1536, when she was sent to the Tower for a time after involving herself in a misalliance with Lord Thomas Howard.

Any one of these royal ladies could have been the sitter in this portrait.

The only authenticated portrait of Margaret Douglas dates from 1567;[1] a seventeenth-century full-length by Daniel Mytens, said to show her in later life,[2] may not be Margaret at all, as it was described only as 'a Scottish lady in a long mourning habit' in 1639.[3] Neither bears a strong resemblance to the 'Mary Boleyn' portrait, but we might not expect them to, as they were painted at least thirty years later. There is also a tomb effigy in Westminster Abbey, executed after 1578. All these representations show the Countess with a slightly retroussee nose, unlike the rather prominent straight nose of the sitter in our portrait.

The only certain image of Frances Brandon is her tomb effigy in Westminster Abbey, dating from after 1559. There is a portrait in the Royal Collection of the same period, said to be her, but without authentication. That leaves Eleanor Brandon, of whom no portrait is known to exist – claims on the internet that a Holbein drawing of an unknown lady in the Royal Collection is her are unsubstantiated – and for whose portrait there probably would have been little demand.

Yet if one compares facial characteristics in portraits of Charles Brandon, Duke of Suffolk, his wife, Mary Tudor, and his daughter, Mary, Lady Monteagle, it is possible to detect similarities with the portrait said to be of Mary Boleyn, notably the large nose, which is evident in the wedding portrait of Brandon (1515), the Holbein sketch of Lady Monteagle and also in a drawing done in 1515 of Mary Tudor. The shape of the chin is exactly the same as Mary Tudor's in the two surviving French portraits of her, and the setting of the eyes and eyebrows like those of Charles Brandon. This is subjective evidence, of course, but added to the other clues, it suggests that what we have here may be a portrait of Frances Brandon, painted to mark the solemnising of her marriage to Henry Grey, Marquess of Dorset, which was celebrated in May 1533, shortly before Anne Boleyn's coronation. The costume is of that period, and this identification of the sitter would explain the ermine and the existence of several copies of the portrait, for Frances was the King's niece and the daughter of one of the foremost peers in England by a princess of the blood. Nevertheless, given the absence of any contemporary likeness of these royal ladies, we cannot say with certainty that the sitter in the 'Mary Boleyn' portrait is one of them. It is most unlikely, however, that it depicts Mary Boleyn.

How, then, did this portrait come to be associated with Mary? The answer is not far to seek. For centuries, it was common for names to be inscribed on portraits, or labels added, on the feeblest assumptions as to identity, and in more recent times, many have been shown to have been incorrect. Although Mary's name appears on at least one version of this picture, it has been written in a much later hand. Once an error like this had been made, it was easily replicated, with the false identification coming to be accepted as authentic. Most examples have been corrected in the light of recent research, yet even today some are the subject of dispute, such as two Holbein drawings said, on shaky authority, to be of Anne Boleyn.

A fine but unfinished portrait of Mary's first husband, William Carey, was until fairly recently in the private Irish collection of Henry A. Fitzhugh, and portrays a richly dressed, young and attractive man with brown hair, a short beard and a strong nose, with eyes that markedly resemble those of his Tudor cousins. Carey holds a book, with one finger marking a page, which suggests that he wished to be seen as a man of learning or piety. The portrait was overpainted in the sixteenth century, and has recently been cleaned, with the restoration revealing an underpainting of a woman's head that much resembles Holbein's drawing of a lady of the Zouche family (labelled 'M. Souch') in the Royal Collection.[4]

David Starkey has credibly suggested that this portrait of William Carey may have been painted by Hans Holbein, who was working in England in 1526–8, under the patronage of Sir Thomas More, and in 1532–43 for Henry VIII.[5] The quality of the painting, the realism of the features and the portrait beneath in Holbein's style might suggest that, as does the fact that Holbein painted every one of the colleagues who worked with Carey to organise a major court reception in 1527[6] at a time when he was executing his first works for the court.

The sitter was identified as William Carey in 1959 on the evidence of a coat of arms on an inferior Elizabethan portrait of the same man, which bears the date 1526, and gives the age of the sitter – who is holding a pair of gloves instead of a book – as thirty.[7] Back in 1959, it was thought that the pioneering miniaturist Lucas Horenbout – who was working at the English court under the lucrative patronage of Henry VIII from at least April 1524, and who painted the earliest English portrait miniatures – executed this picture,[8] but tree-ring dating on the wood panel carried out by John Fletcher in 1971 proved that that portrait could not have been painted before 1570, and that it probably dated from 1575–90. Thus it was probably based either on the Fitzhugh portrait, which must have been painted after Carey's death, or on a lost portrait or miniature from life.

We know that William Carey's son, Henry, Lord Hunsdon, commissioned portraits of his cousin Elizabeth I and other family members, so it is likely that he also commissioned one of his father – probably this one – and perhaps a companion portrait of his mother, Mary Boleyn. It is likely that Hunsdon wanted these paintings for the long gallery that he added to Brooke House in Hackney, which he owned from 1578 to 1583.[9] It is also possible that he commissioned them to hang in Hunsdon House, in time for Elizabeth I's visit in September 1571.

It has been said that that dating the portrait to after 1570 would explain why the haircut, bonnet and neckline – which would have been seen in a miniature – are accurate for 1526, while the horizontally banded sleeves are more in keeping with the costume of *c.*1550–*c.*1570.[10] Yet such banding and slashing is seen in male costume from the 1520s to Elizabethan times, and in 1526 would have been at the height of Burgundian fashion;[11] moreover, the sleeves in the portrait match the part of the doublet that would have been visible in a miniature. So although it has been put forward that this portrait was based on a miniature by Horenbout,[12] it is also possible that it derives from a half-length panel painting.

It may be that the addition of the date 1526 on the Elizabethan copy of Carey's portrait was based on information given by Lord Hunsdon, or taken from another picture, perhaps the lost original of the Fitzhugh portrait, which might just have fitted into Holbein's

first sequence of courtier portraits. The Fitzhugh picture itself must
be later, for the female portrait beneath dates from after 1532. That
does not, of course, preclude its being by Holbein, or a member of
his workshop or follower, but it must have been a copy of an original painting or drawing from life, possibly done in 1526 and now
lost, for by the earliest time the copy could have been painted,
William Carey had been dead for at least four years.

Thus we have two later paintings, one of which was probably
based on a lost original dated 1526, possibly by Horenbout, and the
other possibly by Holbein, executed in 1527 as part of a sequence
of portraits of Carey's colleagues at court.[13]

Who would have commissioned the Fitzhugh portrait? We could
be more certain if we knew the provenance of the painting, and
whether it descended through the Carey family. It is more likely that
the original had been commissioned by Carey himself, and was later
inherited by Mary Boleyn. Carey had not lived to fulfil his potential, and there would not have been much demand for a copy of his
portrait some years after his death, unless a family member or friend
commissioned one privately. Was it Mary herself? In 1539–40 she
came into part of her inheritance, and it is just possible that she
wanted another painting of her first husband to hang in one of the
houses that were now hers.

It has been suggested[14] that a miniature of a lady in the collection
of the Duke of Buccleuch by Lucas Horenbout depicts Mary Boleyn.
The costume worn by the sitter is that of the early to mid 1520s;
there has been some repainting of her features at one time.[15]
Erroneously labelled 'Katherine of Aragon', and first recorded in the
collection of Charles II (reigned 1660–85), it has been claimed in
recent years that this miniature is an early portrait of Anne Boleyn,
but there is no convincing evidence to support that identification,
while the woman depicted is blonde, and bears little resemblance to
Anne Boleyn in authenticated portraits.

It has also been claimed that the brooch on her breast depicts
Anne's falcon badge, but some have noticed that the 'wings' appear
to point downwards on either side, while those of Anne's falcon
sweep upwards towards the right. The brooch is so small that it is
impossible, even through magnification, to obtain a clear image of
it, but – as can be plainly seen in a second version of the miniature
– it actually bears an image of a kneeling woman wearing a white

girdled gown with a low square neck and long hanging sleeves. This second version, previously in the Watney Collection at Cornbury Park, is now in the Royal Ontario Museum in Toronto, and was once thought to depict Katherine of Aragon and, later, Jane Seymour, on the grounds that it had once been owned by a collateral descendant, Charles Seymour (1662–1748). In this version, the sitter is wearing a different hood, a black damask gown and an ornate pendant with three drop pearls, which is not seen in the Buccleuch version. The brooch is the same, though.

Lucas Horenbout had worked at the court of Margaret of Austria, and may well have known Sir Thomas Boleyn, who might even have been instrumental in bringing the artist's family to England; Lucas's father Gerard had been an illuminator and court painter to the Archduchess, and his sister Susanna was skilled in the same fields. As discussed above, it has been suggested that Mary's first husband, William Carey, was a patron of Lucas Horenbout, on the grounds that it was Horenbout who painted a lost portrait of Carey, probably in 1526.[16]

Although we cannot be certain that Carey patronised Horenbout or the up-and-coming Holbein, an artist of some skill painted his portrait, so to that extent he could be described as a patron of the arts. It has been stated that he actually introduced Horenbout to the English court[17] – although too little is known of the circumstances in which Horenbout arrived to say that for certain – and that he assembled his own collections of art.[18] That is unlikely, given that he lived in a cramped courtier lodging. One or two portraits, of himself and perhaps his wife – desirable objects that were effective statements of his high office and his importance in the court – did not make a collection.

The theory has been put forward that, if Horenbout painted William Carey, it followed that he might have painted Mary as well, as one of his first commissions in England in 1526.[19] Yet with William Carey's patronage of Horenbout uncertain, there is nothing to link this miniature to Mary Boleyn, unless, of course, her father commissioned it – although, again, his link with Horenbout is not proven.

Certainly the miniature dates from the mid-1520s. The Toronto version is inscribed ANNO XXV, showing that the sitter was in her twenty-fifth year; and it is possible that Mary could have been born in 1500, making her twenty-four in 1524/5, which would coincide with Horenbout's first year in England. The brooch is possibly symbolic – a kneeling woman represented deference, humility and subordination, and was often a ritual image suggesting the marriage bond, so this sitter is almost certainly a married woman. It could also represent a mythological or allegorical figure.

At that time, however, the portrait miniature had only just been introduced into England, and was an expensive novelty, sought after by a king and nobles eager to be at the forefront of artistic fashion. With Horenbout, the chief master of the form, being a court painter, most early English miniatures are therefore of royalty, with only a few exceptions. The sitter in this pair of miniatures, however, does not resemble any royal lady of the mid-1520s. The age of the sitter excludes Katherine of Aragon and Mary Tudor, Duchess of Suffolk. It is of course possible that, if Sir Thomas Boleyn was responsible for bringing Horenbout to England, he then commissioned a work or works to demonstrate the limner's craft in order to win his protégé commissions; it follows too that he might have chosen one of his daughters as a sitter. If this is Mary – and that is a big 'if' – the portrait could have been painted to mark the birth of her daughter; and if that daughter had been fathered by Henry VIII, there was all the more reason to commission a likeness.

Normally, the existence of duplicated portraits suggests that there was some demand for the image of an important or royal personage, but it is credible in this case that a second miniature may have been painted for William Carey. Furthermore, the suggested Boleyn link to Horenbout is strengthened by the fact that the latter was appointed King's Painter in 1531, when Anne Boleyn was riding high in the King's favour; this grant of office was confirmed three years later, on the day before George Boleyn was made Lord Warden of the Cinque Ports.[20] All this is speculation, though, and without any more evidence to go on, the identity of the sitter in these miniatures must remain in question.

Select Bibliography

Primary Sources

Ambassades en Angleterre de Jean du Bellay, 1527-29 (ed. V.L. Bourilly and P. de Vassière, Paris, 1905)

An English Garner (8 vols., ed. Edward Arber, London, 1877-92)

Anselme, Père (Father Anselm of the Virgin Mary): *Histoire généalogique de la maison royale de France, et des grands officiers de la couronne* (2 vols., Paris, 1674)

The Antiquarian Repertory: A Miscellany, intended to Preserve and Illustrate Several Valuable remains of Old Times (4 vols., ed. F. Grose and T. Astle, London, 1775-84, 1808)

Bellay, Martin and Guillaume: *Mémoires* (4 vols., ed. V.L. Bourrilly and F. Vindry, Paris, 1908-19)

Bibliothèque Nationale, Paris MS. fr.7853, f.305b

Blackwood, Adam: *Martyre de la Reyne d'Éscosse* (Edinburgh, 1587; Antwerp, 1588)

Bourbon, Nicolas: *Nicolae Borbonii Vandoperani Lingonensis, Nugarum libri octo* (Lyons, 1538; Basel, 1540)

Brantôme, Pierre de Bourdeille, Seigneur de: *Ouvres Complètes* (12 vols., ed. Ludovic Lalanne, Librairie de la Société de l'Histoire de France, Paris, 1864-96)

Brodeau, Jean: *La vie de Maistre Charles Dumoulin, advocate au parlement de Paris* (Paris, 1654)

Calendar of the Close Rolls preserved in the Public Record Office: Henry VII (2 vols., London, 1955-63)

Calendar of Inquisitions Post Mortem: Henry VII (2 vols., London, 1915)

Calendar of Letters, Despatches and State Papers relating to Negotiations between England and Spain, preserved in the Archives at Simancas and Elsewhere (17 vols., ed. G.A. Bergenroth, P. de Goyangos, Garrett Mattingley, R. Tyler et al., H.M.S.O., London, 1862-1965)

Calendar of Letters and State Papers relating to English Affairs, preserved principally in the Archives of Simancas, Vols. 1-4, Elizabeth I, 1558-1603 (Vaduz, 1971)

Calendar of Patent Rolls: Henry VII: 1485-1509 (2 vols., London, 1914-16)

Calendar of Patent Rolls for the Reign of Henry VIII, 1509-1547 (incorporated in *Letters and Papers, Foreign and Domestic, of the Reign of Henry VIII* (21 vols. in 33 parts, ed. J.S. Brewer, James Gairdner, R. Brodie et al., 1862-1932)

Calendar of the Patent Rolls preserved in the Public Record Office, Mary and Philip and Mary (4 vols., ed. A.E. Stamp, London, 1937-9)

Calendar of State Papers, Domestic Series, for the Reigns of Edward VI, Mary, Elizabeth I, 1547-1625 (12 vols., ed. Robert Lemon and Mary Anne Everett Green, London, 1856-72)

Calendar of State Papers, Foreign Series, of the Reign of Elizabeth (23 vols., ed. Joseph Stevenson and A.J. Crosby et al., London, 1863-1950)

Calendar of State Papers: Ireland: Elizabeth I, 1588-92 (ed. Hans Claude Hamilton, London, 1974)

Calendar of State Papers and Manuscripts existing in the Archives and Collections of Milan, Vol. 1, 1385-1618 (ed. Allen B. Hinds, London, 1912)

Calendar of State Papers and Manuscripts relating to English Affairs preserved in the Archives of Venice and in the other Libraries of Northern Italy (7 vols., ed. L. Rawdon-Brown, Cavendish Bentinck et al., H.M.S.O., London, 1864-1947)

Calendar of State Papers relating to Scotland and Mary, Queen of Scots, 1547-1603 (12 vols., ed. Joseph Bain, W.K. Boyd and M.S. Giuseppi, Edinburgh, 1898-1969)

Camden, William: *Annales rerum Anglicarum et Hibernicarum regnante Elizabetha* (London, 1615)

Camden, William: *Reges, Reginae, Nobilis et alii, in Ecclesia Collegiata B. Petri Westmonasterii sepulti* (London, 1600)

Carey, Sir Robert: *Memoirs of the Life of Robert Carey, Baron of Leppington and Earl of Monmouth, written by himself* (written before 1627; ed. John Boyle, Earl of Cork and Orrery, London, 1759; ed. F.H. Mares, Oxford, 1972)

Carles, Lancelot de: *Letter containing the criminal trial brought against the Queen Anne Boleyn of England* (MSS Fr. 1742 and 2370, Bibliothèque

Nationale, Paris, written 1536, published Lyons, 1545, of which a copy is in the British Library; published as 'Épistre contenant le procès criminel faict a l'encontre de la royne Anne Boullant d'Angleterre' (in *La Grande Bretagne devant l'Opinion Française* by Georges Ascoli, Paris, 1927)

Cavendish, George: *The Life and Death of Cardinal Wolsey* (London, 1557; ed. R. Sylvester, Early English Texts Society, 1959; ed. Roger Lockyer, The Folio Society, 1962)

Cavendish, George: *Metrical Visions* (published in Vol. 2 of S.W. Singer's edition of George Cavendish's *The Life of Cardinal Wolsey*, London, 1825)

The Chronicle of Calais in the Reigns of Henry VII and Henry VIII, to the year 1540 (attributed to Richard Turpin; ed. J.G. Nichols, Camden Society, 25, 1846)

The Chronicle of King Henry VIII of England (*Crónica del Rey Enrico Otavo de Inglaterra*, sometimes attributed to Antonio de Guaras; also known as 'The Spanish Chronicle'; ed. M.A.S. Hume, 1889)

Clifford, Henry: *Life of Jane Dormer, Duchess of Feria* (1643; ed. E.E. Estcourt and J. Stevenson, 1887)

Correspondence de l'Empereur Maximilien Ier et de Marguerite d'Autriche sa Fille, Gouvernante de Pays Bas (ed. Le Glay, André Joseph, Paris, 1839)

Cotton MSS, British Library

Cranmer, Thomas: *Miscellaneous Writings and Letters of Thomas Cranmer* (ed. J.E. Cox, Parker Society, Cambridge, 1846)

Dugdale, William: *Monasticon Anglicanum* (6 vols., ed. J. Caley, H. Ellis and B. Bandine, London, 1817-30)

Egerton MSS (British Library)

English Historical Documents, 5, 1485-1558 (ed. C.H. Williams and D.C. Douglas, London, 1967)

Fénelon, Bertrand de Salignac de la Mothe: *Correspondance Diplomatique* (Paris, 1838)

Four Years at the Court of Henry VIII: Selections from Despatches written by Sebastian Giustiniano, January 12 1515 to July 26 1519 (4 vols., trans. and ed. L. Rawdon Brown, London, 1854)

Foxe, John: *History of the Acts and Monuments of the Church* (*Foxe's Book of Martyrs*) (1563; ed. G. Townshend and S.R. Cattley, 8 vols., London, 1837-41)

Fuller, Thomas: *History of the Worthies of England* (London, 1662)

Gardiner, Stephen: *The Letters of Stephen Gardiner* (ed. James Arthur Muller, Cambridge, 1933)

Hall, Edward: *The Triumphant Reign of King Henry the Eighth* (London, 1547; 2 vols., ed. C. Whibley and T.C. and E.C. Jack, London, 1904)

Harington, Sir John, et al.: *Nugae Antiqua, being a Miscellaneous Collection of Original Papers in Prose and Verse; written during the reigns of Henry VIII, Edward VI, Queen Mary, Elizabeth and King James* (ed. Henry Harington, London, 1779, 1804)

Harington, Sir John: *A Tract on the Succession to the Crown* (1602; ed. Sir Clements Robert Markham, Roxburghe Club, New York, 1970)

Harleian MSS, British Library

Harpsfield, Nicholas: *The Life and Death of Thomas More, Knight* (London, c.1557; ed. E.V. Hitchcock and R.W. Chambers, Early English Texts Society, London, 1935)

Harpsfield, Nicholas: *A Treatise on the Pretended Divorce between King Henry VIII and Katherine of Aragon* (ed. N. Pococke, Camden Society, 2nd Series, 21, London, 1878)

Hatfield MSS: The Salisbury (Cecil) Manuscripts and Papers (Hatfield House, Hertfordshire)

Herbert, Edward, Ist Baron Herbert of Cherbury: *The Life and Raigne of King Henry the Eighth* (London, 1649)

Hostillers' Books (Durham Cathedral Muniments, Durham University Library)

'Household Expenses of the Princess Elizabeth during her Residence at Hatfield October 1, 1551 to September 30, 1552' (ed. Viscount Strangford, *Camden Miscellany*, 2, Old Series 55, London, 1853)

Inventories of the Wardrobe, Plate, Chapel Stuff etc. of Henry Fitzroy, Duke of Richmond and Somerset. . . (ed. John Gough Nichols, Camden Society, Old Series 61, London, 1854)

Lansdowne MSS, British Library

Latymer, William: Treatise on Anne Boleyn (Bodleian Library, Oxford, MS. Don. C.42)

Leland, John: *The Itinerary of John Leland in or about the years 1535-1543* (5 vols., ed. Lucy Toulin Smith, London, 1906-10)

Leti, Gregorio: *Vita di Elisabetta* (Amsterdam, 1692)

The Letters of King Henry VIII (ed. Muriel St Clair Byrne, London, 1936)

Letters of Mary, Queen of Scots (ed. Agnes Strickland, London, 1848)

Letters and Papers, Foreign and Domestic, of the Reign of Henry VIII (21 vols.

in 33 parts, ed. J.S. Brewer, James Gairdner, R. Brodie et al., 1862–1932)

Letters of the Queens of England, 1100-1547 (ed. Anne Crawford, Stroud, 1994)

Letters of Royal and Illustrious Ladies of Great Britain (3 vols., ed. Mary Anne Everett Wood, London, 1846)

The Lisle Letters (6 vols., ed. Muriel St Clair Byrne, London and Chicago, 1981)

The Love Letters of Henry VIII (ed. Henry Savage, London, 1949)

The Love Letters of Henry VIII (ed. Jasper Ridley, 1988)

The Love Letters of Mary, Queen of Scots, to James, Earl of Bothwell (ed. Hugh Campbell, London, 1825)

Mander, Karel van: *Schilderbook* (1604; trans. Constant van der Wall, New York, 1936)

The Manuscripts of J. Eliot Hodgkin Esq., F.S.A., of Richmond, Surrey (Historical Manuscripts Commission, 15, 2)

Meteren, E. van: *Historie der Nederlandsche . . . oorlogen ende geschiedenissen* (Delft, 1599, 1609)

National Archives (Public Record Office): C142: Inquisitions Post Mortem E326: Ancient Deeds SP1: State Papers

Naunton, Sir Robert: *Fragmenta Regalia* (London, 1653; ed. Edward Arber, London, 1879, 1896)

Newton, Thomas: *An Epitaph upon the Worthy and Honourable Lady, the Lady Knowles* (London, 1569)

Original Letters Illustrative of English History (11 vols. in 3 series, ed. Sir Henry Ellis, London, 1824, 1827 and 1846)

'Papers relating to Mary, Queen of Scots, communicated by General Sir William Knollys' (ed. William Knollys, *Philobiblon Society Miscellanies*, 14-15, 1872-6)

Parker, Matthew: *The Correspondence of Matthew Parker, 1535-1575* (ed. J. Bruce and T. Perowne, Parker Society, 1853)

The Paston Letters, 1422-1509 (3 vols., ed. James Gairdner, Edinburgh, 1910)

The Privy Purse Expenses of King Henry the Eighth from November MDXIX to December MDXXXII (ed. Sir Nicholas Harris Nicolas, London, 1827)

Pole, Reginald: *Pro ecclesiasticae unitatis defensione (A Defence of the Unity of the Church)* (Rome, 1538, based on an open letter sent to Henry VIII in 1536)

Puttenham, George: *The Art of English Poesie* (London, 1589; ed. G.D. Willcock and Alice Walker, London, 1936)

Rastell, William: Life of Sir Thomas More (fragment in the Arundel MSS, British Library)

Robinson, C.: 'Carey, Barons Hunsdon, etc.' (*Herald and Genealogist*, 8 vols., London, 1867)

Roper, William: *The Life of Sir Thomas More, Knight* (*c.*1556; ed. E.V. Hitchcock, Early English Texts Society, 197, 1935)

The Rutland Papers: Original Documents illustrating the Courts and Times of Henry VII and Henry VIII, selected from the private archives of His Grace the Duke of Rutland (ed. William Jordan, Camden Society, Old Series, 21, London, 1842)

Rymer, Thomas: *Foedera, Conventiones, Et. . . Acta Publica inter Reges Angliae* (London, 1704–17)

Sander, Nicholas: *Rise and Growth of the Anglican Schism* (*De Origine ac Progressu Schismatis Anglicani*) (Rome, 1585; ed. and trans. David Lewis, London, 1877)

Skelton, John: *The Book of the Laurel* (ed. Frank Walsh Brownlow, Delaware, 1990)

Sloane MSS, British Library

Smyth, John: *The Berkeley Manuscripts: Lives of the Berkeleys* (ed. Sir John Maclean, Gloucester, 1883)

State Papers of the Reign of Henry VIII (11 vols., Records Commissioners, 1831–52)

Statutes of the Realm (11 vols., Records Commissioners, London, 1810–28)

Stow, John: *A Survey of London* (London, 1598; Stroud, 1994)

Testimenta Vetusta (ed. Nicholas Harris Nicholas, London, 1826)

Thomas, William, Clerk of the Council to Edward VI: *The Pilgrim: A Dialogue on the Life and Actions of King Henry the Eighth* (1546; ed. James Anthony Froude, London, 1861)

Tillet, Jean du: *Receuil des Rois de France* (Paris, 1580)

Tottel's Miscellany (ed. H.E. Rollins, Cambridge, Mass., 1965)

Weever, John: *Ancient Funeral Monuments within the United Monarchies of Great Britain, Northern Ireland and the Islands Adjacent* (London, 1631)

Worde, Wynkyn de: *The Manner of the Triumph at Calais and Boulogne* (London, 1532; printed in *Tudor Tracts*, ed. A.F. Pollard, London, 1903)

Wriothesley, Charles, Windsor Herald: *A Chronicle of England in the Reigns of the Tudors from 1485 to 1559* (2 vols., ed. William Douglas Hamilton, Camden Society, 2nd Series, 10 and 20, 1875, 1877)

Wyatt, George: *Extracts from the Life of the Virtuous, Christian and Renowned Queen Anne Boleigne* (published privately, 1817, and publicly as an appendix to Vol. 2 of S.W. Singer's edition of George Cavendish's *The Life of Cardinal Wolsey*, London, 1825)

Secondary Sources

Aikin, Lucy: *Memoirs of the Court of Elizabeth, Queen of England* (London, 1818)

Albert, Marvin H.: *The Divorce* (London, 1966)

Anne Boleyn (ed. Frederic P. Miller, Agnes F. Vandome and John McBrewster, Mauritius, 2009)

Ashdown, Dulcie M.: *Ladies in Waiting* (London, 1976)

Asquith, Clare: *Shadowplay: The Hidden Beliefs and Coded Politics of William Shakespeare* (New York, 2005)

Astor, Gavin, 2nd Baron Astor of Hever: *Hever in the 20th Century* (no publisher cited, 1973; reprinted 2003)

Aungier, George James: *The History and Antiquities of Syon Monastery, the Parish of Isleworth and the Chapelry of Hounslow* (London, 1840)

Bagley, J.J.: *Henry VIII and His Times* (London, 1962)

Baker, John Austin: *The Living Splendour of Westminster Abbey* (Norwich, 1977)

Ball, W.E.: 'Old Heraldic Glass in Brasted Church' (*The Antiquary*, 42, 1906)

Barnes, N., and Newman, L.: *Transactions* (Rochford Hundred Historical Society, 17, 1973)

Barnwell, Edward Lowry: *Perrot Notes: Some Account of the Various Branches of the Perrot Family* (London, 1867)

Barrett, C.R.B.: *Essex: Highways, Byways and Waterways* (London, 1893)

Beauclerk-Dewar, Peter, and Powell, Roger: *Right Royal Bastards: The Fruits of Passion* (Burke's Peerage, 2006; republished as *Royal Bastards: Illegitimate Children of the British Royal Family*, Stroud, 2008)

Beckingsale, B.W.: *Elizabeth I* (London, 1963)

Bell, Doyne C.: *Notices of the Historic Persons Buried in the Chapel of St Peter ad Vincula in the Tower of London, with an Account of the Discovery of the Supposed Remains of Queen Anne Boleyn* (London, 1877)

Benton, P.: *The History of the Rochford Hundred* (Rochford, 1882)

Bernard, G.W.: *Anne Boleyn: Fatal Attractions* (Yale, 2010)

Bernard, G.W.: *The King's Reformation: Henry VIII and the Making of the English Church* (Yale, 2005)

Bernard, G.W.: 'The Rise of Sir William Compton, Tudor Courtier' (*English Historical Review*, 96, 1981)

Bindoff, S.T.: *The House of Commons, 1509-1558* (3 vols., London, 1982)

Birch, Thomas: *Memoirs of the Reign of Queen Elizabeth* (2 vols., London, 1754)

Black, J.B.: *The Reign of Elizabeth, 1558-1603* (Oxford, 1959)

Blomefield, Francis, and Parkin, Charles: *An essay towards a topographical description of the county of Norfolk, Vol. 6* (London, 1807)

The Book of Beauty, or Regal Gallery for 1848 (ed. the Countess of Blessington, London, 1848)

Borman, Tracy: *Elizabeth's Women: The Hidden Story of the Virgin Queen* (London, 2009)

Bowle, John: *Henry VIII: A Biography* (London, 1965)

Brewer, J.S.: *The Reign of Henry VIII: From His Accession to the Death of Wolsey, Vol. 2* (London, 1884)

Briis-sous-Forges (www.mairie-de-briis-sous-forges.fr)

Brigden, Susan: *New Worlds, Lost Worlds: The Rule of the Tudors, 1485-1603* (London, 2000)

Brigden, Susan, and Wilson, Nigel: 'New Learning and Broken Friendship' (*English Historical Review*, Vol. 112, No. 446, April 1997)

British History Online (www.british-history.ac.uk)

The British Library (www.bl.uk)

Broadway Jan: 'John Smyth of Nibley: a Jacobean man-of-business and his service to the Berkeley family' (*Midland History*, Vol. 24, 1999)

Bruce, Marie Louise: *Anne Boleyn* (London, 1972)

Brysson Morrison, N.: *The Private Life of Henry VIII* (London, 1964)

Burke, S. Hubert: *Historical Portraits of the Tudor Dynasty and the Reformation Period* (4 vols., London, 1879-83)

Cannon, John, and Hargreaves, Anne: *The Oxford Book of Kings and Queens of Britain* (Oxford, 2001)

Carlton, Charles: *Royal Mistresses* (London and New York, 1990)

Carroll, Leslie: *Royal Affairs* (New York, 2008)

Castelli, Jorge H.: 'Tudor Place' (www.tudorplace.com)

Chapman, Hester W.: *Anne Boleyn* (London, 1974)

Childe-Pemberton, William S.: *Elizabeth Blount and Henry VIII, with some account of her surroundings* (London, 1913)

Claremont, Francesca: *Catherine of Aragon* (London, 1939)

Clark, Andrew: *The Life and Times of Anthony Wood, Antiquary of Oxford, 1632-1695, described by himself* (5 vols., Oxford Historical Society, 1891-1900)

Clark, Michael: *Rochford Hall: The History of a Tudor House* (Stroud, 1990)

Cloake, John: *Palaces and Parks of Richmond and Kew, Vol. I: The Palaces of Shene and Richmond* (Chichester, 1995)

Clutterbuck, Robert: *The History and Antiquities of the County of Hertford* (3 vols., 1827)

Colvin, H.M.: *History of the King's Works, Vol. 4, 1485-1660* (London, 1982)

The Complete Peerage (ed. G.H. White et al., St Catherine's Press, 1910-1959)

Cook, Petronelle: *Queen Consorts of England: The Power behind the Throne* (New York, 1993)

Craster, H.H.E.: *A History of Northumberland, Vol. 8* (Newcastle, 1907)

Croft, P., and Hearn, K.: '"Only Matrimony makes Children to be certain": Two Elizabethan Pregnancy Portraits: Lady Cecil and Lady Knollys' (*British Art Journal*, 3, Autumn 2002)

The Crown and Local Communities in England and France in the Fifteenth Century (ed. J.R.L. Highfield and Robin Jeffs, Stroud, 1981)

Cryer, L.R.: *A History of Rochford* (London, 1978)

Currie, Dr A.S.: 'Notes on the Obstetric Histories of Katherine of Aragon and Anne Boleyn' (*Edinburgh Medical Journal*, 1, 1888)

Denny, Joanna: *Anne Boleyn* (London, 2004)

Denny, Joanna: *Katherine Howard: A Tudor Conspiracy* (London, 2005)

Dictionary of National Biography (22 vols., ed. Sir Leslie Stephen and Sir Sidney Lee, 1885-1901; Oxford, 1998 edition)

Dixon, Philip: *Excavations at Greenwich Palace, 1970-71: An Interim Report* (Greenwich and Lewisham Antiquarian Society, London, 1972)

Doran, Susan: *The Tudor Chronicles 1485-1603* (London, 2008)

Edwards, D.: *The Edwardes Legacy* (Baltimore, 1992)

Elton, G.R.: *Studies in Tudor and Stuart Politics and Government* (Cambridge, 1983)

Emerson, Kate: 'A Who's Who of Tudor Women' (www.kateemerson historicals.com)

English Heritage: National Monuments Record (www.pastscape.org)

Erickson, Carolly: *Anne Boleyn* (London, 1984)

Erickson, Carolly: *The First Elizabeth* (London, 1999)

Erickson, Carolly: *Great Harry* (London, 1980)

Erickson, Carolly: *Bloody Mary* (London, 1978)

L'Estrange, A.G.: *The Palace and the Hospital, or Chronicles of Greenwich* (2 vols., London, 1886)

Fedden, Robin, and Kenworthy-Browne, John: *The Country House Guide* (London, 1979)

Fletcher, Benton: *Royal Homes Near London* (London, 1930)

Fletcher, John: 'A Portrait of William Carey and Lord Hunsdon's Long Gallery' (*Burlington Magazine*, 1981)

Fletcher, Stella: *Cardinal Wolsey: A Life in Renaissance Europe* (London, 2009)

Flood, J.L.: '"Safer on the Battlefield than in the City": England, the "sweating sickness" and the Continent' (*Renaissance Studies*, Vol. 17, No. 2, June 2003)

Flügel, J.C.: 'On the Character and Married Life of Henry VIII' (in *Psychoanalysis and History*, ed. Bruce Mazlish, New York, 1971)

Foster, Joseph: *The Royal Lineage of our Noble and Gentle Families, together with their Paternal Ancestry* (London, 1884)

Fox, Julia: *Jane Boleyn, The Infamous Lady Rochford* (London, 2007)

Fraser, Antonia: *The Six Wives of Henry VIII* (London, 1992)

Friedman, Dennis: *Ladies of the Bedchamber: The Role of the Royal Mistress* (London, 2003)

Friedmann, Paul: *Anne Boleyn: A Chapter of English History, 1527-1536* (2 vols., London, 1884; reprinted, ed. Josephine Wilkinson, Stroud, 2010)

Froude, James Anthony: *The Divorce of Catherine of Aragon* (London, 1891)

Froude, James Anthony: *History of England* (London, 1856-70)

Gainey, James: *The Princess of the Mary Rose* (East Wittering, 1986)

Gairdner, James: 'The Age of Anne Boleyn' (*English Historical Review*, 9, 1895)

Gairdner, James: 'Mary and Anne Boleyn' (*English Historical Review*, 8, 1893)

Gairdner, James: 'Mary and Anne Boleyn' (*English Historical Review*, 10, 1895)

Garrett, Christina Hallowell: *The Marian Exiles* (Cambridge, 1938)

Given-Wilson, Chris, and Curteis, Alice: *The Royal Bastards of Medieval England* (London, 1984)

Glenne, Michael: *Katherine Howard: The Story of Henry VIII's Fifth Queen* (London, 1948)

Grattan Flood, W.H.: 'Richard Davy' (*The Musical Times*, August, 1921)

Griffiths, Elizabeth: 'The Boleyns at Blickling, 1450-1560' (*Norfolk Archaeology*, 40, 2009)

Guy, J.A.: *The Cardinal's Court* (Hassocks, 1977)

Gwyn, Peter: *The King's Cardinal: The Rise and Fall of Thomas Wolsey* (London, 1990)

Hackett, Francis: *Henry the Eighth* (London, 1929)

Haigh, Christopher: *English Reformations: Religion, Politics and Society under the Tudors* (Oxford, 1993)

Hamer, Colin: *Anne Boleyn: One short life that changed the English-speaking world* (Leominster, 2007)

Hamy, Alfred: *Entrevue de François Premier avec Henri VIII a Boulogne-sur-Mer en 1532* (Paris, 1898)

Harben, Henry: *A Dictionary of London* (London, 1918)

Hare, Augustus J. C.: *Walks in London* (Vol. 2, London, 1878)

Harris, Barbara J.: *English Aristocratic Women, 1450-1550* (Oxford, 2002)

Harris, J.: 'The Prideaux Collection of Topographical Drawings' (*Architectural History*, 7, 1964)

Hart, Kelly: *The Mistresses of Henry VIII* (London, 2009)

Hasler, P.W.: *The House of Commons 1558-1603* (3 vols., London, 1981)

Hasted, Edward: *The History and Topographical Survey of Kent* (12 vols., Canterbury, 1797-1801)

Henry VIII: A European Court in England (ed. David Starkey, London, 1991)

Henry VIII: Man and Monarch (ed. Susan Doran and David Starkey, The British Library, London, 2009)

Hever Castle and Gardens (guidebooks, Norwich, 2008, and earlier undated editions)

Hilliam, David: *Kings, Queens, Bones and Bastards* (Stroud, 1998)

Hobden, Heather: *Tudor Bastard: Henry FitzRoy, Duke of Richmond and Somerset, and his mother, Elizabeth Blount* (Lincoln, 2001)

Hoskins, Anthony: Lady Antonia Fraser's views regarding the Careys' paternity and Anthony Hoskins' paper (unpublished article, 1995, kindly sent to the author)

Hoskins, Anthony: 'Mary Boleyn's Carey Children – Offspring of Henry VIII?' (*Genealogy Magazine*, Vol. 25, March 1997, No. 9)

Hughes, Jonathan: 'Mary Stafford (c.1499-1543)' (*Oxford Dictionary of National Biography*, Oxford, 2004-9)

Hughey, Ruth Willard: *John Harington of Stepney: Tudor Gentleman: His Life and Works* (Columbus, Ohio, 1971)

Hui, Roland: 'A Reassessment of Queen Anne Boleyn's Portraiture' (www.geocities.com)

Hume, David: *The History of Great Britain* (6 vols., Edinburgh and London, 1754-62)

Hume, Martin A.S.: *The Wives of Henry the Eighth* (London, 1905)

Hutchinson, Robert: *House of Treason: The Rise and Fall of a Tudor Dynasty* (London, 2009)

Ives, Eric: *The Life and Death of Anne Boleyn, 'The Most Happy'* (Oxford, 2004)

James, Susan: *Catherine Parr: Henry VIII's Last Love* (Stroud, 2008)
Jansen, Sharon L.: *Dangerous Talk and Strange Behaviour: Women and Popular Resistance to the Reforms of Henry VIII* (New York, 1996)
Jenkins, Simon: *England's Thousand Best Houses* (London, 2003)
Jenkyns, Richard: *Westminster Abbey* (London, 2004)
Jenner, Heather: *Royal Wives* (London, 1967)
Jollet, Etienne: *Jean & François Clouet* (Paris, 1997)
Johnson, Paul: *Elizabeth I: A Study in Power and Intellect* (London, 1974)
Jones, Philippa: *The Other Tudors: Henry VIII's Mistresses and Bastards* (London, 2009)

Kelly, Henry Ansgar: *The Matrimonial Trials of Henry VIII* (Stanford, California, 1976)
King, Tim: 'Henry VIII's secret heirs link Tudors to House of Windsor' (*The Daily Telegraph*, 27 May 1997)
Knecht, Robert J.: *Francis I* (Cambridge, 1984)
Knowles, D.: 'The Matter of Wilton' (*Bulletin of the Institute of Historical Research*, 31, 1958)

Lacey, Robert: *The Life and Times of Henry VIII* (London, 1972)
Lancelott, Francis: *The Queens of England and their Times* (New York, 1858)
Law, Ernest P.A.: *A Short History of Hampton Court* (London, 1906)
Levin, Carole: 'Sister-Subject, Sister-Queen: Elizabeth I among her Siblings' (*Faculty Publications*, University of Nebraska, 2006)
Lindsey, Karen: *Divorced, Beheaded, Survived: A Feminist Reinterpretation of the Wives of Henry VIII* (Reading, Mass., 1995)
Lingard, John: *The History of England* (8 vols., 1819-30)
Lloyd, Stephen: *Portrait Miniatures from the Collection of the Duke of Buccleuch* (Scottish National Portrait Gallery, 1996)
Loades, David: *Elizabeth I: The Golden Reign of Gloriana* (The National Archives, 2003)
Loades, David: *Henry VIII: Court, Church and Conflict* (The National Archives, 2007)
Loades, David: *The Six Wives of Henry VIII* (Stroud, 2009) (first published as *Henry VIII and His Queens*, Stroud, 1994)

Loades, David: *Henry VIII: King and Court* (Andover, 2009)
Loades, David: *Mary Tudor: A Life* (Oxford, 1989)
Loades, David: *The Tudor Queens of England* (London, 2009)
Lofts, Norah: *Anne Boleyn* (London, 1979)
Losing Your Head Over Henry: Mary Boleyn (information sheet from Hever
    Castle, undated)
Luke, Mary M.: *Catherine the Queen* (London, 1967)

Mackie, J.D.: *The Earlier Tudors, 1485-1558* (Oxford, 1952)
MacNalty, Arthur S.: *Henry VIII, A Difficult Patient* (London, 1952)
Martienssen, Anthony: *Queen Katherine Parr* (London, 1973)
Mary Boleyn (www.elizabethan-era.org.uk)
Mary Boleyn (www.englishmonarchs.co.uk)
Mary Boleyn (www.wikipedia.org)
Mathew, David: *The Courtiers of Henry VIII* (London, 1970)
Mattingly, Garrett: *Catherine of Aragon* (London, 1942)
McBride, Kari Boyd: *Biography of Aemilia Lanier* (University of Arizona,
    2008)
McClure, N.E.: *Letters and Epigrams of Sir John Harington* (Philadelphia,
    1930)
Meyer, G.J.: *The Tudors: The Complete Story of England's Most Notorious
    Dynasty* (New York, 2010)
Mongello, Marilee: Mary Boleyn (www.englishhistory.net)
Morant, Philip: *The History and Antiquities of the County of Essex, Vols. 1
    and 2* (London, 1768)
Morley, Henry, and Griffin, William Hall: *English Writers: An Attempt
    towards a History of English Literature, Vol. 8* (London, 1887)
Morton Bradley, M.: *Elizabeth Blount of Kinlet* (Kidderminster, 1991)
Murphy, Beverley A.: *Bastard Prince: Henry VIII's Lost Son* (Stroud,
    2001)
Murrell, Jim: Manuscript Notes on the Conservation of the Buccleuch
    Collection of Portrait Miniatures, 1977-80 (MSS, Victoria and Albert
    Museum)

Nash, Joseph: *The Mansions of England in Olden Time* (4 vols., London,
    1838-49; abridged edition London, 1906)
Neale, J.E.: *Queen Elizabeth I* (London, 1934)
Newman, John: *Buildings of England: West Kent and the Weald* (London, 1980)
Noble, Mark: 'History of the Beautiful Elizabeth Blount' (*The
    Genealogist*, 2, 1803)
Norris, Herbert: *Tudor Costume and Fashion* (London, 1938)
Norton, Elizabeth: *Anne Boleyn, Henry VIII's Obsession* (Stroud, 2008)

Norton, Elizabeth: *She Wolves: The Notorious Queens of England* (Stroud, 2008)
Norwich Cathedral: Church, City and Diocese, 1096-1996 (ed. Ian Atherton, Eric Fernie, Christopher Harper-Bill and A. Hassell Smith, London, 1996)

Online Family Trees (www.gw1.geneanet.org)
The Oxford Book of Royal Anecdotes (ed. Elizabeth Longford, Oxford, 1989)
The Oxford Companion to Irish History (ed. S.J. Connolly, Oxford, 1998)

Paget, Gerald: *The Lineage and Ancestry of H.R.H. Prince Charles, The Prince of Wales* (London, 1977)
Paget, Hugh: 'Gerard and Lucas Hornebolte in England' (*Burlington Magazine*, 101, 1959)
Paget, Hugh: 'The Youth of Anne Boleyn' (*Bulletin of the Institute of Historical Research*, 55, 1981)
Pailthorpe, Richard; Martyn, Topher; Shrimpton, Colin; Baxter, Clare: *Syon: London Home of the Duke of Northumberland* (Derby, 2003)
Panton, Kenneth: *London: A Historical Companion* (Stroud, 2001)
Parmiter, Geoffrey de C.: *The King's Great Matter* (London, 1967)
Perry, Maria: *Sisters to the King: The Tumultuous Lives of Henry VIII's Sisters – Margaret of Scotland and Mary of France* (London, 1998)
Perry, Maria: *The Word of A Prince: A Life of Elizabeth I* (Woodbridge, 1990)
Phillips, Charles: *The Illustrated Encyclopaedia of the Castles, Palaces and Stately Houses of Britain and Ireland* (London, 2007)
Plowden, Alison: *The House of Tudor* (London, 1976)
Plowden, Alison: The Other Boleyn Girl (www.bbc.co.uk)
Plowden, Alison: *Tudor Women: Queens and Commoners* (London, 1979)
Porter, Linda: *Mary Tudor: The First Queen* (London, 2007)
Powell, Roger: *Royal Sex: Mistresses and Lovers of the British Royal Family* (Stroud, 2010)
Poynton, F.J.: *Miscelleanea, Genealogica et Heraldica* (London, 1880)
Prévost, M.: 'Anecdotes historiques sur Limours' (Documents pour l'histoire du département de Seine-et-Oise, Publications de la Société Archéologique de Rambouillet, 1978, University of Michigan)

Reilly, E.G.S.: *Historical Anecdotes of the Families of Boleyn, Carey, Mordaunt, Hamilton and Jocelyn* (Newry, 1839)

The Renaissance at Sutton Place (The Sutton Place Heritage Trust, 1983)

Rex, Richard: *Henry VIII* (Stroud, 2009)

Rex, Richard: *The Tudors* (Stroud, 2002)

Richardson, Douglas: *Plantagenet Ancestry* (Baltimore, 2004)

Richardson, Ruth Elizabeth: *Mistress Blanche, Queen Elizabeth I's Confidante* (Little Logaston, 2007)

Richardson, Walter C.: *Mary Tudor: The White Queen* (London, 1970)

Rickman, Johanna: *Love, Lust and Licence in Early Modern England: Illicit Sex and the Nobility* (Farnham, 2008)

Ridley, Jasper: *Elizabeth I* (London, 1987)

Ridley, Jasper: *Henry VIII* (London, 1984)

Ridley, Jasper: *The Life and Times of Mary Tudor* (London, 1973)

Ridley, Jasper: *The Tudor Age* (London, 1988)

Riordan, Michael: 'William Carey, Courtier (c.1496-1528)' (*Oxford Dictionary of National Biography*, Oxford, 2004-9)

Rival, Paul: *The Six Wives of Henry VIII* (London, 1937)

Rivals in Power: Lives and Letters of the Great Tudor Dynasties (ed. David Starkey, London, 1990)

Robinson, C.J.: 'Valentine Carey, D.D., Bishop of Exeter' (*The Herald and Genealogist*, Vol. 4, London, 1867)

Rollins, Hyder Edward: 'The Troilus-Cressida Story from Chaucer to Shakespeare' (*Journal of the Modern Language Association of America*, 32, 1917)

Rootsweb: Finding Our Roots Together (www.rootsweb.ancestry.com)

Round, J.H.: *The Early Life of Anne Boleyn: A Critical Essay* (London, 1886)

Rowse, A.L.: *The Elizabethan Renaissance: The Life of the Society* (London, 1971)

Royal Commission on Historical Monuments in Essex, 1923

Scarisbrick, Diana: 'Jewellery in Tudor and Jacobean Portraits at New Haven' (*Apollo*, November 1987)

Scarisbrick, J.J.: *Henry VIII* (London, 1968)

Scudamore/Skidmore (www.skidmoregenealogy.com)

Sergeant, Philip W.: *The Life of Anne Boleyn* (London, 1924)

Seward, Desmond: *Prince of the Renaissance* (London, 1973)

Shelley, A: 'Dragon Hall, King Street, Norwich: Excavation and Survey of a Late-Medieval Merchant's Trading Complex' (*East Anglian Archaeology*, 112, 2005)

The Shell Guide to England (ed. John Hadfield, London, 1970)

Simpson, Richard: *The School of Shakespeare* (London, 1878)

Sitwell, Edith: *The Queens and the Hive* (London, 1963)
Smith, Lacey Baldwin: *Henry VIII: The Mask of Royalty* (London, 1971)
Smith, Lacey Baldwin: *A Tudor Tragedy: The Life and Times of Catherine Howard* (London, 1961)
Somerset, Anne: *Elizabeth I* (London, 1991)
Somerset, Anne: *Ladies in Waiting* (London, 1984)
Starkey, David: *The Reign of Henry VIII: Personalities and Politics* (London, 1991)
Starkey, David: *Six Wives: The Queens of Henry VIII* (London, 2003)
Stogdon, Catalina: 'In Anne Boleyn's Footsteps' (*Daily Telegraph*, 24 September, 2009)
Stone, Lawrence: 'Ages of Admission to Educational Institutions in Tudor and Stuart England: A Comment' (*History of Education*, 6, February 1977)
Strickland, Agnes: *Lives of the Queens of England* (8 vols., London, 1851; 6 vols., Bath, 1972)
Strong, Roy: *Artists of the Tudor Court: The Portrait Miniature Rediscovered, 1520-1620* (Victoria and Albert Museum, London, 1983)
Strong, Roy: *The English Renaissance Miniature* (London, 1983, revised edition 1984)
Strong, Roy: *Gloriana: The Portraits of Queen Elizabeth I* (London, 1987)
Strong, Roy: *Portraits of Queen Elizabeth I* (Oxford, 1963)
Strong, Roy: *Tudor and Jacobean Portraits* (2 vols., London, 1969)
Struthers, Jane: *Royal Palaces of Britain* (London, 2004)

Tallis, Nicola: Mary Boleyn: An Introduction (unpublished MS., 2009)
Tazon, Juan E.: *The Life and Times of Thomas Stukeley, 1525-1578* (Burlington, 2003)
Thoms, William J.: *Anecdotes and Traditions* (Camden Society, 5, London, 1839)
Thornton-Cook, Elsie: *Her Majesty: The Romance of the Queens of England, 1066-1910* (New York, 1926)
Thurley, Simon: *The Royal Palaces of Tudor England* (Yale, 1993)
Tighe, W.J.: 'The Herveys: Three Generations of Tudor Courtiers' (*Proceedings of the Suffolk Institute of Archaeology and History*, 36, 1988)
Tompkins, H.W.: *'Standard' Guide to Rochford* (Southend, 1923)
Tremlett, Giles: *Catherine of Aragon, Henry's Spanish Queen* (London, 2010)
Trowles, Tony: *Treasures of Westminster Abbey* (London, 2008)
Tucker, M.J.: 'The Ladies in Skelton's Garland of Laurel' (*Renaissance Quarterly*, 22, 1969)
Tunis, David L.: *Fast Facts on the Kings and Queens of England* (Milton Keynes, 2006)

Turvey, Roger: *The Treason and Trial of Sir John Perrot* (University of Wales, 2005)

Tytler, Sarah: *Tudor Queens and Princesses* (London, 1896; reprinted New York, 2006)

Unlocking Essex's Past: From Heritage Conservation at Essex County Council (www.unlockingessex.essexcc.gov.uk)

Van Duyn Southworth, John: *Monarch and Conspirators: The Wives and Woes of Henry VIII* (New York, 1973)

Varlow, Sally: *The Lady Penelope: The Lost Tale of Love and Politics in the Court of Elizabeth I* (London, 2007)

Varlow, Sally: 'Sir Francis Knollys's Latin Dictionary: New Evidence for Katherine Carey' (*Bulletin of the Institute of Historical Research*, 2006)

Victoria County Histories (www.britishhistory.ac.uk)

Walder, John: *All Colour Book of Henry VIII* (London, 1973)

Waldherr, Kris: *Doomed Queens* (New York, 2008)

Warnicke, Retha: 'Anne Boleyn's Childhood and Adolescence' (*Historical Journal*, 28, 4, 1985)

Warnicke, Retha: *The Rise and Fall of Anne Boleyn: Family Politics at the Court of Henry VIII* (Cambridge, 1989)

Warwick Castle (guidebooks, Birmingham, 1994, 2002)

Weir, Alison: *Elizabeth the Queen* (London, 1998)

Weir, Alison: *Henry VIII: King and Court* (London, 2001)

Weir, Alison: *The Lady in the Tower: The Fall of Anne Boleyn* (London, 2009)

Weir, Alison: *The Six Wives of Henry VIII* (London, 1991)

Weir, Alison: The Wives of Henry VIII: A Domestic History of the Reign (unpublished MS., 1024 pages, 1974)

Westminster Abbey: Official Guide (London, 1953, 1966)

Wilkinson, Josephine: *The Early Loves of Anne Boleyn* (Stroud, 2009)

Wilkinson, Josephine: *Mary Boleyn* (Stroud, 2009)

Williams, Neville: *Henry VIII and His Court* (London, 1971)

Williams, Neville: *The Life and Times of Elizabeth I* (London, 1972)

Wilson, Derek: *Henry VIII: Reformer and Tyrant* (London, 2009)

Wilson, Derek: *In the Lion's Court: Power, Ambition and Sudden Death in the Reign of Henry VIII* (London, 2001)

Woods, Susan: *Lanyer: A Renaissance Woman Poet* (Oxford and New York, 1999)

The World Roots Genealogy Archive: European Royalty and Nobility (www.worldroots.com)

Wright, Thomas: *The County of Essex* (London, 1836)
Wright, Thomas: *The History of Ireland* (3 vols., London, 1855)
Wright, Thomas: *Queen Elizabeth and her Times*, Vol. 1 (London, 1838)

Miscellaneous Websites

www.britishlistedbuildings.co.uk
www.château.médiéval.fr
www.derkeiler.com (for the Stafford family, with extensive references)
www.gilles.maillet.free.fr
www.teachergenealogist.com
www.vivies.com

Notes and References

Abbreviations:

L. & P.   *Letters and Papers, Foreign and Domestic, of the Reign of Henry VIII*

S. C.   Spanish Calendar: *Calendar of Letters, Despatches and State Papers relating to Negotiations between England and Spain, preserved in the Archives at Simancas and Elsewhere*

V. C.   Venetian Calendar: *Calendar of State Papers and Manuscripts relating to English Affairs preserved in the Archives of Venice and in the other Libraries of Northern Italy*

V. C. H.   *Victoria County Histories*

Introduction

   1 Tallis

1: 'The Eldest Daughter'

   1 Loades: *Henry VIII: Court, Church and Conflict*
   2 Blomefield
   3 *The Complete Peerage*
   4 Griffiths
   5 For Blickling Hall, to which there are many references in this chapter, I am indebted in several instances to the paper of Elizabeth Griffiths, who discovered that Sir Geoffrey Boleyn built a house on the site. The date 1452 is inferred from internal evidence in *The Paston Letters*; Blomefield gives it as 1450.

6 Wilkinson: *Mary Boleyn*

7 Ibid.; Griffiths; Leland

8 *The Paston Letters*; National Archives: Ancient Deeds: C.137,862,5972

9 *The Paston Letters*

10 *The Complete Peerage*; his will was proved on 2 July that year.

11 Stow

12 *Calendar of Inquisitions Post Mortem: Henry VII*

13 Ibid.; her age is given as twenty or more in the Inquisition Post Mortem on her mother, taken in November 1485.

14 *The Complete Peerage*

15 *The Oxford Companion to Irish History*

16 Michael Clark

17 Harleian MSS

18 *Calendar of Patent Rolls: Henry VII: 1485-1509*; Blomefield

19 *L. & P.*; in 1529, at the legatine court convened at Blackfriars to try Henry VIII's nullity suit against Katherine of Aragon, Boleyn gave his age as fifty-two.

20 *Calendar of Patent Rolls: Henry VII: 1485-1509*; Wilkinson: *Mary Boleyn*; Griffiths; *The Crown and Local Communities in England and France in the Fifteenth Century*

21 Meyer

22 *L. & P.*

23 Cited by Ives.

24 Brewer

25 *L. & P.*

26 Surrey is known to have been resident at Sheriff Hutton Castle only between 1489 and 1499, when he was serving as Lieutenant of the North. Anne Bourchier had married Lord Dacre probably in 1492; Elizabeth Tylney died in 1497. Her daughters Elizabeth and Muriel are given their maiden name and style, so were not yet married when the poem was written (Muriel married before 1504). For Skelton and this poem, see Rollins; Tucker; Morley and Griffin; Brownlow in Skelton, John: *The Book of the Laurel*; *The Complete Peerage*.

27 *L. & P.*

28 For example, *Anne Boleyn*; Jones

29 For example, Warnicke: *The Rise and Fall of Anne Boleyn*; Claremont

30 For example, Loades: *The Six Wives of Henry VIII*; Plowden: The Other Boleyn Girl

31 Not her son, Henry, as Hart states.

32 Round is incorrect in asserting that Hunsdon was mistaken here, and that Boleyn was created Lord Rochford to him and his heirs

male, and Earl of Wiltshire and Ormond to him and his heirs
general; the earldom of Wiltshire was granted to him in tail male,
the others in tail general; see *The Complete Peerage.*

33 *Calendar of State Papers, Foreign Series, of the Reign of Elizabeth*
34 Round
35 *The Complete Peerage*; Broadway. On the death of Queen Elizabeth
   in March 1603, George Carey became sole heir to Thomas Boleyn,
   Earl of Wiltshire and Ormond, and when he died without male
   issue six months later, his daughter Katherine Carey inherited his
   claim to the earldom. When she died in 1635, her son, George
   Berkeley, born in 1613, succeeded her in her apparent right to the
   earldom of Ormond, even though that earldom was in fact still
   held by the Butlers.
36 MS. in the Chapter House, Westminster Abbey
37 Tallis; Bernard: *Anne Boleyn*; Sergeant
38 Sergeant
39 *The Complete Peerage*; Starkey: *Six Wives*
40 Ives; *Calendar of the Close Rolls preserved in the Public Record Office:
   Henry VII.* I am indebted to Douglas Richardson for kindly
   drawing my attention to this reference.
41 Barbara Harris
42 Ibid.
43 As before, I am grateful to Douglas Richardson for this information.
44 Ives
45 Warnicke: 'Anne Boleyn's Childhood'
46 Warnicke: *The Rise and Fall of Anne Boleyn*; Wilkinson: *Mary Boleyn*
47 Bell. For a fuller discussion of the examination of the bones, see
   Weir: *The Lady in the Tower.*
48 For example, Warnicke: *The Rise and Fall of Anne Boleyn*; Jones
49 The best source is *The Complete Peerage.*
50 Paget: 'The Youth of Anne Boleyn'; Warnicke: 'Anne Boleyn's
   Childhood'. For the full text of the letter, in context, see p. 31.
51 Ives; Bernard: *Fatal Attractions*
52 S. C.
53 Round
54 Plowden: The Other Boleyn Girl
55 Powell
56 Hughes
57 Powell
58 Ibid.; Mongello
59 Powell states that Mary Boleyn was born around 25 March 1498, 'at

the same time as the Princess Mary', but the latter had been born two years earlier.

60 Powell

61 Brewer, in *L. & P.*; *The Complete Peerage*

62 Somerset: *Ladies in Waiting*; Hoskins; Hackett; Williams: Henry *VIII and His Court.* Tunis has Mary born in 1504 at 'Hever Castle in Chilton Foliat', but Hever is in Kent, not Wiltshire, while Chilton Foliat was possibly the birthplace of Mary's first husband, William Carey.

63 Warnicke: *The Rise and Fall of Anne Boleyn*

64 Bernard: *Anne Boleyn*

65 *Metrical Visions*

66 *Ambassades en Angleterre de Jean du Bellay*

67 Powell

68 Blomefield

69 Ibid.; Griffiths; Shelley

70 *L. & P.*

71 *The Rutland Papers*

72 *Calendar of Patent Rolls: Henry VII: 1485–1509*

73 *Calendar of the Close Rolls preserved in the Public Record Office: Henry VII*; Griffiths; *Norwich Cathedral: Church, City and Diocese, 1096–1996*

74 *Calendar of Patent Rolls: Henry VII: 1485–1509*; *Calendar of the Close Rolls preserved in the Public Record Office: Henry VII*; *L. & P.*; Blomefield. Sir William's will is given in *Testimenta Vetusta.*

75 *Calendar of Patent Rolls: Henry VII: 1485–1509*

76 *Calendar of the Close Rolls preserved in the Public Record Office: Henry VII*, where he is described as 'late of Blickling, Co. Norfolk'.

77 Blomefield

78 *L. & P.* This overturns John Newman's assertion that Hever was never the Boleyns' chief residence, as they did nothing to 'transform their house into a worthy expression of their ambitions'. But the works at Hever carried out by Sir Geoffrey Boleyn, and, more importantly, by Sir Thomas, prove rather the contrary. Moreover, there are very few references to Thomas Boleyn being in Norfolk during the reign of Henry VIII.

79 Norton: *Anne Boleyn*

80 Cited by Norris.

2: 'The Best of Husbands'

1 *L. & P.*
2 Ibid.; Starkey: *Six Wives*
3 *L. & P.*
4 Rymer; Wilkinson: *Mary Boleyn*
5 *L. & P.*
6 Warnicke: *The Rise and Fall of Anne Boleyn*
7 Stow; Panton. Sir Thomas More had studied at New Inn from 1494 to 1496 before going on to do law at Lincoln's Inn. New Inn survived to be acquired by the London County Council in 1899 and was demolished in 1902 to make way for a road linking Holborn and the Strand.
8 The word means a setting of precious stones so closely set that no metal shows.
9 *S. C.*
10 Hart
11 For further information on Henry VIII's obsession with hygiene, see Weir: *Henry VIII: King and Court*.
12 *V. C.*
13 *S. C.*
14 *L. & P.*
15 *S. C.*
16 *L. & P.*
17 Sloane MSS
18 *V. C.*
19 *S. C.*
20 Mathew
21 Hart gives his name as Chapuys, but Eustache Chapuys did not take up his post until 1529. The ambassador at this time was Luis Caroz.
22 *S. C.*
23 For example, Norton: *Anne Boleyn*; Jones; Hart; Williams: *Henry VIII and His Court*; Powell; Wilkinson: *Mary Boleyn*
24 *L. & P.*
25 Powell
26 Walder
27 Lewis, in Sander
28 *L. & P.*
29 *Pro ecclesiasticae unitatis defensione*, published in 1538 and based on an open letter sent to Henry in 1536.

30 *L. & P.*
31 Ibid.
32 Ibid.
33 Ibid.
34 *Annales rerum Anglicarum et Hibernicarum regnante Elizabetha*
35 Further evidence for the existence of Rastell's life of More is in Arundel MS. 152 in the British Library, in which a reference is made to 'certain brief notes appertaining to Bishop Fisher, collected out of Sir Thomas More's Life, written by Mr Justice Rastell'.
36 Camden: *Annales rerum Anglicarum et Hibernicarum regnante Elizabetha*
37 For a general discussion of 'The Garland of the Laurel', see Tucker; Rollins; Brownlow, in Skelton.
38 *S. C.*
39 Jones
40 Ibid.
41 Van Duyn Southworth
42 Luke
43 Rival
44 Glenne
45 Walder
46 Luke
47 Thornton-Cook
48 Ives; Hart
49 *Calendar of State Papers and Manuscripts existing in the Archives and Collections of Milan*
50 *L. & P.*
51 Ibid.; Anselme; www.gilles.maillet.free.fr
52 Jones; The World Roots Genealogy Archive: European Royalty and Nobility (www.worldroots.com)
53 www.château.médiéval.fr; Online Family Trees (www.gw1.geneanet.org)
54 *S. C.*
55 Cotton MSS Caligula
56 *S. C.*
57 *Inventories of the Wardrobe, Plate, Chapel Stuff etc. of Henry Fitzroy, Duke of Richmond and Somerset*; Fraser
58 National Archives: The King's Book of Payments, E36/215
59 Childe-Pemberton
60 Hall
61 Ibid.; *Inventories of the Wardrobe, Plate, Chapel Stuff etc. of Henry Fitzroy, Duke of Richmond and Somerset*
62 Wilkinson: *Mary Boleyn*

63 Hall. For Jane Popincourt, see Chapter 3.

64 *L. & P.*

65 Jones

66 Jones states that, on this occasion, Elizabeth sang a song she had composed herself, but does not cite the source.

67 *Four Years at the Court of Henry VIII*; Hall

68 Jones

69 Ibid.

70 Ibid.

71 Ibid.

72 Childe-Pemberton

73 From the Eltham Ordinances in *The Antiquarian Repertory*

74 Ibid.

75 Childe-Pemberton. It was largely demolished in the 1540s and only the nave of the former priory survives today as the nave of the parish church. The present house, called Jericho Priory, is eighteenth century, and incorporates a range from the seventeenth century or perhaps earlier; the building known as Jericho Cottage dates from the seventeenth century (data from English Heritage, at www.britishlistedbuildings. co.uk). I should like to thank Karen Gardner for sending me information about Jericho Cottage.

76 Beauclerk-Dewar and Powell

77 Hall

78 Jones, without citing a source, claims that, after the birth, the Queen visited Elizabeth to congratulate her. Given Katherine's anger at the ennobling of Elizabeth's child, this is highly unlikely.

79 National Archives: Inquisitions Post Mortem, C142; Map Room.

80 Beauclerk-Dewar and Powell

81 *L. & P.*; *The Complete Peerage*

82 *L. & P.*

83 Ibid.

84 Ibid.

85 Somerset: *Ladies in Waiting*

86 *L. & P.*

87 Ibid.

88 Ibid.

89 Ibid.

90 Ibid.; *The Complete Peerage*

91 *The Complete Peerage*

92 Ibid.

93 *L. & P.*

94 Ibid.

95 Ibid.; *The Complete Peerage*
96 Cited by Beauclerk-Dewar and Powell.

3: *'Into the Realm of France'*

1   L. & P.
2   Ibid.
3   Ibid.
4   Ibid.; Rymer
5   L. & P.
6   Loades: *The Tudor Queens of England*
7   Martienssen
8   Rival
9   Erickson: *Anne Boleyn*
10 Fraser
11 Loades: *The Tudor Queens of England*
12 Claremont
13 Erickson: *Bloody Mary*
14 Norton: *Anne Boleyn*
15 Martienssen
16 Barbara Harris
17 Loades: *The Tudor Queens of England*
18 Herbert
19 Grattan Flood
20 Hobden
21 It was suggested to me by a correspondent that 'My Lady Carey's Dompe', a mournful dance of a type peculiar to the sixteenth and seventeenth centuries, which comes from the earliest collection of English music for the virginals, was composed for Mary Boleyn when she was married to William Carey, and that it might be associated with her affair with Henry VIII. This composition has been dated to *c.*1524/5, which would place it in the right period, yet it could also have been written at any time between 1500 and 1540 or later; and it could not have been named after Mary, because she was not styled Lady Carey – William Carey was never knighted. The Lady Carey in the title must have belonged to one of the senior lines of the Carey family. Certainly this music has never been associated with Mary Boleyn. Some say this dompe was a traditional Irish melody composed by Turlough O'Carolan. The name is associated with the saying 'down in the dumps', and there is evidence that dompes were played at funerals.
22 L. & P.

23 Hart. For the full texts of Mary's two letters, see pp. 199 and 201 et seq.
24 Barbara Harris
25 Martienssen
26 Wilkinson: *Mary Boleyn*
27 Plowden: The Other Boleyn Girl
28 Wilkinson states that Mary was launched at court before Anne (*Mary Boleyn*).
29 Ibid.
30 Denny: *Anne Boleyn*
31 Manuscripts of J. Eliot Hodgkin
32 Perry: *Sisters to the King*
33 Paget: 'The Youth of Anne Boleyn'
34 Brewer, in *L. & P.*; Gairdner: 'The Age of Anne Boleyn' and 'Mary and Anne Boleyn'
35 Hackett; Plowden: *Tudor Women*, corrected in The Other Boleyn Girl; Somerset: *Ladies in Waiting*; Lofts; Bruce; Erickson: *Anne Boleyn*; Chapman; Sergeant; Smith: *A Tudor Tragedy*
36 *L. & P.*; Paget: 'The Youth of Anne Boleyn'
37 *Original Letters Illustrative of English History*
38 *L. & P.*
39 *Correspondence de l'Empereur Maximilien Ier et de Marguerite d'Autriche*
40 Ibid.
41 *Calendar of State Papers and Manuscripts existing in the Archives and Collections of Milan*
42 Warnicke: *The Rise and Fall of Anne Boleyn*
43 Ibid.
44 Norton: *Anne Boleyn*
45 Carlton
46 Erickson: *Anne Boleyn*
47 Brysson Morrison
48 Glenne
49 Luke
50 Martienssen
51 Erickson: *Bloody Mary*
52 For a discussion of the portraits said to be of Mary Boleyn, and those of her first husband, William Carey, see Appendix II.
53 Paget: 'The Youth of Anne Boleyn'; Ives; Perry: *Sisters to the King*
54 Paget: 'The Youth of Anne Boleyn'; Ives
55 Warnicke: *The Rise and Fall of Anne Boleyn*, 'Anne Boleyn's Childhood'

56 Letter recently acquired by Lincoln Cathedral Library. I am grateful to Dr Nicholas Bennett, Vice Chancellor and Librarian at Lincoln Cathedral, for kindly sending me a transcript.

57 For example, Brewer, in *L. & P.*; Meyer; Hackett; Brysson Morrison; Lindsey; Sergeant. Warnicke incorrectly asserts that it was Anne (*The Rise and Fall of Anne Boleyn*, 'Anne Boleyn's Childhood').

58 *L. & P.*

59 Bibliothèque Nationale, Paris MS. fr.7853, f.305b; Ives

60 Bibliothèque Nationale, Paris MS. fr.7853, f.305b; Bernard: *Anne Boleyn*; Lindsey

61 Ives

62 Bibliothèque Nationale, Paris MS. fr.7853, f.305b; cf. Denny: *Anne Boleyn*

63 Ives

64 Hall

65 Ibid.

66 Perry: *Sisters to the King*

67 Jones

68 Hart

69 *L. & P.*; Perry: *Sisters to the King*

70 Erickson: *Anne Boleyn*; Hart; Wilkinson: *Mary Boleyn*

71 Jones

72 Ibid.

73 *L. & P.*

74 Ibid.

75 *V. C.*

76 Ibid.

77 Ibid.; Hall

78 Hall

79 For Mary Tudor's sojourn in France, see chiefly Perry: *Sisters to the King*; Walter C. Richardson; Gainey

80 *V. C.*

81 *L. & P.*

82 Cited by Seward

83 *L. & P.*

84 Cotton MS. Vitellius; *L. & P.*

85 *L. & P.*

86 Ibid.

87 Denny: *Anne Boleyn*

88 Perry: *Sisters to the King*

89 *L. & P.*

90 Ibid.
91 Ibid.
92 Wilkinson: *Mary Boleyn*

4: 'A Very Great Whore'?

1 Plowden: *Tudor Women*
2 *V. C.*
3 Carlton; *V. C.*
4 *L. & P.*
5 Cited by Seward.
6 Brantôme
7 Carlton
8 *L. & P.*; this statement was not written by King François himself, as Jones states.
9 Denny: *Anne Boleyn*
10 Powell
11 Porter
12 *L. & P.*
13 For example, Wilkinson, in *Mary Boleyn*.
14 Ridley, in *The Love Letters of Henry VIII*
15 Warnicke: *The Rise and Fall of Anne Boleyn*
16 Jones
17 Ridley, in *The Love Letters of Henry VIII*
18 Luke
19 Erickson: *Anne Boleyn*
20 Wilkinson: *Mary Boleyn*
21 Denny: *Anne Boleyn*
22 Rival
23 Ibid.
24 Luke
25 Ibid.
26 Bruce. She dates Mary's liaison with François to the period when she was supposedly serving Queen Claude.
27 Hart
28 Bruce
29 Plowden: The Other Boleyn Girl
30 Jollet; Seward
31 Cf. Norton: *Anne Boleyn*; Lindsey; *Losing Your Head Over Henry: Mary Boleyn*
32 Including myself in previous books.
33 Carroll

34 Varlow: *The Lady Penelope*
35 Jones
36 Denny: *Anne Boleyn*
37 Ibid.
38 Norton: *Anne Boleyn*
39 Denny: *Anne Boleyn*
40 Ibid.; Norton: *Anne Boleyn*; Wilkinson: *The Early Loves of Anne Boleyn*
41 Wilkinson: *The Early Loves of Anne Boleyn*
42 Ibid.
43 S. C.
44 Cf. Lofts
45 Bruce
46 Fraser
47 For example, Savage, in *The Love Letters of Henry VIII*
48 Erickson: *Bloody Mary*
49 Hackett
50 Sergeant
51 Jenner
52 Norton: *Anne Boleyn*
53 Jones
54 Loades: *Henry VIII: King and Court*
55 Fraser
56 *Rivals in Power*
57 Luke
58 Martienssen
59 Rival
60 Hackett
61 Hart
62 Varlow: *The Lady Penelope*
63 Hart
64 For Mary's letter, see Chapter 11.
65 Glenne
66 Denny: *Anne Boleyn*
67 Ibid.
68 Norton: *Anne Boleyn*
69 L. & P.
70 S. C.
71 L. & P.
72 Erickson: *Anne Boleyn*
73 Seward
74 Ibid.
75 Knecht

76 Wilkinson: *Mary Boleyn*
77 Ibid.
78 MacNalty
79 Ridley: *Henry VIII*; Denny: *Anne Boleyn*
80 Ridley: *Henry VIII*
81 *V. C.*
82 Plowden: *Tudor Women*; Erickson: *Great Harry, Anne Boleyn*; Walder; Luke; Norton: *Anne Boleyn*; Hart; Hughes
83 Bruce; Hackett
84 Hackett
85 Ibid.
86 Round, although Martienssen for one repeats this as fact.
87 Denny: *Anne Boleyn*; Norton: *Anne Boleyn*
88 Martienssen
89 Chapman, who states that Mary, and not Anne, had been sent to the court of the Archduchess Margaret.
90 Powell. John Walder states that Mary came home in the early 1520s, but she was married in England in February 1520.
91 Ives; Norton: *She Wolves*; Michael Clark; Denny: *Anne Boleyn*; Fraser; Loades: *The Six Wives of Henry VIII*; Bernard: *Anne Boleyn*; Jones
92 Denny: *Anne Boleyn*
93 *The Chronicle of King Henry VIII of England*
94 *L. & P.*
95 Loades: *The Tudor Queens*
96 Ridley: *Henry VIII*; Brysson Morrison; Fraser; Loades: *The Six Wives of Henry VIII*; Plowden: The Other Boleyn Girl; Luke; Powell, who states that Mary filled Elizabeth Blount's place; and Jones, who asserts that this was how she came to Henry's attention.
97 Luke
98 Perry: *Sisters to the King*
99 Loades: *The Six Wives of Henry VIII*
100 Not Elizabeth Howard, Lady Boleyn, as Warnicke states in *The Rise and Fall of Anne Boleyn*.
101 Cited by Erickson in *The First Elizabeth*.
102 Jones
103 Ibid.; Norton: *Anne Boleyn*; Wilkinson: *The Early Loves of Anne Boleyn*
104 For example, Erickson in *The First Elizabeth*, and your author in earlier books. I can trace no contemporary source for the French King saying that Mary was 'always good for a ride' (Hobden) or the claim that, 'according to François, Mary "did service" to male members of the court too' (Fox).

105 Jones
106 Prévost
107 The relation is identified elsewhere, less credibly, as William du Moulin de l'Hospital, seigneur of Fontenay-sous-Briis, a descendant of 'Louis Boulen', who is mentioned in a notarial contract of 1460; Moulin's wife was called Catherine, and they had married in 1510; he too died in 1548.
108 www.mairie-de-briis-sous-forges.fr
109 That of M. Marcel Mouton, a romantic poet who lived in the tower in the nineteenth century and claimed to have documents relating to Anne's sojourn there. According to him, the facts were beyond doubt, although certain authors had contested them (Prévost).
110 Warnicke: 'Anne Boleyn's Childhood'
111 See, for example, Bruce.
112 Prévost
113 Norton: *Anne Boleyn*
114 Denny: *Anne Boleyn*
115 Sergeant
116 Andrew Clark; *Tottel's Miscellany*
117 Stone
118 *L. & P.*
119 Ives
120 Erickson: *Anne Boleyn*
121 Chapman
122 Michael Clark
123 *L. & P.*
124 Cited by Michael Clark.
125 *L. & P.*

5: 'William Carey, of the Privy Chamber'

1 Denny: *Katherine Howard*; Powell; Wilkinson: *Mary Boleyn*
2 Hart
3 Foster; www.teachergenealogist.com
4 Hart
5 Warnicke: *The Rise and Fall of Anne Boleyn*
6 Not a week before the wedding, as Hart states.
7 Warnicke: *The Rise and Fall of Anne Boleyn*
8 Starkey says he was a Gentleman of the Privy Chamber in 1519, but he is not referred to as such until 1526 (the Eltham Ordinances, in *The Antiquarian Repertory*); he was Esquire of the

Body in June 1524 (*L. & P.*). A grant to him as 'esquire' in 1526, and a description of him as an esquire at the time of his death, refer to his status, not his office.

9 *The Rutland Papers*
10 Jones
11 Powell
12 Plowden: *Tudor Women, The House of Tudor*
13 Denny: *Anne Boleyn*
14 Lofts
15 Luke
16 Hackett
17 *The Reign of Henry VIII*
18 Hall
19 Powell
20 Denny: *Anne Boleyn*; Plowden: The Other Boleyn Girl
21 Denny: *Katherine Howard*
22 Bruce
23 Hart
24 Jones
25 Warnicke: 'Anne Boleyn's Childhood'
26 Ibid.
27 Warnicke: *The Rise and Fall of Anne Boleyn*
28 Wilkinson: *Mary Boleyn*
29 Varlow: *The Lady Penelope*
30 Hart; Wilkinson: *Mary Boleyn*
31 Cf. Hart
32 Bruce
33 For example, Luke.
34 *L. & P.* Some sources incorrectly give the date as 1521, e.g. Friedmann; J.J. Scarisbrick; Fraser; Martin Hume; Erickson: *Anne Boleyn*; Norton: *Anne Boleyn*; Williams: *Henry VIII and His Court*; Plowden: The Other Boleyn Girl
35 *L. & P.*
36 Thurley; Carroll
37 *L. & P.*
38 For example, Hart.
39 By her second husband, Sir Robert Spencer.
40 Warnicke: *The Rise and Fall of Anne Boleyn*. Erickson incorrectly assumes that, on marriage, Mary became known as 'Mary Boleyn Carey', but that is a later American form of name unknown in Tudor England.
41 It is also given as Karry or Cary in early documents, and

variously as Carey, Cary, Care, Caree, Carre or Karre in Tudor sources.

42 Some genealogies give the date 1479, eight years after his father's death!

43 Chilton had been owned by the Saxon King Harold before the Norman Conquest of 1066, and soon after that the manor became part of the Honour of Wallingford. From 1156, it was held by the Foliots, who gave it its later name (which is now spelt Foliat). The manor passed to their descendants, the Teys family, in 1289, and then, in 1367, to the Lords Lisle. In 1439, it came into the possession of Eleanor, the wife of Edmund Beaufort, Duke of Somerset, and from 1467 to her death in 1505, Chilton Foliat and the surrounding manors were held jointly by her seven daughters – among whom was William Carey's grandmother, Eleanor Beaufort – and their husbands, and by her grandson, Henry Stafford, Duke of Buckingham, whose lands were declared forfeit after he was attainted and executed in 1483. In 1505, Chilton Foliat and the other manors reverted to the Crown, and from 1519, they were held by the successive queens of Henry VIII. William's father was probably allowed to remain there as a tenant of the Crown.

44 For example, Wilkinson in *Mary Boleyn*.

45 Foster; www.teachergenealogist.com

46 He is sometimes styled 'of Pleshey Castle' – then also spelt Plashy – but this castle was in the hands of the Crown from 1397 to the reign of Edward VI (1547–53) and, according to *L. & P.*, John Carey was merely its constable (Unlocking Essex's Past).

47 *L. & P.*

48 Starkey, in *The Renaissance at Sutton Place*, gives his date of birth as c.1500 but cites no source, while Wilkinson states in *Mary Boleyn* that William's date of birth is not known.

49 Wilkinson: *Mary Boleyn*. She also suggests that William had become Courtenay's ward on the death of Sir Thomas Carey in 1500, but – as has been shown – Thomas Carey did not die until 1536.

50 *L. & P.*

51 Ibid.

52 Ibid.

53 Ibid.

54 Ibid.

55 Ibid.

56 Ibid.

57 Ibid.

58 *The Rutland Papers*

59 *L. & P.*

60 Ibid.

61 Ibid.

62 Starkey, in *The Renaissance at Sutton Place*

63 *Four Years at the Court of Henry VIII*

64 Wilkinson: *Mary Boleyn*

65 Cited by Loades: *The Tudor Queens*

66 Starkey, in *The Renaissance at Sutton Place*

67 Fox says that Carey played tennis; while this is likely, for it was one of the King's favourite sports, I can find no contemporary source to support this statement.

68 The words are quoted from his song, 'Pastime With Good Company'.

69 The Eltham Ordinances, in *The Antiquarian Repertory*

70 Hall

71 *Henry VIII: A European Court in England.* For a discussion of William Carey's portraits, see Appendix II.

72 The Careys' house stood in a field south-east of the parish church, where a few mounds are all that remain to indicate its site. It was William Carey's nephew, Sir Edward Carey of Aldenham (the son of his older brother, Sir John Carey), the Master and Treasurer of Elizabeth I's jewels and plate, who bought the manor and the Elizabethan house from Paul Stepneth in 1589, and was buried in the parish church in 1618. His son, the colonist and politician Lucius Carey, 1st Viscount Falkland, was born at Aldenham in 1576. The house was remodelled around 1632, and ten years later it was sold by the 2nd Viscount to Sir John Harby, a staunch Royalist; in 1664, it was bought by Denzil Holles, the statesman and author who had been one of the five M.P.s whom Charles I famously had tried to arrest in 1642. The Careys' former home was finally pulled down in 1711.

Investigating the possibility that William and Mary Carey had lived in another property in Aldenham, I discovered that three other substantial houses had once stood there. Pennes Place, named after a local family who had held lands in the village since the thirteenth century, was demolished sometime after 1559. Later called Aldenham Hall, it had been built before 1485, when it was purchased from Ralph Penne by Humphrey Coningsby, who owned it until his death in 1535. A 'fair house of brick', orginally called Wigbournes, was owned in the sixteenth century by the Wigbourne and Wrence families. It was rebuilt in 1632, and forms the core of the present Aldenham House – the name was changed around 1769 – which was remodelled in the early eighteenth century, and practically rebuilt in the nineteenth, when the magnificent gardens were laid out; its garden is on the site of the double moat of Pennes Place. Today, Aldenham House is home to Haberdashers' Aske's public school. Neither of these properties can have been the residence of William Carey and Mary Boleyn, nor are the couple linked to any lesser properties in the area, while their names appear nowhere in the records of the village.

The manor of Titburst and Kendals to the south-east of the parish had been left to Henry VIII in 1509 by his grandmother, Lady Margaret Beaufort, William Carey's kinswoman; in 1530, it was granted to Henry Fitzroy, Duke of Richmond. (*V. C. H.: Hertfordshire*, www.british-history.ac.uk)

73 Warnicke: *The Rise and Fall of Anne Boleyn*
74 Warnicke also claims that Mary was never a maid of honour to Katherine of Aragon because she was too young, having been born in 1508 (*sic*).
75 Warnicke: 'Anne Boleyn's Childhood'; Barbara Harris
76 Barbara Harris
77 Starkey: *The Reign of Henry VIII*
78 Cavendish: *The Life and Death of Cardinal Wolsey*
79 *The Rutland Papers*
80 *L. & P.*
81 *The Chronicle of Calais; The Rutland Papers*
82 *The Rutland Papers.* For general references to the Field of Cloth of Gold quoted in the text, see this source and, principally, *The Chronicle of Calais; V. C.; S. C.; L. & P.*, and Hall.
83 *L. & P.; The Rutland Papers*
84 *The Chronicle of Calais; L. & P.*
85 Hall
86 Ibid.
87 Ibid.
88 Ibid.
89 Ibid.
90 *V. C.*
91 Ibid.
92 *L. & P.*
93 Wilkinson: *Mary Boleyn*. He is incorrectly listed in this contemporary source as 'Sir William Carey', although he was never knighted.
94 *L. & P.*
95 Hall
96 Ibid.

97   *V. C.*
98   Luke
99   Denny: *Anne Boleyn*
100 *L. & P.*
101 Ibid.; *The Complete Peerage*
102 Ibid.
103 Ibid.

6: *'The Assault on the Castle of Virtue'*

1   Burke
2   Murphy
3   Ridley: *Henry VIII*; Sergeant
4   *The Book of Beauty*
5   Ridley: *Henry VIII*
6   Denny: *Anne Boleyn*
7   *L. & P.*; Elton: *Studies in Tudor and Stuart Politics and Government*;
     Warnicke: 'Anne Boleyn's Childhood'
8   *L. & P.*
9   Luke
10 Hackett
11 Fox; Erickson: *Anne Boleyn*
12 Denny: *Anne Boleyn, Katherine Howard*
13 Erickson: *Bloody Mary*
14 Loades: *The Tudor Queens, Henry VIII: Court, Church and Conflict*
15 Norton: *Anne Boleyn*
16 Ibid.
17 Ives speculates that the liaison might just be dated to the 1510s;
     Ridley says that it was going on in February 1516, at the time of
     the Princess Mary's christening (*The Life and Times of Mary Tudor*),
     and Loades states that Mary was sharing Henry VIII's bed during
     the years when Anne Boleyn was at the French court (i.e. between
     the spring of 1515 and the spring of 1522). Plowden thinks that the
     affair probably began in 1519 (The Other Boleyn Girl). It has been
     suggested that Henry probably became interested in Mary during
     Elizabeth Blount's pregnancy in 1519, and that she supplanted
     Elizabeth in 1519 or 1520 (Loades: *The Tudor Queens*; *Henry VIII*;
     Court, Church and Conflict; Cannon and Hargreaves). Denny assumes
     that their liaison began early in 1520: 'By April 1522 . . . Mary had
     been Henry's mistress for two years'.
        It has been claimed that Reginald Pole referred to Henry being
     the first to spoil Mary, and some have inferred from that that the

affair took place before her marriage, as Pole does not refer to her as a married woman (Beauclerk-Dewar and Powell); but Pole actually wrote that the King had 'first violated and for a long time after kept [Mary] as [his] concubine', meaning that the violation came first, not that the King was the first man to sleep with her.

Several writers state that Mary was married to William Carey during her affair with the King (Lindsey; Luke; Hamer; Denny: *Anne Boleyn*; Jones), or that she was perhaps given Carey as a reward when Henry had finished with her (Lindsey). Jones states, as if it were an established fact, that 'as soon as Henry declared his interest in her, she was found a husband', and that the affair began either before or 'shortly after' the wedding. Powell writes that she became the King's mistress after her marriage, suggesting that the affair 'almost certainly' began in 1520, either during the visit of the Emperor Charles V to England in May, or at the Field of Cloth of Gold. Van Duyn Southworth, Johnson and Hackett suggest a date of 1520–1, Hackett romantically imagining Henry noticing Mary's 'warm consoling gaze' at the Field of Cloth of Gold in 1520.

Nicholas Sander stated in 1585 that Henry brought Mary to court and 'ruined her' after her father returned from France in March 1520; of course, she was already at court by then. Friedman states that 'the affair between the King and Mary Boleyn began almost immediately after she married William Carey'. Ashdown firmly states that Mary became the King's mistress in 1521, 'the same year in which she married William Carey (*sic.*)' (*Ladies in Waiting*). Ridley thinks that 'she was probably Henry's mistress both before and after the marriage' (*Henry VIII*), Norton that, by the time of Anne Boleyn's return to England early in 1522, Mary was 'well-established as Henry VIII's mistress' (*Anne Boleyn*). Murphy and Mathew wisely state only that the affair began after her marriage to Carey, Rex that it flourished in the early 1520s (*The Tudors*). Wilson writes that it started in 1524–5 (*In The Lion's Court*). Warnicke dates it as late as 1525, purely on the grounds that, in that year, the King became 'increasingly alienated' from Queen Katherine after her nephew, the Emperor Charles V, jilted the Princess Mary in order to marry the fabulously wealthy Isabella of Portugal ('Anne Boleyn's Childhood'). Round also suggests that the affair 'may not improbably be placed as late as 1525', the year in which Thomas Boleyn was ennobled and there was 'a change in Henry for the worse' after he ceased having sexual relations with Queen Katherine. According to Round, 'there

is nothing to prove that [the affair] belongs to an earlier date'.
All this is speculation.

18 Ives; Haigh; Murphy
19 Cf. Parmiter; Starkey: *Six Wives*; Hart; Fox; Stella Fletcher;
    Wilkinson: *The Early Loves of Anne Boleyn*
20 Fraser
21 Norton: *Anne Boleyn*. She states elsewhere that there is no evidence
    that Elizabeth Howard was Henry's mistress.
22 Rex: *Henry VIII*
23 Thornton-Cook
24 Jones
25 Hackett
26 Hackett; Hart; Wilkinson: *Mary Boleyn*. Wilkinson may be correct in
    suggesting that Sir William Compton probably approached Mary on
    the King's behalf.
27 Hobden
28 Jones
29 Hart
30 Loades: *The Tudor Queens*
31 L. & P.
32 Luke
33 *Four Years at the Court of Henry VIII*
34 *English Historical Documents, 5, 1485–1558*
35 L. & P.
36 Ibid.; Herbert
37 Wilkinson: *Mary Boleyn*
38 L. & P.
39 Cavendish: *The Life and Death of Cardinal Wolsey*
40 Wyatt
41 For this pageant, see Hall and L. & P.
42 Wilkinson: *The Early Loves of Anne Boleyn*. Although it has long
    been assumed that the Countess of Devon was Katherine of York,
    Wilkinson is correct in identifying her as Gertrude Blount, whose
    mother-in-law, Katherine of York, daughter of Edward IV and aunt
    of Henry VIII, would surely have been referred to as the Dowager
    Countess. Besides, Katherine of York was then forty-three, and
    rather old to be dancing in a court pageant.
43 Tallis
44 Luke
45 Bruce
46 Wilkinson: *Mary Boleyn*
47 L. & P.

48 Murphy

49 Fox

50 For example, Friedmann; Michael Clark; Erickson: *Anne Boleyn*;
    Hackett; Starkey: *Six Wives*; Martin Hume; Albert; Norton: *Anne
    Boleyn*; Sergeant; Murphy; Powell; Varlow: *The Lady Penelope*

51 Hackett

52 Varlow: *The Lady Penelope*

53 Ibid.; Bagley; Bruce; Jones

54 Chapman

55 Ibid.

56 Ibid.

57 Ibid.

58 Ibid.

59 Ibid.; *The Complete Peerage*

60 *State Papers of the Reign of Henry VIII*

61 *L. & P.*

62 Ibid.

63 Ball

64 *L. & P.*

65 Ibid.

66 Ibid.

67 Powell

68 *L. & P.*

69 Childe-Pemberton

70 Ibid.; Murphy

71 Murphy

72 Norton: *Anne Boleyn*

73 *Six Wives*

74 *L. & P.*

75 Erickson: *Anne Boleyn*

76 Norton: *Anne Boleyn*

77 *L. & P.*

78 Lofts

79 *L. & P.*

80 Ibid.

81 Ibid.

82 Ives; Warnicke: *The Rise and Fall of Anne Boleyn*; Friedmann;
    Hoskins; Loades: *The Six Wives of Henry VIII*; Jones; Fox; Stella
    Fletcher; Hutchinson; Varlow: *The Lady Penelope*

83 Plowden: The Other Boleyn Girl

84 *L. & P.*; Ives

85 *L. & P.*

86 Which I have not been able to trace; it is not to be identified with Wickford, as that name derives from the Saxon word *wic*, meaning a dwelling place, fort or spring, and all early versions of the name Wickford are spelt with an 'i'.

87 *L. & P.*

88 Ibid.

89 Ibid.

90 Ibid. The annuity of £100 came 'out of the Earl of Derby's lands'.

91 Ibid.. Herbage was the right to graze cattle, and pannage the right to allow pigs to go into woodland to root for masts and nuts.

92 Robinson; *V. C. H.: Wiltshire*

93 *L. & P.*

94 Ibid.

95 *V. C. H.: Essex*

96 *L. & P.*

97 Ibid.

98 Hoskins says 1527, but in *L. & P.* this grant is correctly listed in the early months of 1526, as Warnicke (*The Rise and Fall of Anne Boleyn*) and others have rightly accepted.

99 *L. & P.*; these lands would be sold off in 1552 and 1553 by William's son, Henry Carey.

100 Hall

101 For example, Bowle; Ridley: *Henry VIII*; Chapman; James

102 *S. C.*

103 Hall

104 *L. & P.*; Cotton MSS Vespasian; *The Antiquarian Repertory*

105 *L. & P.*

106 Erickson: *Anne Boleyn*

107 *L. & P.*

108 Erickson: *Anne Boleyn*; Jones

109 Carlton

110 Luke

111 Friedman

112 Wyatt

113 Powell

7: 'Living in Avoutry'

1 For a broader discussion, see Given-Wilson and Rickman.

2 *S. C.*

3 *L. & P.*

4 Barbara Harris

5 *V. C.*
6 Wilkinson: *The Early Loves of Anne Boleyn*
7 Brysson Morrison
8 Ridley: *Henry VIII*; Wilkinson: *The Early Loves of Anne Boleyn*
9 Wilson: *In the Lion's Court*
10 Murphy
11 Luke; Denny: *Katherine Howard*
12 Erickson: *Anne Boleyn*
13 Lindsey
14 Varlow: *The Lady Penelope*
15 Claremont
16 Bruce
17 Luke
18 Chapman
19 Erickson: *Bloody Mary*
20 Fraser
21 Brysson Morrison
22 Martin Hume
23 Chapman
24 Ibid.
25 Wilkinson: *The Early Loves of Anne Boleyn*
26 Denny: *Anne Boleyn*; Wilkinson: *The Early Loves of Anne Boleyn*
27 Hart
28 Benton Fletcher
29 *L. & P.*; Hoskins; Wilkinson: *Mary Boleyn*. Wilkinson sees this grant as marking the end of Henry VIII's affair with Mary Boleyn.
30 Powell
31 Hoskins
32 Colvin
33 Ibid.
34 Dixon
35 *L. & P.*
36 Not Cardinal Wolsey, as Hart suggests.
37 Hart
38 Ibid.
39 Ibid.
40 Tallis
41 Friedmann
42 Denny: *Anne Boleyn*
43 Norton: *Anne Boleyn*; Mathew
44 Sergeant
45 Luke

46 Ibid.
47 Bruce
48 Warnicke: *The Rise and Fall of Anne Boleyn*
49 Denny: *Anne Boleyn*
50 Luke
51 Contrary to Hart's claim that 'we have no evidence of her ever exercising patronage'.
52 Hostillers' Books, Durham Cathedral Muniments
53 *L. & P.*; Dugdale; Ives; Douglas Richardson; Craster. Thomas Gardiner was the son of William Gardiner of London by Helen (or Ellen), a bastard daughter of Henry VIII's great-uncle, Jasper Tudor, Earl of Pembroke, and thus cousin to the King.
54 Hutchinson
55 Lacey
56 Jones
57 Bruce
58 Erickson: *Bloody Mary*
59 Hart
60 Bagley
61 *L. & P.*
62 Wilkinson: *Mary Boleyn*
63 Starkey: *Six Wives*; Luke
64 Beckingsale
65 Loades: *The Tudor Queens*; Hoskins; Hart
66 Flügel
67 Warnicke: 'Anne Boleyn's Childhood'
68 Hoskins
69 Loades: *The Tudor Queens, The Six Wives of Henry VIII*
70 Murphy
71 Ibid.
72 Loades: *Mary Tudor*
73 *L. & P.*
74 S. C.
75 Hackett
76 Smith: *Henry VIII: The Mask of Royalty*
77 S. C.
78 Ibid.; *L. & P.*
79 Puttenham. A varlet was an attendant or page, but the word could also mean a rascal or knave.
80 Hoskins
81 *L. & P.*
82 *State Papers of the Reign of Henry VIII*

83 *L. & P.*
84 Ibid.
85 Erickson: *Anne Boleyn*

8: 'Hiding Royal Blood'

1 Not 1529–30, as was once claimed, or 1526, as claimed by Bernard (Anne Boleyn), or 1525, the date sometimes given, since her brother was almost certainly born that year, while Jones is incorrect in saying that Mary 'finally became pregnant in June 1525', and in claiming that there is still 'some dispute' as to which of her children was born first.

2 There is no evidence that the child was christened Katherine Mary Carey, as Tunis calls her; middle names were virtually unknown in early Tudor England.

3 Bruce

4 Hoskins and Wilkinson (*Mary Boleyn*) give the year as 1526. Hoskins has argued that the grant of February 1527 (*sic.*) – which in fact belongs to 1526 – marks the first birthday of Mary's son, yet it is far more likely that Henry Carey was born in 1525. Murphy has muddled the dates, saying that Henry was born in 1524 and Katherine in 1526. Rootsweb and other websites claim that Henry was born – and later married – at Hengrave Hall in Suffolk, but I can find no contemporary evidence for this, and no link between the Careys and Thomas Kytson, the wealthy cloth merchant who built Hengrave between 1525 and 1538. Nor can I find any evidence to support Claremont's claim that there was a second daughter of the marriage called Mary.

5 *L. & P.*

6 Starkey: *Six Wives*; Bernard: *Anne Boleyn*; Fox. Bruce gives the date incorrectly as 1524, Erickson (*Anne Boleyn*) as 1522 or thereabouts, Loades (*The Six Wives of Henry VIII*) as 1527, while Beauclerk-Dewar and Powell assert that 'the uncertain date of [Henry Carey's] birth makes it possible, though not probable, that he had been conceived when Mary Boleyn was Henry VIII's mistress'.

7 Hoskins; Hilliam; Waldherr; Carlton; Erickson: *Anne Boleyn, The First Elizabeth*; Denny: *Anne Boleyn, Katherine Howard*; Tunis; Jones; Hart; Fox; Stella Fletcher; Bernard: *The King's Reformation*. Warnicke (*The Rise and Fall of Anne Boleyn*) claims the son was the King's child, on the grounds that Mary had been Henry's mistress in 1525.

8 Hackett

9 Rex: *Henry VIII*

10 Starkey: *Six Wives*; Wilkinson: *Mary Boleyn*
11 Jones
12 Powell
13 Hoskins
14 Doran
15 Martienssen
16 *L. & P.*; Douglas Richardson, in a letter to the author; Levin
17 Michael Clark; Sergeant
18 Warnicke: 'Anne Boleyn's Childhood'
19 *V. C.*
20 Wilkinson: *Mary Boleyn*
21 Cf. Plowden: The Other Boleyn Girl
22 *L. & P.*; Aungier
23 It is clear that Hale was not referring to Henry Carey being banished from the court because the boy was 'an idiot', as Erickson claims (*Anne Boleyn*); there is no evidence whatsoever for this.
24 *L. & P.*
25 Bernard: *Anne Boleyn*
26 Mattingly
27 *L. & P.*
28 Hoskins; Varlow: *The Lady Penelope*
29 Hoskins: Lady Antonia Fraser's views regarding the Careys' paternity and Anthony Hoskins' paper.
30 Rex: *Henry* VIII; Starkey: *The Reign of Henry VIII*
31 Bagley
32 *L. & P.*
33 If the landowner had no son, his property went to his legitimate brothers or nephews (Barbara Harris).
34 Barbara Harris
35 For example, Wilkinson: *Mary Boleyn*; Hoskins
36 Murphy; Harleian MSS. Hart gives the date incorrectly as 1532.
37 Hoskins; L'Estrange
38 Hoskins
39 Wilkinson: *Mary Boleyn*
40 See Weir: *The Lady in the Tower* for a fuller discussion.
41 Wilkinson: *Mary Boleyn*
42 For a fuller discussion of the subject of Henry's alleged impotence in 1536, see Weir: *The Lady in the Tower*.
43 Wilkinson: *Mary Boleyn*
44 Hoskins
45 Murphy
46 Hoskins

47 Murphy

48 *V. C.*

49 Denny: *Katherine Howard*

50 Ibid.; Hoskins; Hart

51 Hoskins: Lady Antonia Fraser's views regarding the Careys' paternity and Anthony Hoskins' paper.

52 For example, Loades: *Henry VIII: Court, Church and Conflict*; Fraser

53 For this dictionary, see Varlow: 'Sir Francis Knollys's Latin Dictionary: New Evidence for Katherine Carey', *The Lady Penelope*.

54 Ibid.; Croft and Hearn

55 Croft and Hearn

56 Diana Scarisbrick

57 Varlow: *The Lady Penelope*

58 Varlow: 'Sir Francis Knollys's Latin Dictionary: New Evidence for Katherine Carey'

59 Private collection, on loan to Shakespeare's Globe, London.

60 Varlow: *The Lady Penelope*

61 Ives; he asserts that the affair ended in or before 1526 and that Henry Carey was Mary's first child.

62 Varlow: *The Lady Penelope*

63 Ibid.

64 Ibid.

65 Hughes

66 Hoskins: Lady Antonia Fraser's views regarding the Careys' paternity and Anthony Hoskins' paper.

67 Wilkinson (*Mary Boleyn*) has suggested that a miniature attributed to Levina Teerlinc of Lady Katherine Grey with her son, Edward Seymour, at Belvoir Castle, Rutland, is in fact a likeness of Katherine Carey, but the sitter in that portrait is clearly the same lady as depicted in another Teerlinc miniature in the Victoria and Albert Museum, whose identification as Katherine Grey is based on a very early inscription on the back. Moreover, she has a circular miniature of her husband, Edward Seymour, Earl of Hertford, attached by a ribbon to her bodice.

68 By, for example, Warnicke: *The Rise and Fall of Anne Boleyn.*

69 Varlow: 'Sir Francis Knollys's Latin Dictionary: New Evidence for Katherine Carey'; Jones

70 *The Lady Penelope*

71 *The Complete Peerage*; *Dictionary of National Biography*; Gerald Paget; Hoskins; Jones

72 Cited by Beauclerk-Dewar and Powell; see their book for Perrot, also Turvey; Barnwell

73   *L. & P.*

74   Beauclerk-Dewar and Powell

75   Jones

76   For example, Jones, who tells an unfounded tale about Henry visiting the Perrots in Pembrokeshire and enjoying the hunting there, as well as the lady of the house.

77   Turvey

78   *Calendar of State Papers: Ireland: Elizabeth I, 1588–92*

79   Cited by Simpson.

80   Wright: *The History of Ireland*

81   Notably by Jones, who accepts that he was Henry's son.

82   Cited by Simpson.

83   Edwards

84   Murphy says March 1525.

85   Edwards; Murphy; Hart

86   See McClure; Hughey

87   According to a recent theory, Joan Dingley was not so lowly born, but is to be identified with Joan, the daughter of a Gloucestershire gentleman, John Moore, who married one James Dingley (Jones); but in his will of 1547, Malte referred to Etheldreda's mother as 'Joan Dingley, now the wife of one Dobson', and since Joan Moore subsequently married Michael Ashfield and Thomas Parker, that theory must fall.

88   Jones

89   *L. & P.*

90   Cited by Poynton.

91   Harington et al.

92   Ibid.

93   *L. & P.*

94   Ibid.

95   Hughey

96   Cited by Hughey.

97   *Calendar of the Patent Rolls preserved in the Public Record Office, Mary and Philip and Mary*

98   Hughey

99   Ibid.; Levin

100 Hughey

101 Levin

102 *L. & P.; The Complete Peerage*

103 Ridley, in *The Love Letters of Henry VIII*; Norton: *Anne Boleyn*; Murphy; Ives

104 *The Complete Peerage*

105 L. & P.
106 Given-Wilson
107 Fraser
108 V. C.

9: 'The Sister of Your Former Concubine'

1 Hart; Jones; Williams: *Henry VIII and His Court*
2 Wilkinson: *Mary Boleyn*
3 Friedman
4 L. & P.; Rex: *Henry VIII*; Carlton; Erickson: *Anne Boleyn*; Hamer; Jones
5 Jones
6 L. & P.
7 Wilkinson (*Mary Boleyn*) claims that the King paid £521.8s.6½d. (£168,000) for the *Mary Boleyn*, but what L. & P. III 3358 (the source she cites) actually records is that wages, rewards and victualling for its seventy-nine-strong crew came to £352.8s.6½d. (£113,500).
8 Antonia Fraser believes that the liaison was over by 1524; Hoskins (also in Lady Antonia Fraser's views regarding the Careys' paternity) is incorrect in claiming that she is the only historian who believes the affair ended prior to 1526. David Starkey suggests that it ceased around Christmas 1524, after Mary became pregnant with her husband's child (*Six Wives*), a view echoed by Jones; Loades (*The Six Wives of Henry VIII*) and Norton say it was over by 1525 (although Norton opts for 1526 elsewhere), Loades (*Mary Tudor*) and Wilkinson (*Mary Boleyn*) stating that it had lasted three years; Erickson cautiously opts for the mid-1520s (*Great Harry*) or by the summer of 1525 (*Anne Boleyn*), Parmiter, Doran, Ashdown (*Ladies in Waiting*), Hart, Stella Fletcher and Wilkinson (*The Early Loves of Anne Boleyn*) for 1525, Wilkinson (*Mary Boleyn*) for the autumn of 1525, Varlow (*The Lady Penelope*) for when Henry 'transferred his affections to Anne some time near the end of 1525', while Ives, Scarisbrick, Plowden (The Other Boleyn Girl) and Denny (*Anne Boleyn*) think it ended in or before 1526.
9 Hoskins
10 Cf. Fraser
11 Powell
12 Lindsey; Jenner
13 Bruce
14 Denny: *Anne Boleyn*

15 Ibid.; Carroll
16 Wilkinson: *Mary Boleyn*.
17 As Jones claims.
18 Carroll
19 Fox
20 Beauclerk-Dewar and Powell
21 Denny: *Katherine Howard*
22 Beauclerk-Dewar and Powell
23 Walder
24 Thornton-Cook
25 Porter
26 Ridley, in *The Love Letters of Henry VIII*; Savage, in *The Love Letters of Henry VIII*; Thornton-Cook; Jones
27 Scarisbrick, for example.
28 Jones is incorrect in stating that the first evidence of Henry's interest in Anne dates from 1528.
29 Wilkinson: *Mary Boleyn*
30 L. & P.
31 Warnicke: *The Rise and Fall of Anne Boleyn*
32 Cavendish: *The Life and Death of Cardinal Wolsey*; L. & P.
33 L. & P.
34 Cavendish: *The Life and Death of Cardinal Wolsey*
35 L. & P.; Bernard: 'The Rise of Sir William Compton, Tudor Courtier'
36 L. & P. It has been suggested (Jansen) that the Mrs Amadas who was arrested in 1533, and who had been courted by Henry VIII, was not the wife of Robert, Master of the Jewel House, but of John Amadas (before 1489–1554/5), one of the King's Serjeants-at-Arms (L. & P.), who owned properties in Kent, Devon and Cornwall. He had married by 1519, but his wife's name is unknown; she was dead by 1542, when he remarried. However, the entry relating to moneys owed by Robert Amadas appears immediately after that relating to 'Mrs Amadas's treason in L. & P. July 1533, and refers to information laid by her, so it seems incontestable that the two are connected.
    Robert Amadas was dead before August 1533, when Elizabeth, who seems to have been released from custody without punishment, married Sir Thomas Neville.
37 Loades: *Henry VIII: Court, Church and Conflict*
38 Hall
39 Now in the Vatican Library.
40 L. & P.

41 Norton: *She Wolves*

42 Fox

43 Bruce

44 Luke

45 Hackett

46 Lacey

47 Flügel; Smith: *Henry VIII: The Mask of Royalty*

48 Erickson: *Anne Boleyn*

49 Ibid.

50 Lacey

51 Norton: *Anne Boleyn*

52 Luke

53 Round, who thought that Thomas Boleyn owed his ennoblement
    to Mary becoming the King's mistress; Friedmann concurs, stating
    that it was Boleyn who 'reaped the golden harvest', not Mary or
    her husband.

54 Cf. Wilkinson: *Mary Boleyn*

55 Fox

56 *The Rutland Papers*

57 L. & P.; Cotton MSS Vespasian; *The Antiquarian Repertory*

58 Starkey, in *The Renaissance at Sutton Place*

59 L. & P.

60 Ibid.

61 See, for example, Wilkinson: *Mary Boleyn*

62 L. & P.

63 Hall; *Henry VIII: A European Court in England*. For Holbein's
    possible portrait of William Carey, see Appendix II.

64 Kelly

65 S. C.; Sander

66 Gwyn

67 S. C.

68 Kelly

69 *The Complete Peerage*

70 S. C.

71 Wilson: *Henry VIII: Reformer and Tyrant*

72 Wilkinson: *Mary Boleyn*

73 Ives; Fraser; Bernard: *Anne Boleyn*. The late Abbess's name is some-
    times incorrectly given as Elizabeth Shelford.

74 Starkey: *Six Wives*

75 L. & P.

76 As Bowle claims.

77 L. & P.; Knowles

78 Denny: *Anne Boleyn*
79 See Chapter 10.
80 *L. & P.*
81 *Ambassades en Angleterre de Jean du Bellay, 1527–29*
82 Hall
83 *L. & P.*
84 *V. C.*; Flood
85 Starkey, in *The Renaissance at Sutton Place*
86 Wilkinson: *Mary Boleyn*; Flood
87 *Ambassades en Angleterre de Jean du Bellay, 1527–29*
88 Gardiner
89 *Ambassades en Angleterre de Jean du Bellay, 1527–29*
90 *L. & P.*
91 Ibid.; Hall
92 *Ambassades en Angleterre de Jean du Bellay, 1527–29*
93 *L. & P.*
94 Starkey, in *The Renaissance at Sutton Place*
95 Mattingly
96 *L. & P.*
97 Hall
98 *Ambassades en Angleterre de Jean du Bellay, 1527–29*
99 *L. & P.*
100 Ibid.
101 Warnicke: *The Rise and Fall of Anne Boleyn*

10: 'In Bondage'

1 William Carey's Inquisition Post Mortem is in *L. & P.*; Benton; *V. C. H.: Buckinghamshire and Cambridgeshire*.
2 *L. & P.*
3 Ibid.
4 Wilkinson: *Mary Boleyn*. These were the manors of 'Tracies [Traceys], Stansford [Stanford] Rivers and Suttons, and appurtenances there and in High Ongar, Essex'. Formerly owned by the Duke of Buckingham, they had been granted to William Carey and Mary his wife on 18 June 1524 (*L. & P.*). I am indebted to Josephine Wilkinson for this reference.
   The three manors all lay south-west of Chipping Ongar. There is no evidence that their lords were ever in residence in the early sixteenth century. There is a record of Mary holding a manorial court at Stanford Rivers in 1534, but that manor – and probably the others – had reverted to the Crown by 1544 (*V. C. H.: Essex*).

5 Walder
6 Hackett
7 Bruce
8 Albert
9 Lofts
10 Ibid.
11 *L. & P.*
12 Fox
13 Wilkinson: *Mary Boleyn*
14 *L. & P.*
15 Lindsey; Denny: *Anne Boleyn*
16 Warnicke: *The Rise and Fall of Anne Boleyn*
17 Erickson: *Bloody Mary*
18 Cf. Brewer, in *L. & P.* Wilkinson suggests that Henry referred the matter to Boleyn in case Mary was trying to tempt her father 'to act inappropriately' (*Mary Boleyn*); this seems unlikely, given Henry's comments.
19 Lindsey
20 *L. & P.* Carroll, without citing a scource, says the King also gave her an elaborately wrought golden cup.
21 Tunis's statement that Mary remarried in 1528, six years before she actually did so, is unfounded.
22 *L. & P.*
23 Ives
24 Friedmann
25 *L. & P.*
26 Denny: *Anne Boleyn*
27 *L. & P.*
28 Ibid.
29 Ibid.
30 Now in Corpus Christi College, Cambridge.
31 L. & P.
32 Brewer, in *L. & P.*
33 S. C.
34 Ibid.
35 Ibid.
36 *The Complete Peerage*; *L. & P.*
37 *The Privy Purse Expenses of King Henry the Eighth from November MDXIX to December MDXXXII*; Wilkinson (*Mary Boleyn*) states that Mary was styled 'Lady Rochford' from June 1525, when her father was created Viscount Rochford, but that title rightly belonged to her mother.

38 L. & P.; Warnicke: *The Rise and Fall of Anne Boleyn*
39 *The Privy Purse Expenses of King Henry the Eighth from November MDXIX to December MDXXXII*
40 Warnicke: *The Rise and Fall of Anne Boleyn*
41 Hall
42 L. & P. It is sometimes claimed, incorrectly – for example, by Sergeant – that Mary was given the shirt by Henry, but the entry in L. & P. is clear, while women did not wear shirts anyway.
43 L. & P.
44 V. C.; L. & P. gives just ten or twelve.
45 S. C.
46 L. & P.
47 S. C.
48 Ibid.
49 For the Calais trip, see chiefly Hall; du Bellay; *Calendar of State Papers and Manuscripts existing in the Archives and Collections of Milan;* V. C..; Worde; L. & P.; S. C.; *The Chronicle of Calais; An English Garner,* Hamy.
50 Hall
51 Colvin
52 Ibid.
53 S. C.
54 V. C.
55 Worde. Ives suggests that the name 'my Lady Mary' does not refer to Mary Boleyn, and that Wynkyn de Worde was deliberately fed false information that the King's daughter Mary – 'my Lady Mary' – was present and willing to give place to Anne Boleyn. Ives says that Mary Boleyn would not have taken precedence over the Countess of Derby and Lady FitzWalter; yet Anne Boleyn – until recently only the Lady Anne Boleyn – had taken precedence over all other ladies of rank, at the King's instance, and Mary was her sister. Furthermore, as Lady Mary Rochford, Mary was entitled to be called 'my Lady Mary'.
56 Hall
57 L. & P.; *Losing Your Head Over Henry: Mary Boleyn;* Lindsey; Wilkinson: *Mary Boleyn;* Bindoff
58 *The Lisle Letters;* L. & P.
59 Hall
60 S. C.
61 Ibid.
62 Wilkinson: *Mary Boleyn*
63 L. & P.

64 Somerset: _Ladies in Waiting_; Warnicke: _The Rise and Fall of Anne Boleyn_
65 Latymer
66 Foxe
67 L. & P.
68 Ibid.
69 _Statutes of the Realm_
70 L. & P.
71 Hall
72 Not her mother, as Wilkinson (_Mary Boleyn_) states; her mother would have been styled Countess of/Lady Wiltshire, not Lady Boleyn.
73 L. & P.
74 _The Chronicle of King Henry VIII of England_
75 Hall
76 Cranmer
77 _State Papers of the Reign of Henry VIII_
78 Varlow: _The Lady Penelope_
79 Ibid.
80 S. C.
81 Ibid.

11: 'High Displeasure'

1 S. C.
2 Ibid.
3 Smith: _A Tudor Tragedy_
4 Fraser
5 Sergeant
6 L. & P.
7 Bindoff
8 L. & P.
9 This is inferred from the fact that William became a Gentleman Pensioner around 1540, and they were required to handle a wide range of weapons and cut a fine figure on horseback.
10 Savage, in _The Love Letters of Henry VIII_
11 L. & P.
12 Ibid. He was not a hanger-on at court, as Hughes claims.
13 Those of William Stafford (c.1259–1315?), who married Isabella, daughter of Robert de Stafford, and Sir John Stafford (c.1315–c.1370), who married Margaret, daughter of Ralph, 1st Earl of Stafford.

14   *Calendar of Inquisitions Post Mortem: Henry VII*, although in 1517, his age is given as forty-two, thus placing his birth in 1475, not 1478.

15   *L. & P.*

16   *V. C. H.: Staffordshire*

17   Contrary to what Jones states.

18   *V. C. H.: Hertfordshire*

19   *L. & P.*

20   Ibid. It is unlikely that this was the King's fool, William Somer(s), who is said to have been brought to court and immediately appointed to that post by an impressed Henry VIII in 1525; although he may have been under twenty-one, the upper age for wardship, in 1529, he was not the heir to an estate.

21   *L. & P.*

22   *The Chronicle of Calais*

23   *L. & P.*

24   Ibid.

25   Ibid.

26   Ibid.

27   Chapman

28   Ives

29   *S. C.*

30   *L. & P.*

31   *S. C*

32   *L. & P.*

33   *S. C.*

34   *L. & P.*

35   Ibid.

36   In *L. & P.*

37   Hackett

38   Hart

39   Lindsey

40   Ibid.

41   *L. & P.*

42   I can find no source for Jones's statement that Henry wrote to Lord Rochford, asking him to contact his father about helping Mary, and that the couple were given Rochford Hall; Fox states that Mary lived there with her father's blessing prior to his death, but does not cite any source, and in fact Mary inherited that house from her grandmother in 1540 (although livery of her lands was not granted until 1543). It has been claimed elsewhere that Cromwell insisted that Wiltshire help his daughter, and that an

angry Wiltshire flatly refused to do so; again, I can find no contemporary evidence for this, and it would appear that this episode has been confused with the events following William Carey's death, when Henry VIII stepped in to insist that Boleyn succour Mary.

43 Lindsey
44 Hart
45 Denny: *Katherine Howard*; Hart. Neither cites a source for the gift of the cup.
46 Denny: *Anne Boleyn*
47 Porter
48 Ibid.
49 Walder
50 Friedmann. As Wilkinson (*Mary Boleyn*) points out, sources naming him Edward have probably confused him with Stafford's eldest son by his second wife. His date of death is sometimes given as 1545, without any source being cited.
51 Erickson: *Anne Boleyn*
52 Warnicke: *The Rise and Fall of Anne Boleyn*
53 Latymer; Bourbon; *L. & P.*; Warnicke: *The Rise and Fall of Anne Boleyn*
54 Bourbon
55 Denny: *Anne Boleyn*
56 S. C.
57 Hughes
58 Varlow: 'Sir Francis Knollys's Latin Dictionary: New Evidence for Katherine Carey'
59 *L. & P.*
60 *The Chronicle of Calais*
61 *V. C.*
62 *The Chronicle of Calais*
63 Ibid.; *V. C.*
64 *The Chronicle of Calais*
65 Ibid.
66 *L. & P.* The same source also records that, at some point during her widowhood, Mary, 'lately wife to William Carey, deceased', was granted the wardship of one William Bailey, with his lands in Wiltshire, Kent and Hertfordshire. This is mentioned in an undated grant of 1546. It may also have been for Katherine Carey's maintenance.

12: 'A Poor Honest Life'

1 *L. & P.*. Josephine Wilkinson, in conversation with the author, has raised the possibility that the 'sister' referred to by Pio was not Mary but Jane Parker, Lady Rochford, with either the term 'sister' being used interchangeably with 'sister-in-law', or Pio being in error: after all, he got it wrong about Anne's miscarriage. Pio obviously had heard of Mary, and he might have assumed she was the one attending Anne. But Mary had been banished from court, and it seems curious that she would be allowed back to comfort Anne only to vanish again afterwards. I am most grateful to Dr Wilkinson for kindly agreeing to my publishing her theory in this book.
2 Wriothesley; Hall
3 Van Duyn Southworth; Sergeant
4 Wilkinson: *Mary Boleyn*
5 For a full account of Anne's fall, see Weir: *The Lady in the Tower*, also Ives; Bernard: *Anne Boleyn*
6 Weir: *The Lady in the Tower*
7 *S. C.* It was Froude who first deduced that these were the grounds on which the marriage was annulled.
8 Ridley: *Henry VIII*
9 *Statutes of the Realm*
10 Ibid.
11 Ridley: *Henry VIII*; Kelly
12 Bagley
13 Brigden
14 *The Complete Peerage*
15 Tallis
16 Hare; *Westminster Abbey: Official Guides*
17 Cotton MSS Cleopatra
18 Cited by Beauclerk-Dewar and Powell.
19 Naunton
20 Dating from 1513 and now in the British Library.
21 Cited by Sitwell.
22 Cited by Rowse.
23 *L. & P.*
24 Brigden and Wilson
25 Tighe
26 *L. & P.*
27 Brigden and Wilson
28 Walder

29 *L. & P.*
30 Ibid.
31 Ibid.
32 Ibid. Denny (*Anne Boleyn*) is incorrect in following Strickland's long discredited theory that the Countess died in 1512, whereupon Thomas Boleyn supposedly took a second wife who came from 'inferior gentry' stock.
33 *L. & P.*
34 Ibid.; *The Lisle Letters*; Ives
35 National Archives: Exchequer Inquisition Post Mortem, 639/4,493/4. Wiltshire did not end his life in disgrace, as Griffith states.
36 *L. & P.*
37 Ibid.
38 *The Complete Peerage*
39 *L. & P.*
40 Ibid.
41 Ibid.
42 Ibid.; *The Chronicle of Calais*; Weir: *The Six Wives of Henry VIII*
43 *L. & P.*
44 Ibid.
45 Ibid.
46 Ibid.
47 Ibid.
48 The post cannot have been secured for Katherine by Mary Boleyn, as Jones claims, for Mary was probably still in Calais at that time, and had no influence at the English court, which she probably never visited after 1534.
49 *L. & P.*
50 Ibid.
51 For Rochford Hall, see Michael Clark; Wright: *The County of Essex*; Benton; Barnes and Newman; Tompkins; Cryer; Barrett; Stogdon; Royal Commission on Historical Monuments in Essex. From the eleventh century to the fourteenth, the manor had been the property of the de Essex and de Rochford families. In 1342, after the de Rochford line had died out, Edward III granted the manor to William de Bohun, Earl of Northampton, and thence it had come into the possession of the Crown through the marriage of Bohun's granddaughter Mary to the future Henry IV. Henry IV restored the manor to another granddaughter of William de Bohun, Joan FitzAlan, Lady Bergavenny, who bequeathed it on her death in 1435 to James Butler, 5th Earl of Ormond (the 'White Earl'), Mary Boleyn's great-uncle, who was created Earl of Wiltshire in 1449. It was this James

Butler who, in the 1450s, dismantled the old manor house and built in its place the mansion that would become Rochford Hall.

The fifth Earl, a stout Lancastrian, was attainted and executed in 1461 for supporting the wrong side in the Wars of the Roses, and the manor again reverted to the Crown. It remained in the royal gift throughout the Yorkist period, but was restored, with all the other family estates, to Thomas Butler, 7th Earl of Ormond, by the first Tudor King, Henry VII, soon after his accession in 1485.

52 Rochford Hall was solidly constructed of red brick and Kentish ragstone, with walls up to three feet thick, and was moated on at least three sides. The bricks were similar to those used for Hampton Court in the 1530s, and the woodwork was of the same style as that used in the 1540s for the Lieutenant's Lodging – the present Queen's House – in the Tower of London. Rochford Hall was a gabled house, built around three or four courtyards, and boasted at least three octagonal towers (of the twelfth or thirteenth century), perpendicular door arches, and high, twisting Tudor chimneys. There were east, west and middle wings, leading southwards from the north wing, and a great hall and chapel, testifying to the high status of the hall's occupants. Tradition has it that the original chapel was largely destroyed by a great fire before 1461.

53 Michael Clark. This suggests that Stafford retained his association with, or stayed on at, Rochford Hall after his stepson, Henry Carey, inherited it.

54 Barrett

55 Wilkinson (*Mary Boleyn*) gives this as Hendon.

56 Wilkinson (*Mary Boleyn*) gives this as Bransted.

57 *L. & P.*

58 Fox

59 *L. & P.*; Ball

60 The date is recorded by Sir Francis Knollys in his Latin dictionary.

61 *L. & P.*

62 Warnicke: *The Rise and Fall of Anne Boleyn*; Hasler

63 There is no evidence to support claims that Katherine was appointed a companion to Anne of Cleves and went to live with her at Hever, one of the properties the former Queen had been given as part of her nullity settlement.

64 *L. & P.*

65 Wilkinson (*Mary Boleyn*) gives this as Leith.

66 *L. & P.* Within three years, Henry VIII had sold Henden to Sir Thomas Gresham (*L. & P.*).

67 Ibid.; Bindoff
68 *L. & P.*
69 Ibid.
70 Ibid.
71 Ibid. Letters Patent are legal instruments in the form of an open letter from a monarch to a subject, granting lands, offices, rights or titles.
72 Bindoff. They did not, as Denny (*Anne Boleyn*) states, live there as newlyweds.
73 *L. & P.*
74 Ibid.
75 Ibid.
76 Ibid.
77 Ibid.
78 Ibid.
79 Blomefield; Round
80 For a fuller discussion, see Weir: *The Lady in the Tower*; Borman.
81 *L. & P.*
82 Ibid.
83 Ibid.
84 According to her Inquisition Post Mortem in the National Archives, cited by Round.
85 Beauclerk-Dewar and Powell
86 *L. & P.*
87 Michael Clark
88 Cited by Tallis.
89 Also cited by Tallis.
90 It has been established that the diapered bricks used for the present church tower are the same as those used for Rochford Hall, and that they are similar to those used at Hampton Court in the 1530s.
91 Savage, in *The Love Letters of Henry VIII*

Appendix I: 'Of Her Grace's Kin'

1 For his later career, see Bindoff.
2 *L. & P.*
3 Ibid.
4 Ruth Richardson
5 Hoskins
6 For details of the Carey children's lives, see, for example: Michael Clark; Beauclerk-Dewar and Powell; *The Complete Peerage*; The Dictionary of National Biography; Varlow (both titles).
7 Michael Clark; Hughes

8 Bindoff. Again, there is no evidence that they married at Hengrave Hall, Suffolk, as asserted in Rootsweb.

9 Beauclerk-Dewar and Powell

10 Varlow: 'Sir Francis Knollys's Latin Dictionary: New Evidence for Katherine Carey'; Carey

11 Naunton

12 Varlow: *The Lady Penelope*

13 Ibid.

14 Michael Clark

15 Ibid.

16 '*Household Expenses of the Princess Elizabeth during her Residence at Hatfield October 1, 1551 to September 30, 1552*'

17 I am indebted to Peter Steward for information about Philadelphia Carey; he lives in a property she once owned at Hambleden, near Henley-on-Thames.

18 For example, Fox.

19 Hughes

20 Hoskins

21 Varlow: *The Lady Penelope*

22 *Calendar of State Papers relating to Scotland and Mary, Queen of Scots, 1547–1603*

23 Lansdowne MSS

24 *Letters of Mary, Queen of Scots*

25 *The Love Letters of Mary, Queen of Scots, to James, Earl of Bothwell*

26 I am indebted to Douglas Richardson, the author of *Plantagenet Ancestry*, for drawing my attention to these letters and laying out these arguments.

27 Jones says £400.

28 *The Complete Peerage*

29 Hoskins; Bindoff; Clutterbuck

30 L. & P.

31 *Calendar of Letters and State Papers relating to English Affairs, preserved principally in the Archives of Simancas, Vols.1–4, Elizabeth I, 1558–1603*

32 Rowse

33 Cited by Somerset: *Elizabeth I*

34 Aikin

35 Naunton

36 Ibid.

37 Ibid.

38 Ibid.

39 Hoskins

40 Cited by Johnson
41 National Archives: SP 15/17/113
42 Cited by Rowse.
43 Brewer
44 Naunton
45 Cited by Neale.
46 Black
47 Collection of the late Lord Berkeley, Hunsdon's descendant.
48 Strong: *Gloriana: The Portraits of Queen Elizabeth I*
49 Asquith
50 Ibid.
51 Doran
52 Of course, there are other theories as to her identity; I am grateful
    to Dr Katharine Craik of Oxford Brookes University for kindly
    sending me a reading list on the 'Dark Lady'.
53 Beauclerk-Dewar and Powell
54 There are several studies of Emilia Lanier; see, for example,
    McBride; Woods.
55 Naunton; Fuller
56 Not the Sanctuary, as Fox states.
57 Stow
58 Michael Clark; *The Complete Peerage*; Jones
59 Varlow: *The Lady Penelope*
60 *Westminster Abbey: Official Guide*; Jenkyns; Trowles
61 Hoskins
62 Baker
63 Jenkyns
64 Birch; David Hume; Strickland
65 Carey
66 Varlow: 'Sir Francis Knollys's Latin Dictionary: New Evidence for
    Katherine Carey'
67 Ibid.
68 Ibid.
69 Ibid.
70 Lansdowne MSS; *Letters of Royal and Illustrious Ladies of Great
    Britain*; Garrett
71 Varlow: *The Lady Penelope*
72 Fenelon
73 Newton. Jones is incorrect in stating that Elizabeth affectionately
    called Katherine her 'Crow': that was the nickname she gave to
    another close friend, Lady Norris.
74 Varlow: *The Lady Penelope*

75 Ruth Richardson

76 Borman

77 'Papers relating to Mary, Queen of Scots, communicated by General Sir William Knollys'

78 Fenelon, citing Nicholas White, confidant of William Cecil and future Master of the Rolls in Ireland.

79 'Papers relating to Mary, Queen of Scots, communicated by General Sir William Knollys'; Varlow: *The Lady Penelope*

80 'Papers relating to Mary, Queen of Scots, communicated by General Sir William Knollys'. Jones incorrectly says that it was Elizabeth who blamed Queen Mary for causing Sir Francis to be away from home.

81 Wright: *Queen Elizabeth and her Times*

82 'Papers relating to Mary, Queen of Scots, communicated by General Sir William Knollys'

83 Hatfield MSS; Varlow: 'Sir Francis Knollys's Latin Dictionary: New Evidence for Katherine Carey'

84 Ibid.; *Dictionary of National Biography*

85 Hatfield MSS; *Westminster Abbey: Official Guide*; Trowles

86 *Calendar of State Papers, Domestic Series, for the Reigns of Edward VI, Mary, Elizabeth I, 1547–1625*

87 Carroll; Tallis; Hoskins; Hart

Appendix II: Portraits of 'Mary Boleyn' and William Carey

 1 In the Royal Collection, showing her mourning her murdered son, Henry Stewart, Lord Darnley.

 2 Now in Leeds City Art Galleries.

 3 Strong: *Tudor and Jacobean Portraits*

 4 *Henry VIII: A European Court in England*; Starkey, in *The Renaissance at Sutton Place*

 5 *Henry VIII: A European Court in England*

 6 Ibid.

 7 Ibid.; Paget: 'Gerard and Lucas Hornebolte in England'

 8 Paget: 'Gerard and Lucas Hornebolte in England'

 9 John Fletcher. Brooke House was badly damaged by a bomb during the Blitz of 1940, and demolished in 1954/5, the cost of repairing it having been deemed prohibitive.

10 John Fletcher

11 Norris

12 John Fletcher

13 Mander

14 Hui

15 Murrell
16 Hui; John Fletcher; Ives; Hart
17 Jones; Hart
18 Jones
19 Hui
20 Strong: *The English Renaissance Miniature*

Genealogical Tables

Table 1: The Boleyns

Sir Geoffrey Boleyn 1406?-63 m. Anne 1425?-84 dr. of Thomas, Lord Hoo and Hastings

Thomas 1445-71

Sir William Boleyn 1451?-1505 m. Margaret 1465-1539/40 dr. of Thomas Butler Earl of Ormond

James m. Alice Filby a knight

other issue

Anne c.1475-1556 m. Sir John Shelton c.1472-1539 (issue)

Thomas Boleyn 1477-1539 Earl of Wiltshire and Ormond m. Elizabeth d.1538 dr. of Thomas Howard, 2nd Duke of Norfolk

Anne 1478-9

John 1481-4

Anthony 1483-93

Amata 1485?-1543 m. Sir Philip Calthorpe 1481-1549 (issue)

Alice 1487?-1538 m. Sir Robert Clere 1453?-1529 (issue)

William 1491-1571 a knight

Edward 1496-by 1536 a knight m. Anne 1497-after 1536 dr. of Sir John Tempest

James 1493?-1561 a knight m. Elizabeth dr. of John Wood

Anne (or Margaret) m. Sir John Sackville 1484?-1557

MARY BOLEYN c.1498-1543 m. 1 William Carey 1496?-1528 2 William Stafford 1512?-56 (issue, d. young)

George 1503?-36 Viscount Rochford m. Jane d.1542 dr. of Henry Parker, Lord Morley

Anne c.1501-36 m. Henry VIII King of England 1491-1547

Katherine Carey 1524-69 (see Table 4)

Henry Carey 1525-96 (see Table 3)

Elizabeth I Queen of England 1533-1603

Table 2: The Carey Connections (simplified)

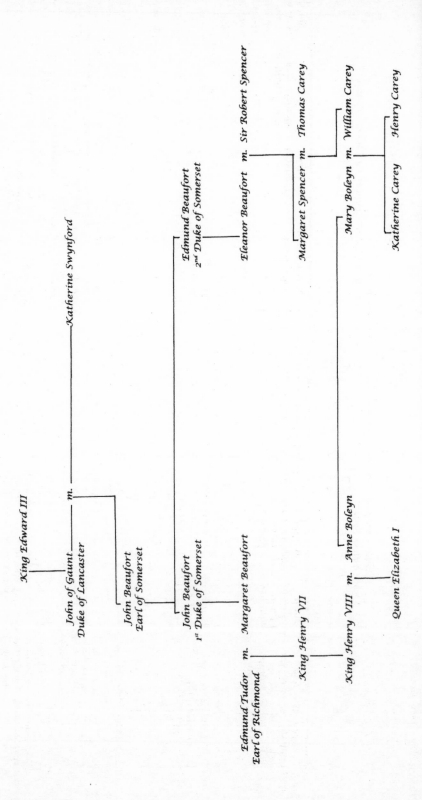

Table 3: The Carey Family

Thomas Carey of Chilton Foliat 1465?-1536 — m. — Margaret dr. of Sir Robert Spencer by Eleanor Beaufort

Children:

- Sir John Carey of Thremhall Priory 1491?-1552 m. Joyce 1495-1559 dr. of Sir Edmund Denny
- Anne 1493?-1550? nun at Wilton?
- Margaret 1495?-1550/60 nun at Wilton?
- William 1496?-1528 m. Mary Boleyn 1498?-1543
- Edward 1498-1560
- Eleanor d. after 1528 nun at Wilton
- Mary 1501?-60 m. Sir John Delaval 1493-1552

Son of Sir John Carey and Joyce:

- Sir Edward Carey of Aldenham 1540?-1618 → Viscounts Falkland

Children of William Carey and Mary Boleyn:

- Katherine Carey 1524-69 (see Table 4)
- Henry Carey 1525-96 1st Lord Hunsdon — m. — Anne 1529-1607 dr. of Sir Thomas Morgan

Children of Henry Carey and Anne:

- George 1547-1603 2nd Lord Hunsdon m. Elizabeth Spencer (issue)
- Katherine 1548?-1603 m. Charles Howard 1st Earl of Nottingham 1536-97 (issue)
- Philadelphia 1527?-1627 m. Thomas 10th Lord Scrope of Bolton 1562-1609 (issue)
- John 1556-1617 3rd Lord Hunsdon m. Mary Hyde d.1627 (issue)
- Edmund 1557?-1637 a knight m.1 Mary Crocker m.2 Elizabeth Neville m.3 Judith Humphrey (issue)
- Robert 1560-1639 1st Earl of Monmouth m. Elizabeth Trevannion d.1641? (issue)
- Margaret m. Sir Edward Hoby 1560-1617
- Henry, Thomas, Thomas, William and one other, d. young

Table 4: The Knollys Family

Katherine Carey 1524-69 — m. — Sir Francis Knollys 1514?-1596

Children:

- **Henry** 1541-83/96 m. Margaret Cave d.1606 (issue)
- **Mary** b.1542 d. young
- **Lettice (Laetitia)** 1543-1634 — m.1 Walter Devereux 1st Earl of Essex 1539-76 (issue); m.2 Robert Dudley Earl of Leicester 1533-88; m.3 Sir Christopher Blount 1565?-1601
- **Edward** 1546-75 M.P.
- **William** 1545-1632 1st Earl of Banbury — m.1 Dorothy Bray 1530-1605 (issue); m.2 Elizabeth Howard 1586-1658
- **Maud** b.1548 d. young
- **Elizabeth** b.1549 m. Sir Thomas Leighton 1535?-1611?
- **Robert** 1550-1619 m. Katherine Vaughan
- **Richard** 1552-1596 M.P. m. Joan Heigham d.1631 (issue)
- **Anne** 1555-after 1608 m. Thomas West Lord de la Warre 1556?-1602 (issue)
- **Thomas** 1558-after 1596 a knight m. Odella de Morada
- **Katherine** 1559-1632 — m.1 Gerald Fitzgerald Lord Offaly 1559-1580/5 (issue); m.2 Sir Philip Boteler
- **Cecily** and one other, d. young
- **Dudley** b.&d.1562
- **Francis** a knight 1553-1648 m. Lettice Barrett (issue)

Children of Lettice (by Walter Devereux):

- **Penelope Devereux** 1562?-1607
- **Robert Devereux** 2nd Earl of Essex 1565-1601 (issue)

Table 5: The Stafford Family

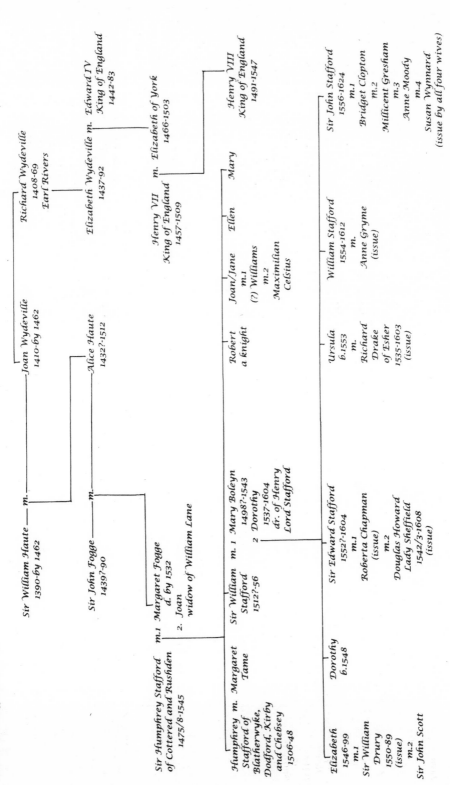

Index